3704722377

Android Forensics

WITHDRAWN

Investigation, Analysis, and Mobile Security for Google Android

D1579149

Android Forensics

Investigation, Analysis, and Mobile Security for Google Android

Andrew Hoog

John McCash, Technical Editor

AMSTERDAM • BOSTON • HEIDELBERG • LONDON
NEW YORK • OXFORD • PARIS • SAN DIEGO
SAN FRANCISCO • SINGAPORE • SYDNEY • TOKYO

Syngress is an imprint of Elsevier

SYNGRESS.

Acquiring Editor: Angelina Ward
Development Editor: Heather Scherer
Project Manager: Danielle S. Miller
Designer: Russell Purdy

Syngress is an imprint of Elsevier
225 Wyman Street, Waltham, MA 02451, USA

© 2011 Elsevier, Inc. All rights reserved.

No part of this publication may be reproduced or transmitted in any form or by any means, electronic or mechanical, including photocopying, recording, or any information storage and retrieval system, without permission in writing from the publisher. Details on how to seek permission, further information about the Publisher's permissions policies and our arrangements with organizations such as the Copyright Clearance Center and the Copyright Licensing Agency, can be found at our website: www.elsevier.com/permissions.

This book and the individual contributions contained in it are protected under copyright by the Publisher (other than as may be noted herein).

Notices
Knowledge and best practice in this field are constantly changing. As new research and experience broaden our understanding, changes in research methods or professional practices may become necessary. Practitioners and researchers must always rely on their own experience and knowledge in evaluating and using any information or methods described herein. In using such information or methods they should be mindful of their own safety and the safety of others, including parties for whom they have a professional responsibility.

To the fullest extent of the law, neither the Publisher nor the authors, contributors, or editors, assume any liability for any injury and/or damage to persons or property as a matter of products liability, negligence or otherwise, or from any use or operation of any methods, products, instructions, or ideas contained in the material herein.

Library of Congress Cataloging-in-Publication Data
Application submitted

British Library Cataloguing-in-Publication Data
A catalogue record for this book is available from the British Library.

ISBN: 978-1-59749-651-3

For information on all Syngress publications visit our website at www.syngress.com

Transferred to Digital Printing in 2012

Dedication

To my beautiful spouse who has endured my extended absenteeism as I wrote this book. She is my motivation, my friend, my partner, and the root of my happiness. This book is dedicated to her.

And to my wonderful daughters. You light up our lives and know more about Android forensics than any other 6-year-olds. May your lives be full of learning, success, and happiness.

Park Library
University of Gloucestershire
The Park
Cheltenham
GL50 2RH
Tel. 01242 714333

Contents

Acknowledgements

I now understand that the phrase "It takes a village…" applies equally to writing a book as it does to raising children. As such, I wish to acknowledge the village:

- My family (see Dedication).
- Lee Haas, for excellent editing and attempts to keep me on schedule
- Ted Eull, who coined to term "deHOOGification," which provides an immense service to you, the reader, as the ideas bouncing around in my head don't always come out that clear when I persist them to words. Ted is also a great friend and all around swell guy. Many thanks to his better half for her patience in putting up with the long hours racked up by motivated geeks at a tech start-up.
- Chris Triplett, for diving head first into Android and doing an amazing job at it. Chris is also excellent at patching drywall and providing some comic relief by applying farm English to digital forensics.
- Katie Strzempka, for generally taking care of that other book ("iPhone and iOS Forensics"). Please buy that one too, seriously.
- My parents, Stevie and Al, who set me on the correct path from the start and were always there to remind me if I swerved off a bit.
- To Harmonee and Hadabogee, whose help with our daughters, dinner, and other areas is immensely appreciated.
- To the men and women who bravely serve the public interest in Local, State, and Federal law enforcement and other government agencies. We appreciate all that you do to protect and serve our communities and countries.
- To Google, for seeing the value in Android and creating a new paradigm of openness for mobile devices.
- To Apple, for providing the opposite paradigm.
- And finally to the reader. I hope that you find this book useful and certainly do appreciate your support.

Introduction

The Android mobile platform has quickly risen from its first phone in October 2008 to the most popular mobile operating system in the world by early 2011. The explosive growth of the platform has been a significant win for consumers with respect to competition and features. However, forensic analysts and security engineers have struggled as there is a lack of knowledge and supported tools for investigating these devices. This book seeks to address issues not only by providing in-depth insights into Android hardware, software, and file systems but also by sharing techniques for the forensic acquisition and subsequent analysis of these devices. For readers with limited forensic experience, this book creates step-by-step examples that use free, open source utilities so the reader can directly participate in the examples. As the free Android software development kit provides a full Android emulator, readers do not even need to possess an Android device.

As Android devices grow in numbers, an increased awareness of the data they possess will equally grow. Unfortunately, much of that interest will come from cyber criminal organizations who realize that successful attacks against the platform will yield significant results as the devices contain enormous quantities of personal and business information. The solution to this threat requires a deep understanding of the platform not only from core Android developers and manufacturers but also from app developers and corporate security officers. More secure apps will prevent loss of sensitive information as well as strong policies that can be put in place by IT security managers.

Although most of the discussed statistics about Android focus on smartphones and now tablets, there are many more devices that currently or in the near future will run Android. Some examples include vehicles, televisions, GPS, gaming devices, netbooks, and a wide variety of other consumer devices. Android will be present in an increasingly significant percentage of investigations for both forensic analysts and security engineers. Finally, the appeal of Android is not specific to any particular country or region and as such will impact individuals, corporations, and agencies throughout the world.

The following paragraphs contain a brief summary of each of the chapters.

CHAPTER 1

This chapter provides not only a history of the Android platform but also discusses the Android Open Source Project (AOSP), the internationalization of the platform, the Android Market, a brief Linux tutorial, and a quick fb-non-chapter to Android forensics. It also provides a step-by-step tutorial for creating an Ubuntu-based virtual machine (VM), which will be used throughout the book in examples. The Ubuntu VM is a highly recommended component of this book and can also be used outside of the book for Android forensic cases.

CHAPTER 2

In this chapter, a wide array of Android-supported hardware and device types is covered. Although the hardware compatibility is great for manufacturers, wireless providers, and ultimately consumers, this diversity poses challenges for forensic analysts and security engineers. Understanding the hardware components, device types, and boot process for Android will aid in your overall understanding of Android and assist in both forensic and security investigations.

CHAPTER 3

This chapter covers the various Android releases, the Android software development kit (SDK), the Davlik virtual machine, key components of Android security, and several other concepts core to Android forensics such as the Android debug bridge (adb) and the USB debugging setting. Step-by-step examples include installing the SDK on Linux, OS X, and Windows as well as creating an Android virtual device that can be used to test forensic techniques.

CHAPTER 4

This chapter covers the information needed to understand how data are stored on an Android device. This includes reviewing the methods in which data are stored (shared preferences, files, SQLite, and network) as well as the types of memory used in an Android device such as RAM and the all important NAND flash. The various file systems the reader might encounter in an Android device are also covered in great detail including the YAFFS2, EXT, FAT32/FAT16, and a variety of low-level file systems.

CHAPTER 5

This chapter covers the security of Android devices, data, and apps. A review not only of how data can be exfiltrated from an Android device is covered but also of how an Android device can be used as an active attack vector. After discussing several overarching security concepts, this chapter provides specific advice for three primary audiences: individuals, corporate security, and app developers. As the growth of Android continues, issues of data security will be increasingly important and this chapter provides a thorough and practical fb-non-chapter to this important topic.

CHAPTER 6

This chapter covers specific techniques that are useful in the forensic acquisition of Android devices. After clarifying the different types of acquisitions and providing procedures for handling an Android device, seven different strategies for circumventing a pass code are discussed. Next, techniques and a specific script for acquiring an SD card and, if present, the Embedded MultiMediaCard (eMMC) are covered. Logical acquisition techniques are then covered including ones built into Android and the SDK, a solution free to law enforcement and government agencies called AFLogical, and finally a review of six commercial forensic software packages. Finally, techniques for acquiring a physical image of the NAND flash are described in detail including six strategies for gaining root privileges and the AFPhysical technique developed by viaForensics.

CHAPTER 7

In this final chapter, strategies and specific utilities are provided, which enable a forensic analyst or security engineer to analyze an acquired Android device. Although many of the techniques used in traditional forensic investigations are applicable in Android forensics analysis, the new file system and the underlying hardware characteristics require new techniques. Without these new techniques, little content and value can be extracted from an Android physical acquisition. Beyond providing the background and actual utilities, an overview of Android's directory structure as well as an in-depth analysis of 11 important applications that provide significant data about the device are given. Armed with this knowledge, a forensic analyst or security engineer can investigate any Android device they encounter.

WEBSITE

For companion material including code, programs and updates please visit: http://viaforensics.com/education/android-forensics-mobile-security-book/

About the Author

Andrew Hoog is a computer scientist, certified forensic analyst (GCFA and CCE), computer and mobile forensics researcher, former adjunct professor (assembly language), and cofounder of viaForensics, an innovative digital forensic and security firm. He divides his energies between investigations, forensic software development, and research in digital forensics and security. He also has two patents pending in the areas of forensics and data recovery. He lives in Oak Park, IL, where he enjoys spending time with his family, traveling, great wine, science fiction, and tinkering with geeky gadgets.

About the Technical Editor

John McCash (CompTIA Sec+, GCIH, GAWN, GCFA, EnCE, GREM, SANS Lethal Forensicator) is a 23-year IT veteran. He has specialized in Security for the last 15 years, and Forensics for the last 4 years. McCash has extensive experience in digital forensics, security/system/network administration, and incident response on diverse platforms in very heterogeneous environments. He obtained his BS and MS in CS at Bradley University in 1988. Currently John works for a major telecommunications equipment provider, and is a semiregular contributor to the SANS Forensic Blog.

CHAPTER 1

Android and mobile forensics

INFORMATION IN THIS CHAPTER

- Android platform
- Linux, Open source software and forensics
- Android Open Source Project
- Internationalization
- Android Market
- Android forensics

INTRODUCTION

Digital forensics is an exciting, fast-paced field that can have a powerful impact on a variety of situations including internal corporate investigations, civil litigation, criminal investigations, intelligence gathering, and matters involving national security. Mobile forensics, arguably the fastest growing and evolving digital forensic discipline, offers significant opportunities as well as many challenges. While the interesting part of Android forensics involves the acquisition and analysis of data from devices, it is important to have a broad understanding of both the platform and the tools that will be used throughout the investigation. A thorough understanding will assist a forensic examiner or security engineer through the successful investigation and analysis of an Android device.

> **TIP**
>
> **Book corrections, updates, and software**
>
> All corrections, updates, and even software samples for this book will be maintained online at the following web page:
>
> http://viaforensics.com/education/android-forensics-mobile-security-book/
>
> Please check the web site as over time it will evolve and provide significant and increasing value to the reader. Beyond corrections and updates, some of the software referenced in the book will be available for download.

ANDROID PLATFORM

Android is an open source mobile device platform based on the Linux 2.6 kernel and managed by the Open Handset Alliance, a group of carriers, mobile device and component manufacturers, and software vendors.

Table 1.1 Total US Smartphone Subscribers, Ages 13+, November 2010	
Platform	**Share (%) of Smartphone Subscribers**
RIM	33.5
Google	26.0
Apple	25.0
Microsoft	9.0
Palm	3.9

Android has made a significant impact on the smartphone market and, consequently, in the area of forensics. Two years and one month after the first Android device was introduced (October 2008), Android became the second largest smartphone platform capturing 26.0% of the 61.5 million US smartphone subscribers (comScore reports, n.d.). Table 1.1 shows the top smartphone platforms as of November 2010, according to comScore, Inc.

But Android's influence extends well beyond the US market. According to Gartner, Inc., the Android operating system (OS) was the second most popular during the third quarter of 2010 and accounted for 25.5% of worldwide smartphone sales (Gartner says, n.d.), as shown in Table 1.2.

According to the web site Google Investor, Google CEO Eric Schmidt reported that over 350,000 Android devices were being activated each day as of February 2011 (Google investor, n.d.). These statistics focus on the smartphone market, which is only one of the many types of Android devices available in the market.

The open source nature of Android has not only established a new direction for the industry, but also has enabled developers, code savvy forensic analysts, and

Table 1.2 Worldwide Smartphone Sales to End Users by Operating System in Third Quarter of 2009–2010 (in Thousands of Units)

Company	Units—3rd Qtr 2010	Market Share (%)—3rd Qtr 2010	Units—3rd Qtr 2009	Market Share (%)—3rd Qtr 2009
Symbian	29,480.1	36.6	18,314.8	44.6
Android	20,500.0	25.5	1424.5	3.5
iOS	13,484.4	16.7	7040.4	17.1
Research in motion	11,908.3	14.8	8522.7	20.7
Microsoft Windows mobile	2247.9	2.8	3259.9	7.9
Linus	1697.1	2.1	1918.5	4.7
Other OS	1214.8	1.5	612.5	1.5
Total	80,532.6	100.0	41,093.3	100.0

(unfortunately) sophisticated criminals to understand the device at the most fundamental level. As the core platform quickly matures and continues to be provided free of charge, carriers and hardware vendors alike can focus their efforts on customizations intended to retain their customers.

History of Android

For over three decades, companies have invested significant resources into research and development of handheld computing devices in the hopes that they would open new markets. As with traditional computers, the hardware components central to building such devices have advanced significantly and now provide a small, though powerful, mobile platform for handheld computers.

A central figure in the development of Android is Andy Rubin whose past employers include robotics firms, Apple, WebTV, and Danger Inc. His previous company, Danger Inc., developed a smartphone and support OS most recognized from the T-Mobile Sidekick. This mobile operating system, DangerOS, was built using Java. It provided a software development kit and had some of the features found in current smartphones. In 2004, Rubin left Danger and tinkered with several new ideas. He again returned to smartphone development and teamed with several engineers from past companies. The company Rubin formed in 2003 was called Android, Inc.

While the team began development, Rubin was actively marketing Android to both potential investors and wireless carriers. One of the companies he spoke with was Google, who subsequently acquired Android in July 2005. The acquisition, combined with new patents and services involving mobile and a large bid for wireless spectrum, fueled significant speculation that Google was developing their own smartphone and perhaps was aiming to be a full wireless carrier.

However, on November 5, 2007, Andy Rubin announced a more ambitious plan on the official Google blog (Official Google blog, n.d.):

> *Android is the first truly open and comprehensive platform for mobile devices. It includes an operating system, user-interface and applications—all of the software to run a mobile phone, but without the proprietary obstacles that have hindered mobile innovation. We have developed Android in cooperation with the Open Handset Alliance, which consists of more than 30 technology and mobile leaders including Motorola, Qualcomm, HTC and T-Mobile. Through deep partnerships with carriers, device manufacturers, developers, and others, we hope to enable an open ecosystem for the mobile world by creating a standard, open mobile software platform. We think the result will ultimately be a better and faster pace for innovation that will give mobile customers unforeseen applications and capabilities.*

One week later, Google released an early look at the Android software development kit (SDK) to developers. This allowed Google to create the first Android Developer Challenge, which ran from January 2008 through April 2008. Google set aside $1,000,000 to reward the most innovative Android apps. The top 50 apps are available for review at http://code.google.com/android/adc/adc_gallery/.

In August 2008, Google announced the availability of the Android Market where developers could upload their apps for mobile device owners to browse and install. The initial release did not support paid apps. However, that feature was added in early 2009. Finally, October 2008 marked both the official release of the Android Open Source Project (AOSP) (Bort, n.d.) and the first publicly available Android smartphone, the T-Mobile G1.

Since inception, the Android ecosystem has grown significantly and is comprised of diverse groups of contributors. Table 1.3 summarizes significant milestones for the Android platform.

Open Handset Alliance

The Open Handset Alliance (OHA) is a collaboration among mobile technology companies including wireless carriers, handset and component manufacturers, software developers, and other support and integration companies. The alliance, established on November 5, 2007, originally had 34 members. However, by January 2011 there were nearly 80 members.

The OHA is committed "to accelerate innovation in mobile and offer consumers a richer, less expensive, and better mobile experience" (Alliance FAQ, n.d.) with the primary focus on the coordination, development, and release of Android devices. Google is the driving force behind both the OHA and AOSP. Some have complained that the alliance is simply a marketing technique that offers little value to the members or consumers. However, new members have joined throughout 2010 and the OHA will undoubtedly continue well into the future. The members, as of

Table 1.3 Android Milestones

Date	Event
July 1, 2005	Google acquires Android, Inc.
November 12, 2007	Android launched
August 28, 2008	Android Market announced
September 23, 2008	Android 1.0 platform released
October 21, 2008	Android released as open source software
February 13, 2009	Android Market: USA takes paid apps
March 12, 2009	Android Market: UK takes paid apps
April 15, 2009	Android 1.5 (Cupcake) platform released
September 16, 2009	Android 1.6 (Donut) platform released
October 5, 2009	Android 2.0/2.1 (Eclair) platform released
May 20, 2010	Android 2.2 (Froyo) platform released
May 23, 2010	Android 2.2. for Nexus One phones released
December 6, 2010	Android 2.3 (Gingerbread) platform released
February 2, 2011	Android 3.0 (Honeycomb) preview released

February 3, 2011, listed in Table 1.4, are grouped by mobile operators, handset manufacturers, semiconductor companies, software companies, and commercialization companies (Alliance members, n.d.).

Android Features

While we explore the various Android device types more in the next chapter, there are several features common to most Android devices that we can discuss here.

First, Android was engineered from the beginning to be online, whether using cellular networks such as Global System for Mobile Communications and Code Division Multiple Access (GSM/CDMA) or wireless networks (Wi-Fi). Regardless of the venue, the ability to be online is a core feature of any Android device. Many of the devices are indeed smartphones and thus support sending and receiving phone calls, text messages, and other services found on cellular networks. Interacting with the device is typically via a touch screen, but many devices also allow for keyboards or other buttons, which support user interaction.

A second core feature of Android devices is the ability to download and install applications (apps) from the Android Market. This is a primary feature to many users because it allows them to extend the functionality of the device. These apps also typically happen to be a rich source of information for forensic analysts.

The final core feature is the ability for users to store their data on the devices. This, of course, is the basis for the forensics work covered in detail in this book. Most Android devices come with some on-device storage using flash (NAND) memory as well as an external SD card that is portable and intended to store larger amounts of data. Some recent HTC devices are now shipping with an emulated SD card which is a separate USB device ID mapped to the NAND and presented as an SD card. The emulated SD cards are typically formatted with Microsoft's FAT32 file system.

Supported Cellular Networks

As smartphones are the largest category of Android devices, it is important to understand the various cellular technologies Android currently supports.

The first Android device, the HTC DREA100 or T-Mobile G1, was a Global System for Mobile Communications (GSM) phone. GSM is the most widely used and supported cellular system with excellent support throughout the world. Major wireless providers in the United States that support GSM include AT&T and T-Mobile. The GSM system leverages a subscriber identity module (SIM) or universal subscriber identity module (USIM) to identify the user to the cellular network.

The next cellular system supported by Android is the Code Division Multiple Access, often referred to as CDMA. CDMA is the technique used to encode and send the voice, data, and control signals used by a CDMA phone. It is popular in the United States, but less so around the world. In the United States, the primary technology standard used is called CDMA2000. Major carriers include Verizon Wireless, Sprint, U.S. Cellular, and Cricket Communications.

The final cellular system supported by Android is the Integrated Digital Enhanced Network, or iDEN, whose primary attraction is its support of the

Table 1.4 Open Handset Alliance Members

Company Type	Companies
Mobile operators	• Bouygues Telecom • China Mobile Communications Corporation • China Telecommunications Corporation • China Unicom • KDDI Corporation • NTT DoCoMo, Inc. • Softbank Mobile Corp. • Sprint Nextel • T-Mobile • Telecom Italia • Telefónica • Telus • Vodafone
Handset manufacturers	• Acer Inc. • Alcatel Mobile Phones • ASUSTeK Computer Inc. • CCI • Dell • FIH • Garmin • Haier Telecom (Qingdao) Co., Ltd • HTC Corporation • Huawei Technologies • Kyocera • Lenovo Mobile Communication Technology Ltd • LG • Motorola • NEC Corporation • Samsung Electronics • Sharp Corporation • Sony Ericsson • Toshiba Corporation • ZTE Corporation
Semiconductor companies	• AKM Semiconductor Inc. • Audience • ARM • Atheros Communications • Audience • Broadcom Corporation • CSR Plc. • Cypress Semiconductor Corp. • Freescale Semiconductor • Gemalto • Intel Corporation • Marvell Semiconductor, Inc. • MediaTek, Inc. • MIPS Technologies, Inc.

Table 1.4 Open Handset Alliance Members *(Continued)*

Company Type	Companies
	• Nvidia Corporation • Qualcomm • Renesas Electronics Corp. • ST-Ericsson • Synaptics, Inc. • Texas Instruments Inc. • Via Telecom
Software companies	• Access Co., Ltd • Ascender Corp. • Cooliris, Inc. • eBay Inc. • Google Inc. • LivingImage Ltd • Myriad • Motoya Co., Ltd • Nuance Communications, Inc. • NXP Software • OMRON Software Co., Ltd • PacketVideo (PV) • SkyPop • SONiVOX • SVOX • VisualOn Inc.
Commercialization companies	• Accenture • Aplix Corp. • Borqs • L&T Infotech • Noser Engineering Inc. • Sasken Communication Technologies Limited • SQL Start International Inc. • TAT The Astonishing Tribe AB • Teleca AB • Wind River Systems • Wipro Technologies

popular push-to-talk (PTT) feature. In the United States, the only large carrier supporting iDEN is Sprint Nextel (who also owns Boost Mobile). Motorola, the developer of iDEN, also developed the Motorola i1, the first Android phone supporting iDEN.

Google's Strategy

Android is clearly a powerful mobile device platform which costs an enormous amount in development. So why did Google give Android away for free?

The answer starts with Google's clearly defined mission (Corporate information: about, n.d.):

> *Google's mission is to organize the world's information and make it universally accessible and useful.*

Cell phones are the most popular consumer device, numbering over 4 billion, so by providing an advanced mobile stack at no cost, Google believes they are fulfilling the universally accessible portion of their mission. But, obviously there must still be some benefit for Google. When more people are online, more people use search, which ultimately drives ad revenue—Google's primary source of income. In a March 2009 interview, Andy Rubin explained:

> *Google has a great business model around advertising, and there's a natural connection between open source and the advertising business model. Open source is basically a distribution strategy, it's completely eliminating the barrier to entry for adoption.*
>
> **(Krazit, n.d.)**

One of the criticisms of Android is that the market is now highly fragmented with different versions and variations of Android—a direct result of how Google releases Android to the manufacturers. This is in contrast to other devices, such as the iPhone where Apple has total control over the hardware and OS and significant influence over third-party application. Rubin defends this model, however. In the same interview, Rubin further commented on this aspect (Krazit, n.d.):

> *Controlling the whole device is great, (but) we're talking about 4 billion handsets. When you control the whole device the ability to innovate rapidly is pretty limited when it's coming from a single vendor. You can have spurts of innovation. You can nail the enterprise, nail certain interface techniques, or you can nail the Web-in-the-handset business, but you can't do everything. You're always going to be in some niche. What we're talking about is getting out of a niche and giving people access to the Internet in the way they expect the Internet to be accessed. I don't want to create some derivative of the Internet, I don't want to just take a slice of the Internet, I don't want to be in the corner somewhere with some dumbed-down version of the Internet, I want to be on the Internet.*

So by creating a mobile OS that meets the demands of the consumer as well as the needs of the manufacturers and wireless carriers, Google has an excellent distribution platform for their revenue-generating search and advertising business.

Apps

One important way by which Android supports innovation beyond the core mobile stack is by enabling the development and distribution of third-party apps on Android. As of January 2011, over 200,000 Android apps have been developed. This, of course, is similar to the strategy Apple developed. However, there are key differences in their approach. Apple maintains tight control over their App Store, requiring developers to submit to a sometimes lengthy review process and providing Apple with the final approval for an app. Apps can be denied based on a number of criteria, most notably if they contain any content Apple feels is objectionable. Google, on the other hand, requires very little review to publish an app in the Android Market. While Google has the ability to ban a developer, remove an app from the Android Market, and even remotely uninstall apps from Android devices, in general their approach to app management is hands off.

Nexus Phones

In January 2010, Google released its own smartphone, the Nexus One (N1) shown in Fig. 1.1. The N1 was developed by HTC and, by all accounts, was an ideal model for how manufacturers should develop their phones. The processor was extremely fast (1 GHz), it was running the latest version of Android, and it had innovations such as three microphones which survey background noise and blend your voice to create the most clear conversation possible.

The N1 was sold directly by Google and was sold unlocked—a move many analysts saw as a direct challenge to the carrier lock-in model where customers must sign a two-year agreement to get a discount on the device. The N1 was also available through T-Mobile for a reduced price, provided the user signs an extended contract. In the end, the sales for the N1 were not overwhelming and there was speculation that Google failed in their implementation (Fig. 1.1).

FIGURE 1.1

Google Nexus One by HTC.

FIGURE 1.2

Google Nexus S by Samsung.

However, at the time, Google was also trying to demonstrate how they believed an Android phone should be released and maintained. To the surprise of many, one year later Google released the Nexus S manufactured by Samsung, shown in Fig. 1.2. One interesting feature of the Nexus S was that it ran on Android 2.3 that allowed the native ability to make Voice over IP (VoIP) phone calls. If a device has a data connection, whether it is Wi-Fi.com or some other network, then it can send and receive phone calls using any number of popular VoIP services. In the United States, the phone was sold only through Best Buy stores and service was available through T-Mobile (Fig. 1.2).

It is unclear what Google's overall goals are with the Nexus line of smartphones. However, it is clear they intend to release Google phones and eventually may offer consumers a new flexibility in how they purchase and use smartphones.

LINUX, OPEN SOURCE SOFTWARE, AND FORENSICS

Open source software has had a tremendous impact on the digital forensics discipline. Forensic tools that are released as free open source software have tremendous advantages over closed source solutions including the following:

- The ability to review source code and understand exact steps taken
- The ability to improve the software and share enhancements with entire community
- The price

While many of the free, open source software packages do not offer a commercial support model, some companies specialize in providing support. For example, Red Hat has built a significant business providing support and services for the Linux OS. In addition, the maintainers of many free, open source software packages are generally very accessible and responsive to inquiries and can often provide far superior support as they directly maintain the software.

The most significant and important example of free, open source software is the Linux OS. Linux is not only a critical component of Android but can also be used as a powerful forensic tool.

Brief History of Linux

There have been many books written about Linux and dedicating only one section to such an important OS is difficult. There are also many fantastic online resources for Linux some of which focus on Linux as a forensic tool.

In 1991, Linus Torvalds was a University of Helsinki student when he decided to develop a terminal emulator that he could use to connect to the University's systems. The code was developed specifically for his computer, which had an Intel 386 processor. After he completed the initial development, he realized that code could actually form the basis of an OS and he posted the following famous messages on the Usenet newsgroup comp.os.minix (Torvalds, 1991):

```
Path: gmdzi!unido!mcsun!news.funet.fi!hydra!klaava!torvalds
From: torva...@klaava.Helsinki.FI (Linus Benedict Torvalds)
Newsgroups: comp.os.minix
Subject: Free minix-like kernel sources for 386-AT
Keywords: 386, preliminary version
Message-ID: <1991Oct5.054106.4647@klaava.Helsinki.FI>
Date: 5 Oct 91 05:41:06 GMT
Organization: University of Helsinki
Lines: 55

Do you pine for the nice days of minix-1.1, when men were men and wrote
their own device drivers? Are you without a nice project and just dying
to cut your teeth on a OS you can try to modify for your needs? Are you
finding it frustrating when everything works on minix? No more all-
nighters to get a nifty program working? Then this post might be just
for you :-)

As I mentioned a month(?) ago, I'm working on a free version of a
minix-lookalike for AT-386 computers.  It has finally reached the stage
where it's even usable (though may not be depending on what you want),
and I am willing to put out the sources for wider distribution.  It is
just version 0.02 (+1 (very small) patch already), but I've successfully
run bash/gcc/gnu make/gnu-sed/compress etc under it.

<snip>

I can (well, almost) hear you asking yourselves "why?".  Hurd will be
out in a year (or two, or next month, who knows), and I've already got
minix.  This is a program for hackers by a hacker.  I've enjouyed doing
it, and somebody might enjoy looking at it and even modifying it for
their own needs.  It is still small enough to understand, use and
modify, and I'm looking forward to any comments you might have.

<snip>
```

Reading this post, the mentality of many avid Linux users is captured in the desire to understand, modify, create, and otherwise tinker with complex systems (often referred to as a hacker mentality). The newsgroup Linus posted on was for the Minix OS, which at the time was the OS of choice for many people wanting to test and develop a Unix-like OS. However, there were licensing restrictions as well as technical limitations of Minix that Linus wanted to overcome.

Over nearly 20 years, Linux has matured significantly and is used on many PCs, servers, and now mobile devices. There are literally thousands of powerful tools available as well as complete development environments for many programming languages. The are many distributions that focus on different needs including servers, workstations, laptops, embedded devices, security suites, and many more.

Installing Linux in VirtualBox

Linux is a truly amazing OS and we will use its power throughout this book in examples intended for the reader to follow along and complete. All examples in this book are performed on an Ubuntu 10.10 64-bit desktop install running as a virtual machine (VM). While the virtual machine software from several vendors is compatible (including VMWare Fusion running on Mac OS X), this book is focused on options that are free, open, or both. In this instance, VirtualBox is both open source software and freely available.

> **NOTE**
>
> This Ubuntu VM will be used extensively through the book for all examples. Subsequent chapters will build upon this base install by adding more tools and scripts. Readers are encouraged to create this Ubuntu VM and follow along with all examples to maximize knowledge. The Ubuntu VM can be used directly for Android forensic cases.

VirtualBox is now owned by Oracle and is distributed under the GPLv2 license. There is a section on Oracle's web site that addresses frequently asked questions about licensing.

You can download VirtualBox for many operating systems including Microsoft Windows, Mac OS X, and Linux (2.4 and 2.6) from http://www.virtualbox.org/. After you install VirtualBox, you will see the Oracle VM VirtualBox Manager, shown in Fig. 1.3, where you create and manage new VMs.

When you create the new VM, make sure you have enough hard drive space (at least 20 GB is recommended) and as much RAM as you can spare. For the Android build, Google recommends at least 1536 MB (1.5 GB) (Get Android source code, n.d.).

Using the VirtualBox Manager graphical user interface (GUI) to set the new virtual machine is straightforward. However, if you have access an Ubuntu Linux 64-bit workstation or server, but do not have the ability to run desktop

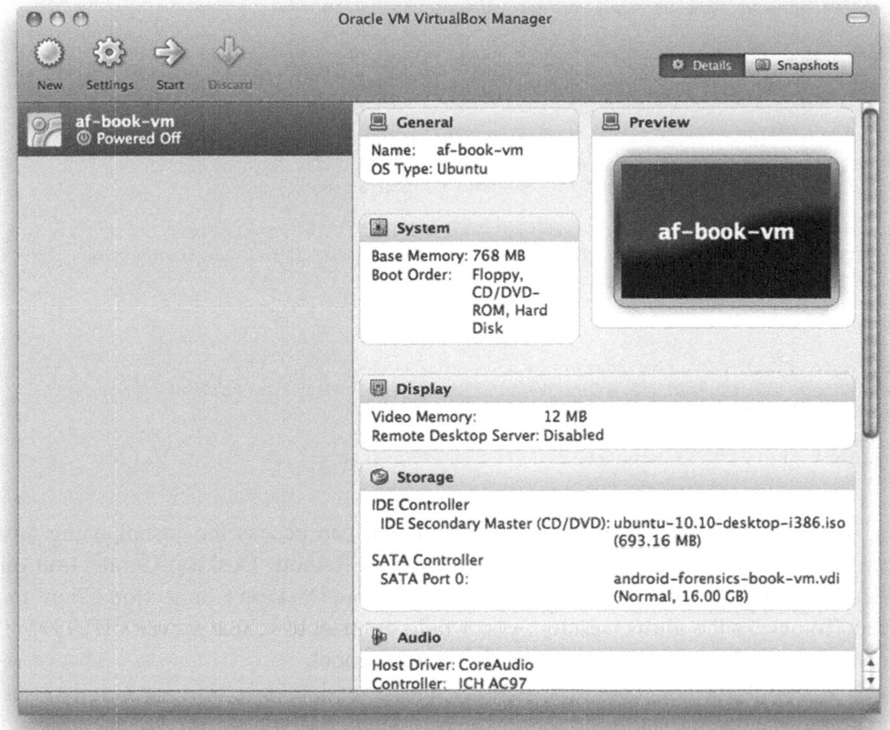

FIGURE 1.3

Oracle VM VirtualBox Manager for OS X.

applications, here are the steps you can follow to setup, configure, and run the new VM (VirtualBox 3.2.10).

From an ssh session, it is best to use the program "screen" so that if you lose connection to the server, your VM remains active. Then, follow these steps:

```
mkdir -p ~/vbox
cd ~/vbox
wget http://ubuntu.mirrors.pair.com/releases/maverick/ubuntu-10.10 -desktop
-amd64.iso

VBoxManage createvm -name af-book-vm -ostype Ubuntu -register

VBoxManage modifyvm af-book-vm --memory 1536 --acpi on --boot1 dvd \
--nic1 bridged --usb on --usbehci on --vrdp on --vrdpport 3392 \
--clipboard bidirectional --pae on --hwvirtex on --hwvirtexexcl on
  --vtxvpid on \
--nestedpaging on --largepages on
```

```
VBoxManage modifyvm af-book-vm --bridgeadapter1 eth0

VBoxManage storagectl af-book-vm --name "IDE Controller" --add ide

VBoxManage createvdi --filename ~/vbox/af-book-vm.vdi \
--size 20000 --register

VBoxManage storageattach af-book-vm --storagectl "IDE Controller" \
--port 0 --device 0 --type hdd --medium ~/vbox/af-book-vm.vdi

VBoxManage storageattach af-book-vm --storagectl "IDE Controller" \
--port 1 --device 0 --type dvddrive --medium ~/vbox/ubuntu-10.10-desktop
-i386.iso

VBoxHeadless -startvm af-book-vm -p 3392 &

#need to eject DVD, the restart
VBoxManage storageattach af-book-vm --storagectl "IDE Controller" --port 1 \
--device 0 --type dvddrive --medium none

#restart the virtual machine
VBoxHeadless -startvm af-book-vm -p 3392
```

At this point, the VM will start up and you can access the install using any Remote Desktop Protocol (RDP) viewer such as Remote Desktop Connection on Windows, rdesktop on Linux, or Microsoft's Remote Desktop Connection Client for Mac. To access the above session, you would connect to <host server's IP:3392>. From there, follow the install until it is time to reboot.

If you shutdown or reboot the VBoxHeadless session ends; you can simply issue the command again to start the server backup. Then, RDP back into the machine and install openssh server so that we can use ssh instead of the less efficient RDP:

```
sudo apt-get install openssh-server
```

Now you can find the virtual machine's IP address by running ifconfig and looking at the "inet addr" for eth0. You can use your favorite ssh program (if on Windows, try Putty for a great, free client) and ssh into the virtual machine.

The Sleuth Kit (TSK)

Brian Carrier has an excellent open source forensic toolkit called The Sleuth Kit (TSK), which will be discussed in this section. Examples throughout this book will leverage TSK extensively. Brian developed and continues to maintain TSK and provides an enormous service to our industry. If you are not familiar with TSK, visit the web site at http://sleuthkit.org/ and consider using the programs. There is quite a bit of information on TSK's web site as well as many forensic blogs and books. If you are going to follow the examples in this book, you should install TSK on the Linux workstation with the following command:

```
sudo apt-get install sleuthkit
```

Hopefully others can follow in Brian's footsteps and provide such important toolkits and service to the forensic community.

Disable Automount

It is critical that forensic workstations do not have automount enabled which, as the name infers, will automatically mount a file system when one is found on a device connected. The option to disable automount in Ubuntu is done per user, so if the workstation will have more than one user account, please make sure you change each of them:

```
gconf-editor
```

Then navigate to apps > nautilus > preferences and ensure the "media_automount" and "media_automount_open" options are unchecked as illustrated in Fig. 1.4.

You can then close the Gnome Configuration editor. Now, automount is disabled. For typical users, this is more work. However, for a forensic analyst, it is an absolute necessity (as is the use of hardware write blockers).

Linux and Forensics—Basic Commands

Before we setup and configure a Linux forensic workstation, it is helpful to provide an overview of Linux's relevance to forensics. A Linux workstation is a powerful tool for forensic investigation due to the wide support for many file systems, the advanced tools available, and the ability to develop and compile source code. However, since many examiners are not familiar with Linux, the following sections provide a breakdown of some of the more common Linux commands including a description of the command, its general usage, and one or more examples of how the command can be applied.

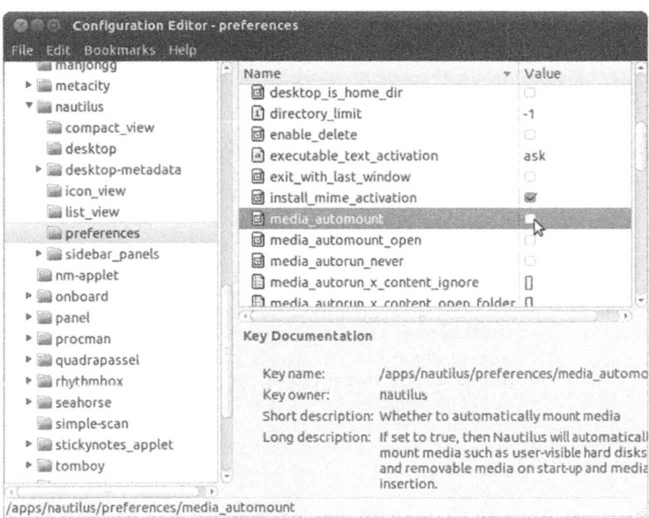

FIGURE 1.4

Disable automount on Ubuntu.

man

The "man" command pulls up online manuals for the requested command in the terminal window. The manual will provide a detailed description of the command as well as its usage (including all the options or "flags" for that command).

```
$  man [-k keywords] commands
```

In the following examples, the first command lists the beginning of the manual page for the "mount" command, while the second searches all manuals containing the characters "grep", a powerful searching tool.

```
$ man mount
MOUNT(8)                    Linux Programmer's Manual                    MOUNT(8)

NAME
       mount - mount a filesystem

SYNOPSIS
       mount [-lhV]

       mount -a [-fFnrsvw] [-t vfstype] [-O optlist]

       mount [-fnrsvw] [-o option[,option]...]  device|dir

       mount [-fnrsvw] [-t vfstype] [-o options] device dir

DESCRIPTION
       All files accessible in a Unix system are arranged in one big tree, the
       file hierarchy, rooted at /.  These files can be spread out  over  sev-
       eral  devices.  The mount command serves to attach the filesystem found
       on some device to the big file tree. Conversely, the umount(8)  command
       will detach it again.

       The standard form of the mount command, is
<snip>

$ man -k grep
bzegrep (1)          - search possibly bzip2 compressed files for a regular
                       expression
bzfgrep (1)          - search possibly bzip2 compressed files for a regular
                       expression
bzgrep (1)           - search possibly bzip2 compressed files for a regular
                       expression
egrep (1)            - print lines matching a pattern
fgrep (1)            - print lines matching a pattern
git-grep (1)         - Print lines matching a pattern
grep (1)             - print lines matching a pattern
pgrep (1)            - look up or signal processes based on name and other
                       attributes
rgrep (1)            - print lines matching a pattern
xzegrep (1)          - search compressed files for a regular expression
xzfgrep (1)          - search compressed files for a regular expression
xzgrep (1)           - search compressed files for a regular expression
zegrep (1)           - search possibly compressed files for a regular
                       expression
zfgrep (1)           - search possibly compressed files for a regular
                       expression
zgrep (1)            - search possibly compressed files for a regular
                       expression
zipgrep (1)          - search files in a ZIP archive for lines matching a
                       pattern
```

help

The "help" command displays information on the requested command, including usage and examples, similar to "man." Some commands use the --help notation while others simply use -h or -help.

```
$ mount --help

Usage: mount -V                 : print version
       mount -h                 : print this help
       mount                    : list mounted filesystems
       mount -l                 : idem, including volume labels
So far the informational part. Next the mounting.
The command is 'mount [-t fstype] something somewhere'.
Details found in /etc/fstab may be omitted.
       mount -a [-t|-O] ...     : mount all stuff from /etc/fstab
       mount device             : mount device at the known place
       mount directory          : mount known device here
       mount -t type dev dir    : ordinary mount command
Note that one does not really mount a device, one mounts
a filesystem (of the given type) found on the device.
One can also mount an already visible directory tree elsewhere:
       mount --bind olddir newdir
or move a subtree:
       mount --move olddir newdir
One can change the type of mount containing the directory dir:
       mount --make-shared dir
       mount --make-slave dir
       mount --make-private dir
       mount --make-unbindable dir
One can change the type of all the mounts in a mount subtree
containing the directory dir:
       mount --make-rshared dir
       mount --make-rslave dir
       mount --make-rprivate dir
       mount --make-runbindable dir
A device can be given by name, say /dev/hda1 or /dev/cdrom,
or by label, using  -L label  or by uuid, using  -U uuid.
Other options: [-nfFrsvw] [-o options] [-p passwdfd].
For many more details, say man 8 mount.
```

cd

This command is used to change into another directory. In Linux, the special character ~ is used to represent the current user's home directory. For example, the user ahoog has a home directory on a Linux system at /home/ahoog. From anywhere in the file system, you can use ~ to refer to /home/ahoog. This works well for documentation so throughout this book we refer to ~ and, even if you have setup a different user name, the command will still function as expected.

```
$ cd ~                     (changes into the current user's home directory from
                           anywhere)
$ cd ~/Desktop/Projects    (changes into the "Projects" folder located on the
                           user's Desktop)
$ cd ..                    (changes directories up 1 level, back into "Desktop")
$ cd ../../                (changes directories up 2 levels)
$ cd                       (also changes into the user's home directory from
                           anywhere)
$ cd /                     (changes into the root file system folder from
                           anywhere)
```

mkdir

The "mkdir" command creates a directory in the current location, unless otherwise specified.

```
$ mkdir android                        (creates the "android" folder in the
                                        current directory)
$ mkdir -p ~/android/forensics/book    (creates the full path of directories even
                                        if top levels do not exist)
```

rmdir/rm

This command removes existing directories or files based on the flags specified. The "rmdir" command will only remove empty folders. If there are files within the directory, these will first need to be removed prior to running the "rmdir" command. The "rm" command can be used to remove both files and folders, and will prompt the user prior to removing. You can override the prompt with the -f option but use with caution, hence the phrase "rm minus rf" or rm -rf.

```
$ rmdir android                        (removes only an empty folder)
$ rmdir -p ~/android/forensics/book    (removes each folder within the specified
                                        path)
$ rm -r android                        (removes the specified folder and all of
                                        its contents)
$ rm -rf android                       (removes the specified folder and all of
                                        its contents without prompting)
$ rm test.txt                          (deletes the specified file)
$ rm *.txt                             (deletes all .txt files within the current
                                        directory)
$ rm *                                 (deletes all files within the current
                                        directory)
```

nano

The "nano" is a terminal based editor that allows the creation and modification of text files. To create a file, simply type the command.

```
$ nano
```

Typing "nano" will open the text editor within the terminal window or ssh session, allowing the user to enter the contents they wish as shown in Fig. 1.5.

When the text has been entered, pressing Control X will exit the text editor and prompt you to save the file. In this case, we set the file name to newfile.txt.

To modify an existing file, simply follow the nano command with the file name or full path and file name if the file is in a different directory:

```
$ nano /etc/apt/sources.list
```

ls

This command lists files and folders. The "ls" command without any options specified will list the file/folder names only in the current directory. Adding the "-lh"

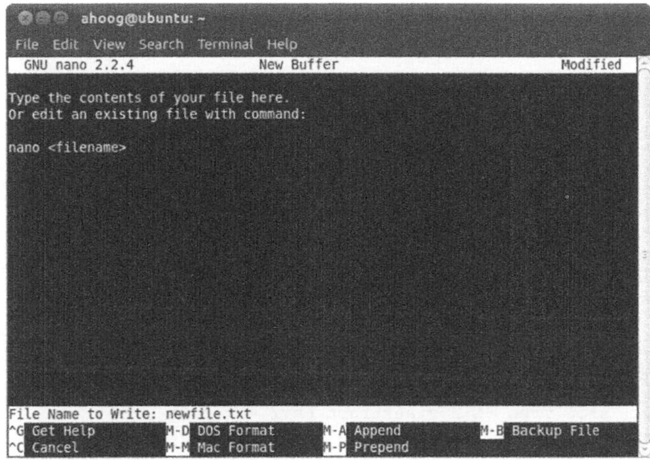

FIGURE 1.5

Create file using "nano."

option will provide a long list with more details including permissions, ownership, size, and date and time stamps.

```
ahoog@ubuntu:~/src$ ls
dc3dd-7.0.0          md5deep-3.7          viaextract-python
dc3dd-7.0.0.tar.gz   md5deep-3.7.tar.gz   yaffs2-old
download             viaextract_env       yaffs2-older.tgz

ahoog@ubuntu:~/src$ ls -lh
total 9.0M
drwxr-xr-x 10 ahoog ahoog 4.0K 2011-02-12 13:21 dc3dd-7.0.0
-rw-r--r--  1 ahoog ahoog 4.2M 2011-02-12 13:12 dc3dd-7.0.0.tar.gz
-rw-r--r--  1 ahoog ahoog 4.2M 2010-08-19 18:23 download
drwxr-xr-x  6 ahoog ahoog 4.0K 2011-02-18 07:21 md5deep-3.7
-rw-r--r--  1 ahoog ahoog 256K 2010-12-17 09:33 md5deep-3.7.tar.gz
drwxr-xr-x  6 ahoog ahoog 4.0K 2011-02-16 11:54 viaextract_env
drwxr-xr-x  6 ahoog ahoog 4.0K 2011-02-16 11:21 viaextract-python
drwxr-xr-x  8 ahoog ahoog 4.0K 2011-02-18 07:13 yaffs2-old
-rw-r--r--  1 ahoog ahoog 460K 2011-02-18 07:11 yaffs2-older.tgz
```

tree

The "tree" command shows the hierarchy of folders for the directory specified. If no parameters are specified, the current directory will be used. In Linux, the current directory is referred to as a single "." while one directory up is a double period "..". In the following output, the current directory is used, which happens to be the current user's home directory. The user can specify how many directory levels they wish to view with the "-L" flag. In the first example, one level is shown. Whereas in the second example, two levels of the source directory and files are displayed. Don't forget: you can learn all the details of a command by examining the man page (man tree) or specifying the command's help parameter (tree --help).

```
ahoog@ubuntu:~/src$ tree -L 1
.
├── dc3dd-7.0.0
├── dc3dd-7.0.0.tar.gz
├── download
├── md5deep-3.7
├── md5deep-3.7.tar.gz
├── viaextract_env
├── viaextract-python
├── yaffs2-old
└── yaffs2-older.tgz

5 directories, 4 files

ahoog@ubuntu:~/src$ tree -L 2 viaextract_env/
viaextract_env/
├── bin
│   ├── activate
│   ├── activate_this.py
│   ├── easy_install
│   ├── easy_install-2.6
│   ├── pilconvert.py
│   ├── pildriver.py
│   ├── pilfile.py
│   ├── pilfont.py
│   ├── pilprint.py
│   ├── pip
│   ├── pisa
│   ├── python
│   └── xhtml2pdf
├── include
│   └── python2.6 -> /usr/include/python2.6
├── lib
│   └── python2.6
└── src
    └── viaextract -> /home/ahoog/src/viaextract-python/trunk/viaextract/

7 directories, 13 files
```

less

The "less" command displays specified files one page at a time. This command is commonly used in conjunction with other commands to show output one page at a time. The following command will display the contents of the sanitize-csv.sh file one screen at a time within the terminal window. Once you are in the less utility, there are a few key commands to remember:

- h: access help menu
- q: quit help menu
- spacebar: display one screen/page down
- b: display one screen/page up
- /: search for a pattern
- Enter: move one line down
- y: move one line up

There are many more commands and tricks to this powerful utility so read the help screens, the man page, or simply search the Internet for more helpful tips.

```
ahoog@ubuntu:~$ less sanitize-csv.sh
#!/bin/bash

# create a new directory to store the sanitized files
mkdir sanitized

#for each file ending with .csv
for f in *.csv
do
        #read the top 1 row of the file and save it to the sanitized directory
        #with the same filename followed by -1strowonly
        head -1 "$f" > sanitized/"$f"-1strowonly
done

#create a "tar gzip" archive of the file so it is easier share
tar czvf AFlogical-sanitized.tgz sanitized/*
sanitize-csv.sh (END)
```

cat

The “cat” command outputs the contents of a file to the screen or to a new file if specified (without retaining the format of the file).

```
ahoog@ubuntu:~/Desktop$ cat android.txt
android forensics is so much fun.

This file contains unnecessary information used to display the workings of the
"cat" command.

The "cat" command can be used in conjunction with "less" in order to display
the contents of a
file one page at a time.
```

This command can also be used to combine multiple files into one (i.e., often referred to as concatenating files).

```
$ cat file1.txt file2.txt file3.txt > final.txt
```

find

The “find” command is used to search for files in a directory hierarchy. The following command will list all of the files, including the full path, contained on the specified user’s home directory.

```
ahoog@ubuntu:~$ find ~
/home/ahoog
/home/ahoog/scalpel-1.60
/home/ahoog/scalpel-1.60/README
/home/ahoog/scalpel-1.60/dirname.h
/home/ahoog/scalpel-1.60/base_name.c
/home/ahoog/scalpel-1.60/dig.c
/home/ahoog/scalpel-1.60/prioque.h
/home/ahoog/scalpel-1.60/scalpel.o
/home/ahoog/scalpel-1.60/files.c
/home/ahoog/scalpel-1.60/helpers.o
<snip>
```

The output of the find command can also be used in another command. For example, the following will run the "md5sum" command on the files from the "find" command. Several parameters are specified:

- find: the command
- ~: find files in the current user's home directory
- -type f: only list regular files (do not list directories)
- -exec: run the following command
- sha256sum : the utility that calculates a file's sha256 hash
- { } \;: crazy shell escapes and notations!

```
ahoog@ubuntu:~$ find ~ -type f -exec sha256sum {} \;
1d4b6d9e7930e1bd186de982e21ad0d4dab92239920dea791dc25f2d0ffe92cb
/home/ahoog/scalpel-1.60/README
a771570f4b3ebfb212b39abaeff92cc7b4c116b920b726f6f6cabc78092b5d5b
/home/ahoog/scalpel-1.60/dirname.h
95d9d2243444b3e53eb2b449bd9052050bb4bb7d12d9d9bcaae2802de61feab1
/home/ahoog/scalpel-1.60/base_name.c
70babfb49c46a989f8d034b5e7438d5f51fe115a0ce61e6fdac6f0619d47d581
/home/ahoog/scalpel-1.60/dig.c
a5456e609810bca0730768a9d07b8c591246f1448c72b7d107d8b7ebd90f8fef
/home/ahoog/scalpel-1.60/prioque.h
f2364fd3caac10a297ec93123da6503b621cb65a98efaab6ca6fa5aeeccb6c32
/home/ahoog/scalpel-1.60/scalpel.o
d9c2351cc1fa8a8e4ea874005b756d89fa722de051d9e23dd2cd7b3988ce7122
/home/ahoog/scalpel-1.60/files.c
58c10d10cb629c95a81035fd73c553fa0c9ca2bbcacd184b9533f342285cf554
/home/ahoog/scalpel-1.60/helpers.o
<snip>
```

If you run a command against the results of a large number of files, you can run into issues. In those cases, you should research piping the output of the file command to a utility called xargs.

With most Linux commands, you can also save the output of a command into a file. For example, the output from the same command above can be saved in the user's home directory in a file called md5.txt:

```
ahoog@ubuntu:~$ find ~ -type f -exec sha256sum {} \; > ~/sha256sum.txt
```

The output of the find command run against the sha256sum utility is redirected to the sha256sum.txt file in the user's home directory.

chmod

Short for "change mode," this command changes file or folder permissions. Many examples are provided in the following list. Note that these commands must either be run in the directory in which "textfile.txt" is stored, or the full path to the file must be provided.

```
*Provides details on the file permissions for "textfile.txt"
   ahoog@ubuntu:~/Desktop$ ls -l textfile.txt
   -rw-r--r-- 1 ahoog ahoog 264 2011-03-01 12:17 textfile.txt

*Gives read, write, and execute permissions for the owner, and read and execute
permissions for group and world.
   ahoog@ubuntu:~/Desktop$ chmod 755 textfile.txt

   ahoog@ubuntu:~/Desktop$ ls -l textfile.txt
   -rwxr-xr-x 1 ahoog ahoog 264 2011-03-01 12:17 textfile.txt

*Gives read, write, and execute permissions for the owner, and execute
permissions for group and world.
   ahoog@ubuntu:~/Desktop$ chmod 711 textfile.txt

   ahoog@ubuntu:~/Desktop$ ls -l textfile.txt
   -rwx--x--x 1 ahoog ahoog 264 2011-03-01 12:17 textfile.txt

*Gives read, write, and execute permissions for the owner, and read-only
permissions for group and world.
   ahoog@ubuntu:~/Desktop$ chmod 744 textfile.txt

   ahoog@ubuntu:~/Desktop$ ls -l textfile.txt
   -rwxr--r-- 1 ahoog ahoog 264 2011-03-01 12:17 textfile.txt
```

The "chmod" command can also be run on a group of files or a folder.

```
$ chmod 755 *           (Changes permissions of all files in the current
                         directory)
$ chmod -R 444 Files/   (Changes permissions of the "Files" directory and all of
                         the files within it)
```

chown

The "chown" command changes the owner or group of a specified file or directory. In the following example, the original owner and group of "textfile.txt" was ahoog. The chown command changed the owner to "root." This command required "sudo."

```
ahoog@ubuntu:~/Desktop$ ls -l textfile.txt
-rwxr--r-- 1 ahoog ahoog 264 2011-03-01 12:17 textfile.txt

ahoog@ubuntu:~/Desktop$ sudo chown root textfile.txt
[sudo] password for ahoog:

ahoog@ubuntu:~/Desktop$ ls -l textfile.txt
-rwxr--r-- 1 root ahoog 264 2011-03-01 12:17 textfile.txt
```

sudo

Preceding any command with "sudo" gives the user elevated permissions, allowing them to run a command as a super user or another user. Sudo is required to run certain commands such as apt-get (to install software), chown (to change ownership if you are not the owner), mount, accessing raw disk devices, and many other commands depending on the files it must access. To use sudo, simply precede the command with "sudo," which will then prompt you for your password. Then log the command in the sudo logs:

```
ahoog@ubuntu:~$ sudo xxd /dev/sda1 | less
[sudo] password for ahoog:
```

apt-get

The "apt" part of the apt-get command stands for Advanced Packaging Tool and allows the user to install and uninstall software, upgrade existing software, or even perform system updates. To run this command, sudo permissions are required.

```
$ sudo apt-get install scalpel      (Installs scalpel software package)
[sudo] password for ahoog:

$ sudo apt-get remove scalpel       (Uninstalls scalpel software package)
[sudo] password for ahoog:

$ sudo apt-get update               (Updates the APT package index, which stores
                                     packages available for download)
[sudo] password for ahoog:

$ sudo apt-get upgrade -u           (Upgrades APT package versions, including
                                     security updates; should be run after
                                     update)
[sudo] password for ahoog:
```

grep

The "grep" command searches through a file, or list of files and folders, for a specified phrase. It is equivalent to opening a document and doing a "find" for a certain phrase. The search is case sensitive, so if you are unsure if a letter is capitalized or lower case, then you should specify the "-i" (case insensitive) flag. This option will take longer, depending on the size of the file that is being searched.

General usage is:

```
$ grep keyword file.txt
```

The following contains several examples of the usage of "grep."

```
$ grep Forensics androidBook.txt          (will search for "forensics" in the
                                           specified file)
$ grep -i forensics androidBook.txt       (will search for "forensics", case
                                           insensitive, in the specified file)
$ grep "list of files" androidBook.txt    (will search the specified file for
                                           "list of files", case sensitive)
```

The next command searches the contents of all files on the user's desktop for the word "unnecessary." The results show that this word was found in "textfile.txt," and there are also matches for this word in "WXP-PRO-OEM.iso." Because this is a binary file, further techniques will need to be performed to make the content viewable.

```
ahoog@ubuntu:~/Desktop$ grep unnecessary *
android.txt:This file contains unnecessary information used to display the
workings of the "cat" command.
Binary file WXP-PRO-OEM.iso matches
```

As you use Linux more extensively for forensic investigations, grep will become an indispensable utility.

Piping and Redirecting Files (| and >)

The pipe character "|" (located above the "Enter" key on most keyboards) allows the output of one command to be sent to another for further processing. Output can also be redirected into another file using ">".

The following command takes the results of "cat file.txt" and pipes it to the "less" command, allowing the user to view the contents one page at a time.

```
$ cat file.txt | less
```

The next command searches for "android" in "ch1.xml" using the grep command and then takes the results of that search and performs another search, case insensitive, for "forensics." The final results are then piped through "less" to be displayed one page at a time.

```
$ grep android ch1.xml | grep -i forensics | less
```

Redirecting output from a command can also be helpful. The following command takes the output of "book.txt" (using the "cat" command) and copies the output into a file on the user's desktop called "newdocument.txt."

```
cat ch1.xml > ~/Desktop/new-ch1.xml
```

Redirection can be very helpful while running the "strings" command on a particular file or even an entire disk image, which will be explored further in Chapter 7.

ANDROID OPEN SOURCE PROJECT

The open strategy behind Android naturally led to the release of the Android source code through the AOSP on October 21, 2008. The site states (Get Android source code, n.d.):

> *We created Android in response to our own experiences launching mobile apps. We wanted to make sure that there would always be an open platform available for carriers, OEMs [original equipment manufacturers], and developers to use to make their innovative ideas a reality. We wanted to make sure that there was no central point of failure, where one industry player could restrict or control the innovations of any other. The solution we chose was an open and open-source platform.*

The development strategy focuses on flagship devices (for instance, the Nexus series), which allows Google to absorb much of the risk with a new platform. The manufacturers can then use the latest release of Android on their devices while the AOSP develops the next major release.

AOSP Licenses

The AOSP is governed by two primary software licenses, the Apache Software License 2.0 (Apache 2.0 or ASL2.0) and the GNU Public License v2 (GPLv2). The GPLv2 is a far more restrictive license that forces contributors to distribute all of their source code under the same license. Google felt this would limit the commercial backing of Android, so the GPLv2 primarily covers the use of the Linux kernel core to Android only.

The Apache 2.0 license, however, is more accepted by commercial entities because it is less restrictive and does not force companies to open source all of their related software. The AOSP addresses the question of why they chose the Apache 2.0 license (Licenses, n.d.):

> *We are sometimes asked why Apache Software License 2.0 is the preferred license for Android. For userspace (that is, non-kernel) software, we do in fact prefer ASL2.0 (and similar licenses like BSD, MIT, etc.) over other licenses such as LGPL.*
>
> *Android is about freedom and choice. The purpose of Android is to promote openness in the mobile world, but we don't believe it's possible to predict or dictate all the uses to which people will want to put our software. So, while we encourage everyone to make devices that are open and modifiable, we don't believe it is our place to force them to do so. Using LGPL libraries would often force them to do so.*
>
> *Here are some of our specific concerns:*
>
> *1. LGPL (in simplified terms) requires either: shipping of source to the application; a written offer for source; or linking the LGPL-ed library dynamically and allowing users to manually upgrade or replace the library. Since Android software is typically shipped in the form of a static system image, complying with these requirements ends up restricting OEMs' designs. (For instance, it's difficult for a user to replace a library on read-only flash storage.)*
>
> *2. LGPL requires allowance of customer modification and reverse engineering for debugging those modifications. Most device makers do not want to have to be bound by these terms, so to minimize the burden on these companies we minimize usage of LGPL software in userspace.*
>
> *3. Historically, LGPL libraries have been the source of a large number of compliance problems for downstream device makers and application developers. Educating engineers on these issues is difficult and slow-going, unfortunately. It's critical to Android's success that it be as easy as possible for device makers to comply with the licenses. Given the difficulties with complying with LGPL in the past, it is most prudent to simply not use LGPL libraries if we can avoid it.*

> *The issues discussed above are our reasons for preferring ASL2.0 for our own code. They aren't criticisms of LGPL or other licenses. We do feel strongly on this topic, even to the point where we've gone out of our way to make sure as much code as possible is ASL2.0. However, we love all free and open source licenses, and respect others' opinions and preferences. We've simply decided that ASL2.0 is the right license for our goals.*

Development Process

The AOSP is a very sophisticated and complex open source project, requiring the coordination of many developers across the world. As such, the AOSP has a defined set of roles and processes that must be followed to contribute to the project. The roles include the following:

- Contributor/developers: individuals and corporations who contribute code to the project
- Verifiers: individuals who test code changes
- Approvers: individuals who are experienced developers and decide whether a change will be included or excluded
- Project leads: typically Google employees who are responsible for the overall management of the AOSP project

Anyone can download, compile, and enhance the AOSP project. Figure 1.6 illustrates the development process.

Value of Open Source in Forensics

Not many forensic examiners will, or need to, contribute directly to the AOSP. However, there is tremendous value in downloading the software. For example, when examining a Yet Another Flash File System2 (YAFFS2) physical image from an Android 1.5 device, the phrase "silly old name" frequently appears when using strings to extract ASCII text. For most file systems, the examiner would have to simply conjecture as to the relevance of "silly old name." However, by downloading the source code, an examiner can quickly search for the phrase, identify the code, and examine it for additional information. In this case, when the object header for a YAFFS2 object (e.g., a file) is updated, the name field is set to "silly old name" under certain circumstances.

From the AOSP in file kernel/fs/yaffs2/yaffs_guts.c, there is a function called yaffs_UpdateObjectHeader. The comment in the code and function header reads:

```
/* UpdateObjectHeader updates the header on NAND for an object.

 * If name is not NULL, then that new name is used.
 */
int yaffs_UpdateObjectHeader(yaffs_Object * in, const YCHAR * name, int force,
       int isShrink, int shadows)
```

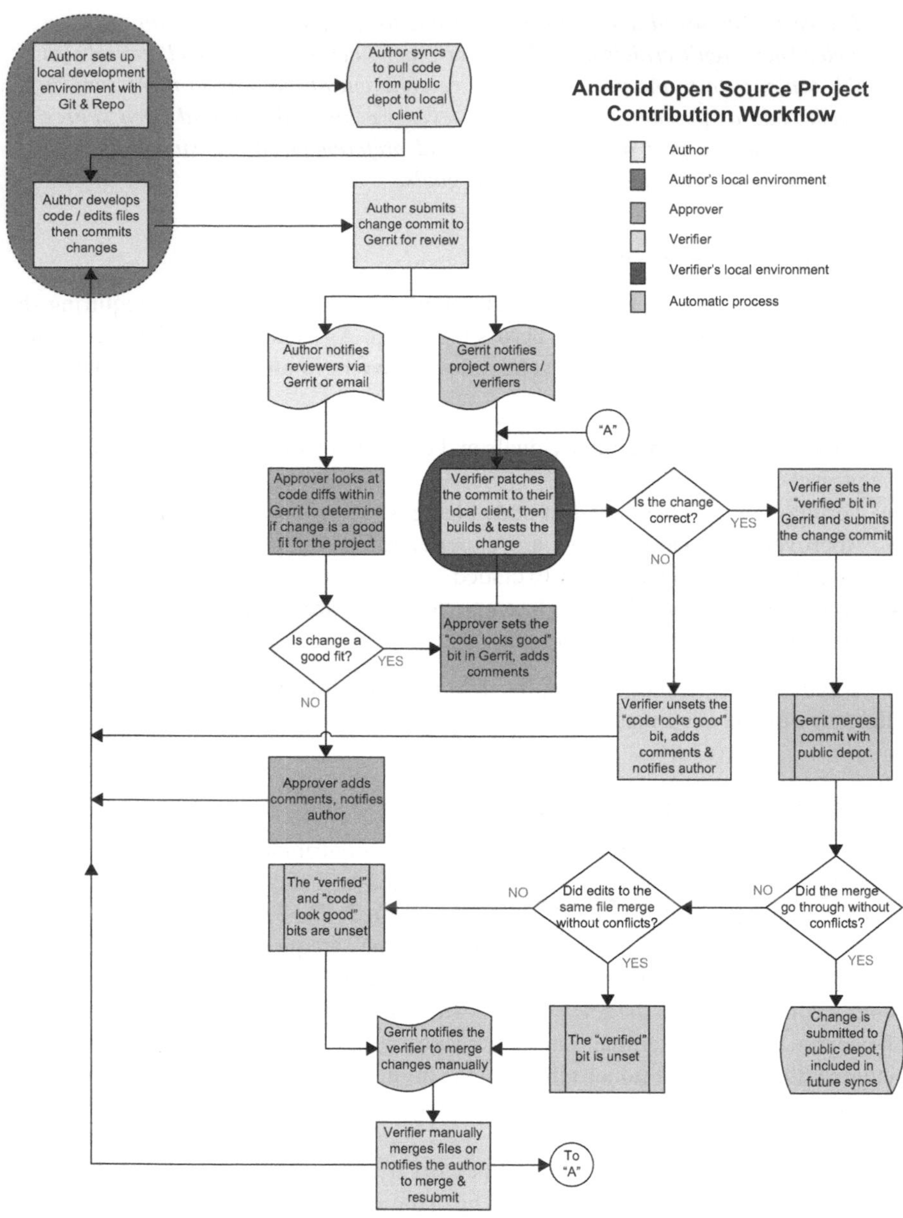

FIGURE 1.6

AOSP development process.

A variable called "oldName" is created with the contents "silly old name":

```
yaffs_strcpy(oldName,_Y("silly old name"));
```

And the name field of the object header being updated is set to "oldName" when the previous "ChunkId" is greater than 0:

```
if (prevChunkId > 0) {
 result = yaffs_ReadChunkWithTagsFromNAND(dev, prevChunkId,
     buffer, &oldTags);

 yaffs_VerifyObjectHeader(in,oh,&oldTags,0);

 memcpy(oldName, oh->name, sizeof(oh->name));
}
```

The code also checks to see if the original call to the function passed in a new name for the object. If a new name value was not provided to the function, the value of oldName (which is still "silly old name") is used:

```
if (name && *name) {
   memset(oh->name, 0, sizeof(oh->name));
   yaffs_strncpy(oh->name, name, YAFFS_MAX_NAME_LENGTH);
  } else if (prevChunkId>=0) {
   memcpy(oh->name, oldName, sizeof(oh->name));
  } else {
   memset(oh->name, 0, sizeof(oh->name));
  }
```

While not every examiner is comfortable interpreting a programmer's code (C in this case), clearly this information could be useful in a forensic examination. And, of course, there are many other situations, such as how SMS messages are time stamped or how geo-tagging is implemented, which could bring tremendous value to an examination.

Downloading and Compiling AOSP

Hopefully the value of referring to the Android source code was demonstrated in the previous YAFFS2 example. The following section highlights the steps you should follow to download and compile the latest release from the AOSP. While Android 2.2 and earlier versions would compile on 32-bit machines, the latest version of the AOSP (Android 2.3) and forward require a 64-bit computer.

Using the Ubuntu VM we previously built, we can now start updating the stock Ubuntu install and then build Android from source code.

```
#add repository needed for sun-java6-jdk
sudo add-apt-repository "deb http://archive.canonical.com/ lucid partner"

#update installed packages
sudo apt-get update
sudo apt-get upgrade -u
sudo reboot
```

```
#install packages needed to build Android
sudo apt-get install git-core gnupg flex bison gperf libsdl1.2-dev libesd0-dev \
libwxgtk2.6-dev squashfs-tools build-essential zip curl libncurses5-dev \
zlib1g-dev sun-java6-jdk pngcrush g++-multilib lib32z1-dev lib32ncurses5-dev \
lib32readline5-dev gcc-4.3-multilib g++-4.3-multilib

#make directories and repo utility
mkdir -p ~/bin
mkdir -p ~/android
curl http://android.git.kernel.org/repo > ~/bin/repo
chmod 755 ~/bin/repo

#initialize Android git archive
cd ~/android
time ~/bin/repo init -u git://android.git.kernel.org/platform/manifest.git

#download source files
time ~/bin/repo sync

#build Android
cd ~/android
source build/envsetup.sh
lunch
time make
```

Congratulations, you have built Android from source (or started the build—it takes a while).

Now, if you come across an aspect of Android you need to understand better, you can search the source code and learn more about it. Table 1.5 charts the core Android

Table 1.5 Core Android Projects

Project	Description
bionic	C runtime: libc, libm, libdl, dynamic linker
bootloader/legacy	Bootloader reference code
build	Build system
dalvik	Dalvik virtual machine
development	High-level development and debugging tools
frameworks/base	Core Android app framework libraries
frameworks/policies/base	Framework configuration policies
hardware/libhardware	Hardware abstraction library
hardware/ril	Radio interface layer
kernel	Linux kernel
prebuilt	Binaries to support Linux and Mac OS builds
recovery	System recovery environment
system/bluetooth	Bluetooth tools
system/core	Minimal bootable environment
system/extras	Low-level debugging/inspection tools
system/wlan/ti	TI 1251 WLAN driver and tools

project, which you will find maps roughly to the directories in the Android source tree. The project information can be found on the AOSP site at https://sites.google.com/a/android.com/opensource/projects, which provides a brief description of each project function.

INTERNATIONALIZATION

Android has broad support for international languages and locales throughout the platform. This not only allows the phone to display menus, web sites, and other aspects of the graphical user interface in many languages, but there is also support for input in a variety of international keyboard formats.

Unicode

The key to Android's ability to support a multitude of languages is the ability to encode and decode characters in Unicode, the industry standard encoding scheme that supports over 600 languages (Languages and scripts, n.d.).

> **TIP**
>
> **Cuneiform support**
>
> For those curious and adventurous readers, Unicode does support Cuneiform, although we are still waiting for someone to implement the Android user interface in Sumero-Akkadian Cuneiform. The full list of Unicode supported languages and scripts can be viewed at http://unicode.org/repos/cldr-tmp/trunk/diff/supplemental/languages_and_scripts.html

Keyboards

Android supports many different types of keyboards, sometimes referred to as the input method. For example, when running an Android virtual device (AVD), the emulator allows you to change the language of the keyboard input as shown in Fig. 1.7.

The ability to handle various languages is simply built into the AVD system. This has important implications in a forensic investigation where analysts must remain vigilant and consider that some data could be encoded in an unexpected language.

The same feature of the ADV is available on the physical Android devices as well. For example, on the HTC Incredible distributed in the United States by Verizon Wireless, there is a setting called Language and Keyboard. You can select from two languages for the phone user interface: English and Español. Then, under the Text settings, you can choose your Touch Input settings. From here, you can specify the keyboard type (QWERTY, Phone Keypad, or Compact QWERTY), select from over 20 international keyboards, specific options for Chinese Text input (Traditional or

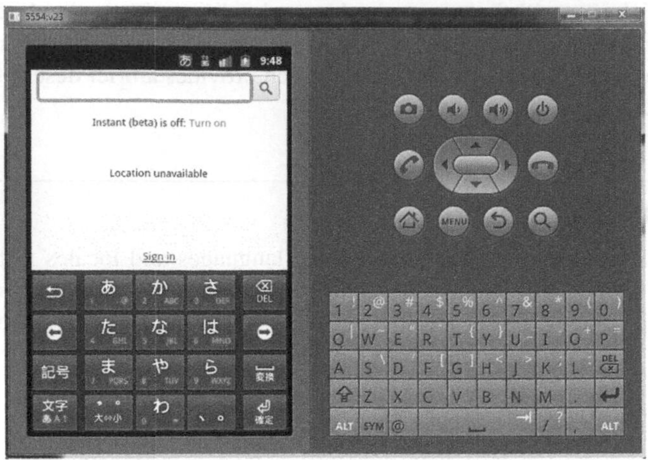

FIGURE 1.7

Android virtual device with Chinese number pad.

Simplified Chinese), and a number of other options. The latest version of Android (Gingerbread, 2.3) now supports 57 languages (Android 2.3 platform, n.d.).

Finally, Android supports third-party keyboards that the user can install. An alternative keyboard that is gaining popularity is called Swype that allows the user to drag their finger across the keyboard to each letter in one continuous motion. The software is then able to determine, with high probability, what word you were typing. The software supports multiple languages and is a good example of a pluggable keyboard input.

Custom Branches

As Android was released as open source, anyone (including you after following the steps above!) can download and then customize the Android source code. While many people who undertake this ultimately release their changes back to Google for inclusion into Android, some people fully branch the code and release their own version of Android.

Aftermarket Firmware

Perhaps the most prolific example of custom Android branches (also called Mods, firmware, and ROMs) comes from the Android hacking and enthusiast community. The community is a very large and diverse group of individuals who are motivated to develop, experiment, and otherwise hack Android. Some of their work may involve gaining root permissions on an Android device, enabling new features, or simply bragging about their latest customization. The community is passionate, prolific, and a terrific source of information (as well as misinformation) and they respond to many requests for help. Serious Android researchers would be remiss if they ignored this community. However, the sheer volume of information makes it a very time-consuming endeavor.

One of the most popular communities is called XDA Developers, self-described as "the largest Internet community of smartphone enthusiasts and developers for the Android and Windows Mobile platforms" (xda-developers, n.d.). Their web site has over 3.2 million registered users and runs a truly impressive forum.

Many of the custom Mods are released on XDA and often the developers themselves are active in the community. Perhaps the most popular aftermarket firmware is CyanogenMod. This firmware is based on the AOSP. It adds new features and attempts to increase the performance and reliability of the device over Android-based ROMs released by the vendors and carriers directly (CyanogenMod, n.d.). Currently CyanogenMod supports 17 different smartphone and tablet devices from six manufacturers: Commitva, Dell, HTC, Motorola, Samsung, and Viewsonic. These aftermarket firmwares have root access enabled on the device which, as we will discuss in Chapter 6, is key to obtaining a physical acquisition of the device.

OPhone OS

The Open Mobile Phone OS (OPhone OS) is based on Android and developed by Borqs, a Chinese software developer. OPhone OS was designed for Chinese government-owned China Mobile, the largest mobile carrier in the world with over 500 million subscribers. In June 2010, OPhone OS 2.0 was released in Beijing, and while Borqs/OPhone OS is relatively unknown outside of China, they clearly play an important and growing role in the Android ecosystem. Inside China, Borqs CEO stated they only work with one carrier, China Mobile, because "you cannot serve two masters" in that country (China's OPhone, n.d.).

So, they reserve the name OPhone OS for their China Mobile software. However, according to their web site, they also develop another branch of Android software that they call Android+ (China's OPhone, n.d.). In their press release, Borqs explains the Dell Aero is outfitted with their Android+ software, which includes an Apple-esque user interface, and that their software is also being distributed by Dell in Brazil and Mexico.

Android on iPhone (and Other non-Android Devices)

Perhaps one of the most controversial aftermarket firmwares is the one that enables Android to run on an iPhone. Since many mobile devices are based on the ARM processor, the porting process is achievable. This allows Android to run on devices designed to run other OSs like Windows Mobile, Symbian, iOS, and others. There's nothing quite like showing an Apple fanboy your beautiful iPhone running Android!

ANDROID MARKET

The Android Market is an avenue for third-party developers to release their applications to anyone who owns an Android device. The Android Market was first announced on August 28, 2008 on the Google Developer blog as "an open content distribution system that will help end users find, purchase, download and install various types of content on their Android-powered devices" (Android developers blog, n.d.). When the market was first released in October 2008, it did not support paid apps. However, by early 2009 the Android Market supported paid applications in both the United States and United Kingdom. By January 2011, the Android Market supported paid apps in 29 countries (Supported locations, n.d.). Several other countries, most notably India, can use the Android Market but currently cannot install paid apps.

Google's light-handed approach to managing the Android Market is in stark contrast to Apple's tight management of their App Store. While the Android Market does have Terms of Service for users (Android Market terms, n.d.) and an Android Market Developer Distribution Agreement (Android Market developer, n.d.) for developers, apps are released to the market without an approval process. Instead, Google believes that the app ratings will weed out apps that are buggy or show little merit.

To release an app into the Android Market, developers must be registered, pay a $25 fee, and sign their app with a private key which will uniquely identify them to the market. When a user purchases an app, the developer receives 70% of the purchase price with the remaining 30% going to Google (and, at times, the carrier involved). Initially, users had a 48 h window of time where they could return the apps. However, in December 2010, Google shortened that window to 15 min.

Google has the ability to remotely remove an app not only from the Android Market, but also directly from an Android device. The Remote Application Removal Feature is a security control Android possesses where a dangerous application could be removed from active circulation in a rapid and scalable manner to prevent further exposure to users (Android developers blog: exercising, n.d.). The security control was first exercised in June 2010 when a security researcher distributed a proof of concept app which could allow it to download and install another app on the device (Mills, n.d.).

In the open spirit of Android, Google also does not preclude users from directly installing apps on their phone from the developers' web site, nor does it preclude the development of a competing app marketplace. There are several alternatives to the Android Market, most of which are small in comparison. Also, several large companies have either announced or indicated their intentions to create an alternative app store, including Amazon, Best Buy, and Verizon.

Installing an app

To install an app from the Android Market, shown in Fig. 1.8, a user must first run the Market app and sign in with a Gmail account. This account allows the user to purchase paid apps through a Google Checkout account with address and credit card information. Recently, Google has partnered with some carriers so an app can be

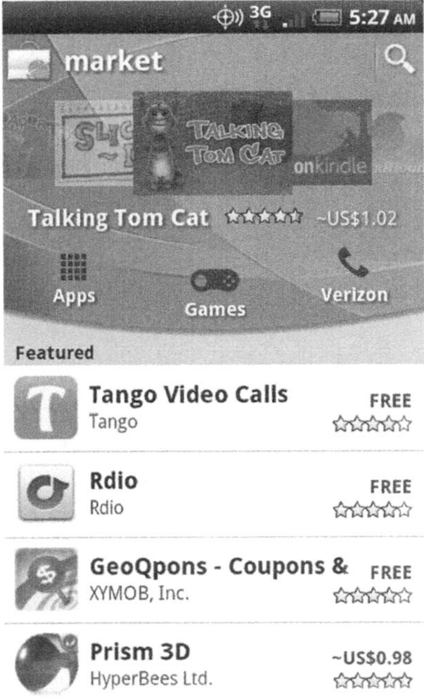

FIGURE 1.8

Android Market on HTC Incredible running Android 2.2.

purchased and placed on the subscribers' monthly wireless carrier bill instead of the Google Checkout credit card.

The Market app allows the user to search for apps and to browse by topic or popularity. Once an app is selected, a dedicated app page is displayed from which the user may install the app. The dedicated page also provides general information such as description, number of downloads, average rating, detailed reviews, related apps, developer info and, finally, an opportunity to provide feedback or flag the app as inappropriate.

As we will discuss, permissions are a central component to Android security. Once a user decides to install an app, they are presented with the screen that displays all of the permissions an app is requesting, as seen in Fig. 1.9. At this point, the user can accept the permissions and proceed with the install or go back to the previous screen.

The app is then downloaded and installed and the results are displayed in the notification bar at the top of the device. From there, the user can run the application or access it anytime from the list of applications.

To remove an application, the user can access the device's Settings and choose the Application setting. From there, they can Manage applications (see Fig. 1.10), which displays a list of apps with various characteristics such as downloaded, running, and on SD card.

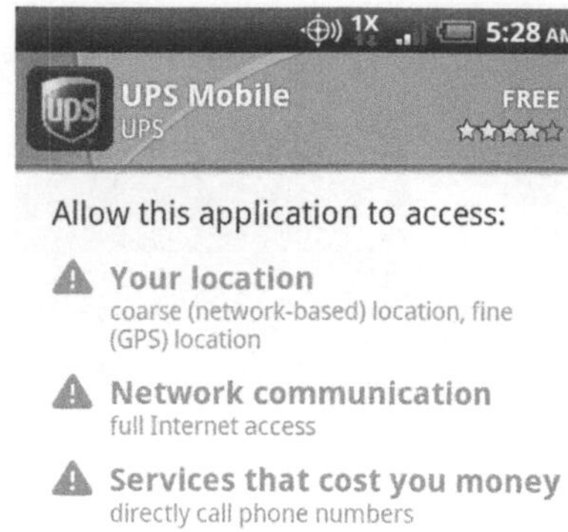

FIGURE 1.9

Android app permissions.

FIGURE 1.10

Manage applications.

FIGURE 1.11

Application information, including uninstall.

By selecting an app, the user can then see the Application info screen which shows various information about the apps and allows the user options to Force stop, Clear data, Clear cache, and Uninstall as shown in Fig. 1.11.

Application Statistics

The Android Market is growing quickly. Six months after its release, T-Mobile's Chief Technology Officer, Cole Brodman, commented that users needed more filters to successfully locate apps from the nearly 2300 apps on the Market (Lawson, n.d.). By January 2011, over 200,000 apps were on the Market with 27,227 added in November 2010 alone (Android Market statistics, n.d.). Estimates place the number of downloaded apps at over 2.5 billion.

Obviously, apps are a key area of focus for both security and forensics. In Chapter 4, we will explore in great detail how apps persist data to an Android device, what types of information are stored, and how data can be recovered and analyzed.

ANDROID FORENSICS

Clearly there is a need for Android forensics. Smartphones in general are perhaps the one electronic device that knows the most about an individual. For most people, their smartphone is rarely more than a few feet from them at any point of time—including while sleeping. The device blends both personal and corporate information and has the ability to store vast amounts of data including text messages, e-mails, GPS locations, picture, videos, and more. And people tend to be more honest with their smartphone than any other person or device. Why? Because people feel the device is secure and can provide them with answers to questions they may choose not to share with anyone else. More than one forensic examiner has quipped, "You are what you Google," clearly a byproduct of seeing firsthand the honesty with which people use their smartphones.

Challenges

Of course, nothing worth doing is easy and both mobile forensics and Android forensics in particular have a host of challenges that must be overcome.

A fundamental goal in digital forensics is to prevent any modification of the target device by the examiner. However, mobile phones lack traditional hard drives that can be shutdown, connected to a write blocker, and imaged in a forensically sound way. Any interaction with the smartphone will change the device in some way. As such, the examiners must use their judgment when examining a mobile device and if the device is modified, they must explain how it was modified and—as importantly—why that choice was made.

Some forensic examiners take exception to this approach and debates have ensued. However, techniques that may alter a computer targeted for forensic examination have been used for some time. For example, often a live memory analysis is necessary in an investigation of a malware attack. Similarly, if a hard drive is encrypted, an examiner must image the device while it is still running or they run the risk of never having the ability to access the data on the drive. Other good examples are systems that must remain online due to complex environments, typically found in cases involving larger corporate servers. While every examiner should strive to not change the device they are investigating, it is rarely possible in the mobile world. So, if the device cannot be modified, then the only other choice would be to not examine the device. Clearly this option is not acceptable as evidence from mobile forensics is a critical component in many investigations and has even solved many crimes.

Further complicating Android forensics is the sheer variety of devices, Android versions, and applications. The permutations of devices and Android versions alone are in the thousands and each device plus platform has unique characteristics. While a logical analysis of every Android phone is achievable, the vast combinations make the full physical acquisition of *every* Android device likely unachievable. Even a minor difference in the Android version may require extensive testing and validation in high-stakes cases.

SUMMARY

Android is a fast growing, feature-rich, and exciting mobile platform. The combination of features, connectivity, and popularity naturally lead to a growing need for Android forensics. While the difficulty of mobile forensics is increasing, the value is increasing as well. The open source aspect of Android greatly assists in the fundamental understanding a forensic analyst requires, making Android an ideal platform to work on.

References

Alliance, F. A. Q. (n.d.). *Open Handset Alliance*. Retrieved January 3, 2011, from http://www.openhandsetalliance.com/oha_faq.html.

Alliance Members. (n.d.). *Open Handset Alliance*. Retrieved March 9, 2011, from http://www.openhandsetalliance.com/oha_members.html.

Android developers blog: Android Market: a user-driven content distribution system. (n.d.). Retrieved January 9, 2011, from http://android-developers.blogspot.com/2008/08/android-market-user-driven-content.html.

Android developers blog: Exercising our remote application removal feature. (n.d.). Retrieved January 9, 2011, from http://android-developers.blogspot.com/2010/06/exercising-our-remote-application.html.

Android Market developer distribution agreement. (n.d.). Retrieved January 9, 2011, from http://www.android.com/us/developer-distribution-agreement.html.

Android Market terms of service. (n.d.). Retrieved January 9, 2011, from http://www.google.com/mobile/android/market-tos.html.

Android Market statistics from AndroLib, Androlib, Android applications and games directory. (n.d.). Retrieved January 9, 2011, from http://www.androlib.com/appstats.aspx.

Android 2.3 platform, & Android developers. (n.d.). Retrieved January 8, 2011, from http://developer.android.com/sdk/android-2.3.html#locs.

Bort, D. (n.d.). *Android is now available as open source*. Android Open Source Project. Retrieved January 3, 2011, from https://sites.google.com/a/android.com/opensource/posts/opensource.

China's OPhone to find its way to US as Android+. (n.d.). Retrieved January 8, 2011, from http://www.borqs.com/news.jsp.

Corporate information: About. (n.d.). Google. Retrieved January 4, 2011, from http://www.google.com/corporate/.

comScore reports November 2010 U.S. mobile subscriber market share. (n.d.). comScore. Inc. Retrieved January 9, 2011, from http://www.comscore.com/Press_Events/Press_Releases/2011/1/comScore_Reports_November_.

CyanogenMod, About the Rom, CyanogenMod. (n.d.). Retrieved January 8, 2011, from http://www.cyanogenmod.com/about.

Gartner says worldwide mobile phone sales grew 35 percent in third quarter 2010; smartphone sales increased 96 percent. (n.d.) Technology Research & Business Leader Insight. Gartner Inc. Retrieved March 9, 2011, from http://www.gartner.com/it/page.jsp?id=1466313.

Get Android source code, Android open source. (n.d.). Retrieved March 9, 2011, from http://source.android.com/source/download.html.

Google Investor: Google android activating 350,000 devices daily (data visualization video) "Top global smartphone platform." (n.d.). Retrieved March 9, 2011, from http://googinvestor.blogspot.com/2011/03/google-android-activations-350k-daily.html.

Krazit, T. (n.d.). *Google's Rubin: Android "a revolution." Digital Media—CNET News. Technology News—CNET News*. Retrieved January 5, 2011, from http://news.cnet.com/8301-1023_3-10245994-93.html.

Licenses. (n.d.). *Android open source*. Retrieved January 5, 2011, from http://source.android.com/source/licenses.html.

Languages and scripts. (n.d.). *Unicode Consortium*. http://unicode.org/repos/cldr-tmp/trunk/diff/supplemental/languages_and_scripts.html.

Lawson, S. (n.d.). *Android Market needs more filters, T-Mobile says*. ITworld, IT news, technology analysis and how-to resources. Retrieved January 9, 2011, from http://www.itworld.com/personal-tech/64481/android-market-needs-more-filters-t-mobile-says.

Mills, E. (n.d.). *Google remotely wipes apps off Android phones*. InSecurity Complex—CNET News. Technology News—CNET News. Retrieved January 9, 2011, from http://news.cnet.com/8301-27080_3-20008922-245.html.

Official Google Blog: Where's my Gphone? (n.d.). Retrieved January 2, 2011, from http://googleblog.blogspot.com/2007/11/wheres-my-gphone.html.

Supported locations for merchants—Android Market help. (n.d.). Retrieved January 9, 2011, from http://www.google.com/support/androidmarket/bin/answer.py?hl=en&answer=150324.

Torvalds, L. (1991, October 5). *Free minix-like kernel sources for 386-AT—comp.os.minix*. Google Groups. Retrieved March 3, 2011, from http://groups.google.com/group/comp.os.minix/msg/2194d253268b0a1b.

xda-developers. (n.d.). Retrieved January 8, 2011, from www.xda-developers.com/.

CHAPTER

Android hardware platforms 2

INFORMATION IN THIS CHAPTER

- Overview of core components
- Overview of different device types
- Read-only memory and boot loaders
- Manufacturers
- Specific devices

INTRODUCTION

Android was designed to be compatible with a wide array of hardware. This is achieved, in large part, through the Linux kernel, which over the years has evolved to support a large variety of hardware. This is an important characteristic of the platform as it allows manufacturers freedom to design, procure, or otherwise integrate the ideal components of the Android device. This strategy has led to the development of powerful dual core Android devices capable of significant processing as well as entry-level devices targeted to entry-level wireless plans. Although the hardware compatibility is great for manufacturers, wireless providers, and ultimately consumers, the diversity poses challenges for forensic analysts and security engineers. Understanding the hardware components, device types, and boot process for Android will aid in your overall understanding of Android.

OVERVIEW OF CORE COMPONENTS

Android was developed to support a wide range of devices and manufacturers. As such, any list of major components will likely be outdated as soon as it is printed. However, there are some consistent components found in Android devices, which are beneficial to discuss. The following components comprise the core of an Android device.

Central Processing Unit

The central processing unit (CPU) is a term quite familiar to most forensic analysts, and there are no surprises in its role on Android devices. The CPU is responsible for executing operating system (OS) and application code and coordinating or controlling other core components including the network, storage, displays, and input devices.

From the beginning, most (if not all) Android devices utilize ARM processors as their CPU, which are powerful enough for the mobile platform but designed for low power consumption—a key aspect in maximizing battery life.

However, corporations and enthusiasts alike have ported Android to other platforms. On the corporate front, Intel has ported Android to their Atom processors. Similarly, Google has ported Android in their Google TV product, which is built on top of Android. There are also projects, such as Android-x86 (Android-x86, n.d.), that have released ported versions of Android running on Intel's x86 architecture. Some of the platforms supported include many of the Eee PC models and the Lenovo ThinkPad x61 Tablet.

Baseband Modem/Radio

The baseband modem and radio are hardware and software systems that provide Android devices a connection to the cellular network. This allows both voice and data communication from the device.

Instead of occupying the main CPU with these activities, device designers typically leverage a dedicated component to manage the complexities of cellular communication. Thus, although the CPU may direct the overall activities of the device, the baseband modem manages cellular communication.

Throughout this book, we will use the terms *baseband*, *baseband modem*, and *radio* interchangeably. Although these systems are complex and certain nuances may be overlooked in this definition, the distinctions are not significant for forensic analysts.

Memory (Random-Access Memory and NAND Flash)

Android devices, because they are at some level simply computers, need various types of memory to operate. The two primary types of memory required are volatile (random-access memory [RAM]) and nonvolatile (NAND flash) memory.

The RAM is used by the system to load, execute, and manipulate key parts of the OS, applications, or data. RAM is volatile, meaning that it does not preserve its state without power.

However, NAND flash memory (we will refer to this memory simply as NAND flash) is nonvolatile, and thus, the data are preserved after the device has been powered off. The NAND flash is used to store the boot loader, OS, and user data. It is therefore a critical component of any forensic investigation and is similar to a hard drive in a forensic investigation of a laptop, desktop, or server. NAND flash also has unique properties that make it ideal for mobile devices while at the same time presenting a number of challenges for programmers (which often yield unique opportunities for forensic analysts). These characteristics will be explored in detail in Chapter 4.

From a hardware perspective, mobile devices obviously have significant space limitations. Often, the RAM and NAND flash memory are manufactured into a simple component referred to as the multichip package (MCP). When examining

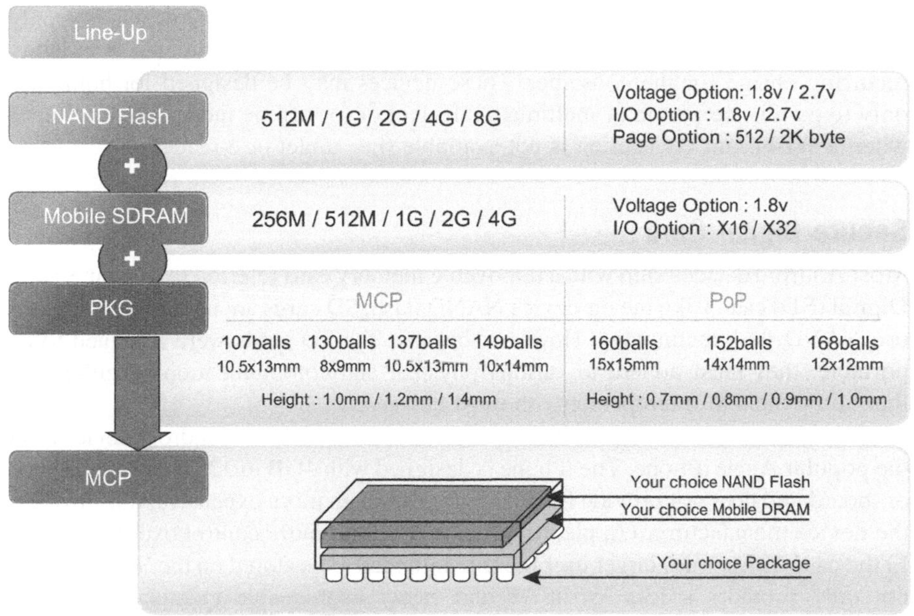

FIGURE 2.1

MCP architecture (Mobile Memory, n.d.).

Android device components, generally the NAND flash and RAM will be packaged as an MCP.

Although Fig. 2.1 is specific to the memory manufacturer Hynix (used in the Dell Streak and other Android devices), this overall architecture is a good depiction of MCP components that include not only the NAND flash and RAM but also the packaging options to suit various devices.

Global Positioning System

Undoubtedly one of the most important innovations in mobile devices since the inclusion of cellular communication has been integration of the Global Positioning System (GPS) into the core offering. This functionality not only identifies the location of the device using the GPS satellite network but also allows for applications such as point-to-point directions, position-aware applications, and, undoubtedly, many more interesting uses in the future.

Wireless (Wi-Fi.com and Bluetooth)

Beyond the cellular networks, most devices allow for additional wireless technologies, such as Wi-Fi.com for high-speed data connection and Bluetooth for connections to external devices such as headsets, keyboards, printers, and more. In fact, some devices may omit the cellular network connection, which not only reduces the cost and complexity of the device but also eliminates a monthly recurring charge for the consumer. These devices may be designed for home use only (e.g., a home phone or multimedia device) or for offline mode for those times when a Wi-Fi.com connection is not available (i.e., tablet or e-reader).

Secure Digital Card

Most Android devices ship with a removable memory card referred to as their Secure Digital (SD) card. Like the on-device NAND flash, SD cards are nonvolatile and also use NAND flash technology. However, because the SD cards were designed to be portable, they must adhere to various physical and communication specifications that allow them to interoperate with most devices.

The SD card is one obvious design difference between most Android devices and the popular Apple iPhone. The iPhone is designed with 4GB to 32GB of NAND flash on-board and does not provide for SD cards. Although more expensive, this provides the device manufacturer (Apple, in this case) with far more control over the device. In the case of Android, larger user files are intended to be stored on the SD card. This not only provides a less expensive and easily upgradeable memory option for consumers but is also portable, so if a consumer purchases a new phone, they can easily transfer data using their existing SD card.

Recent HTC phones (notably the HTC Incredible) have provided the standard SD card interface but did not ship with an SD card installed. Instead, they created an emulated SD card by carving a portion of the on-board NAND memory and presenting it as an SD card. This adds additional complexity for the forensic analysts. Analysts must first determine whether there is an SD card, an emulated SD card, or some other means of user data storage (in addition to the on-board NAND flash).

Screen

The screen on an Android device is obviously a critical component. It is the primary interface for user interaction, not only through the visual display but also by responding to the user's touch. The technologies behind the display are the focus of intense development. Early iterations included a liquid crystal display and a second layer that detects user input on the screen. Recent improvements include higher display resolution, brighter screens, more sensitive and complicated user touch interactions, and reduced power consumption. In fact, some recent Android smartphones, such as those using Samsung's Super AMOLED technology, have been well received by consumers due largely to the screen capabilities.

Camera

Initially cameras on smartphones were used to take pictures. Although an exciting development at the time, there has been significant innovation in this area too. Most devices now also support video recording (some in high definition). Of course, cameras have increased in their quality and now often include an integrated flash.

Recently, some devices include two cameras. The first, on the back of the device, is used for external pictures and videos. A second front-facing camera allows for new applications such as videoconferencing.

Most Android devices also combine the camera functionality with the GPS; hence, you can record not only the date and time of a picture but also the GPS coordinates. You can then easily upload or share the picture using the network or perhaps send them through the Multimedia Messaging Service (MMS) of the cellular provider.

One interesting development in this area is the use of cameras to read bar codes. Specialized applications leverage the camera to take a picture of a bar code and then analyze the data. It might look up product reviews, determine the best price, or automatically check you into a restaurant's application so that you can rate experiences. Perhaps in the future, these apps may even allow you to pay for items you wish to purchase.

An early implementation of this is a Google app called Goggles. The user can take a picture of anything, and the app attempts to identify the object. An interesting example, provided by Google, was tourists using the app to identify landmarks they were visiting.

Keyboard

You might think that there is little innovation possible with a keyboard; however, this is certainly not the case. Most Android devices come with an on-screen keyboard thanks to touch screen technology. A number of devices also have a hardware-based keyboard.

The powerful software keyboards can adapt to the screen orientation (i.e., if you rotate the screen 90 degrees, the keyboard will also rotate) and can support multiple languages.

There are also companies developing more efficient ways to input text to a device. One such company, Swype Inc., developed a keyboard where the user does not select individual keys for each letter. Instead, for each word they simply start with the first letter and then swipe their finger around the keyboard (without picking it up) to each subsequent letter until they are done. The Swype keyboard then determines the likely word and completes it (or offers suggestions). This approach has proven to be quite successful, and we expect to see more Swype technology (or similar innovations) integrated into the Android keyboard.

Battery

Battery life has always been a major concern for smartphone adopters. You may love your phone but hate its battery life. The more people use the device—and the components that make it so powerful—the more battery consumed. Great care is taken in minimizing power consumption. However, most people find they must charge their phones every day.

Over time, improvements in the hardware, software, and battery technology may lead to less frequent charging. There are some interesting research initiatives in this area such as recharging your phone without wires, leveraging the movement of the human body for continuous recharging, or simply creating more powerful batteries. Whatever the improvements, they will be welcomed by consumers.

For forensic analysts, one thing to bear in mind is that the SD card is often located behind the battery. So, to access the SD card (and determine the exact device type and identification), you generally have to remove the battery (thus powering off the device). There are various considerations here, which we will cover in Chapter 6.

Universal Serial Bus

Most Android devices support several Universal Serial Bus (USB) interfaces that can be accessed from computers. The cables may vary between devices, but in general, the USB interface allows most modern OSs connectivity to the device. The following are some common interfaces exposed by Android devices:

1. Charge only: the device can be recharged over the USB cable
2. Disk interface: portions of the device, including the SD card, emulated SD card, and other disk interfaces, are presented and accessible to the OS as a Mass Storage Device
3. Vendor-specific interfaces: these include custom synchronization protocols, emulated CD-read-only memory (ROM) drives for software installs, and specialized connections for sharing the phone's Internet connection
4. Android Debug Bridge (ADB): an interface that provides the user access to a shell prompt on the device as well as other advanced features

In Chapter 3, we will explore the disk interface and the ADB interface, both of which are critical components in the forensic investigation of an Android device.

Accelerometer/Gyroscope

Android can detect and change the user interface based on how the device is held or rotated. This is typically achieved through an accelerometer that detects the size and direction a device has been accelerated (or positioned). Typically, this is used to change the display between landscape and portrait.

The latest version of Android (2.3 as of this writing) now supports a gyroscope, which is more sensitive and sophisticated than an accelerometer. The gyroscope is a more responsive and accurate measure of device movement—key for advanced game development.

Speaker/Microphone

Finally, a smartphone or tablet is not that interesting without the ability to hear or produce sound. Like the other components, the speaker and microphone continue to mature with each iteration. For instance, some Android devices contain two or three microphones that, combined with the Android software, have the ability to detect and cancel out background noise to provide better sound quality. In perhaps some of the most stunning technological development of this decade, the speaker phones have evolved to the point where they can actually be used in real conversation!

OVERVIEW OF DIFFERENT DEVICE TYPES

From these core components, designers have created a wide variety of device types. Back in October of 2008, the T-Mobile G1 (HTC Dream 100) was just released, and it was quite easy to track the Android devices and types. It was simply the G1. And the only device type was a smartphone. Of course, there were already blog posts flying around about new device types but that was all speculation.

However, by the end of 2010, not only had the number of Android devices grown tremendously but also the types of devices. There are many web sites that attempt to track Android devices; however, most are incomplete. One decent reference that is useful while preparing to examine a new Android device is PDAdb.net, which tracks significant information about current and future devices. Currently, they are tracking over 300 devices running Android, which you can search from their PDAmaster page (Main Page, n.d.).

The primary device types remain smartphones and tablets, but there are a growing number of ultraportable computers (we will call them netbooks) as well as e-readers. On the innovation front, Google TV devices (running Android) are beginning to hit the market, a few media players exist, and a number of automotive companies have announced that they will run Android as part of their media and navigation systems. And finally, there is an entire group that falls under the "other" category, which may remain as one-off devices or could certainly go mainstream. Examples include appliances, gaming devices, GPS receivers, home phones and audio devices, photo frames, and printers. The following sections detail some of these device types.

Smartphone

Smartphones are the most popular type of Android devices. They contain nearly all of the components described above and are generally the most well known. As of October 2010, Android devices represent 22% of the smartphone market in the United States (Nielsen Wire, n.d.) and are growing quickly. It is widely accepted that Android will surpass the iPhone and perhaps will ultimately be the most popular smartphone platform.

Tablet

Even though tablet computers have been around for decades, it appears that the confluence of hardware, software, mobile networks, and applications may finally yield a viable market. There are a number of Android tablets on the market. However, the most recent and widely publicized device is the Samsung Galaxy Tab™. The 7-inch device has essentially all the components of an Android smartphone but in a larger form factor. Although tablets may support cellular data connections (as the Galaxy Tab does), they are typically limited to data and Short Message Service/MMS and do not support cellular voice calls. However, with the convergence of voice and data, we expect tablet devices to support Voice over Internet Protocol phone and video calls soon.

Netbook

Netbooks are highly portable laptops with low power consumption and are a good candidate for Android. It is important to note that Android is different from another Google project called Chromium OS, which "is an open-source project that aims to build an OS that provides a fast, simple, and more secure computing experience for people who spend most of their time on the web" (Chromium OS, n.d.). Android was developed first and is far more mature than Chromium OS.

A number of Android netbooks that are now available share common characteristics with tablets, except netbooks have a full hardware keyboard and generally a larger hinged screen. Often, the primary data storage medium for netbooks is NAND flash. However, there is no technical reason why a more traditional hard drive could not be used.

Google TV

Google, like many companies in the past, is trying to bridge the gap between viewing broadcast television and Internet content. The devices span from full television sets with Android built in, to set-top boxes that connect to existing televisions. But the key is leveraging Android as the base OS, integrating the Internet and television shows, and providing a framework for developers to create new applications specific for the new medium.

Vehicles (In-board)

An area that holds exciting possibilities is the integration of Android devices into automobiles, typically as part of the navigation/heads-up display or entertainment system. To date, such systems are specific to each vehicle manufacturer, which has resulted in systems that vary greatly in features, stability, and effectiveness. If manufacturers integrated the full functionality of the ever-evolving Android OS, it would allow them to focus on the user experience instead of the fundamental building blocks. Users would find consistency between different vehicles and with the Android devices. And developers could target applications specific to the needs of vehicles and have a wider distribution market. Finally, there may be a host of additional interested players, such as insurance agencies, attorneys, research organizations, forensic analysts, and more, who could analyze information from these systems in many ways.

The first car in production running Android is the Roewe 350 developed and distributed in China by Shanghai Automotive Industry Corporation. In addition, many US-based car makers have announced support for Android ranging from connectivity with smartphones through full integration of the Android OS into their vehicles.

Global Positioning System

As mentioned previously, most Android devices have GPS built into their hardware. When GPS first became available to consumers, the manufacturers created custom OSs to manage their devices. Although most still leverage their custom system, several have moved to the Android OS. As such, forensic analysts might encounter dedicated GPS devices that run Android.

Other Devices

There are a growing number of new Android devices that will be hopelessly out-of-date as soon as they are mentioned. Android is just too good of a deal for manufacturers to pass up. The OS is free, mature, and allows for proprietary development. It also provides a mechanism for application development, whether internal or through third parties. So many manufacturers are foregoing the expensive OS development, maintenance, and support and instead building on top of Android. Here are some examples of additional Android device types:

- Home appliances such as washing machines and microwaves
- E-readers such as Barnes and Noble's Nook
- Media players
- Office equipment such as copying machines
- Home phones, audio and video (e.g., photo frames) devices
- Dedicated gaming devices
- Printers

As you can tell, there are many ways in which manufacturers will leverage Android that will certainly keep the forensic analyst's job interesting (as if it was not already).

ROM AND BOOT LOADERS

Android devices, like any other computer, have a fairly standard boot process which allows the device to load the needed firmware, OS, and user data into memory to support full operation. Although the boot process itself is well defined, the firmware and ROM varies by manufacturer and by device. The goal of this section is to provide a high-level overview of the Android boot process, as techniques addressed later in this book will interact with the device at various levels. This overview is intended to be a high level because an in-depth description of the Android or Linux boot process could easily require an entire book on its own.

Much of the information in this section is based on a post titled "The Android boot process from power on" by Mattias Björnheden of the Android Competence Center at Enea (Björnheden, n.d.). In the post, Mattias identifies seven key steps to the Android boot process:

1. Power on and on-chip boot ROM code execution
2. The boot loader
3. The Linux kernel
4. The init process
5. Zygote and Dalvik
6. The system server
7. Boot complete

We will examine each of these steps in detail.

Power On and On-chip Boot ROM Code Execution

When an Android device is first powered on, a special boot ROM code paired with the CPU is executed to (1) initialize the device hardware and (2) locate the boot media. The ROM code is specific to the CPU the device is using. This step in the boot process is similar to the basic input-output system used to boot computers.

For example, a CPU popular with the hardware hacking community is the Texas Instrument OMAP3530 ARM-compatible CPU that has a 3444-page *Technical Reference Manual* available publicly (Public Version of OMAP35xx, 2010). Although reading the technical manual is not for everyone, it provides enormous detail and insight into how the CPU initializes and loads an OS. On page 3373, the manual provides a flowchart detailing the overall booting sequence. The ROM code, which starts the entire process, is hard coded at address 0x00014000, so that when power is applied to the device, the CPU knows exactly where to locate the boot ROM to start the boot sequence.

Once the device hardware is initialized, the ROM code scans until it finds the boot media (which Android devices store on the NAND flash) and copies the initial boot loader to internal RAM. Then execution jumps from the boot ROM to the freshly loaded code in RAM as shown in Fig. 2.2.

Boot Loader (Initial Program Load/Second Program Loader)

The boot loader, now copied from the boot media, is executed in internal RAM. This step is similar to the boot loader found when booting computers such as Windows, Mac, and Linux. A typical computer boot loader, such as GRUB for Linux, allows the user to select which OS they want to boot and loads it accordingly.

For an Android device, the boot loader has two distinct stages: the initial program load (IPL) and the second program loader (SPL). The IPL is responsible for detecting and setting up external RAM, an essential component needed to boot and

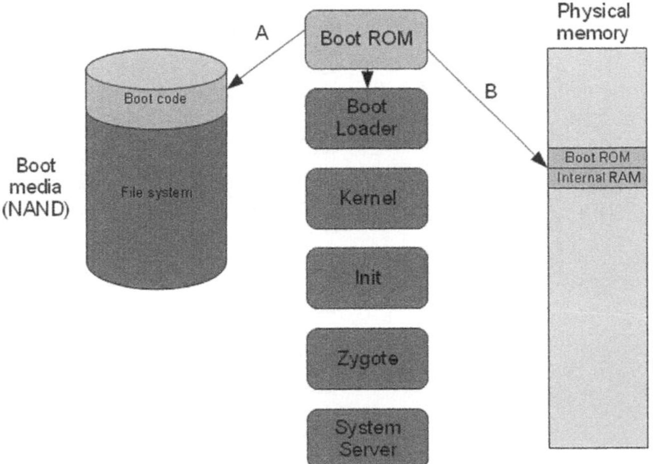

FIGURE 2.2

Power on and on-chip boot ROM code.

operate the device. Once external RAM is prepared, the IPL copies the SPL into RAM and then transfers execution to the SPL.

The SPL is responsible for not only loading the Android OS but also providing access to alternative boot modes such as fastboot, recovery, or other modes designed to update and debug or service the device. The SPL is generally provided by the manufacturer. However, the Android community actively creates their own SPLs (and other custom images) that enable additional features and functionality. In a typical boot scenario, the SPL will initialize hardware components such as the clock, console, display, keyboard, and baseband modem as well as file systems, virtual memory, and other features required to operate the device.

The SPL then locates the Linux kernel on the boot media, copies it to RAM, loads boot parameters, and finally transfers execution to the kernel. Figure 2.3 illustrates this process.

Linux Kernel

There have been volumes written on the Linux kernel and much of it is available online. For this book, we simply acknowledge that the Linux kernel is now controlling the device. After setting up additional features on the device, the root file system is read from the NAND flash, which will provide access to system and user data shown in Fig. 2.4.

The Init Process

Once the kernel has access to the system partition, it can process the init scripts that start key system and user processes. This is similar to the /etc/init.d scripts found on

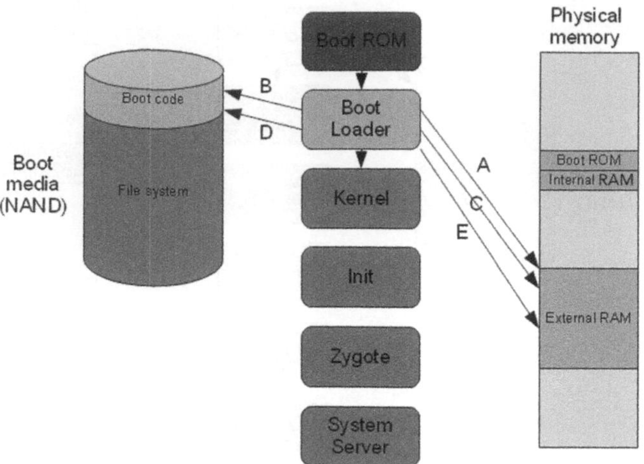

FIGURE 2.3

Boot loader.

traditional Linux devices. For Android, the init.rc is typically located on the root file system and provides the kernel with the details on how to start core services.

On an HTC Incredible running Android 2.2, the init.rc and init.inc.rc files contain over 650 lines and provide substantial insight into the device setup. The selected portions of the /init.rc file are as follows:

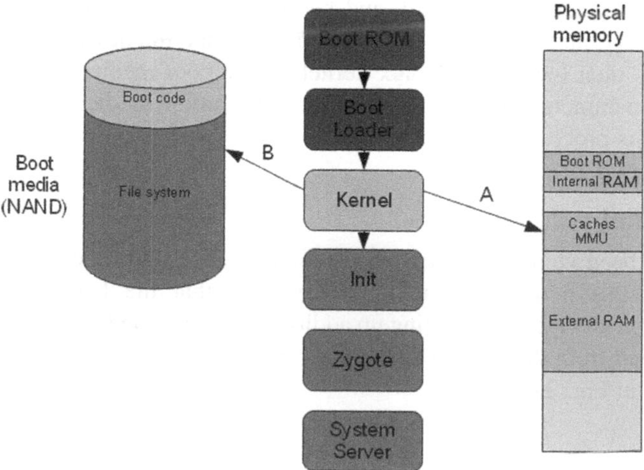

FIGURE 2.4

Linux kernel.

```
on init

sysclktz 0

loglevel 3

# setup the global environment
    export PATH /sbin:/system/sbin:/system/bin:/system/xbin
    export LD_LIBRARY_PATH /system/lib
    export ANDROID_BOOTLOGO 1
    export ANDROID_ROOT /system
    export ANDROID_ASSETS /system/app
    export ANDROID_DATA /data
    export EXTERNAL_STORAGE /mnt/sdcard
    export ASEC_MOUNTPOINT /mnt/asec

# Backward compatibility
    symlink /system/etc /etc
    symlink /sys/kernel/debug /d

# create mountpoints
    mkdir /mnt 0775 root system
    mkdir /mnt/sdcard 0000 system system

# Backwards Compat - XXX: Going away in G*
    symlink /mnt/sdcard /sdcard

    mkdir /system
    mkdir /data 0771 system system
    mkdir /cache 0770 system cache
    mkdir /config 0500 root root

    # Directory for putting things only root should see.
    mkdir /mnt/secure 0700 root root

    # Directory for staging bindmounts
    mkdir /mnt/secure/staging 0700 root root

    # Directory-target for where the secure container
    # imagefile directory will be bind-mounted
    mkdir /mnt/secure/asec  0700 root root

    # Secure container public mount points.
    mkdir /mnt/asec  0700 root system
    mount tmpfs tmpfs /mnt/asec mode=0755,gid=1000

    mount rootfs rootfs / ro remount

    write /proc/sys/kernel/panic_on_oops 1
    write /proc/sys/kernel/hung_task_timeout_secs 0
    write /proc/cpu/alignment 4
    write /proc/sys/kernel/sched_latency_ns 5000000
    write /proc/sys/kernel/sched_wakeup_granularity_ns 100000
    write /proc/sys/kernel/sched_min_granularity_ns 100000
    write /proc/sys/kernel/sched_compat_yield 1
    write /proc/sys/kernel/sched_child_runs_first 0

# mount mtd partitions
    # Mount /system rw first to give the filesystem a chance to save
    a checkpoint
    mount yaffs2 mtd@system /system
    mount yaffs2 mtd@system /system ro remount
```

```
# We chown/chmod /data again so because mount is run as root + defaults
mount yaffs2 mtd@userdata /data nosuid nodev
chown system system /data
chmod 0771 /data
```

From a forensic standpoint, the HTC Incredible changes how the browser stores cache after the boot process is complete. The contents of /bootcomplete.inc.rc are quite telling:

```
rm -r /data/data/com.android.browser/cache
mkdir /app-cache/com.android.browser
chmod 755 /app-cache/com.android.browser
chownto /app-cache/com.android.browser /data/data/com.android.browser
mkdir /app-cache/com.android.browser/cache
chmod 755 /app-cache/com.android.browser/cache
chownto /app-cache/com.android.browser/cache /data/data/com.android.browser
ln -s /app-cache/com.android.browser/cache /data/data/com.android.browser/cache
rm -r /data/app-cache
rm -r /data/DxDrm
```

As you can see, once the device has completed the boot process, the browser cache is moved from the user data partition stored on the NAND flash into a temporary RAM disk (tmpfs) located at /app-cache. This means that when the device is powered down, any data written to /app-cache will be lost as shown in Fig. 2.5.

In summary, the init.rc is a fundamental step in the setup of the Android device and can be carefully studied to understand how a particular Android device is configured and operates.

Zygote and Dalvik

In Chapter 3, we will cover the specifics of the individual virtual machine each user application is provided as a runtime sandbox. The Dalvik virtual machine is the technology Google selected to create this application sandbox. At startup, the Zygote sequence essentially sets up the Java runtime environment and registers a socket with the system; hence, new applications that need to initialize can request a new Dalvik virtual machine. Without the Zygote service, the Android kernel could run. However, no applications would operate including built-in applications such as the phone, browser, and other core features as illustrated in Fig. 2.6.

System Server

The core features of the device mentioned in the previous section are started by the system server. Once the Java runtime is set up and the Zygote process is listening, the system server is started. This runs core features such as telephony, network, and other fundamental components that the device and other applications rely upon. Figure 2.7 illustrates how the system server runs.

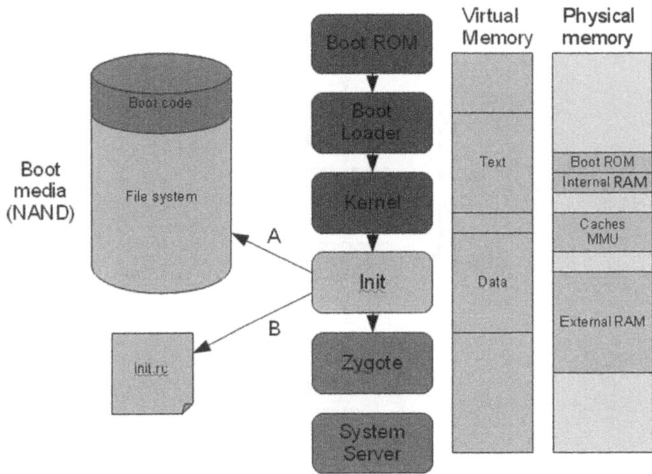

FIGURE 2.5

Init process.

The system finally sends a standard broadcast action called ACTION_BOOT_COMPLETED, which alerts dependent processes that the boot process is complete. The Android system is now fully operational and is ready to interact with the user.

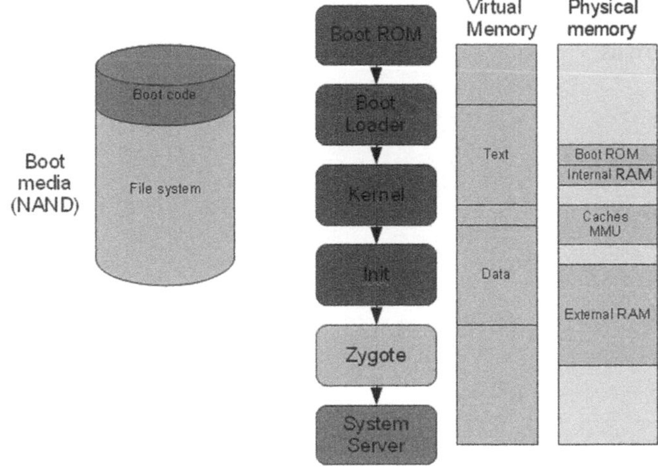

FIGURE 2.6

Zygote and Dalvik.

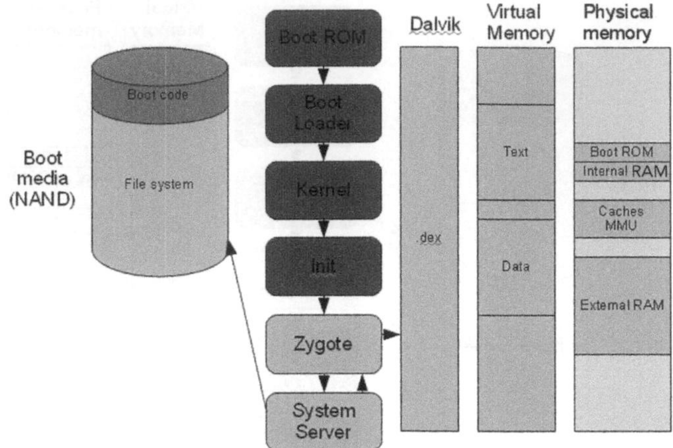

FIGURE 2.7

System server.

MANUFACTURERS

Google's Android strategy has spawned a diverse group of Android device manufacturers. On the Android Developer web site, a list of USB Vendor IDs is maintained and currently tracks 15 manufacturers (Using Hardware Devices, n.d.). The list includes the following:

- Acer
- Dell
- Foxconn
- Garmin-Asus
- HTC
- Huawei
- Kyocera
- LG
- Motorola
- Nvidia
- Pantech
- Samsung
- Sharp
- Sharp
- ZTE

However, once you factor in manufacturers not listed above and devices in the planning phase, there are over 50 different manufacturers of Android devices.

This, of course, presents a unique challenge for forensic investigators and corporate security managers alike. The sheer volume of device manufacturers, device types, and devices results in a complicated array of policies, procedures, techniques, and even USB cables.

ANDROID UPDATES

Android's update models are decentralized, device specific, and are the responsibility of the carrier or device manufacturer, not Google. Although the Open Handset Alliance, largely influenced by Google, is responsible for maintaining the core Android OS, they do not exercise control over specific devices. This decentralized approach impacts the forensic and security procedures for devices in several ways.

First, an analyst is never certain what version of Android a device will have installed. This is in part driven by corporations' quest for the highest possible profit margins. Notably in the United States, if a consumer purchases an Android device with a two-year contract, the carrier has essentially locked the consumer in, because the early termination fees are ever-escalating. As the user is unlikely to upgrade their service or purchase a new phone, they represent a fixed amount of revenue for the carrier. The engineering, development, deployment, and support costs of upgrading an existing Android device are quite steep. Therefore, the carriers can either invest in new Android devices, which generate enormous interest and presumably sales, or maintain an existing device, which brings in very little, if any, additional revenue. More often than not, consumers using older Android phones will remain on older and less functional and less secure versions of Android. This is an issue Google has acknowledged and has stated that they are working to address.

Second, both securing and acquiring a forensic image of an Android device vary greatly between Android versions and device types. For example, the technique an analyst would leverage for an HTC Dream 100 (T-Mobile G1) running Android 1.5 with kernel 2.6.30.4 or earlier is vastly different than the same device running Android 1.6 or a kernel greater than 2.6.30.4. As you can imagine, with more than 50 manufacturers, over 300 Android devices, four major releases and hundreds of minor releases, the possible combinations are vast.

Third, the hardware, drivers, and software used to connect to different Android devices can vary. The Android software development kit (SDK), discussed in Chapter 3, does provide some consistency. However, each manufacturer may have their own set of specific drivers and software. For example, if connecting a Samsung Galaxy S to a computer running Windows, you need to first install specific software provided by Samsung. However, many other devices have standard USB drivers provided by Google via their SDK.

Finally, each manufacturer has their own boot process including the hardware, boot loaders, and ROM firmware. In Chapter 6, we will explore some techniques for exploiting the boot process on devices by various manufacturers.

Custom User Interfaces

Portions of Android are licensed under the Apache 2.0 open source instead of the full GPLv2 open source license. The Apache 2.0 license allows manufacturers and developers the ability to customize certain parts of the Android system, yet relieves them of the obligation to return the source code back to the community. The Apache 2.0 license primarily covers specific drivers for the device where the manufacturer's intellectual property could be compromised and in the area of user interface customization.

By allowing proprietary user interfaces, Google has allowed the manufacturers to tailor a key area to the intended audience and differentiate their Android devices from their competitors. For instance, one Android device may target the teen market and focus on text messaging and social applications, whereas a different device may be primarily targeted to business users. Fundamentally, the devices operate quite similarly. However, the user interface customizations (as well as hardware design implementation) create a unique experience. Table 2.1 describes the custom user interfaces by manufacturers.

Aftermarket Android Devices

As the Android OS is an open source, custom builds have been created, which will run on devices originally released to the market with other OSs. In one infamous example, versions of Android exist which can be installed and run on the iPhone (Linux on the iPhone, n.d.). It is certainly a lot of fun to watch the Apple fanboys react when such a feat has been accomplished. More practically, Android has been ported to many HTC phones that originally shipped with Windows Mobile. And there are many more examples involving devices from companies such as Nokia and even devices in categories other than smartphones.

Although it may not happen too often, it is important to consider the possibility that the Windows phone (or iPhone) you need to forensically analyze may indeed be running Android.

Table 2.1 Custom Android User Interfaces

Manufacturer	Custom User Interface(s)
Motorola	Motoblur
HTC	Sense
Samsung	TouchWiz
Sony Ericsson	Rachael, UX, Nexus
Acer	Touch 3D
Dell	Stage
Viewsonic	TapnTap

SPECIFIC DEVICES

The following devices are used throughout this book, and a brief overview of each device is presented here for reference. Several of these devices were some of the first commercially available Android smartphones and are well understood. They can be purchased at a fairly reasonable price point and may be a great device to populate and experiment on following the examples throughout this book.

T-Mobile G1

The T-Mobile G1 shown in Fig. 2.8 was manufactured by HTC and released to the US market by T-Mobile in October 2008. Like many first-generation devices, there were usability issues with the phone. However, it sold over one million units (Krazit, n.d.) in the first six months and serves as a great reference phone.

Device info:

- Manufacturer: HTC
- Model: G1 (aka: HTC Dream 100)
- Carrier(s): T-Mobile
- Release date: October 2008

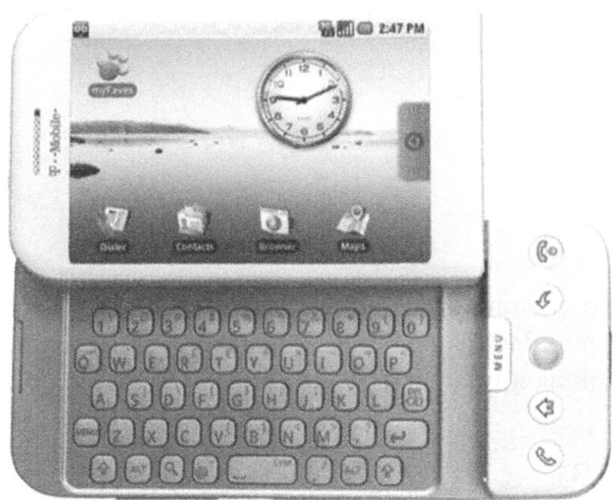

FIGURE 2.8

T-Mobile G1 (DREA100).

Motorola Droid

The Motorola Droid, shown in Fig. 2.9, was manufactured by Motorola and released to the US market by Verizon in November 2009. In the first 74 days, 1.05 million Droid smartphones were sold, making it more popular than the original iPhone

FIGURE 2.9

Motorola Droid (A855).

release in June 2007 (Day 74 Sales, n.d.). The Droid is an excellent reference phone, and if you are contemplating the purchase of a device for testing, you should strongly consider this device.

Device info:

- Manufacturer: Motorola Mobile Devices
- Model: A855
- Carrier(s): Verizon Wireless
- Release date: November 2009

HTC Incredible

The HTC Incredible, pictured in Fig. 2.10, was released on the Verizon network and is also extremely popular in the United States. The device is used extensively throughout this book as a reference phone.

Device info:

- Manufacturer: HTC
- Model: ADR6300
- Carrier(s): Verizon Wireless
- Release date: April 2010

Google Nexus One

As described in Chapter 1, Google released their own smartphone, the Nexus One (N1), in January 2010, shown in Fig. 2.11. The N1 was developed by HTC and, by all accounts, was an ideal model of how manufacturers should develop their phone.

FIGURE 2.10

HTC Incredible.

FIGURE 2.11

Google Nexus One (N1).

The processor was extremely fast (1 GHz), it was running the latest version of Android, and it had innovations such as three microphones that survey background noise and blend your voice to create the most clear conversation possible.

Device info:

- Manufacturer: HTC
- Model: HTC Passion
- Carrier(s): T-Mobile, Verizon, Vodafone
- Release date: January 2010

SUMMARY

Although device components vary, there are several core components common to most devices. A basic understanding of these components, as well as an understanding of the various device types, is sufficient for forensic analysts in many cases. However, it is apparent that there are many other diverse factors that should be considered in an investigation. The high-level overview of the boot process provides a foundation for more in-depth discussions of the processes, which will be further explored. Finally, the overview of manufacturers and devices provides insight into all the various factors that analysts need to consider. The Android Market is fractured and diverse, and forensic analysts need to keep in mind that a "one-size-fits-all" strategy does not work when investigating Android devices.

References

Android-x86—Porting Android to x86. (n.d.). Retrieved March 9, 2011, from http://www.android-x86.org/.

Björnheden, M. (n.d.). *Enea Android Blog: The Android boot process from power on.* Retrieved December 17, 2010, from http://www.androidenea.com/2009/06/android-boot-process-from-power-on.html.

Chromium OS—The Chromium projects. (n.d.). Retrieved December 13, 2010, from http://www.chromium.org/chromium-os.

Day 74 Sales: Apple iPhone vs. Google Nexus One vs. Motorola Droid. (n.d.). The Flurry Blog—Mobile application analytics|iPhone analytics|Android analytics. Retrieved December 18, 2010, from http://blog.flurry.com/bid/31410/Day-74-Sales-Apple-iPhone-vs-Google-Nexus-One-vs-Motorola-Droid.

Krazit, T. (n.d.). *T-Mobile has sold 1 million G1 Android phones.* Wireless—CNET News. Technology news—CNET News. Retrieved December 18, 2010, from http://news.cnet.com/8301-1035_3-10226034-94.html.

Linux on the iPhone. (n.d.). Retrieved December 15, 2010, from http://linuxoniphone.blogspot.com/.

Main Page|PDAdb.net—Comprehensive database of smartphone, PDA, PDA phone, PNA, netbook & mobile device specifications. (n.d.). Retrieved November 28, 2010, from http://pdadb.net/index.php.

Mobile Memory. (n.d.). Hynix. Retrieved March 9, 2011, from http://www.hynix.com/products/mobile/mcp.jsp?menuNo=1&m=4&s=4.

Nielsen Wire. (n.d.). *U.S. smartphone battle heats up: Which is the "most desired" operating system?* Retrieved December 12, 2010, from blog.nielsen.com/nielsenwire/online_mobile/us-smartphone-battle-heats-up/.

Public Version of OMAP35xx. (2010). *Technical reference manual—Version M (SPRUF98M)* Houston, TX: Texas Instruments Incorporated. Retrieved December 17, 2010, from http://focus.ti.com/docs/prod/folders/print/omap3530.html.

Using hardware devices. (n.d.). *Android developers*. Retrieved March 9, 2011, from http://developer.android.com/guide/developing/device.html.

CHAPTER

3 Android software development kit and android debug bridge

INFORMATION IN THIS CHAPTER

- Android platforms
- Software development kit (SDK)
- Android security model
- Forensics and the SDK

INTRODUCTION

The Android software development kit (SDK) provides not only the tools to create applications that run on the Android platform but it also provides documentation and utilities that can assist significantly in the forensic or security analysis of a device. While the Android hardware covered in Chapter 2 plays a major role in the capabilities of a device, the software harnesses these features to ultimately create the experience and functionality consumers seek. A thorough understanding of the Android SDK will provide many insights into the data and the device, as well as important utilities that we will leverage in investigations.

ANDROID PLATFORMS

Android was officially announced in November 2007 but has been under significant development since 2005. This, combined with the large and diverse hardware, which leverages Android, has created a diverse ecosystem adding significant complexity for the forensic analyst or security engineer.

An informative characteristic of Android is the version of the Android platform itself. The platform is a large factor in determining the features a device can support. The official Android platforms are each assigned an application programming interface (API) level, and all the newer versions receive a code name. The current release, as of January 2011, is Android 2.3 which has the code name Gingerbread. The next major release has a code name Honeycomb and appears to

Table 3.1 Android Platforms

Platform	API Level	Code Name	Release Date
Android 2.3.3	10	Gingerbread	February 9, 2011
Android 2.3	9	Gingerbread	December 2010
Android 2.2	8	FroYo	May 20, 2010
Android 2.1	7	Eclair	January 11, 2010
Android 2.0.1	6	Eclair	December 11, 2009
Android 2.0	5	Eclair	October 5, 2009
Android 1.6	4	Donut	September 16, 2009
Android 1.5	3	Cupcake	April 27, 2009
Android 1.1	2	Petit Four	February 9, 2009
Android 1.0	1	N/A	September 23, 2008

target the anticipated growth of tablet devices. Table 3.1 gives the full list of Android platforms including API level, code name, and release date (Android timeline, n.d.).

While many Android versions exist, the distribution of each in current devices can have a large impact on forensic analysts and security engineers. Figure 3.1 shows Google's reports of distribution of Android versions based on a two-week survey of devices accessing the Android Market (Platform Versions, n.d.).

To put that in perspective, Table 3.2 shows the total number of devices in circulation in the United States by Android version. These data are based on an

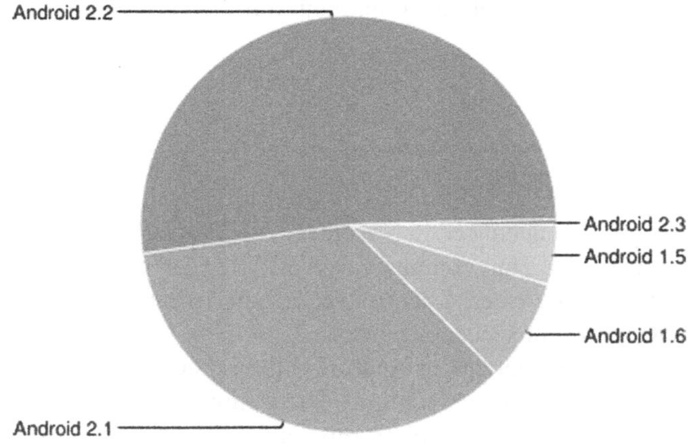

FIGURE 3.1

Distribution of Android devices by platforms, January 2011.

Table 3.2 Approximate Number of Android Devices by Platform in the United States

Android Version	Total Devices
Android 2.3	63,960
Android 2.2	8,282,820
Android 2.1	5,628,480
Android 1.6	1,263,210
Android 1.5	751,530

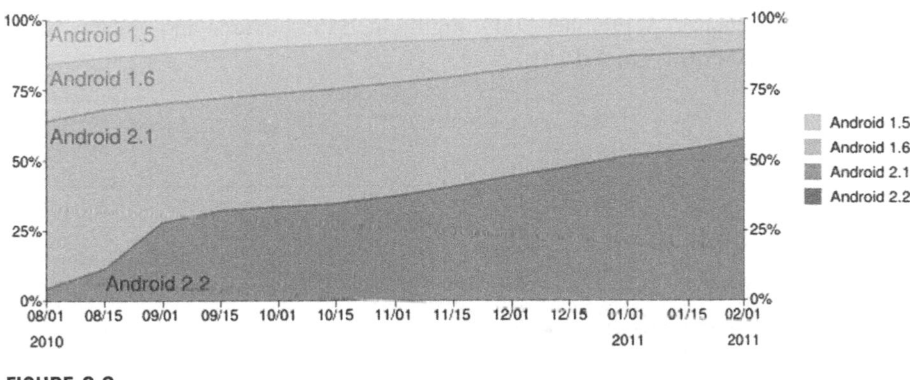

FIGURE 3.2

Historical distribution of Android version from August 2001 through February 2, 2011.

approximate US Android device population of 15.99 million as of November 2011 (comScore Reports, n.d.).

Google also released a graph displaying the historical distribution of Android versions for the seven-month period between August 2010 and February 2, 2011. The data are again based on devices accessing the Android Market but nicely displayed the progress of Android updates over time as shown in Fig. 3.2 (Platform Versions, n.d.).

While some devices will never support the latest version of Android, many do eventually receive the update. Future devices will probably be able to quickly support and upgrade to the latest version. However, from a forensics and security perspective, the older outliers cannot be ignored.

Android Platform Highlights Through 2.3.3 (Gingerbread)

Android is a sophisticated, heavily developed platform and any attempt to fully document all features would encompass a large portion of this book. However, a brief overview of each major release can be helpful so that a forensic analyst is aware of the features a device may support. Generally speaking, the features build on each other so functionality available in Android 1.5 is likely available and improved in Android 2.3.3.

Android 1.5

Android 1.5, released April 2009, highlighted the features and updates listed in Table 3.3 (Android 1.5, n.d.).

Android 1.6

Android 1.6, released September 2009, highlighted the features and updates listed in Table 3.4 (Android 1.6, n.d.).

Table 3.3 Android 1.5 Features and Highlights

New User Features	New Developer Features, APIs, and Technologies	Built-in Applications
• User Interface Refinements, including in-call experience, SMS/MMS and more • Performance Improvements to camera, GPS, browser, and Gmail • On-screen soft keyboard • Home screen widgets • Video recording and playback • Better Bluetooth support and functionality • Browser copy and paste, on-page searching, and more • Contact improvements including pictures, date/time stamps for call logs, and on-touch access to contact methods • View Google Talk friends' status in Contacts, SMS, MMS, Gmail, and e-mail applications • Upload videos to YouTube, pictures to Picasa	• New Linux kernel (version 2.6.27) • SD card file system auto-checking and repair • Improved media framework • Speech recognition framework • Support 26 locales	• Alarm clock • Browser • Calculator • Camcorder • Camera • Contacts • Custom locale (developer app) • Dev. tools (developer app) • Dialer • E-mail • Gallery • IME for Japanese text input • Messaging • Music • Settings • Spare parts (developer app)

Table 3.4 Android 1.6 Features and Highlights

New User Features	New Developer Features, APIs, and Technologies	Built-in Applications
• Quick Search Box for Android • Updated camera, camcorder, and gallery • VPN, 802.1x support • Battery usage indicator • Android Market Updates including categorization, top apps, and screenshots	• 2.6.29 Linux kernel • Expanded search framework • Text-to-speech engine • Support for gestures • New accessibility framework • Expanded support for screen densities and resolutions • Telephony support for CDMA • New version of OpenCore for better audio handling	• All apps in Android 1.5 • Gestures Builder

Androids 2.0 and 2.1

Android 2.0 and 2.1, released October 2009 and January 2010, respectively, highlighted the features and updates listed in Table 3.5 (Android 2.1, n.d.).

Table 3.5 Android 2.0/2.1 Features and Highlights

New User Features	New Developer Features, APIs, and Technologies	Built-in Applications
• Multiple accounts for e-mail and contact syncing, Quick contact feature • Exchange support in e-mail • SMS/MMS search functionality • Many enhancements to camera such as built-in flash, digital zoom, and more • Improvement in Android virtual keyboard • Browser updates include bookmarks with web page thumbnails, double-tap zoom, and HTML5 support • New calendar features such as inviting guests	• Revamped graphics architecture for improved performance that enables better hardware acceleration. • Bluetooth 2.1 • Live Wallpapers API	• Same apps as Android 1.6

Android 2.2

Android 2.2, released May 2010, highlighted the features and updates found in Table 3.6.

Table 3.6 Android 2.2 Features and Highlights

New User Features	New Developer Features, APIs, and Technologies	Built-in Applications
• New Home screen tips widget • The Phone, applications Launcher, and Browser now have dedicated shortcuts on the Home screen • Exchange expanded with addition of numeric pin or alpha-numeric password options to unlock device; Remote wipe; Exchange Calendars are now supported; Auto-discovery; Global Address Lists look-up • Improved camera and gallery • Some devices can be a portable Wi-Fi hotspot that can be shared with up to eight devices. • Multiple keyboard languages • Improved performance in browser, Dalvik VM, graphics, and kernel memory management	• 2.6.32 Linux kernel (support for RAM > 256 MB) • New media framework that supports local file playback and HTTP progressive streaming • Bluetooth improvements including voice dialing over Bluetooth, share contacts with other phones, and better compatibility with vehicles • Android Cloud to Device Messaging • Android Application Error Reports • Apps on external storage • Data backup APIs • Device policy manager	• Same as Android 2.1

Android 2.3

Android 2.3, released December 2010, highlighted the features and updates listed in Table 3.7.

Table 3.7 Android 2.3 Features and Highlights

New User Features	New Developer Features, APIs, and Technologies	Built-in Applications
• UI refinements for simplicity and speed • Faster, more intuitive text input • One-touch word selection and copy/paste • Improved power management • Support for Internet/SIP calling (VoIP) • NFC Reader application lets the user read and interact with near-field communication (NFC) tags. • Downloads management • Camera improvements, support for front- and rear-facing camera	• Linux kernel 2.6.35 • Enhancements for gaming including performance improvements, new sensors, graphics, audio and power management routines • Rich multimedia support such as mixable audio effects • Significant upgrades and enhancements in the Dalvik runtime and supporting libraries • Support for 57 languages/ locales	• Same apps as Android 2.2 • Downloads • Search • Speech Recorder

Table 3.8 Android 2.3.3 Features and Highlights

New User Features	New Developer Features, APIs, and Technologies	Built-in Applications
• Same as Android 2.3	• Improved and extended support for near-field communications (NFCs) • Tweaks to Bluetooth, graphics, media framework, and speech recognition • Support for 57 languages/locales	• Same apps as Android 2.3

Android 2.3.3

Android 2.3.3, released February 2011, highlighted the features and updates found in Table 3.8.

SOFTWARE DEVELOPMENT KIT (SDK)

The Android software development kit (SDK) is the development resource needed to develop Android applications. It includes software libraries and APIs, reference materials, an emulator, and other tools. The SDK is supported in many environments including Linux, Windows, and OS X and can be downloaded free from http://developer.android.com.

The SDK is also a powerful forensic tool used by analysts in many situations to aid in the investigation of an Android device.

SDK Release History

While the Android platforms mark the officially supported releases of Android, the SDK is updated more frequently. Table 3.9 provides the complete SDK release history that can aid in these situations (SDK Archives, n.d.).

Table 3.9 Archived Android Platforms Releases

Platform	API Level	Release Date
Android 1.6 r1	4	September 2009
Android 1.5 r3	3	July 2009
Android 1.1 r1	2	February 2009
Android 1.0 r2	1	November 2008

SDK Install

Since the SDK is critical in the investigation of an Android device, examiners should have a working installation. The following sections provide step-by-step directions for installing the SDK on the supported platforms.

Linux SDK Install

These steps are based on the Ubuntu VM used to download and compile the Android Open Source Project (AOSP) from Chapter 1 which already includes most of the prerequisites including the Java development kit. From a terminal window, install the needed 32-bit libraries:

> **NOTE**
>
> **32-Bit libraries**
>
> Since the Ubuntu VM built in Chapter 1 used the 64-bit version of Ubuntu, we must install the 32-bit libraries to install the SDK. If, however, you are using a 32-bit Linux workstation, you need not complete this step. While the 32-bit workstation can run the SDK, it cannot build the AOSP after version 2.2.

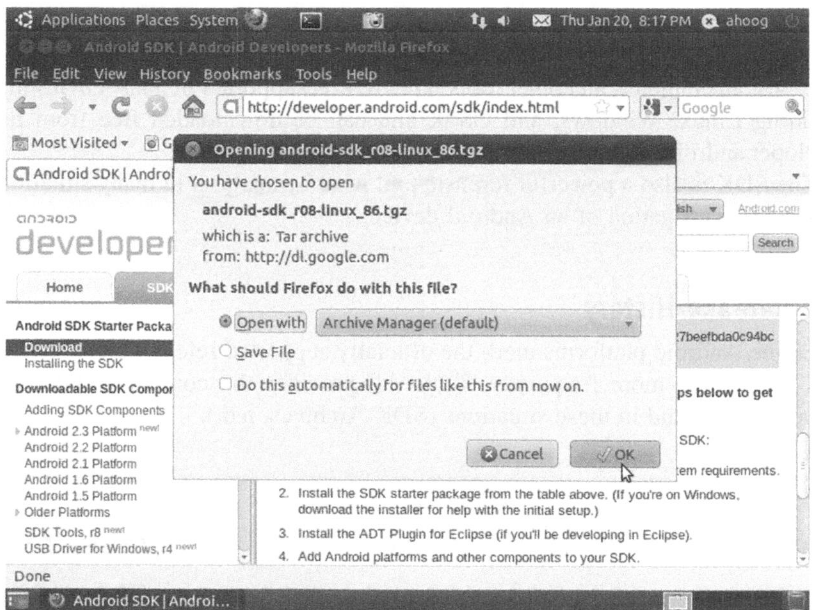

FIGURE 3.3

Download Android SDK for Linux.

```
#install 32-bit libraries
sudo apt-get install ia32-libs
```

Next, start Firefox and navigate to http://developer.android.com/sdk and download the Linux i386 platform (android-sdk_r08-linux_86.tgz, as of January 2011). The default action will open the archive in the archive manager as shown in Fig. 3.3.

Then right click and extract the archive to your home directory as shown in Fig. 3.4.

Next, from the terminal window:

```
#navigate to the tools/ directory in the Android SDK
cd ~/android-sdk-linux_x86/tools

#run android
./android
```

This will run the Android SDK and Android Virtual Device (AVD) manager, which will allow you to download and manage the additional necessary components as shown in Fig. 3.5.

To fully leverage the Android SDK, additional components are required. Minimally, we want to install the platform's specific SDK tools and at least one SDK

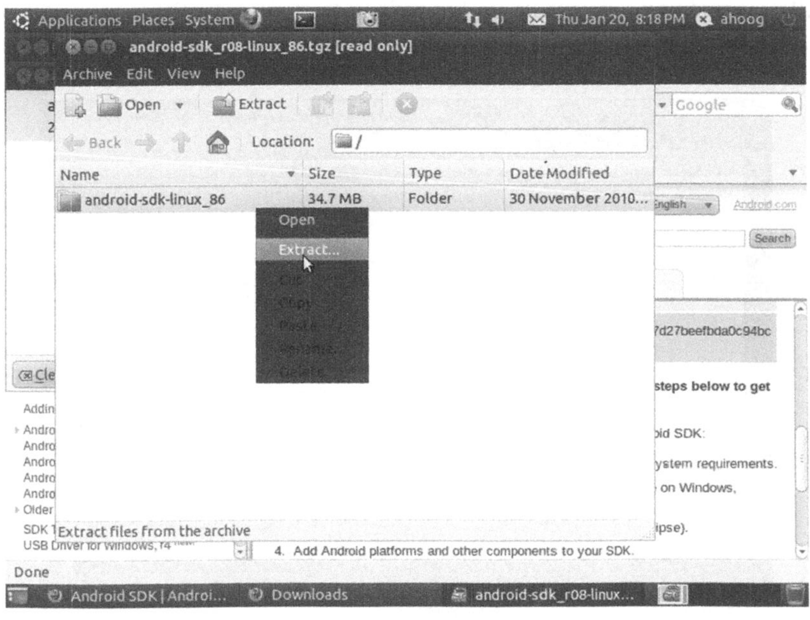

FIGURE 3.4

Extract Android SDK for Linux.

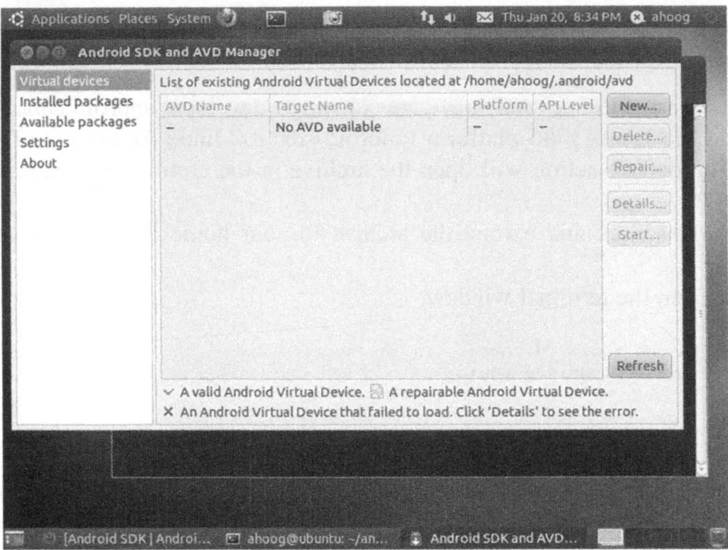

FIGURE 3.5

Android SDK and AVD manager in Linux.

platform (in this case, Android 2.3) so that we can run the emulator. To complete the installation, select the Available packages from the left navigation pane and then the two additional packages as shown in Fig. 3.6.

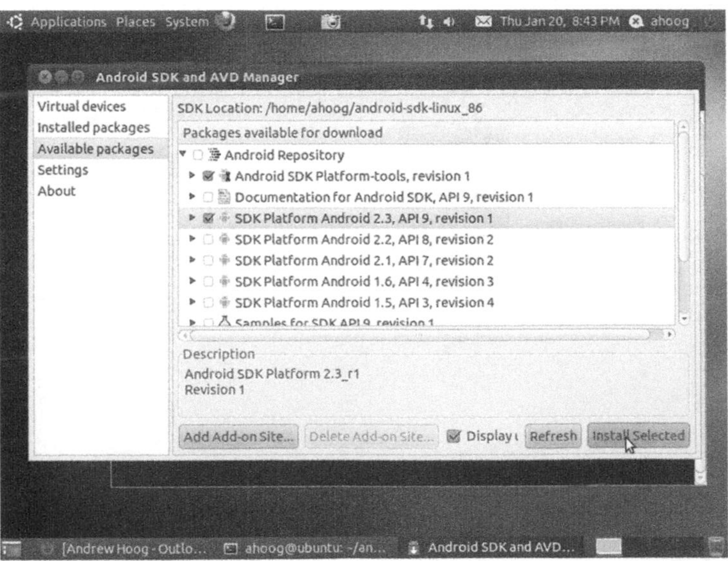

FIGURE 3.6

Select additional Android SDK packages.

And then choose Install Selected. You will be prompted to approve the license for all packages as shown in Fig. 3.7.

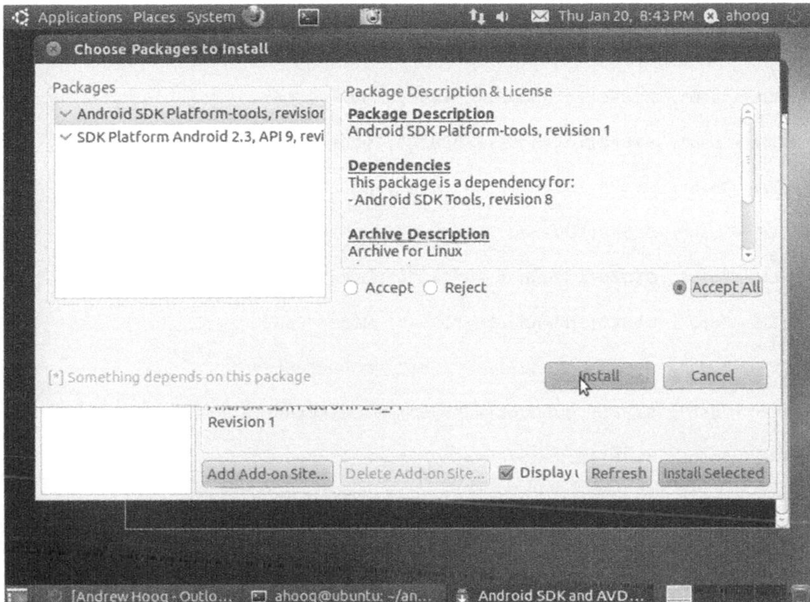

FIGURE 3.7

Accept and install Android SDK packages.

Select Accept All (provided you agree) and then install. The Android SDK and AVD manager will then download and install the components.

Optionally, you may want to add the binary directories to your operating system (OS) execution path so you do not have to specify the full path to the programs each time. In Linux, do the following:

```
# open your .bashrc in an editor
nano -w ~/.bashrc

#add the following line, substituting your login name
export PATH=$PATH:/home/ahoog/android-sdk-linux_86/tools/
export PATH=$PATH:/home/ahoog/android-sdk-linux_86/platform-tools/
```

Save, exit, and then re-open (Ctrl-O) a new shell.

One final step you must take in Ubuntu is to create USB profiles for each Android device manufacturer in the system's configuration, specifically the udev rules. From a terminal session as root, edit/create the udev rule:

```
sudo nano -w /etc/udev/rules.d/51-android.rules
```

Copy the following contents (vendor IDs are supplied on http://developer.android.com/guide/developing/device.html#VendorIds):

```
#Acer
SUBSYSTEM=="usb", SYSFS{idVendor}=="502", MODE="0666"
#Dell
SUBSYSTEM=="usb", SYSFS{idVendor}=="413c", MODE="0666"
#Foxconn
SUBSYSTEM=="usb", SYSFS{idVendor}=="489", MODE="0666"
#Garmin-Asus
SUBSYSTEM=="usb", SYSFS{idVendor}=="091E", MODE="0666"
#HTC
SUBSYSTEM=="usb", SYSFS{idVendor}=="0bb4", MODE="0666"
#Huawei
SUBSYSTEM=="usb", SYSFS{idVendor}=="12d1", MODE="0666"
#Kyocera
SUBSYSTEM=="usb", SYSFS{idVendor}=="482", MODE="0666"
#LG
SUBSYSTEM=="usb", SYSFS{idVendor}=="1004", MODE="0666"
#Motorola
SUBSYSTEM=="usb", SYSFS{idVendor}=="22b8", MODE="0666"
#Nvidia
SUBSYSTEM=="usb", SYSFS{idVendor}=="955", MODE="0666"
#Pantech
SUBSYSTEM=="usb", SYSFS{idVendor}=="10A9", MODE="0666"
#Samsung
SUBSYSTEM=="usb", SYSFS{idVendor}=="400000000", MODE="0666"
#Sharp
SUBSYSTEM=="usb", SYSFS{idVendor}=="04dd", MODE="0666"
#Sony Ericsson
SUBSYSTEM=="usb", SYSFS{idVendor}=="0fce", MODE="0666"
#ZTE
SUBSYSTEM=="usb", SYSFS{idVendor}=="19D2", MODE="0666"
```

And then save the file. Finally, make the file readable by all users:

```
sudo chmod a+r /etc/udev/rules.d/51-android.rules
```

You can either restart the udev daemon or simply reboot.

Windows SDK Install

The latest version of the Android SDK for Windows, shown in Fig. 3.8, is now packaged as an executable installer, which will determine if you have the necessary Java dependencies properly installed and, if not, will download and install them for you. However, the installer will only detect the 32-bit install of the JDK and will not automatically install the JDK on a Windows 7 64-bit install. If you are running a 32-bit version of Windows (such as Windows XP), then the installer may be a good option and you can simply download the package from http://developer.android.com/sdk/index.html and run the installer.

However, many analysts and engineers have moved to 64-bit OSs. To install the Android SDK on Windows, first install the Java SE SDK by downloading it at http://java.sun.com/javase/downloads/. Make sure you install the full SDK.

After the SDK is installed, download the zipped version of the Window's Android SDK at http://developer.android.com/sdk/index.html and extract it to your

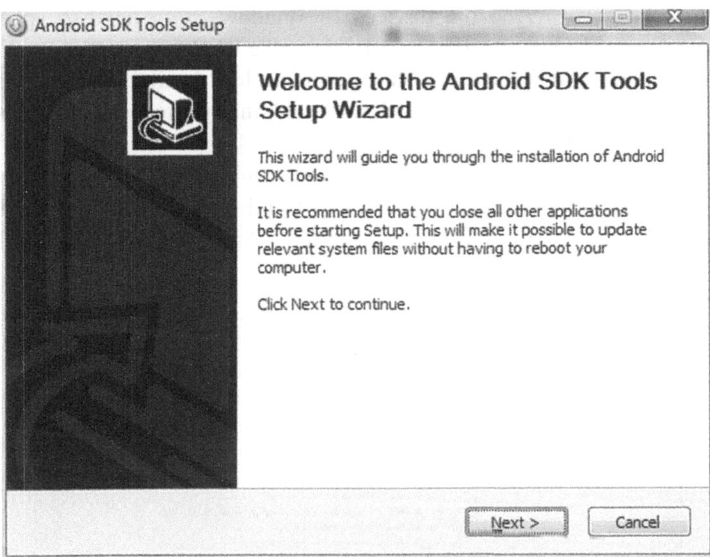

FIGURE 3.8

Android SDK installer for Windows.

hard drive. For our example, we will extract directly to C:\ that will then create the folder C:\android-sdk-windows.

Open that directory and double click SDK Manager.exe to begin the update process. Be sure that you select at least the Android SDK Platform-tools, as in Fig. 3.9, and one release platform (2.3 in this example).

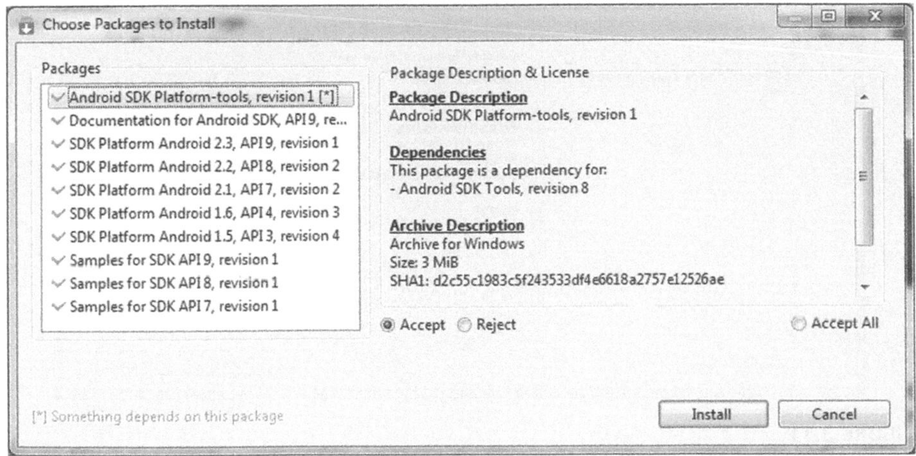

FIGURE 3.9

Android SDK manager for Windows.

When working with Android devices in Windows, you need to specify USB drivers. The Android SDK recently updated how the USB drivers are installed. First, make sure you are running the SDK Manager and select Available packages. Expand Third party Add-ons → Google Inc. add-ons and finally choose Google Usb Driver package as shown in Fig. 3.10.

Then, accept the license and install as shown in Fig. 3.11.

After the USB drivers are installed, you should have all the necessary components. However, to simplify running tools from the Android SDK, you should update

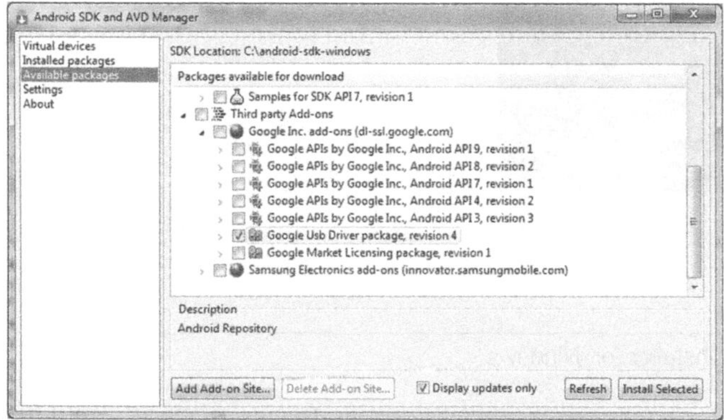

FIGURE 3.10

Google USB driver package for Windows.

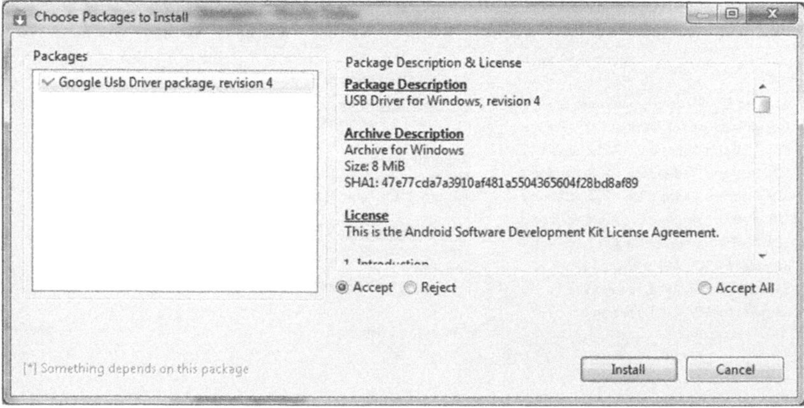

FIGURE 3.11

Accept and install license.

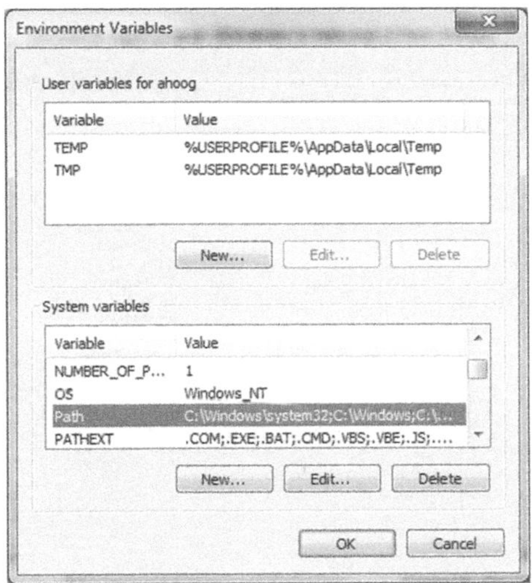

FIGURE 3.12

Update PATH environment variable (Windows 7 64 bit).

your workstation's environment variables, specifically the PATH to executable files. To do this, go to your Control Panel and open the System application. You should then select the tab where you can update the Environment variable, whose location will vary depending on your exact Windows version, shown in Fig. 3.12. Finally, locate the Path system variable, select Edit, and append the full path to your Android SDK platform-tools directory, which in our example would be ;C:\android-sdk-windows\platform-tools.

The ";" is important, as it is the delimiter between path locations. Once you complete this update, make sure you exit and wait for command prompts indicating that the new setting has taken effect.

OS X SDK

To install the Android SDK on OS X, first download the archive from http://developer.android.com/sdk/index.html, from which OS X will then automatically extract.

Navigate to the tools subdirectory as shown in Fig. 3.13, and then double click Android to run the Android SDK and AVD manager as shown in Fig. 3.14.

When the Manager runs, select Available packages, expand Android Repository and then select the Android SDK platform-tools and at least one Android platform as shown in Fig. 3.15.

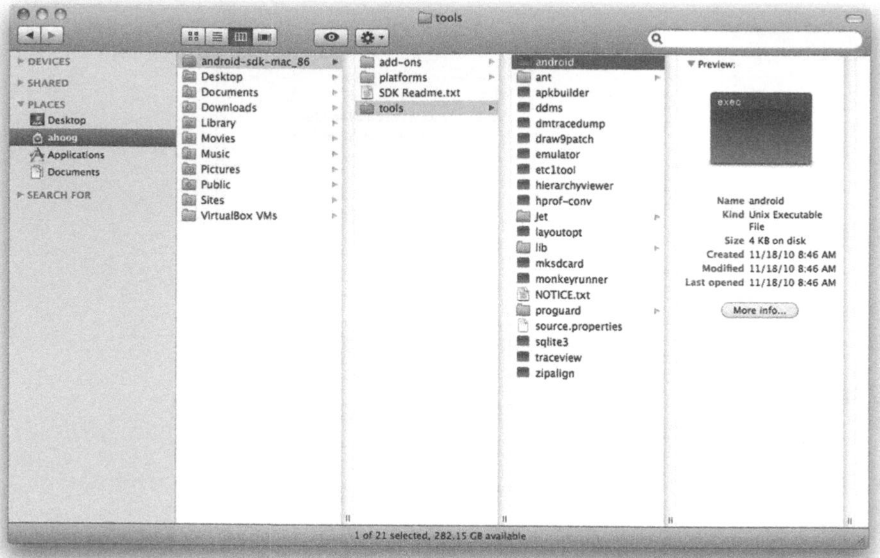

FIGURE 3.13

Extracted Android SDK for OS X.

Then accept the licenses and complete the install. Finally, to simplify running tools from the Android SDK, you should update your executable PATH. On OS X 10.6, run Terminal (Applications → Utilities) and do the following:

```
#edit your bash_profile
nano -w ~/.bash_profile

#add the following line substituting your full path to the platform-tools
directory PATH=$PATH:/Users/ahoog/android-sdk-mac_86/platform-tools

#save with Ctrl-O and then Ctrl-X to exit.  Exit Terminal
exit
```

FIGURE 3.14

Open Android on OS X.

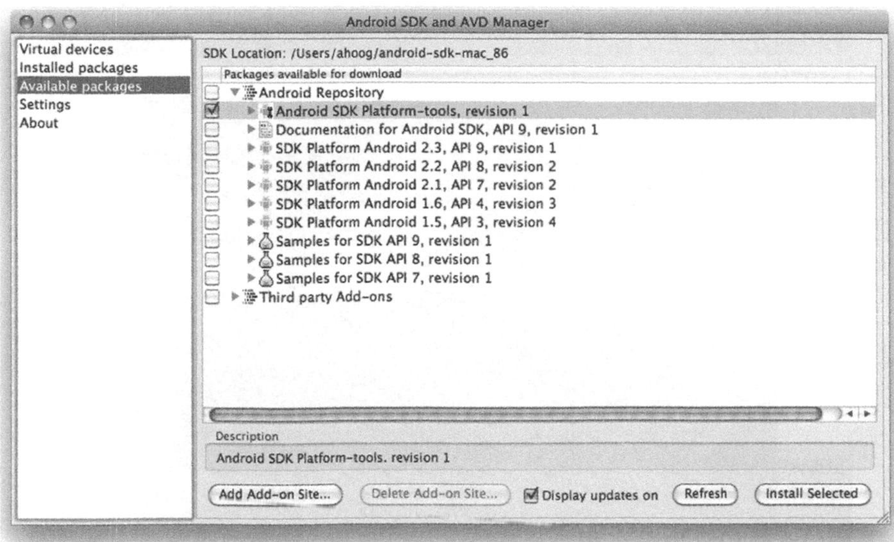

FIGURE 3.15

Install Android SDK components on OS X.

Make sure you fully exit the Terminal app and then restart. From the terminal, type:

```
echo $PATH
```

This should return your executable path with the platform-tools appended.

Android Virtual Devices (Emulator)

Once you have the Android SDK installed on your workstation and have at least one release platform downloaded, you are ready to create an AVD, a virtual mobile device, or emulator, which runs on your computer. The emulator is especially helpful for developers for creating custom applications. However, there is great value for the forensic analyst and security engineer because you can profile how applications execute on a device. This could be important to validate your findings in an investigation, or to test how a forensic tool affects an Android device.

The emulator takes considerable resources, so an ideal workstation would have a newer sufficient CPU and RAM. A bit of patience from the examiner may also be required. To create an AVD, first run the Android SDK and AVD manager application as seen in Fig. 3.16. If you updated your OS's path to include the tools directory in the SDK, you should be able to run Android from a shell, terminal, or command prompt.

In the left pane, select Virtual devices and then select New, as in Fig. 3.17.

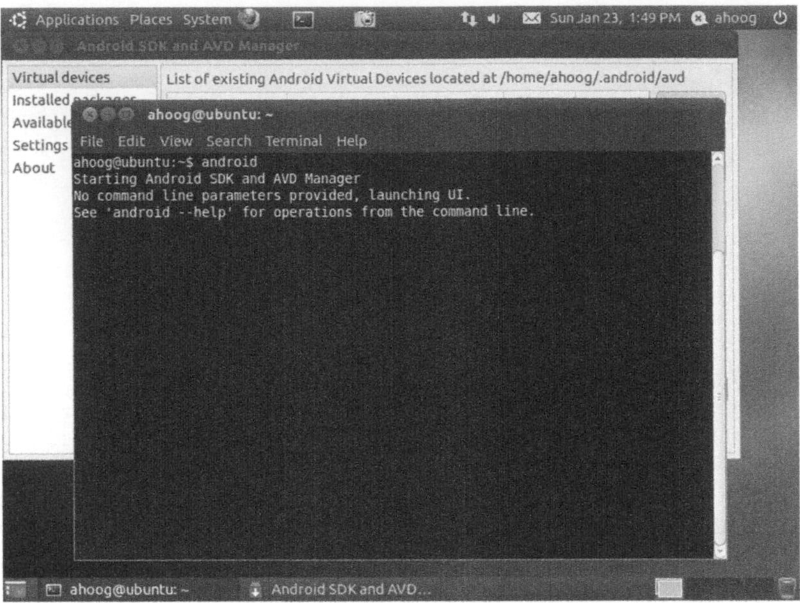

FIGURE 3.16

Start Android SDK and AVD manager.

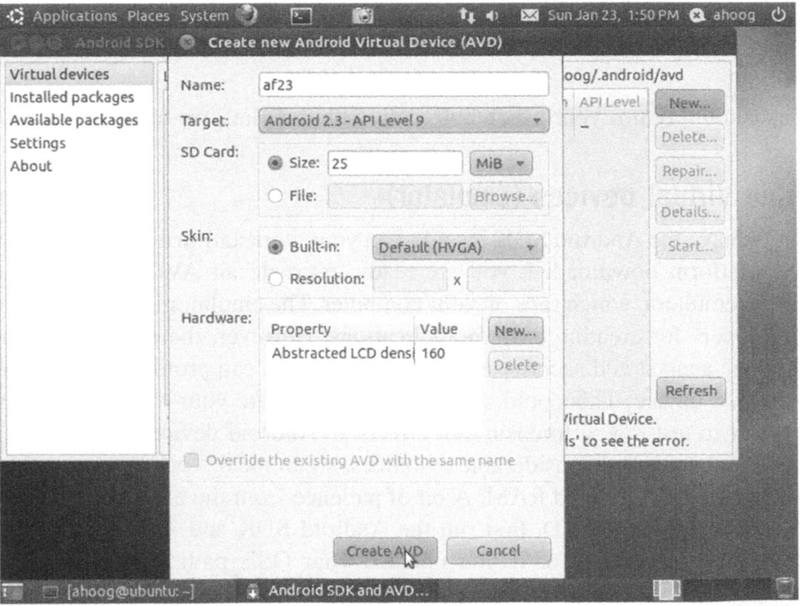

FIGURE 3.17

Creating a new AVD.

Make sure you populate the following fields:

- Name: Provide a name for the virtual device, for example, af23 (Android Forensics 2.3).
- Target: Select the target platform, in this case Android 2.3—API level 9.
- [optional] SD card: Optionally create an SD card for the virtual device.

You can set additional properties. However, for now we will create the most basic AVD. Also, if you encounter an Android device running on an older platform, you can create virtual devices running the older version by simply downloading the Android platform using the Android SDK and AVD manager. When you click Create AVD, the device will be created and you will receive a confirmation screen similar to that shown in Fig. 3.18.

Ensure that the new AVD is highlighted and then click Start, at which point you will be prompted for launch options as shown in Fig. 3.19.

Select any options you wish and click Launch. At this point, the AVD will begin the boot process, which could take a few minutes or longer. During that time, you will see Android starting up. This is illustrated in Fig. 3.20.

Finally, you will be presented with the fully functioning AVD as shown in Fig. 3.21.

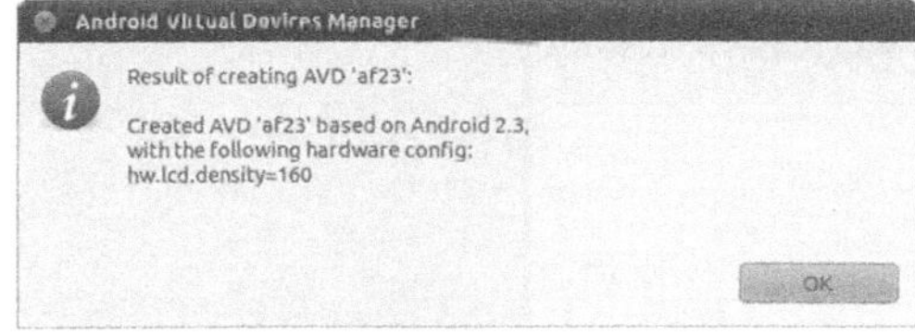

FIGURE 3.18

AVD-created confirmation.

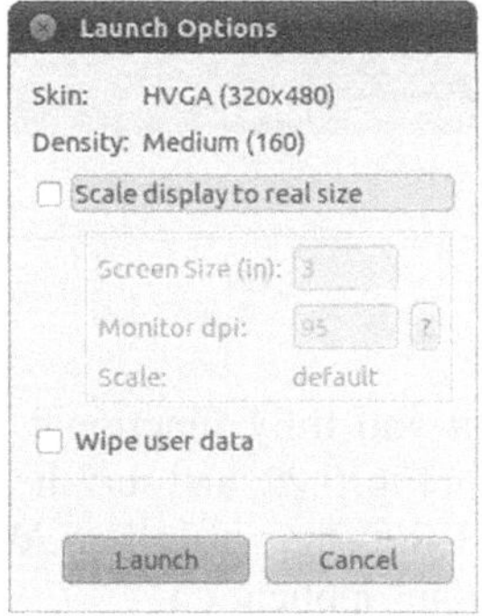

FIGURE 3.19

AVD launch options.

FIGURE 3.20

AVD launching.

FIGURE 3.21

Running AVD.

The AVD is very powerful and fully functional. For example, you can easily jump online, as demonstrated in Fig. 3.22, and surf the web site. You can configure e-mail accounts, send test SMS messages to other AVD and of course, if you are a developer, deploy and test your application.

When an AVD is created and then launched, the data created are valuable for forensic and security research. The files are created in your home directory, which

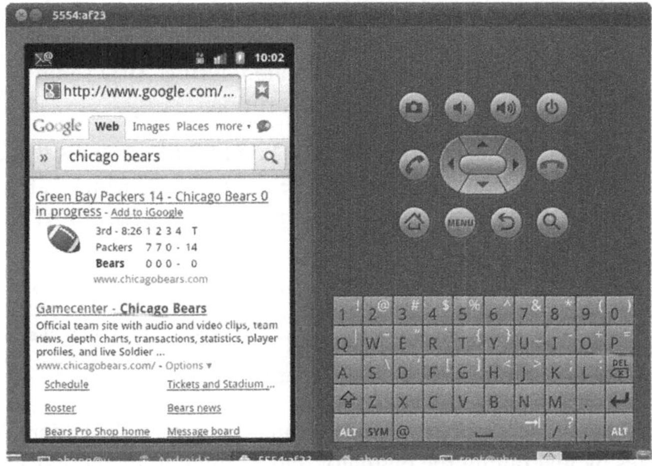

FIGURE 3.22

AVD running browser.

Table 3.10 AVD Storage Directory

Workstation Operating System	AVD Storage Directory	Example
Ubuntu Linux	/home/<username>/.android	/home/ahoog/.android
Mac OS X	/Users/<username>/.android	/Users/ahoog/.android
Windows 7	C:\Users\<username>\.android	C:\Users\ahoog\.android

varies by platform, in a folder called .android (note the dot prefix in the filename). Table 3.10 provides specific OS paths.

Inside AVD's .android directory you will find configuration and data files needed to run the AVD.

```
ahoog@ubuntu:~/.android$ tree
.
├── androidtool.cfg
├── avd
│   ├── af23.avd
│   │   ├── cache.img
│   │   ├── config.ini
│   │   ├── emulator-user.ini
│   │   ├── sdcard.img
│   │   ├── userdata.img
│   │   └── userdata-qemu.img
│   └── af23.ini
├── default.keyset
├── modem-nv-ram-5554
└── repositories.cfg

2 directories, 11 files
```

Files of particular forensic and security interest include the following:

- cache.img: disk image of /cache partition
- sdcard.img: disk image of SD card (if created during AVD setup)
- userdata-qemu.img: disk image of /data partition

The cache.img and userdata-qemu.img are YAFFS2 file systems that are not supported by current forensic software and will be covered in Chapter 4. However, standard forensic tools will work quite well on sdcard.img, which is a FAT32 file system.

```
ahoog@ubuntu:~/.android/avd/af23.avd$ file sdcard.img
sdcard.img: x86 boot sector, code offset 0x5a, OEM-ID "MSWIN4.1", Media
descriptor 0xf8,
sectors 51200 (volumes > 32 MB), FAT (32 bit), sectors/FAT 397, reserved3
0x800000,
serial number 0x1d0e0817, label: "     SDCARD"
```

Forensic analysts and security engineers can learn a great deal about Android and how it operates by leveraging the emulator and examining the network, file system, and data artifacts.

Android OS Architecture

It is important to understand the high-level architecture of Android, especially for security procedures and moving beyond logical forensic analysis.

Android is based on the Linux 2.6 kernel that provides the fundamental software needed to boot and manage both the hardware and Android applications. While the functionality that the kernel provides is quite extensive, we will focus on core areas highlighted in Fig. 3.23.

As illustrated in Fig. 3.23, low-level functions include power management, Wi-Fi.com, display, audio drivers, and more. Perhaps most important from a forensics perspective is the flash memory driver, which will be explored in detail in Chapter 4.

After the kernel, a set of libraries are available, which provide core functionality needed by developers and device owners alike. These include the WebKit library for rendering HTML in both the bundled browser and third-party apps. Other libraries handle fonts, displays, various media, and secure communications using Secure Socket Layers (SSLs). Finally, the SQLite library provides a method for structured data storage on Android and is an area forensic analysts and security engineers will focus on.

The core libraries are then bundled with a custom Java virtual machine (VM) to provide the Android runtime environment, which is where applications run.

Finally, the SDK provides access to these resources via APIs and an application framework. The framework is the primary layer that third-party developers interact with and it provides them abstract access to key resources needed for their application. As we explore logical forensic techniques, an important aspect of the application framework—content providers—will be explained in more detail because they provide the primary mechanism by which we can extract data from an Android device.

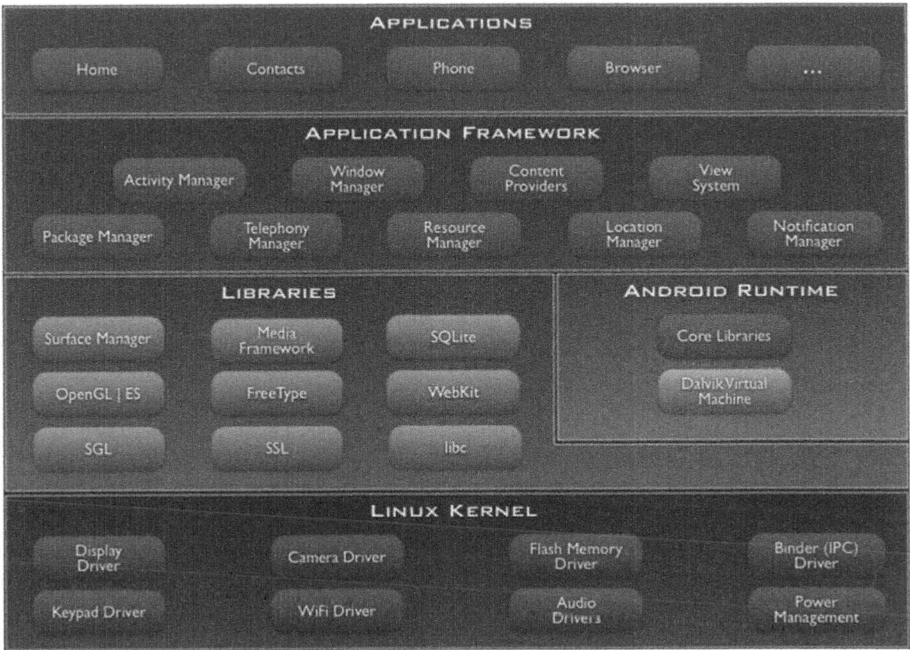

FIGURE 3.23

Android architecture.

Dalvik VM

The Dalvik Virtual Machine (Dalvik VM) was developed by Google to create an efficient and secure mobile application environment.

To achieve the desired security, each application is run on its own Dalvik VM. As such, the Dalvik VM was written so that many VMs could run at once on an Android device. The Dalvik VM relies heavily on the Linux OS to provide low-level functions such as access to core libraries and hardware, threat and security management, memory management, and more.

To achieve efficiency, applications that run in a Dalvik VM have a special format called a Dalvik Executable (.dex) file. Developers write and compile their programs with Sun's Java Development Kit and the resulting byte code is then transformed into a .dex file which provides efficient storage and is optimized for execution in the Dalvik VM. An interesting project developed by JesusFreke, an accomplished and well-known Android hacker, is called smali/baksmali. This project allows a user to decompile a .dex file to determine what an application does (smali, n.d.).

Dalvik is a unique aspect of Android and a critical component in the forensic and security analysis of a device.

Native Code Development

While most Android applications are written in Java using the SDK, Google provides a lower level development platform with their native development kit (NDK). The NDK was first released in June 2009 and has gone through five revisions, with the latest release in November 2010.

The NDK allows developers to write code in C/C++ and compile it directly for the CPU. While this adds complexity to the development process, some developers can benefit from this approach by reusing an existing code base in C/C++ or by implementing certain functions that can be optimized outside the Dalvik VM. The NDK does not allow developers to create full applications that run outside of the Dalvik VM; instead the C/C++ components are packaged inside the application's .apk file and are called by the application within the VM.

At this time, the NDK supports the ARMv5TE and ARMv7-A CPUs, and in the future will support Intel's x86 CPU architecture. When a developer writes code in one platform (e.g., Mac OS X) but compiles it for another CPU, the technique is referred to as cross-compiling an application. The NDK greatly simplifies this process and provides a set of libraries the developer can use.

From a forensics and security viewpoint, cross-compiling is an important component for research and development of new techniques and exploits. While most forensic analysts and security engineers do not need to compile code, understanding how the process works, and what role it plays in the process, is important. For example, the initial Android 1.5 root exploit targeted a Linux kernel bug (CVE-2009-2692) to gain privileges. The initial code was distributed as source code and required cross-compiling. One significant advantage to this approach is that an examiner can describe in exact detail how the device was exploited and, if necessary, provide the source code.

As Android matures, expect to see additional developments in the NDK and natively complied code.

ANDROID SECURITY MODEL

The Android platform implements security through a number of controls designed to protect the user.

When an application is first installed, Android checks the .apk file to ensure it has a valid digital signature to identify the developer. Unlike SSL, the digital certification does not need to be signed by a Certificate Authority. However, the developer must keep the key safe; otherwise someone could sign a malicious application and distribute it as that developer. For example, if a financial institution's digital signature was compromised, a malicious developer could publish an update to the banking application, which steals critical data.

After the .apk file is validated, Android checks the special file created by the developer that specifies, among other items, what access an application needs to the system. For example, an application may request access to the user's contacts, SMS messages, and the network/Internet. If this application adds functionality to the

SMS system, these permissions seem reasonable. If, however, the application simply changes your background images, then a user should question the permission and can choose not to install the application. In practice, users quickly allow all permissions and application requests, and thus may allow a malicious application to install.

After an application has been verified and the user granted the requested permissions, the application can now install on the system. A key part of the Android security model is that each application is assigned a unique Linux user and group ID and runs in its own process and Dalvik VM. During the installation, the system creates a specific directory on the device to store the application's data and only allows that application to access the data leveraging the Linux user ID and group ID permissions. In addition, the application's Dalvik VM is run in its own process as the specific user ID. These key mechanisms enforce data security at the OS level as applications do not share memory, permissions, or disk storage. Applications can only access the memory and data within their Dalvik VM.

Of course, there are a few exceptions to this process. First, a developer can sign more than one application with the same digital certification and specify that it can share the same user ID, process, memory, and data storage as one of their other applications. This situation is exceptional and is most commonly used when a developer has both a free and a paid version. If a user upgrades to the paid version, they can leverage the data accumulated while using the free version and thus no data are lost.

Also, most Android users have the option to allow apps to be installed from non-Market locations and to skip the digital signature check. This option can be accessed from the Applications menu in the device's Settings and, when selected, displays a warning to the user as shown in Fig. 3.24.

FIGURE 3.24

Android setting to allow apps installs from unknown sources.

The most common situation is that users could now install apps from web sites by directly downloading an .apk file. The install process also skips the digital signature check. A recent AT&T phone (Motorola Backflip) removed this option from Android upsetting many users (Android On Lockdown, n.d.). However, a work-around using the Android SDK does exist and will be discussed in Chapter 6.

As a result of the security architecture built into Android, forensic examiners do not have a simple way to extract core user data from a device. Barring exploits, the security architecture is effective in isolating and protecting data between applications.

FORENSICS AND THE SDK

So how is the SDK important in forensics? The SDK not only provides a set of tools and drivers enabling the analysis of Android devices but is also useful for application profiling and other forensic research.

Connecting an Android Device to a Workstation

It is important to note how an Android device actually connects to a VM. Android devices, to date, have a physical USB interface that allows them to connect, share data and resources, and typically to recharge from a computer or workstation. If you are only running a single OS, the USB device should be detected and accessible. However, additional configuration or drivers may be required. If you are running a VM though, you simply want the host OS to pass the connection through to the VM. For example, if your host OS is OS X and you are running VMWare fusion, you select the menus Virtual Machine → USB and then Connect the device (High Android Phone in this case), as shown in Fig. 3.25.

Similarly, when your host OS is Linux, and you are running the VM using Oracle's VirtualBox, you must first ensure that you are a member of the usbusers group. So, from a terminal session, execute the following:

```
#create usbusers group
sudo addgroup usbusers

#Add your username to the userusers group:
sudo usermod -a -G usbusers ahoog
```

Next, you go into the VM's Settings and add a USB Filter for the device, as shown in Fig. 3.26.

Finally, you can connect the USB device as shown in Fig. 3.27.

Finally, here are the steps if you are running the VM headless (VirtualBox 3.2.10 as outlined in Chapter 1). First, you need to install VBox Additions, which will

FIGURE 3.25

Connect USB device to Ubuntu VM in VMWare Fusion.

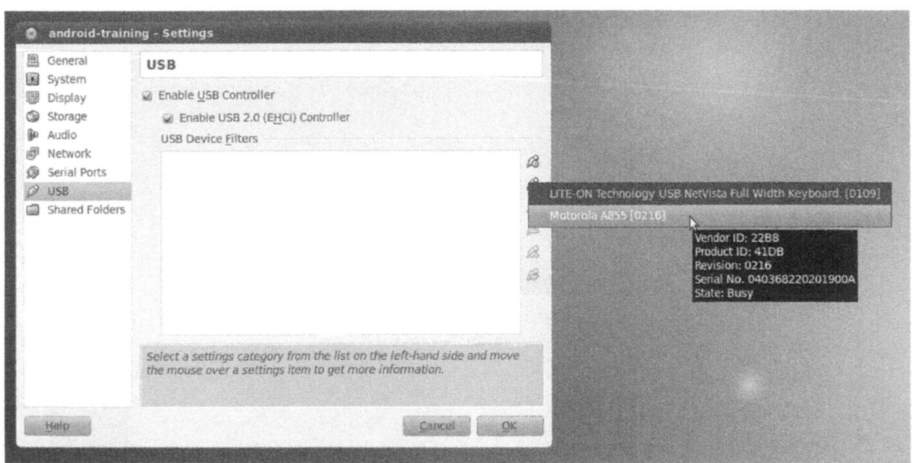

FIGURE 3.26

Adding USB filter on Linux host running Oracle's VirtualBox.

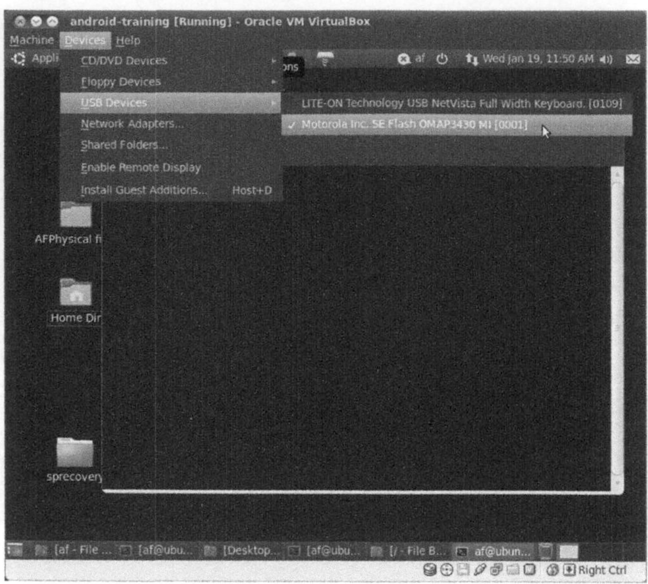

FIGURE 3.27

Connecting USB device on Linux host running Oracle's VirtualBox.

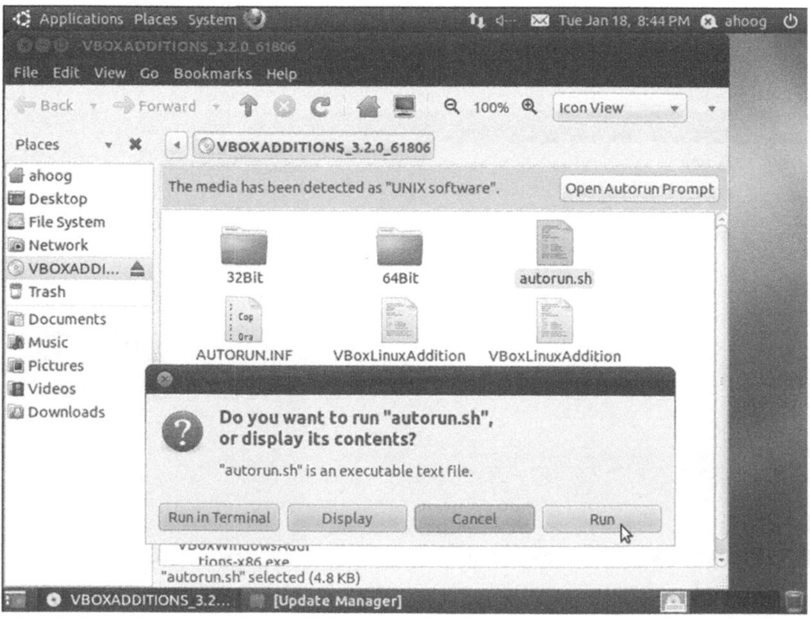

FIGURE 3.28

Install VBox additions over on Ubuntu VM remote desktop protocol.

enable shared folder, better video, USB support (if you downloaded/bought the PUEL edition), and other features. From the host workstation:

```
wget
http://download.virtualbox.org/virtualbox/3.2.0/VBoxGuestAdditions_3.2.0.iso

VBoxManage registerimage dvd ~/VBoxGuestAdditions_3.2.0.iso

VBoxManage storageattach af-book-vm --storagectl "IDE Controller" --port 1
--device 0 \
--type dvddrive --medium ~/VBoxGuestAdditions_3.2.0.iso
```

The DVD should now be available on the Ubuntu VM. Remote desktop into the VM again (see Chapter 1 for necessary steps) and double click VBOX-ADDITIONS_3.2.0_61806 DVD on your desktop to open the DVD. Then double click autorun.sh and select the Run option. You will be prompted for your password after which the install will proceed. Figure 3.28 illustrates this step.

Now that you have VBox Additions installed, you can connect USB devices to your guest OS. But first, you must shutdown the VM. Then, follow these steps:

```
#create usbusers group
sudo addgroup usbusers

#Add your username to the userusers group:
sudo usermod -a -G usbusers ahoog

#Determine attached USB device info
VBoxManage list usbhost

Oracle VM VirtualBox Command Line Management Interface Version 3.2.8
(C) 2005-2010 Oracle Corporation
All rights reserved.

Host USB Devices:

UUID:               b1c23004-db71-49ec-b5cb-348e2038b409
VendorId:           0x0781 (0781)
ProductId:          0x554f (554F)
Revision:           2.0 (0200)
Manufacturer:       Best Buy
Product:            Geek Squad
SerialNumber:       153563119AC07CAD
Address:            sysfs:/sys/devices/pci0000:00/0000:00:1d.0/usb2/2-1/
2-1.5//device:/dev/bus/usb/002/004
Current State:      Busy

#Create the USB filter to connect the device
VBoxManage usbfilter add 0 --target af-book-vm --vendorid 0781
--productid 554F \
--name "Geek Squad" --active yes

#Ensure USB is enabled
VBoxManage modifyvm Win2003SvrR2 --usb on

#Power on the guest (again recommended from inside screen)
VBoxHeadless -startvm af-book-vm -p 3392 &
```

Using this example, the USB device should now be passed through to the VM.

USB Interfaces

While you connect an Android device to your workstation or VM through a single USB port, the hardware and Android itself generally expose more than one virtual USB interface. For example, when you connect the HTC Incredible over USB, you are presented with a menu of four options:

1. Charge only—Charge phone over USB
2. HTC Sync—Sync contacts and calendar
3. Disk drive—Mount as disk drive
4. Mobile Broadband Connect—Smart phone's mobile networks with PC

The default selection, shown in Fig. 3.29, is the Charge only option. Both HTC Sync and Mobile Broadband Connect options are custom options and programs HTC and, at times, the wireless carrier support for the device.

CD-ROM Interface

The disk drive option is more universally used. This option connects the Android device to the workstation as a disk drive. This is one key area where the device exposes multiple USB devices to the workstation. When you first plug HTC

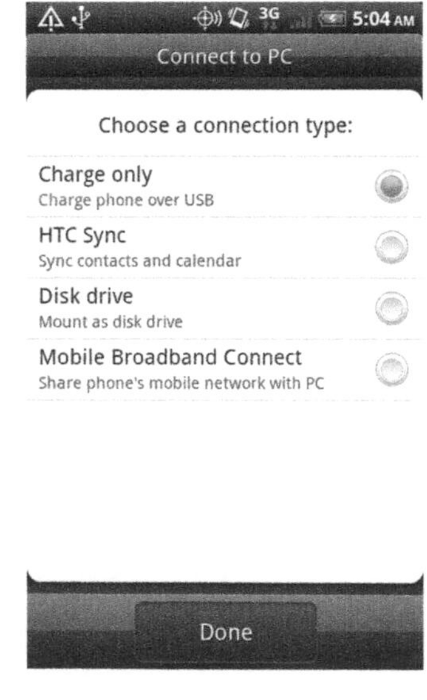

FIGURE 3.29

HTC Incredible connect to PC options.

Incredible into the computer, it actually registers three separate types of drives: one CD-ROM and two USB mass storage devices. The following listing is taken from the Linux workstation's kernel messages with the dmesg command:

```
[  210.336135] usb 1-1: new high speed USB device using ehci_hcd and address 3
[  210.646221] scsi4 : usb-storage 1-1:1.0
[  211.649296] scsi 4:0:0:0: Direct-Access     HTC      Android Phone    0100
PQ: 0 ANSI: 2
[  211.652056] scsi 4:0:0:1: Direct-Access     HTC      Android Phone    0100
PQ: 0 ANSI: 2
[  211.654291] scsi 4:0:0:2: CD-ROM            HTC      Android Phone    0100
PQ: 0 ANSI: 2
[  211.657317] sd 4:0:0:0: Attached scsi generic sg2 type 0
[  211.658364] sd 4:0:0:1: Attached scsi generic sg3 type 0
[  211.661956] sr1: scsi3-mmc drive: 0x/0x caddy
[  211.662569] sr 4:0:0:2: Attached scsi CD-ROM sr1
[  211.662755] sr 4:0:0:2: Attached scsi generic sg4 type 5
[  211.678409] sd 4:0:0:0: [sdb] Attached SCSI removable disk
[  211.686339] sd 4:0:0:1: [sdc] Attached SCSI removable disk
```

As you can see, two Direct-Access drives are found at 4:0:0:0 and 4:0:0:1, and a CD-ROM is found at 4:0:0:2. The CD-ROM contains custom programs and drivers that HTC bundles with the device to enable the syncing and broadband connect features. Obviously, there is no physical CD-ROM. However, a portion of the device's storage is dedicated to the CD-ROM and is formatted as an ISO9660. The host OS can then mount the drive as a CD-ROM and, in Windows, would potentially even support the auto-run feature. Leveraging TSK's fsstat program, we can see more details about the partition:

```
ahoog@ubuntu:~$ sudo fsstat /dev/sr2

=== PRIMARY VOLUME DESCRIPTOR 1 ===
FILE SYSTEM INFORMATION
--------------------------------------------
File System Type: ISO9660
Volume Name: Verizon Mobile
Volume Set Size: 1
Volume Set Sequence: 1
Publisher: Publisher
Data Preparer: Publisher
Recording Application: Application
Copyright:

METADATA INFORMATION
--------------------------------------------
Path Table Location: 23-23
Inode Range: 0 - 9
Root Directory Block: 26

CONTENT INFORMATION
--------------------------------------------
Sector Size: 2048
Block Size: 2048
Total Sector Range: 0 - 2383
Total Block Range: 0 - 2383
```

```
=== SUPPLEMENTARY VOLUME DESCRIPTOR 1 ===
FILE SYSTEM INFORMATION
--------------------------------------------
File System Type: ISO9660
Volume Name:
Volume Set Size: 1
Volume Set Sequence: 1
Publisher:
Data Preparer: Publisher
Recording Application:
Copyright:


METADATA INFORMATION
--------------------------------------------
Path Table Location: 25-25
Root Directory Block: 29
Joliet Name Encoding: UCS-2 Level 1

CONTENT INFORMATION
--------------------------------------------
Sector Size: 2048
Block Size: 2048
Total Sector Range: 0 - 2383
Total Block Range: 0 - 2383
```

As you can tell from the Volume Name, the CD-ROM contains software provided by Verizon to use the additional features of the device.

SD Cards (Removable and Virtual)

Far more important from a forensic standpoint are the SD card(s) available through the device. Placing user's files, especially larger files such as multimedia, is a key strategy in Android. Most Android devices have a removable media slot, which accepts a micro-SD card. The core application data remain on the device (under /data/data), but the files that are likely important in an investigation may also exist on the SD card.

In the previous section, when an Android device was connected via USB, the Linux workstation's kernel messages displayed the various USB devices available. The two SCSI removable disks that were listed, sdb and sdc, represent the SD cards on an HTC Incredible. If you choose the "Mount as disk drive" option under Connect to PC, the following additional messages show up on the kernel messages:

```
[  325.669335] sd 4:0:0:1: [sdc] 3911680 512-byte logical blocks: (2.00 GB/
1.86 GiB)
[  325.672039] sd 4:0:0:1: [sdc] Assuming drive cache: write through
[  325.678282] sd 4:0:0:1: [sdc] Assuming drive cache: write through
[  325.678294]  sdc: sdc1
[  327.671951] sd 4:0:0:0: [sdb] 13844464 512-byte logical blocks: (7.08 GB/
6.60 GiB)
[  327.674074] sd 4:0:0:0: [sdb] Assuming drive cache: write through
[  327.679387] sd 4:0:0:0: [sdb] Assuming drive cache: write through
[  327.679395]  sdb:
```

You will now see additional information about the SD card. The drive sdc has one partition, sdc1. And its size is 2 GB. We can see additional partition information by running TSK's mmls:

```
ahoog@ubuntu:~$ sudo mmls /dev/sdc
DOS Partition Table
Offset Sector: 0
Units are in 512-byte sectors

     Slot     Start        End          Length       Description
00:  Meta     0000000000   0000000000   0000000001   Primary Table (#0)
01:  -----    0000000000   0000000128   0000000129   Unallocated
02:  00:00    0000000129   0003911679   0003911551   DOS FAT16 (0x06)
```

As you will see, the SD card is formatted with a FAT16 file system, but often you will find FAT32 or you might encounter multiple file systems like FAT32 and native Linux file system ext3 and ext4.

More recently, devices also have an emulated or virtual SD card feature that uses the device's NAND flash to create a nonremovable SD card. This more closely models the iPhone where the user data partition is located directly on the NAND flash and cannot be removed. In the previous example, the sdb device provides access to the emulated SD card. Unlike the physical SD card, sdc does not have a partition table and the file system simply starts immediately. To see important information, run TSK's fsstat:

```
ahoog@ubuntu:~$ sudo fsstat /dev/sdb
FILE SYSTEM INFORMATION
--------------------------------------------
File System Type: FAT32

OEM Name: BSD  4.4
Volume ID: 0xc7f80810
Volume Label (Boot Sector): NO NAME
Volume Label (Root Directory):
File System Type Label: FAT32
Next Free Sector (FS Info): 562580
Free Sector Count (FS Info): 13376448

Sectors before file system: 0

File System Layout (in sectors)
Total Range: 0 - 13844463
* Reserved: 0 - 31
** Boot Sector: 0
** FS Info Sector: 1
** Backup Boot Sector: 2
* FAT 0: 32 - 1721
* FAT 1: 1722 - 3411
* Data Area: 3412 - 13844463
** Cluster Area: 3412 - 13844435
*** Root Directory: 3412 - 3475
** Non-clustered: 13844436 - 13844463
```

```
METADATA INFORMATION
--------------------------------------------
Range: 2 - 221456838
Root Directory: 2

CONTENT INFORMATION
--------------------------------------------
Sector Size: 512
Cluster Size: 32768
Total Cluster Range: 2 - 216267

FAT CONTENTS (in sectors)
--------------------------------------------
3412-3475 (64) -> EOF
3476-3539 (64) -> EOF
3540-5267 (1728) -> EOF
5268-7379 (2112) -> EOF
<snip>
```

In this particular case, the file system is in fact FAT32 and you will notice that while the volume has no Label, the OEM Name is set BSD 4.4.

> **WARNING**
>
> **Auto-mounting USB devices**
>
> In the Ubuntu VM configuration section of Chapter 1, the auto-mount feature is disabled to prevent the OS from automatically detecting and mounting USB mass storage devices. Forensic analysts should take extreme precautions to prevent this from happening on a device being investigated. Beyond disabling auto-mount, devices should generally be connected through a USB write blocker.

In Ubuntu, if you do not have auto-mounting of USB devices disabled (which you should in nearly all situations), the SD cards are automatically mounted for you. If the device is attached to a hardware write blocker, mounted read-only, or in a situation where write blocking is not needed (e.g., research and development), you can run the df command in Linux to see where they were mounted:

```
ahoog@ubuntu:~$ df -h
Filesystem            Size  Used Avail Use% Mounted on
/dev/sda1              19G  3.4G   15G  19% /
none                  369M  228K  369M   1% /dev
none                  375M  252K  375M   1% /dev/shm
none                  375M  100K  375M   1% /var/run
none                  375M     0  375M   0% /var/lock
.host:/               931G  663G  269G  72% /mnt/hgfs
/dev/sdc1             1.9G  200M  1.7G  11% /media/E0FD-1813 (physical
                                             2GB SD Card)
/dev/sdb              6.6G  227M  6.4G   4% /media/C7F8-0810 (emmulated SD Card)
```

The physical SD card was mounted on /media/E0FD-1813 and the emulated SD card on /media/C7F8-0810.

On the Android device itself, the two SD cards are mounted as follows:

```
/dev/block/vold/179:9 /mnt/sdcard vfat
rw,dirsync,nosuid,nodev,noexec,relatime,uid=1000,gid=1015,fmask=0702,dmask=0702,
allow_utime=0020,codepage=cp437,iocharset=iso8859-1,shortname=mixed,utf8,
errors=remount-ro 0 0
/dev/block/vold/179:3 /mnt/emmc vfat
rw,dirsync,nosuid,nodev,noexec,relatime,uid=1000,gid=1015,fmask=0702,dmask=0702,
allow_utime=0020,codepage=cp437,iocharset=iso8859-1,shortname=mixed,utf8,
errors=remount-ro 0 0
```

USB Debugging

One final, and very important, USB interface exposes the Android Debug Bridge (ADB) that allows a developer, forensic analyst, or security engineer to communicate and control an Android device over USB. By default, an AVD (running in the emulator) will have USB debugging enabled. However, non-emulator devices must explicitly enable USB debugging. To enable, select Applications → Development from the devices Setting's, as shown in Fig. 3.30. Finally, check USB debugging.

Once set, the device will run the adb daemon (adbd) in the background and wait for a USB connection. The daemon will run under the non-privileged shell user account to limit the access it has to data. AVDs and physical devices that have root access enabled will run adbd as root providing complete access to the system. Additional details on this topic will be covered in Chapter 6.

In newer versions of Android, anytime a device with USB debugging enabled is connected over USB, it will display a security warning as seen in Fig. 3.31.

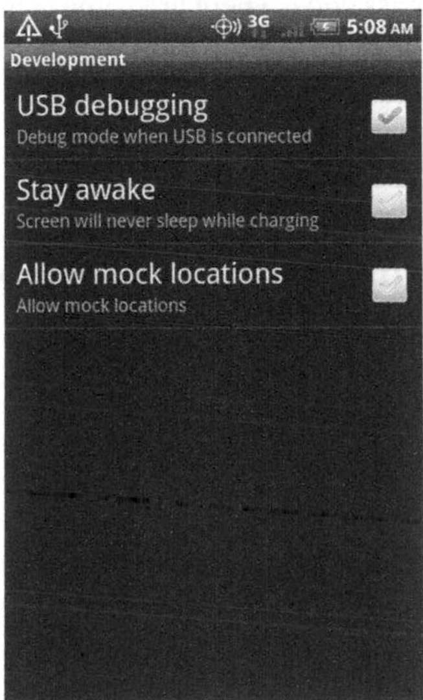

FIGURE 3.30

Enable USB debugging.

FIGURE 3.31

USB debugging warning.

For every current logical Android forensic tool, USB debugging must be enabled. While this is trivial to achieve if the device is unlocked, it is far more difficult if the device has a pass code. There are some techniques that can circumvent the pass code, discussed in Chapter 6. However, they do not work on every platform.

Introduction to Android Debug Bridge

Throughout the rest of this book, we will leverage adb extensively, so covering the basics now is important. There are three primary components involved when utilizing adb:

1. The adbd running on the Android device
2. The adbd running on your workstation
3. The adb client program running on your workstation

As previously covered, when you enable USB debugging on an Android device, the daemon will run and listen for a connection. Communication between the device's adbd and your workstation's adbd takes place over the virtual network running on top of the USB connection. The daemons communicate over their local host on ports 5555 through 5585. When the workstation's adbd detects a new emulator or device, it creates two sequential port connections. The even port communicates with the device's console while the odd port is for adb connections. The local adb client program uses port 5037 to communicate with the local adbd.

The most basic adb command you can issue is the adb devices command, which provides a list of connected devices.

```
ahoog@ubuntu:~$ adb devices
List of devices attached
HT08XHJ00657    device
```

Another important command provides the ability to kill your local adb service. To achieve this, type the following:

```
ahoog@ubuntu:~$ adb kill-server
ahoog@ubuntu:~$ adb devices
* daemon not running. starting it now on port 5037 *
* daemon started successfully *
List of devices attached
HT08XHJ00657    device
```

As you can see, if the adbd on the workstation is not running, it will be automatically started. On Ubuntu, if you ever receive the following response:

```
ahoog@ubuntu:~$ adb devices
List of devices attached
????????????    no permissions
```

it is likely that the connected Android device has a new vendor ID which must be identified (sudo lsusb -v) and added to the udev rule as discussed in the "SDK install" section. In Microsoft Windows, if the Android device is not recognized you will be alerted and you must install the proper USB drivers from Google or the manufacturer.

One powerful adb command all analysts and engineers should know is "adb shell," which allows you to open a shell on the Android device and interact with the system. This is an important feature for anyone exploring Android. For example, start an AVD and follow these steps to view the application data directories on the device:

```
ahoog@ubuntu:~$ adb shell
# cd /data/data
# ls
com.android.sdksetup
com.android.calculator2
com.android.packageinstaller
com.android.providers.userdictionary
com.android.development
com.android.soundrecorder
com.android.providers.drm
com.android.spare_parts
com.android.providers.downloads.ui
com.android.protips
com.android.fallback
com.android.browser
com.android.providers.applications
com.android.netspeed
com.android.wallpaper.livepicker
android.tts
com.android.htmlviewer
```

```
com.android.music
com.android.certinstaller
com.android.inputmethod.pinyin
com.android.providers.subscribedfeeds
com.android.inputmethod.latin
com.android.gallery
com.android.systemui
com.android.contacts
com.android.camera
com.android.term
com.android.speechrecorder
com.android.server.vpn
com.android.quicksearchbox
com.android.defcontainer
com.svox.pico
com.android.customlocale
com.android.providers.settings
com.android.settings
com.android.providers.contacts
jp.co.omronsoft.openwnn
com.android.phone
com.android.launcher
com.android.providers.telephony
com.android.mms
com.android.providers.media
com.android.providers.downloads
com.android.deskclock
com.android.email
```

The functionality of adb has increased with each new SDK and is a very powerful tool. Some of the features will be explored in detail in Chapter 6, including:

1. Running shell commands on the device
2. Installing applications using command line
3. Forwarding ports between your workstation and the device
4. Copying files and folders recursively to and from the device
5. Viewing device log files

Full documentation for the adb command can be found on the Android Developer web site http://developer.android.com/guide/developing/tools/adb.html#commandsummary.

Testing various commands using an Android emulator is an excellent way to understand the tool prior to leveraging it in an investigation.

SUMMARY

The Android SDK not only provides deep insight into the Android platform but also provides powerful tools to investigate a device, from both a forensic and security viewpoint. Once the SDK is installed on a forensic workstation, the examiner has the ability to interact with an Android device connected via USB, provided the USB debugging feature is enabled. Not only is it possible to query information from the device but apps can also be installed, run, and ultimately data extracted from the device. The Android SDK is an important tool used for forensic and security analysis.

References

Android timeline. (n.d.). Android tutorials, news, views and forums, Android Academy. Retrieved March 12, 2011, from http://www.androidacademy.com/1-android-timeline.

Platform Versions, (n.d.). Android developers. Retrieved March 12, 2011, from http://developer.android.com/resources/dashboard/platform-versions.html.

comScore Reports November 2010 U.S. Mobile Subscriber Market Share—comScore, Inc. (n.d.). comScore, Inc.—Measuring the digital world. Retrieved March 12, 2011, from http://www.comscore.com/Press_Events/Press_Releases/2011/1/comScore_Reports_November_2010_.

Android 1.5 Platform. (n.d.). Android developers. Retrieved March 12, 2011, from http://developer.android.com/sdk/android-1.5.html.

Android 1.6 Platform. (n.d.). Android developers. Retrieved March 12, 2011, from http://developer.android.com/sdk/android-1.6.html.

Android 2.1 Platform. (n.d.). Android developers. Retrieved March 12, 2011, from http://developer.android.com/sdk/android-2.1.html.

SDK Archives. (n.d.). Android developers. Retrieved March 13, 2011, from http://developer.android.com/sdk/older_releases.html.

smali-Project Hosting on Google Code. (n.d.). Google code. Retrieved March 13, 2011, from http://code.google.com/p/smali/.

Android On Lockdown: AT&T Removes Best Parts of Android from Backflip (n.d.). AndroidGuys. The trusted source for Android news and opinion, Est. 2007. Retrieved March 13, 2011, from http://www.androidguys.com/2010/03/08/android-lockdown-att-removes-parts-android-backflip/.

CHAPTER

Android file systems and data structures

4

INFORMATION IN THIS CHAPTER

- Data in the shell
- Type of memory
- File systems
- Mounted file systems and directory structures

INTRODUCTION

While the underlying hardware and software powering Android devices is fascinating, the primary focus of forensic analysts and security engineers is to acquire, analyze, and understand data stored on a device. Like other topics discussed, there are many nuances to this that are important to understand for effective analysis including what types of data are stored, where they are stored, how they are stored, and characteristics of the physical mediums on which they are stored. All of these factors play a major role in what data can be recovered and how they can be analyzed.

DATA IN THE SHELL

Forensic analysts are primarily concerned with data artifacts that can be recovered from the devices they investigate. Android is a combination of both well-known artifacts, such as those found in Linux, and entirely new ones, such as the Dalvik VM and the YAFFS2 file system. Adding to the complexity are the varying architectures that different manufacturers embrace.

While no single book or examiner could possibly cover this topic exhaustively, there are certain fundamental concepts common to Android devices. File systems, file, and other artifacts are at the core of what forensic analysts must understand about Android to maximize the effectiveness of their investigations.

What Data are Stored

Android devices store an enormous amount of data, typically combining both personal and work data. Apps are the primary source of these data, and there are a number of sources for apps including:

- Apps that ship with Android
- Apps installed by the manufacturer
- Apps installed by the wireless carrier
- Additional Google/Android apps
- Apps installed by the user, typically from the Android Market

Chapter 7, Android Application and Forensic Analysis, will examine a number of these apps in detail, although it is certainly beyond the scope of this book to cover all possibilities. A sample of data found on Android devices includes the following:

- Text messages (SMS/MMS)
- Contacts
- Call logs
- E-mail messages (Gmail, Yahoo, Exchange)
- Instant Messenger/Chat
- GPS coordinates
- Photos/Videos
- Web history
- Search history
- Driving directions
- Facebook, Twitter, and other social media clients
- Files stored on the device
- Music collections
- Calendar appointments
- Financial information
- Shopping history
- File sharing

App Data Storage Directory Structure

Android applications primarily store data in two locations, internal and external storage, both of which will be covered in more detail later in this chapter. However, it is helpful to have a high-level understanding of the data storage directory structure.

In the external data storage areas (the SD card and emulated SD cards), applications can store data in any location they wish. However, internal data storage is controlled by the Android APIs. When an application is installed (through either the market place or in the build shipped to the consumer), an internal data storage is saved in a subdirectory of /data/data/ named after the package name. For example, the default Android browser has a package name of com.android.browser and, as

Table 4.1 Common /data/data/<packageName> Subdirectories

shared_prefs	Directory Storing Shared Preferences in XML Format
lib	Custom library files an application requires
files	Files the developer saves to internal storage
cache	Files cached by the application, often cache files from the web browser or other apps that use the WebKit engine
databases	SQLite databases and journal files

such, the data files are stored in /data/data/com.android.browser. While applications are not required to store data files, most do.

Inside the applications /data/data subdirectory, there are a number of standard directories found in many applications as well as directories that developers control. The most common standard subdirectories are listed in Table 4.1.

Table 4.1 only presents the most common subdirectories found in an application's /data/data file. As we examine data more closely throughout this book, we will catalog many additional folders and data files.

How Data are Stored

Android provides developers with five methods for storing data to a device. Forensic examiners can uncover data in at least four of the five formats. Therefore, it is important to understand each in detail.

Persistent data are stored to either the NAND flash, the SD card, or the network. Specifically, the five methods are:

1. Shared preferences
2. Internal storage
3. External storage
4. SQLite
5. Network

Beyond the data that app developers store, the Linux kernel and Android stack provide information through logs, debugging, and other standard information services.

Shared Preferences

Shared preferences allow a developer to store key-value pairs of primitive data types in a lightweight XML format. Primitive data types that can be stored in a preferences file include the following:

1. boolean: true or false
2. float: single-precision 32-bit IEEE 754 floating point
3. int: 32-bit signed two's complement integer

4. long: 64-bit signed two's complement integer
5. strings: string value, typically as a UTF-8

With these basic types, developers can create and save simple values that power their application.

Shared preferences files are typically stored in an application's data directory in the shared_pref folder and end with .xml. On our reference HTC Incredible, the Android phone shared preferences directory are five XML files:

```
ahoog@ubuntu:~/data/data/com.android.phone/shared_prefs$ ls -l
total 20
-rw-r----- 1 ahoog ahoog 104 2011-01-23 18:05 cdma_msg_id.xml
-rw-r----- 1 ahoog ahoog 214 2011-01-20 09:34 com.android.phone_preferences.xml
-rw-r----- 1 ahoog ahoog 126 1980-01-06 09:42 _has_set_default_values.xml
-rw-r----- 1 ahoog ahoog 152 2010-09-10 09:46 htc_cdma_settings.xml
-rw-r----- 1 ahoog ahoog 102 2010-09-10 09:48 updateAreaCode.xml
```

The com.android.phone_preferences.xml preferences file has examples of int, boolean, and string preferences:

```
ahoog@ubuntu:~/data/data/com.android.phone/shared_prefs$ cat
com.android.phone_preferences.xml
<?xml version='1.0' encoding='utf-8' standalone='yes' ?>
<map>
<int name="vm_count_key_cdma" value="0" />
<boolean name="pref_key_save_contact" value="true" />
<string name="vm_number_key_cdma">*86</string>
</map>
```

As you can tell, the XML file describes the string encoding type at the start of the file, UTF-8 in this case. There are three preferences that save various settings and characteristics. Perhaps most interesting from a forensics standpoint is the updateAreaCode.xml:

```
ahoog@ubuntu:~/data/data/com.android.phone/shared_prefs$ cat updateAreaCode.xml
<?xml version='1.0' encoding='utf-8' standalone='yes' ?>
<map>
<string name="MDN">312</string>
</map>
```

The mobile directory number (MDN) is queried and the area code for the device is stored in this file, presumably to allow a seven-digit dialing option in areas supporting that feature.

Since many applications take advantage of the lightweight Shared Preferences method for storing key-value pairs, it can be a rich source of forensic data. This is especially true when examiners can recover older or deleted versions of the XML preferences file.

Files on Internal Storage

Files allow developers to store more complicated data structures and are saved in several places on the file internal storage. The files are stored in the application's /data/data subdirectory and the developer has control over the file type, name, and location. By default, the files can only be read by the application and even the device owner is prevented from viewing the files unless they have root access. The developer can override the security settings to allow other processes to read and even update the file.

> **TIP**
>
> **Identifying custom files**
>
> The best way to determine which files in an application's subdirectory fall into this category is by a process of elimination. Basically, any file in the application's /data/data/ subdirectory which is *not* in the shared_prefs, lib, cache, or databases subdirectories is a file the developer created and controls.

Let's examine com.google.android.apps.maps that provides a good example of files saved on internal storage:

```
ahoog@ubuntu:~/data/data/com.google.android.apps.maps$ ls -l
total 24
drwxr-x--x 5 ahoog ahoog 4096 2011-01-18 03:42 app_
drwxr-x--x 3 ahoog ahoog 4096 2010-09-15 10:59 cache
drwxr-x--x 2 ahoog ahoog 4096 2011-01-23 10:30 databases
drwxr-x--x 2 ahoog ahoog 4096 2011-01-23 20:55 files
drwxr-xr-x 2 ahoog ahoog 4096 1980-01-06 09:41 lib
drwxr-x--x 2 ahoog ahoog 4096 2011-01-24 04:13 shared_prefs
```

The application uses most of the storage mechanisms available and stores files on internal storage in both the app_ and files directory. The app_ directory has several subdirectories and a cache_r.m file which is not of a known file format:

```
ahoog@ubuntu:~/data/data/com.google.android.apps.maps$ tree app_/
app_/
├── cache
│   └── cache_r.m
├── debug
└── testdata
```

The files directory stores many data files needed by the application to display and update Google Maps:

```
ahoog@ubuntu:~/data/data/com.google.android.apps.maps$ tree files
files
├── DA_DirOpt_en_US
├── DA_LayerInfo
├── DATA_LATITUDE_WIDGET_MODEL
├── DATA_LAYER_10
├── DATA_LAYER_2
├── DATA_LAYER_20
├── DATA_LAYER_21
├── DATA_LAYER_24
├── DATA_LAYER_25
├── DATA_LAYER_3
├── DATA_LAYER_5
├── DATA_LAYER_6
├── DATA_LAYER_7
```

```
├── DATA_LAYER_8
├── DATA_location_history
├── DATA_OptionDefinitionBlock_en
├── DATA_Preferences
├── DATA_PROTO_SAVED_CATEGORY_TREE_DB
├── DATA_PROTO_SAVED_LAYER_STATE
├── DATA_PROTO_SAVED_RECENT_LAYERS
├── DATA_RemoteStringsBlock_en
├── DATA_Restrictions
├── DATA_Restrictions_lock
├── DATA_SAVED_BGFS_3
├── DATA_SAVED_BGFS_EXTRA_3
├── DATA_SAVED_BGSF_
├── DATA_SAVED_REMOTE_ICONS_DATA_BLOCK
├── DATA_ServerControlledParametersManager.data
├── DATA_STARRING
├── DATA_SYNC_DATA
├── DATA_SYNC_DATA_LOCAL
├── DATA_TILE_HISTORY
├── DATA_Tiles
├── DATA_Tiles_1
├── DATA_Tiles_2
├── DATA_Tiles_3
├── event_store_driveabout
├── event_store_LocationFriendService
├── NavigationParameters.data
├── NavZoomTables.data
├── nlp_GlsPlatformKey
├── nlp_state
└── ZoomTables.data
```

The files clearly indicate data that may be of interest to a forensic analyst or security engineer. A more thorough data analysis of applications and their data stored will be covered in Chapter 7, Android Application and Forensic Analysis.

Files on External Storage

While files stored on the internal device's storage have strict security and location parameters, files on the various external storage devices have far fewer constraints.

First, one important motivation (beyond cost) for using a removable SD card is that the data could be used on other devices, presumably upgraded Android devices. If a consumer purchased a new Android device, inserted their previous SD card containing all of his or her family pictures and videos and found they were unable to access them, they would be quite upset.

In order to facilitate mounting the SD card on desktop computers to share files, SD cards are generally formatted with Microsoft's FAT32 files system. While the file system is widely supported, it lacks the fine grained security mechanism built into file systems such as ext3, ext4, yaffs2, hfsplus, and more. Thus, by default, the files cannot enforce permissions.

For example, the com.google.android.apps.maps application referenced previously also stores data on the SD card in the Android/data subdirectory. The following is a listing of the files and directories from the reference HTC Incredible SD card, mounted at /mnt/sdcard:

```
ahoog@ubuntu:~/htc-inc/mnt/sdcard/Android/data$ tree com.google.android.apps.maps/
com.google.android.apps.maps/
├── cache
│   ├── cache_its.0
│   ├── cache_its.m
│   ├── cache_its_ter.m
│   ├── cache_r.0
│   ├── cache_r.1
│   ├── cache_rgts.0
│   ├── cache_rgts.m
│   ├── cache_r.m
│   ├── cache_vts.0A
│   ├── cache_vts.1
│   ├── cache_vts_GMM.0
│   ├── cache_vts_GMM.1
│   ├── cache_vts_GMM.m
│   ├── cache_vts.m
│   └── cache_vts_tran_GMM.m
├── debug
└── testdata
```

Similarly, the HTC Incredible ships with an emulated SD card that is stored directly on the NAND flash. The emulated SD card is mounted at /mnt/emmc. The following is a listing of a subdirectory that stores album JFIF thumbnail files:

```
ahoog@ubuntu:~/htc-inc/mnt/emmc$ tree Android/data/com.android.providers.media/
└── albumthumbs
    ├── 1283015214003
    ├── 1283015215018
    ├── 1283015215425
    ├── 1283015215861
    ├── 1283015216304
    └── 1283015216711
```

As you can tell, developers have great control over the name, format, and location of files on the external and emulated SD cards.

SQLite

Another NAND/SD card-based storage that developers leverage is a specific type of file—an SQLite database. Databases are used for structured data storage and SQLite is a popular database format appearing in many mobile systems as well as traditional operating systems.

SQLite is popular for many reasons. Notably the entire code base is of high quality, open source, and released to the public domain. The file format and the program itself are very compact and pack significant functionality in less than a few hundred kilobytes. Unlike more traditional relational database management systems (RDBMS), such as Oracle, MySQL, and Microsoft's SQL Server, with SQLite the entire database is contained in a single cross-platform file.

The Android SDK provides dedicated APIs that allow developers to use SQLite databases in their applications. The SQLite files are generally stored on the internal storage under /data/data/<packageName>/databases. However, there are no restrictions on creating databases elsewhere.

SQLite databases are a rich source of forensic data. The built-in Android browser, based on the WebKit Open Source Project (http://webkit.org/), provides a great example. In our referenced HTC Incredible, there were 28 SQLite databases located in subdirectories of /data/data/com.android.webkit. In this instance, the five subdirectories were as follows:

- app_icons: 1 database of web page icons
- app_cache: 1 database containing web application data cache
- app_geolocation: 2 databases relating to GPS position and permissions
- app_databases: 21 databases providing local database storage for supporting web sites
- databases: 3 databases for the browser and browser cache

There is very high potential of recovering forensically valuable data from these files.

Network

The final data storage mechanism available to developers is the network, a key benefit of a device designed to be network aware. Initially, very few applications took advantage of the network as a storage option. However, as the SDK, apps, and devices mature, the network storage option is being leveraged more.

The Android Developer web site provides very few details for those interested in network storage. Their entire documentation is a mere two sentences long (Data storage, n.d.).

You can use the network (when it is available) to store and retrieve data on your own web-based services. To do network operations, use classes in the following packages:

- java.net.*
- android.net.*

The packages referenced in the documentation essentially provide developers with the low-level APIs needed to interact with the network, web servers, and more. Apps that leverage the network require more custom coding and, while all of the forensically interesting data may not be stored on the device, often important configuration and database files are recoverable.

For example (and as a sneak peak to Chapter 7, Android Application and Forensic Analysis), Dropbox is a popular file sharing web site which has mobile apps for Android, Blackberry, and iOS devices. Their current Android application (version 1.0.3.0) has been downloaded from the Android Market over 250,000 times and has over 35,000 user ratings, most quite high. After the app is installed, you can find the application folder at /data/data/com.dropbox.android with four standard directories:

```
ahoog@ubuntu:~/htc-inc/data/data$ tree com.dropbox.android/
com.dropbox.android/
├── databases
│   └── db.db
├── files
│   └── log.txt
├── lib
└── shared_prefs
    └── DropboxAccountPrefs.xml
```

The log.txt is a verbose log of activity and a few lines are provided for reference:

```
ahoog@ubuntu:~/com.dropbox.android$ cat ./files/log.txt
5 1296055108427 com.dropbox.android.provider.DatabaseHelper Creating new Dropbox
database.
4 1296055108459 com.dropbox.android.DropboxApplication Not authenticated, so
authenticating
4 1296055108466 com.dropbox.android.DropboxApplication No stored login token.
4 1296055108702 com.dropbox.android.DropboxApplication Not authenticated, so
authenticating
4 1296055108704 com.dropbox.android.DropboxApplication No stored login token.
4 1296055108704 com.dropbox.android.activity.SimpleDropboxBrowser Didn't
authenticate, redirecting to login
4 1296055108713 com.dropbox.android.DropboxApplication Not authenticated, so
authenticating
4 1296055108714 com.dropbox.android.DropboxApplication No stored login token.
4 1296055134550 com.dropbox.android.DropboxApplication Authenticating username:
book@viaforensics.com
4 1296055136507 com.dropbox.android.DropboxApplication Successfully
authenticated
6 1296055137501 com.dropbox.android.activity.LoginActivity Dismissed nonexistent
dialog box
4 1296055137525 com.dropbox.android.activity.LoginOrNewAcctActivity Successful
account login
4 1296055137549 com.dropbox.android.activity.delegate.MenuDelegate Successful
login
4 1296055137735 com.dropbox.android.activity.SimpleDropboxBrowser Query is:
content://com.dropbox.android.Dropbox/metadata/
6 1296055137742 com.dropbox.android.provider.QueryStatus Querying with query
id: DB2
4 1296055137765 com.dropbox.android.activity.SimpleDropboxBrowser Browsing
URI: content://com.dropbox.android.Dropbox/metadata/
4 1296055138208 com.dropbox.android.provider.ProviderDirSyncThread Directory
changed, going through line-by-line:
content://com.dropbox.android.Dropbox/metadata/
4 1296055161450 com.dropbox.android.activity.delegate.MenuDelegate Importing
Picture from Gallery
6 1296055170307 com.dropbox.android.provider.DropboxProvider Adding new file
(from import, probably): content://media/external/images/media/5
4 1296055170329 com.dropbox.android.taskqueue.TaskQueue Added task to queue:
content://media/external/images/media/5~/
4 1296055170333 com.dropbox.android.taskqueue.TaskQueue Starting up task queue
4 1296055170333 com.dropbox.android.taskqueue.UploadTask Uploading file from
URI: content://media/external/images/media/5
4 1296055170333 com.dropbox.android.taskqueue.DbTaskQueue Task
content://media/external/images/media/5~/ adding to task DB
6 1296055170351 com.dropbox.android.service.ServiceBinderDelegate Unbound
service!
4 1296055170352 com.dropbox.android.taskqueue.UploadTask Uploading file:
/mnt/sdcard/forensics/20110111.1618/387.jpg to / as 387.jpg
4 1296055170367 com.dropbox.android.activity.SimpleDropboxBrowser Browsing URI:
content://com.dropbox.android.Dropbox/metadata/
4 1296055170471 com.dropbox.android.service.DropboxReceiver Connectivity action:
mobile CDMA - EvDo rev. A 2GVoiceCallEnded
4 1296055170471 com.dropbox.android.service.DropboxReceiver Connectivity change!
true
4 1296055170472 com.dropbox.android.taskqueue.DbTaskQueue Adding Uploads from
stored db: 1
```

Some items of potential interest were emphasized in the above listing, specifically:

1. All actions have time stamps
2. Successfully authenticate user, user name provided

3. Picture imported from Gallery
4. Specific file on SD card is uploaded
5. Dropbox service is interrupted by phone call

The app also has a shared preference file:

```
ahoog@ubuntu:~/htc-inc/data/data/com.dropbox.android$ cat
shared_prefs/DropboxAccountPrefs.xml
<?xml version='1.0' encoding='utf-8' standalone='yes' ?>
<map>
<string name="LAST_URI">content://com.dropbox.android.Dropbox/metadata/</string>
<string name="DISPLAY_NAME">Andrew Hoog</string>
<long name="QUOTA_QUOTA" value="2147483648" />
<long name="QUOTA_NORMAL" value="1480890" />
<string name="REFERRAL_LINK">https://www.dropbox.com/referrals/NNNNAN0NnwNNN
</string>
<string name="COUNTRY"></string>
<long name="UID" value="96189742" />
<string name="EMAIL">book@viaforensics.com</string>
<string name="ACCESS_KEY">accesskeyinfohere</string>
<string name="ACCESS_SECRET">accesssecretinfohere</string>
<long name="QUOTA_SHARED" value="0" />
</map>
```

A quick examination of the db.db yields the following data using the sqlite3 command line program (you could also use a graphical SQLite browser to view the database):

```
ahoog@ubuntu:~/htc-inc/data/data/com.dropbox.android/databases$ sqlite3 db.db
SQLite version 3.6.22
Enter ".help" for instructions
Enter SQL statements terminated with a ";"

sqlite> .tables
android_metadata  dropbox           pending_upload

sqlite> .mode line

sqlite> select * from dropbox where _id = 2;
          _id = 2
        _data = /sdcard/dropbox/Android intro.pdf
     modified = Wed, 26 Jan 2011 15:18:40 +0000
        bytes = 176607
     revision = 10
         hash =
         icon = page_white_acrobat
       is_dir = 0
         path = /Android intro.pdf
         root =
         size = 172.5KB
    mime_type = application/pdf
  thumb_exists = 0
   parent_path = /
 _display_name = Android intro.pdf
   is_favorite =
local_modified = 1296055191000
   local_bytes = 176607
local_revision = 10
      accessed =
   sync_status = 2
```

The database provides important forensic and security data about the Dropbox application, device, and ultimately the user and people they might interact with. The "Android intro.pdf" file was automatically synced to the Dropbox account by Dropbox when Android app was installed and logged into. When the shared PDF file was viewed, it was cached on the SD card. Additional metadata about the file and the use of it is contained in the database. Despite Dropbox's extensive use of network data storage for their application, we could still recover useful information.

Kernel, System, and Application Logs

One additional area where forensic analysts and security engineers can locate files and information relevant to an investigation or audit is the standard Linux file system. Unfortunately, that's quite broad and overwhelming, but we can at least provide a starting place to look for relevant information.

Log files and debugging are two common and effective ways in which developers and administrators both maintain their system and their apps. It provides an insight into the apps as well as the system running them. While not true in every case, it is possible to glean important information from an Android device by simply examining the various log and debug files.

Linux kernel logging

The Linux kernel is the low level, abstract interface of the Linux operating system that provides access to the hardware of a device. Since the role of the kernel is central to all functions on the device, the ability to log key events and activities is highly leveraged. The kernel log is accessible on a Linux (and thus Android) device through the command dmesg. This will print to console all available kernel messages, a portion of which is displayed here:

```
ahoog@ubuntu:~$ adb shell dmesg
<6>[151434.178802] batt: SMEM_BATT: get_batt_info: batt_id=2, batt_vol=4211,
batt_temp=264, batt_current=377, eval_current=112, level=96, charging_source=1,
charging_enabled=1, full_bat=1300000, over_vchg=0 at 151435426063278
(2011-01-28 11:28:37.995086662 UTC)
<4>[151574.946685] select 7673 (ogle.android.gm), adj 15, size 4821, to kill
<4>[151574.947418] send sigkill to 7673 (ogle.android.gm), adj 15, size 4821
<4>[151575.003967] deathpending end 7673 (ogle.android.gm)
<4>[151668.188018] mmc1: Starting deferred resume
<6>[151668.195281] incrediblec_sdslot_switchvdd: Setting level to 2850 (Success)
<6>[151668.506591] mmc1: Deferred resume completed
<6>[151674.597320] [dma.c] msm_datamover_irq_handler id 8, result not
valid4000001
<6>[151734.168731] batt: M2A_RPC: level_update: 97 at 151735415412693
(2011-01-28 11:33:37.985015911 UTC)
<6>[151734.173339] batt: batt:power_supply_changed: battery at 151735422126560
(2011-01-28 11:33:37.989654582 UTC)
<6>[151734.190490] batt: SMEM_BATT: get_batt_info: batt_id=2, batt_vol=4212,
batt_temp=281, batt_current=353, eval_current=152, level=97, charging_source=1,
charging_enabled=1, full_bat=1300000, over_vchg=0 at 151735437507419
(2011-01-28 11:33:38.006744426 UTC)
<6>[152004.168853] batt: M2A_RPC: level_update: 98 at 152005415595761
(2011-01-28 11:38:07.985168460 UTC)
```

```
<6>[152004.171142] batt: batt:power_supply_changed: battery at 152005418311825
(2011-01-28 11:38:07.987457279 UTC)
<6>[152004.187622] batt: SMEM_BATT: get_batt_info: batt_id=2, batt_vol=4210,
batt_temp=288, batt_current=265, eval_current=112, level=98, charging_source=1,
charging_enabled=1, full_bat=1300000, over_vchg=0 at 152005434913389 (2011-01-28
11:38:08.003875737 UTC)
```

As you may notice, the data are quite verbose and low level. However, it can provide important time stamps and activities, as well as a wealth of information about the device on boot-up. However, if the device has not been rebooted recently, the initial logs from startup are no longer available.

This command does not require any special permission on the device except that USB debugging must be enabled. If you ran this command on a device or emulator, you would have noticed that far too much data were displayed on your screen. You can determine the total number of lines available in the log by piping (or sending) the contents of dmesg to a program called wc (which stands for word count) and instructing it to count the number of lines:

```
ahoog@ubuntu:~$ adb shell dmesg | wc -l
1859
```

So, on the reference HTC Incredible, we have 1859 lines in the kernel log. If you need to inspect the information more closely, or include it in a report, you can redirect the output of dmesg to a file with the following:

```
ahoog@ubuntu:~$ adb shell dmesg > dmesg.log
```

You can now examine the contents of the available kernel log by opening dmesg.log in a text editor or display program.

logcat

Android has several additional debugging techniques available. One program, logcat, displays a continuously updated list of system and application debug messages.

```
ahoog@ubuntu:~$ adb shell logcat
I/HtcLocationService(  308): agent - search location by name: oak park, country:
united states, state: illinois
I/HtcLocationService(  308): agent - no location was found, total: 0
D/AutoSetting(  308): service - CALLBACK - onGetTimeZoneOffset, result: failed,
zoneId: , offset: 0
D/LocationManager(  308): removeUpdates: listener =
com.htc.htclocationservice.HtcLocationServiceAgent$7@45dfc770
V/AlarmManager(   97): Adding Alarm{463aea28 type 2 com.google.android.location}
Jan 05 05:05:25 pm
I/HtcLocationService(  308): agent - send current location notify intent, name:
Oak Park, state: Illinois, country: United States, lat: 41.8786, lng:
-87.6359,tzid:
D/AutoSetting(  308): service - CALLBACK - onSetWeatherProvider, result: success
I/WSP       (  308): [Receiver] EVENT - CURRENT LOCATION CHANGED
V/AlarmManager(   97): Adding Alarm{46265558 type 0 com.htc.htclocationservice}
Jan 28 09:12:53 am
D/AutoSetting(  308): service - wake lock release
D/LocationManager(  308): removeUpdates: listener =
com.htc.htclocationservice.HtcLocationServiceAgent$7@45dfc770
```

```
V/AlarmManager(   97): Alarm triggering: Alarm{46265558 type 0
com.htc.htclocationservice}
V/AutoSetting(  308): receiver - ***onReceive:
com.htc.app.autosetting.retrylocation
V/AutoSetting(  308): receiver - startAutosettingService, action:
com.htc.app.autosetting.retrylocation,notifyWhenNoResult:false
D/AutoSetting(  308): service - onCreate(),no SharedPreference
D/AutoSetting(  308): service - ***setupWizardIsCompleted: true
D/AutoSetting(  308): service - onStart(), id = 0
D/AutoSetting(  308): service - new wake lock
D/AutoSetting(  308): service - wake lock acquire
D/AutoSetting(  308): service - onStart(), Checking location times = 2
D/AutoSetting(  308): service - onStart(), Checking location change = false
D/AutoSetting(  308): service - onStart(), Set city info = false
D/AutoSetting(  308): service - onStart(), Set network time info = false
D/AutoSetting(  308): service - onStart(), Set network timezone info = true
D/AutoSetting(  308): service - onStart(), Set notify when no result = false
D/AutoSetting(  308): service - ***setupWizardIsCompleted: true
D/AutoSetting(  308): service - ***chkConnected,
mbReqChecking:false,mbApplyAll:true
D/AutoSetting(  308): service - ***Data call is avaiable
D/AutoSetting(  308): service - doAutoSettings(), isNetworkAvailable: true,
isUseWirelessNetworks: true, isTimeAutoState: true
D/LocationManager(  308): requestLocationUpdates: provider = network, listener =
com.htc.htclocationservice.HtcLocationServiceAgent$7@45dfc770
D/LocationManagerService(   97): CdmaCellLocation Unavailable
I/HtcLocationService(  308): agent - search location by name: oak park, country:
united states, state: illinois
V/AlarmManager(   97): Adding Alarm{45fb22a0 type 2 com.google.android.location}
Jan 05 05:04:51 pm
V/AlarmManager(   97): Adding Alarm{45fb0a90 type 2 com.google.android.location}
Jan 05 05:04:51 pm
```

A quick scan of the small log snippet above reveals

- Longitude and latitude data
- Date/time information
- Application details

The logging is very verbose and the sample provided here is just a small sample of what is available. Each log message begins with message type indicator, described in Table 4.2.

Table 4.2 Log Method Types

Message Type	Description
V	Verbose
D	Debug
I	Information
W	Warning
E	Error
F	Fatal
S	Silent

The logcat program also provides logs from the full cellular radio debug, which can be viewed with the following command (only select portions of the radio logs included):

```
ahoog@ubuntu:~$ adb shell logcat -b radio
D/CDMA    ( 193): [CdmaServiceStateTracker] Set CDMA Roaming Indicator to: 128.
mCdmaRoaming = false, isPrlLoaded = true. namMatch = true , mIsInPrl = true,
mRoamingIndicator = 128, mDefaultRoamingIndicator= 64
D/CDMA    ( 193): [CdmaServiceStateTracker] Poll ServiceState done:
oldSS=[0 home Verizon Wireless Verizon Wireless 31000  EvDo rev. A CSS supported
3 20RoamInd: 128DefRoamInd: 64EriInd: 1EriMode: 0RadioPowerSv: falseDefRoamInd:
64EmergOnly: false] newSS=[0 home Verizon Wireless Verizon Wireless 31000  EvDo
rev. A CSS supported 3 20RoamInd: 128DefRoamInd: 64EriInd: 1EriMode:
0RadioPowerSv: falseDefRoamInd: 64EmergOnly: false]
D/CDMA    ( 193): Query NBPCD state: false
D/CDMA    ( 193): will call NBPCD: 7735555555 NBPCD state: false
D/SMS     ( 193): SMS send size=5time=1296219734520
D/RILJ    ( 193): [23001]> RIL_REQUEST_CDMA_SEND_SMS
D/HTC_RIL (  67): ril_func_cdma_send_sms():called
D/HTC_RIL (  67): dump_cdma_sms():uTeleserviceID     = 4098
D/HTC_RIL (  67): dump_cdma_sms():bIsServicePresent = 0
D/HTC_RIL (  67): dump_cdma_sms():uServicecategory  = 0
D/HTC_RIL (  67): dump_cdma_sms():sAddress.digit_mode  = 0
D/HTC_RIL (  67): dump_cdma_sms():sAddress.number_mode = 0
D/HTC_RIL (  67): dump_cdma_sms():sAddress.number_type = 0
D/HTC_RIL (  67): dump_cdma_sms():sAddress.number_plan = 0
D/HTC_RIL (  67): dump_cdma_sms():sAddress.number_of_digits = 10
D/HTC_RIL (  67): dump_cdma_sms():sAddress.digits = [07070305050505050505]
D/HTC_RIL (  67): dump_cdma_sms():sSubAddress.subaddressType = 0
D/HTC_RIL (  67): dump_cdma_sms():sSubAddress.odd = 0
D/HTC_RIL (  67): dump_cdma_sms():sSubAddress.number_of_digits = 0
D/HTC_RIL (  67): dump_cdma_sms():sSubAddress.digits = []
D/HTC_RIL (  67): dump_cdma_sms():uBearerDataLen = 32
D/HTC_RIL (  67): dump_cdma_sms():aBearerData:
[0003202C80010D10654CBCFA20DB979F3C39F2800E0705189249CB1B00080100]
D/HTC_RIL (  67): encode_cdma_sms():encode_index = 51
D/HTC_RIL (  67): ril_func_cdma_send_sms():raw_data:
[00000210020407029DCD158C98800601000820000320 2C80010D10654CBCFA20DB979F3C39F2800
E0705189249CB1B00080100]
D/HTC_RIL (  67): (t=1296219734)>> AT+CMGS=51\r
D/HTC_RIL (  67): RX::> \r\n> ^M
D/HTC_RIL (  67): (t=1296219734)XX \r\n
D/HTC_RIL (  67): (t=1296219734)<< >
D/HTC_RIL (  67): (t=1296219734)>>
00000210020407029DCD158C9880060100082000003202C80010D10654CBCFA20DB979F3C39F2800E
0705189249CB1B00080100^Z
D/RILJ    ( 193): [UNSL]< UNSOL_DATA_CALL_LIST_CHANGED [DataCallState: { cid:
62, active: 1, type: IP, apn: 0, address: 10.237.127.132 }, DataCallState:
{ cid: -1, active: 0, type: , apn: , address:  }, DataCallState: { cid: -1,
active: 0, type: , apn: , address:  }]
```

While the logging is verbose and generally cryptic, scanning the logs above can provide information such as:

- Time of events (in Unix Epoch, e.g., t=1296218163)
- AT commands used by the cellular modem to communicate
- Recipient, size, time, and encoded SMS message
- Device's cellular IP address, networking and location information
- Wireless carrier information

This information is of very low level. However, if such logs are recovered, they can reveal important information about a device.

> **NOTE**
> **Unix Epoch**
> Unix Epoch time is a common format for time stamps in systems based on Unix/Linux. The time stamp is an integer value that represents the number of seconds (or milliseconds) since January 1, 1970. A typical time stamp using seconds will have 10 digits while a time stamp using milliseconds will have 13 digits. Time stamps are covered in more details in Chapter 7.

One final logcat feature is the event logs display:

```
$adb shell logcat -b events
I/db_sample(  193):
[/data/data/com.android.providers.telephony/databases/mmssms.db,INSERT INTO
sms(body, index_on_sim, address, subject, read, type,280,,57]
I/db_sample(  193):
[/data/data/com.android.providers.telephony/databases/mmssms.db,SELECT
transport_type, _id, thread_id, address, body, date, read,170,,35]
```

Again, this log is very verbose. However, as different events within the system occur, they log considerable information here. In the previous log snippet, we can see both an INSERT and SELECT statement on the mmssms.db, which is used to store text messages.

dumpsys

The next logging mechanism is accessed through a command called dumpsys.

Dumpsys provides information on services, memory, and other system details that can provide helpful information. Some of the types of information provided include

- Currently running services
- Dump of each service
- Services, broadcasts, pending intents, activities, and processes in current activity manager state
- Process information including memory, process IDs (PIDs), databases, and more used

Sample sections from the reference HTC Incredible dumpsys are listed next and each include a brief explanation of how the data might be valuable to a forensic analyst or security engineer.

First, you run the dumpsys command as follows:

```
$adb shell dumpsys
Currently running services:
  SurfaceFlinger
  VZW_LOCATION_SERVICE
  accessibility
  account
<snip>
```

The section dumping details of the service "account" has valuable information about the various accounts used on the device.

```
DUMP OF SERVICE account:
Accounts: 10
  Account {name=Backup Assistant, type=com.htc.VzWBASync}
  Account {name=News, type=com.htc.newsreader}
  Account {name=Weather, type=com.htc.sync.provider.weather}
  Account {name=Stocks, type=com.htc.android.Stock}
  Account {name=book@viaforensics.com, type=com.google}
  Account {name=book@viaforensics.com, type=com.htc.android.mail.eas}
  Account {name=Andrew Hoog, type=com.htc.socialnetwork.facebook}
  Account {name=viaforensics, type=com.htc.htctwitter}
  Account {name=viaforensics, type=com.twitter.android.auth.login}
  Account {name=personal@emailaddress.com, type=com.google}
```

You can see not only programs used, but also at times the account name specific to the user. For example, the above reveals:

- Google account with user name book@viaforensics.com
- Exchange ActiveSync (EAS) account with user name book@viaforensics.com (separate from the Google account above)
- Facebook account for Andrew Hoog
- Twitter account for viaforensics
- Google account for personal@emailaddress.com (second one on the device)

Further in the log, the actual time stamps for the last 10 syncs are similarly provided:

```
Recent Sync History
  #1: book@viaforensics.com:com.google com.android.calendar LOCAL @ 2011-01-28
09:52:46 for 0.0s
  #2: book@viaforensics.com:com.htc.android.mail.eas htceas USER @ 2011-01-28
09:51:43 for 34.5s
  #3: book@viaforensics.com:com.google com.android.calendar LOCAL @ 2011-01-28
09:49:25 for 0.0s
  #4: Andrew Hoog:com.htc.socialnetwork.facebook com.htc.socialnetwork.facebook
SERVER @ 2011-01-28 09:48:57 for 0.5s
  #5: book@viaforensics.com:com.google com.android.calendar LOCAL @ 2011-01-28
09:45:30 for 0.0s
  #6: Andrew Hoog:com.htc.socialnetwork.facebook com.htc.socialnetwork.facebook
SERVER @ 2011-01-28 09:44:40 for 1.3s
  #7: book@viaforensics.com:com.htc.android.mail.eas htceas USER @ 2011-01-28
09:44:18 for 1.3s
  #8: viaforensics:com.twitter.android.auth.login
com.twitter.android.provider.TwitterProvider SERVER @ 2011-01-28 09:44:06 for
11.6s
  #9: book@viaforensics.com:com.htc.android.mail.eas htceas USER @ 2011-01-28
09:41:08 for 15.8s
  #10: Andrew Hoog:com.htc.socialnetwork.facebook com.htc.socialnetwork.facebook
SERVER @ 2011-01-28 09:37:27 for 0.1s
```

Another service is humorously named "iphonesubinfo," which obviously has nothing to do with Apple's iPhone despite the similarity in name.

```
DUMP OF SERVICE iphonesubinfo:
Phone Subscriber Info:
  Phone Type = CDMA
  Device ID = A100001829481F
```

Both the phone type and Device ID (changed) are available from this section. The Device ID is not the device's serial number but the Mobile Equipment Identifier (MEID), which uniquely identifies the device on the CDMA network.

Another great source of information is the location service that shows last known location information and time.

```
DUMP OF SERVICE location:
  Last Known Locations:
    passive:
      mProvider=network mTime=1296230208384
      mLatitude=41.8786 mLongitude=-87.6359
      mHasAltitude=false mAltitude=0.0
      mHasSpeed=false mSpeed=0.0
      mHasBearing=false mBearing=0.0
      mHasAccuracy=true mAccuracy=1423.0
      mExtras=Bundle[{networkLocationType=cell, networkLocationSource=cached}]
    gps:
      mProvider=gps mTime=1296157873000
      mLatitude=41.8786 mLongitude=-87.6359
      mHasAltitude=true mAltitude=198.8000030517578
      mHasSpeed=true mSpeed=29.75
      mHasBearing=true mBearing=69.7
      mHasAccuracy=true mAccuracy=2.828427
      mExtras=Bundle[{satellites=11}]
```

Most time stamps in Android are the number of milliseconds since January 1, 1970, which is Unix Epoch time—in milliseconds instead of seconds, however. Since most tools convert Unix Epoch based on seconds, you can divide the number by 1000 and then use a standard formula. If you built the Ubuntu workstation, you can convert using the following command line:

```
ahoog@ubuntu:~$ date -d @1296230208
Fri Jan 28 09:56:48 CST 2011
```

This will output in the workstation's time zone. You can control the time zone, format, and many other parameters with various switches on the command. To see the full possibilities, run "date–help" or "man date."

Examining the three cached locations above, we can see the system cached locations from both GPS satellites and cell towers at the following times:

1. GPS: Thu Jan 27 13:51:13 CST 2011
2. Cell: Fri Jan 28 09:56:48 CST 2011

The locations are accurate for the time recorded and thus provide excellent historical information on the device's location.

The network state section provides additional information, including more detailed information on cell phone towers:

```
network Internal State:
  location Location[mProvider=network,mTime=1296230208384,mLatitude=41.8786,
mLongitude=-87.6359,mHasAltitude=false,mAltitude=0.0,mHasSpeed=false,mSpeed=0.0,
mHasBearing=false,mBearing=0.0,mHasAccuracy=true,mAccuracy=1423.0,mExtras=Bundle
[{networkLocationSource=cached, networkLocationType=cell}]]
  Status 2
  StatusUpdateTime 385403711
  NetworkState 2
  LastCellStateChangeTime 428707868
  LastCellLockTime 0
```

```
 cell state [cid: 277 lac: 3 mcc: 0 mnc: 20 radioType: 2 signalStrength: -85
  neighbors[]
  cell history
    [cid: 4671 lac: 3 mcc: 0 mnc: 20 radioType: 2 signalStrength: -103 neighors[]
    [cid: 277 lac: 3 mcc: 0 mnc: 20 radioType: 2 signalStrength: -103 neighbors[]
    [cid: 4671 lac: 3 mcc: 0 mnc: 20 radioType: 2 signalStrength: -87 neighbors[]
    [cid: 286 lac: 3 mcc: 0 mnc: 20 radioType: 2 signalStrength: -98 neighbors[]
  WifiScanFrequency 60000
  WifiEnabled 0
  WaitingForWifiScan 0
  LastNetworkQueryTime 428712899
  LastSuccessfulNetworkQueryTime 428712926
  Enabled 1
  AirplaneMode 0
  DisabledForAirplaneMode 0
```

One last section to point out, despite the level of technical details, is the memory information section, which is output for each PID:

```
** MEMINFO in pid 454 [com.htc.android.mail] **
                    native   dalvik    other    total    limit   bitmap nativeBmp
            size:    18048     9543      N/A    27591    32768      N/A       N/A
       allocated:    14490     4485      N/A    18975      N/A     1032         0
            free:     1341     5058      N/A     6399      N/A      N/A       N/A
           (Pss):    10644     4839     8651    24134      N/A      N/A       N/A
  (shared dirty):     1348     3924      960     6232      N/A      N/A       N/A
    (priv dirty):    10604     4724     4800    20128      N/A      N/A       N/A

Objects
           Views:        0         ViewRoots:        0
     AppContexts:        0        Activities:        0
          Assets:        3     AssetManagers:        3
   Local Binders:       50     Proxy Binders:       36
Death Recipients:        2
OpenSSL Sockets:        1

SQL
            heap:     3740        memoryUsed:     3740
pageCacheOverflo:     2185  largestMemAlloc:     1667

DATABASES
  Pagesize   Dbsize  Lookaside  Dbname
      1024       21         38  webview.db
      1024      305         52  webviewCache.db
      1024     5662        499  mail.db
      1024        8          0    (attached) people_db
```

This may be useful not only for determining which processes are running, but also for determining the databases they access. For instance, a case may require the investigator to better understand what information is updated when an e-mail is received. In the above listing, you can see that the e-mail application (com.htc.android.mail) updates not only the mail.db, but also two web-related databases attached to the people_db. This information can be very useful when explaining how data on an Android device interrelates.

dumpstate

Another debug command is dumpstate that combines portions of previous debugs with system information. Similar to the other commands, you run the command with the following:

```
$adb shell dumpsys
/data/anr/traces.txt: Permission denied
==========================================================
== dumpstate: 2011-01-28 09:56:27
==========================================================

Build: FRF91
Bootloader: 0.92.0000
Radio: 2.15.00.07.28
Network: Verizon Wireless
Kernel: Linux version 2.6.32.17-g9a2fc16 (htc-kernel@u18000-Build-149)
(gcc version 4.4.0 (GCC) ) #1 PREEMPT Thu Sep 30 18:42:08 CST 2010
Command line: (unknown)
```

The first section displayed on an emulator or device with adbd running as root is stack traces from applications. However, on the reference HTC devices, dumpstate returns a permission denied. Immediately following is basic information about the device, build, radio, network and kernel details. The remaining log contains the sections outlined in Table 4.3.

Table 4.3 Dumpstate Sections

Section	File or Command
Stack traces	N/A
Device info	N/A
System	N/A
Memory info	/proc/meminfo
Cpu info	top -n 1 -d 1 -m 30 -t
Procrank	(procrank)
Virtual memory stats	/proc/vmstat
Vmalloc info	/proc/vmallocinfo
Slab info	/proc/slabinfo
Zoneinfo	/proc/zoneinfo
System log	logcat -v time -d *:v
Event log	logcat -b events -v time -d *:v
Radio log	logcat -b radio -v time -d *:v
Network interfaces	netcfg
Network routes	/proc/net/route
Arp cache	/proc/net/arp
Dump Wi-Fi firmware log	su root dhdutil -i eth0 upload /data/local/tmp/ wlan_crash.dump
System properties	N/A
Kernel log	dmesg
Kernel wakelocks	/proc/wakelocks
Kernel cpufreq	/sys/devices/system/cpu/cpu0/cpufreq/stats/ time_in_state

(Continued)

Table 4.3 Dumpstate Sections *(Continued)*

Section	File or Command
Vold dump	vdc dump
Secure containers	vdc asec list
Processes	ps -p
Processes and threads	ps -t -p -p
Librank	librank
Binder failed transaction log	/proc/binder/failed_transaction_log
Binder transaction log	/proc/binder/transaction_log
Binder transactions	/proc/binder/transactions
Binder stats	/proc/binder/stats
Binder process state	sh -c cat /proc/binder/proc/* -p
File systems and free space	df
Package settings	/data/system/packages.xml: 2011-01-26 09:18:02
Package uid errors	/data/system/uiderrors.txt: 2010-11-14 22:52:26
Last kmsg	/proc/last_kmsg
Last radio log	parse_radio_log /proc/last_radio_log
Last panic console	/data/dontpanic/apanic_console
Last panic threads	/data/dontpanic/apanic_threads
Blocked process wait channels	N/A
Backlights	N/A
Dumpsys	dumpsys

bugreport

The final debugging command further builds on the previous commands and combines the logcat, dumpsys, and dumpstate debug output in a single command, and displays on screen for the purpose of submitting a bug report. The command is run as follows:

```
ahoog@ubuntu:~$ adb bugreport
```

It starts by running dumpstate. When run against the reference HTC Incredible, the output was saved into a file and then a line count was performed:

```
ahoog@ubuntu:~$ adb bugreport > bugreport.log
ahoog@ubuntu:~$ wc -l bugreport.log
42575 bugreport.log
```

As you can see, the report generated over 42,000 lines of debug rich in time stamps, app data, and system information. Parsing this data will yield useful information. However, if the data are processed manually, the task is daunting.

TYPE OF MEMORY

As discussed in Chapter 2, Android devices have two primary types of memory, volatile (RAM) and nonvolatile (NAND flash) memory. Each provides a different insight into the device's data.

RAM

RAM is used by the system to load, execute, and manipulate key parts of the operating system, applications, or data, and is not saved on reboot. Like traditional computers, RAM can contain very important information which applications use to process data. Some examples include the following:

- Passwords
- Encryption keys
- Usernames
- App data
- Data from system processes and services

Recently, solutions for examining Android memory have emerged. One technique was documented by security researcher Thomas Cannon on his blog, which we will step through in detail (Android reverse engineering, n.d.).

Android provides a mechanism for dumping an application's memory to a file by sending the app a special signal (SIGUSR1). To send the signal, you need an app's PID, which you can find with the ps command:

```
ahoog@ubuntu:~$ adb shell ps
USER      PID   PPID  VSIZE  RSS     WCHAN    PC         NAME
root      1     0     348    248    ffffffff 00000000 S /init
root      2     0     0      0      ffffffff 00000000 S kthreadd
root      3     2     0      0      ffffffff 00000000 S ksoftirqd/0
root      28    2     0      0      ffffffff 00000000 S crypto/0
root      39    2     0      0      ffffffff 00000000 S panel_on/0
keystore  72    61    1732   420    ffffffff 00000000 S /system/bin/keystore
shell     76    61    3412   196    ffffffff 00000000 S /sbin/adbd
system    97    68    288408 50100 ffffffff 00000000 S system_server
app_96    193   68    162284 28356 ffffffff 00000000 S com.swype.android.inputmethod
radio     199   68    181376 33452 ffffffff 00000000 S com.android.phone
9997      429   68    187716 34756 ffffffff 00000000 S com.htc.android.mail
app_24    568   68    187796 31064 ffffffff afd0ebd8 S com.google.android.gm
9997      732   68    161816 24492 ffffffff 00000000 S
com.htc.android.mail:directpush
app_103   756   68    150480 23036 ffffffff 00000000 S com.dropbox.android
app_43    1020  68    176632 29472 ffffffff 00000000 S com.google.android.apps.maps
app_43    1132  68    161984 27744 ffffffff 00000000 S
com.google.android.apps.maps:BackgroundFriendService
app_42    1294  68    160680 32672 ffffffff 00000000 S com.facebook.katana
app_4     1355  68    148900 23768 ffffffff 00000000 S com.htc.WeatherWallpaper
shell     1938  76    744    328    c0064900 afd0e88c S /system/bin/sh
shell     1939  1938  892    340    00000000 afd0d97c R ps
```

The ps command lists all system and app processes as well as the parent process id, memory information, and the name. Since a typical device has many running processes, the above listing only displays a portion of the output.

Next, we need to run an interactive shell on the device with root privileges and set /data/misc with sufficient permissions to write and then read the memory dump:

```
ahoog@ubuntu:~$ adb shell
$ su
# chmod 777 /data/misc
```

> **WARNING**
>
> **Changing folder permissions**
>
> The chmod command changes the permissions of the /data/misc folder granting read, write, and execute access to all user accounts on the system. This change is necessary for the successful memory dump. However, this is a system change overtly made by the forensic analyst. If such analysis is warranted, the change should be noted in your report and ideally the folder permissions should be restored to their default setting after the memory dump.

From here, we can send the signal needed to dump memory and display the contents of the directory:

```
# kill -10 1294
# ls -l
drwxrwx--- dhcp     dhcp              2011-01-17 13:18 dhcp
drwxrwx--- system   system            1980-01-06 11:40 vpn
drwxrwx--- system   system            1980-01-06 11:40 bluetooth
drwx------ system   system            1980-01-06 11:40 systemkeys
drwxrwxrwx system   system            1980-01-06 11:41 lockscreen
-rw-r--r-- system   system          1 2011-01-29 15:19 screen_lock_status
-rw-rw---- compass  compass       442 2011-01-29 19:11 AK8973Prms.txt
drwxrwx--- wifi     wifi              2010-08-28 12:06 wifi
drwxrwx--- bluetooth bluetooth          1980-01-06 11:40 bluetoothd
-rw-rw-rw- app_42   app_42    3978523 2011-01-29 19:26 heap-dump-tm1296350817-
                                                       pid1294.hprof
drwx------ keystore keystore          1980-01-06 11:40 keystore
```

The file heap-dump-tm1296350817-pid1294.hprof contains the memory dump and we can exit the interactive adb shell and pull the file to your local workstation for analysis:

```
ahoog@ubuntu:~/memdump$ adb pull /data/misc/heap-dump-tm1296351804-pid1294.hprof
facebook.hprof
1223 KB/s (3977724 bytes in 3.175s)
```

From there, use any memory analysis technique you have at your disposal. For example, you could extract ASCII strings with the command strings:

```
ahoog@ubuntu:~/memdump$ strings gmail.hprof > gmail.str
```

and then view the contents of the file. A quick scan of Gmail's memory provided information about various encryption libraries the app referenced as well as HTTP traffic:

```
POST
/proxy/gmail/a/andrewhoog.com/g/?version=25&clientVersion=25&allowAnyVersion=1
HTTP/1.1
Accept-Encoding: gzip
Content-Length: 29
Host: android.clients.google.com
Connection: Keep-Alive
User-Agent: Android-GmailProvider/156 (inc FRF91); gzip
Cookie: GXAS_SEC=andrewhoog.com=DQAAAJsAAACz6B42ndmh7G5-oRmGrv_78Q-
NxsOMxL256qXfh_Dtkj311Z0uUir7FbGQOK8PsaCi3iXuR1GsqCtV0rOel-07_-
nrjZ7WADRPDYDJ21IYvBfnpaZh7mbMjBpJB4iS6Kvgi1gc8wRJCHhb0aaaaaaaa;
S=gmail=K1XaaaaaaaaaamYA3YypJA:gmproxy=-v0_tVIkUaaaaaaaQ;
GXAS_SEC=andrewhoog.com=DQAAAJwAAAAPCeOv_Xha1i8NCBR5d6hp8wrvO79bW1cweQTUu11d3sVT4
nPcw4wnUfCZAaaav8Cqp-ktu614gW9L2gWCUpuFkjPHGvHiEa4W7P0R-dawWSgk7_wOmaP585kz8Pkoo4
EGYzn9nbQj7X2s5qLfqRwdpRPUMWREKMqaz1g6HgAG5Tsp
Cookie2: $Version=1
: application/vnd.google-x-gms-proto; charset=utf-8
Set-Cookie: XAS_SEC=andrewhoog.com=DQAAAJoAAAAUERMYMdgggggggggiwn1MqWkps31wuuOa
KKe-hKekfgyT7apv6wKpPlycE8PS7S0-gRkmJydqPyDPCgjLXBSw7SVj5Lyp;
Path=/proxy/gmail/a/; Secure
Expires: Sun, 30 Jan 2011 00:16:05 GMT
Transfer-Encoding: chunked
Date: Sun, 30 Jan 2011 00:16:05 GMT
Cache-Control: private, max-age=0
X-Content-Type-Options: nosniff
X-Frame-Options: SAMEORIGIN
X-XSS-Protection: 1; mode=block
Server: GSE
```

The Facebook app, which uses a file format called JSON to encode and transfer data, yielded the following:


```
{"messages":{"unread":0,"most_recent":1296345224},"pokes":{"unread":0,
"most_recent":0},"shares":{"unread":0,"most_recent":0},"friend_requests":[],
"group_invites":[],"event_invites":[18191xxxxxxxxx]}!
:)","time":1296238459,"status_id":1802922removed},"pic_square":"http:\/\/profile.
ak.fbcdn.net\/hprofile-ak-snc4\/hs1323.snc4\/161426_506.jpg"},{"uid":removed,
"first_name":"removed","last_name":"removed","name":"removed
removed","status":{"message":"College friends: do you ever reflect on all the
time we spent driving past removed","time":1296194273,"status_id":10574xxxxxxxx},
{"id":7695xxxxx,"type":"user"
,"pic_square":"http:\/\/profile.ak.fbcdn.net\/hprofile-ak-
snc4\/hs712.ash1\/161111_76xxxxxx_q.jpg","name":"removed"}]},{"name":"places",
"fql_result_set":[{"page_id":1
0823xxxxx,"longitude":-
75.130002,"latitude":40.324749,"description":"","checkin_count":62,"name":
"Pocos"}]}
```


These examples were sanitized prior to inclusion in this book. However, you can see time stamps, profile updates, friend info, check-ins, and more.

Memory analysis of an Android device can provide deep insight into the device's internal structure as well as key information about the device owner. Over time, expect more solutions in the market to address analysis of Android memory.

NAND Flash

Unlike RAM, NAND flash is nonvolatile and thus the data are preserved even when the device is without power or rebooted. The NAND flash is used to store not only system files but also significant portions of the user's data.

NAND flash memory has characteristics very different from the magnetic media found in modern hard drives. These properties make NAND flash ideal storage for mobile devices, while at the same time presenting a number of challenges for programmers and opportunities for forensic analysts.

First, NAND flash has no mechanically moving parts like the spinning platters and arms found in traditional magnetic hard drives. This improves the durability and reduces both the size and power consumption of the device. The memory is distributed as one or multiple chips, which often integrate both NAND flash and RAM (MCP, see Chapter 2) and are directly integrated into the circuit board of the device.

NAND flash also has very high density and is cost effective to manufacture. This, of course, makes it very popular with manufacturers. One side effect of the manufacturing process and technology in general is that NAND flash literally ships with bad blocks directly from the manufacturer. The manufacturer will generally test the memory as part of the manufacturing process and mark bad blocks in a specific structure on the NAND flash, which is described in their documentation. Software, which then directly interacts with the NAND flash, can read the manufacturer's bad block markers and will often implement a bad block table that can logically track the bad blocks on the system and remove them from operation. This greatly speeds up bad block detection and management. So while NAND flash is more physically durable than spinning platters, its error rate is much higher and must be accounted for in development and use.

Another significant limitation of NAND flash is that it has a very limited write/erase life span before the block is no longer capable of storing data. The life span varies by device and is largely impacted by the amount of data stored per NAND flash cell, the central building block for storing the 1 or 0 bit(s). If the cell only stores a single bit (single-level cell or SLC) then the NAND flash is rated around 100k write/erase cycles for one-year data retention. However, NAND flash rarely uses SLC as manufacturers (and consumer) demand more data storage in similarly sized or smaller devices. The technology has moved to multilevel cells (MLC) where a cell can store two, three, or even more bits per cell. However, this not only complicates the manufacturing process and slows down the write/erase cycle, but it also significantly reduces the endurance of the device. A typical MLC NAND flash storing two bits per cell experiences a 10-fold reduction in endurance (measured as one-year data retention) with a value of approximately 10k write/erase cycles. As the bit density per cell increases, the endurance continues to drop, which obviously must be addressed by the controlling device.

Unlike RAM and NOR flash which is also flash memory and typically used in systems such as a computer's Basic Input Output System or BIOS, NAND flash cannot be accessed randomly. Instead, access to data is achieved via an allocation unit, called a page or chunk, which is typically between 512 and 2048 bytes, but generally increases as the overall size of NAND flash increases. Even though NAND flash does not provide the fast random access like RAM, access time is still quite fast because it does not require the mechanical platter and arm movements used in traditional spinning hard drives.

> **NOTE**
>
> **Page versus chunk**
>
> Throughout this book, we will use the word page and chunk synonymously to refer to the low-level data allocation unit referenced in NAND flash. While the allocation unit is usually referred to as a page, the YAFFS2 file system, which is a key component of Android, generally refers to the allocation unit as a chunk.

The chunks are then organized into a larger logical unit called a block, which is typically much larger than a traditional 512B hard drive sector. In most Android devices, the NAND flash blocks contain 64 chunks of data and each chunk is 2048 bytes. Taking 64 × 2 KB yields a block size of 128 KB. Of course, this can and will change over time and is controlled by the NAND flash manufacturers. When a block is allocated for writing, the chunks inside the block are written sequentially.

Another very important characteristic of NAND flash is the operations available for reading and writing:

- Read (page)
- Write (page)
- Erase (block)

While individual chunks can be read or written, the erase operation only functions at the block level. When a block is erased, the entire block is written over with 1's or 0xFF (hex).

> **NOTE**
>
> **NAND flash erase operation**
>
> *The erase operation is the only mechanism by which a 0 can be changed to a 1 in NAND flash.* This point is worth belaboring. In a traditional hard drive, if a value is changed from a 0 to a 1 (or vice versa), the program would simply seek to the value on the hard drive and apply the appropriate voltage to change and store the new value. However, the fundamental architecture of NAND flash provides only one mechanism to change a 0 to a 1 and that is via the erase function that is applied at the block level, not an individual page level. For this reason, a page can only be written once, and if the value of the page needs to change, the entire block must be erased and then the page can be written.

Here is a specific example using a single byte for simplicity: Let's say this particular byte holds the decimal value 179 and we want to add 39 for a total value of 218. For those unfamiliar with converting numbers between base10, hex (base16), and binary (base2), the built-in calculator programs in Windows, Mac OS X, and Ubuntu Linux provide a programmer mode that will perform the conversions. For the numbers above, we have the conversions between numbering systems shown in Table 4.4.

Table 4.4 Decimal, Hex, and Binary Representation of Integers

Decimal (base10)	Hex (base16)	Binary (base2)
179	0xB3	1011 0011
218	0xDA	1101 1010

So the value 179 contains three 0's and two of them need to change to a 1 to present our new value of 218. However, NAND flash cannot make that change without erasing the entire block. So, if this single byte was attempted without the erase, the result would be 146, not 218. Here is how this happened:

```
1011 0011 (original byte, 0xB3 or 179 decimal)
1101 1010 (new byte to write, 0xDA or 218 decimal)
---------
1001 0010 (resulting byte, 0x92 or 146 decimal)
```

As the byte did not contain all 1's (0xFF), the only portions of the write cycle that succeeded were 1's either remaining a 1 or changing to a 0. Anytime the write function encountered a 0 and was requested to change to a 1, it would fail and simply retain the 0 value. The resulting byte was 0x92 or 146 base10—clearly not the value intended. Another way to describe the write function is that it only changes the charged 1 values to a 0 where requested, the equivalent of the "logical and" of the two values.

In summary, a chunk can only be written once, and if it needs to be re-written, the entire block must first be erased.

As you can tell, NAND flash imposes various restrictions and limitations and thus developers and file systems must be flash aware to effectively work within the constraints. Unlike traditional hard drives that ship with firmware to manage the device (including bad block), the NAND flash used in Android devices does not ship with a controller. All management of the memory must be implemented in software interfacing with the NAND flash. Two important techniques deployed are error-correcting code (ECC) and wear-leveling. Both have significant implications for forensics and data recovery.

First, ECC is a technique where an algorithm is used to detect data errors on read or write operations and correct some errors on the fly. Since NAND flash degrades over time through usage, the system must be able to detect when a page or block is going bad and recover the data stored there. After a number of errors or failed operations is exceeded (typically three failed operations), the page or block will be marked bad and added to the bad block table.

The second important algorithm used to effectively manage NAND flash on Android is the wear-leveling code that spreads the writing of data across the entire NAND flash to avoid overutilization of a single area, thus wearing those blocks out more quickly.

Many hardware devices that use NAND flash, such as removable USB thumb drivers and solid state drives (SSD), have controller logic bundled with the device, which provides the functions described above including bad block management, wear-leveling, and error-correcting code. However, Android devices were designed to integrate the NAND flash components directly, and thus a software management layer was needed to provide these important functions. The layer selected to manage the NAND flash was the Memory Technology Device (MTD) system.

MTD was developed to address the need of NAND flash and similar devices due to their unique characteristics. Prior to MTD, Linux supported primarily character devices and block devices. Neither device type addresses the unique properties of the newly developed memory devices. Additionally, while NAND flash was not strictly a block device (like traditional hard drives), exposure of block device characteristics to developers aided in development and support. By leveraging MTD, Android now had the necessary Flash Transition Layer (FTL) needed to effectively interact with the NAND flash. By taking this approach, Android did not lock manufacturers into using a small subset of NAND flash providers and associated controllers. Instead, they are free to use any NAND flash available and then "simply" integrate with MTD, which supports a wide range of NAND flash.

In Android, the MTD provides not only the block interface to the NAND flash but also the ECC, wear-leveling, and other critical functions. The ECC and other chunk metadata are stored in a reserved area called the out of band (OOB) or spare area. The OOB is located directly after each chunk on the NAND flash. While the chunk, block, and OOB layout is configurable, most Android devices to date have a 128 KB block consisting of 64 2,048 byte (2k) chunks each with a 64 byte OOB as shown in Fig. 4.1.

The OOB not only stores information managed by MTD, but can also store metadata critical to the file system, provided the file system is NAND flash aware. While the system presents the block as 128 KB, when you add in the 64 OOB, each 64 bytes in size, there is an additional 4096 bytes (4 KB) bringing the total bytes used on the NAND flash to 132 KB.

On Android devices, you can determine the MTD partitions by viewing the /proc/mtd file. On our reference HTC Incredible, we have the following:

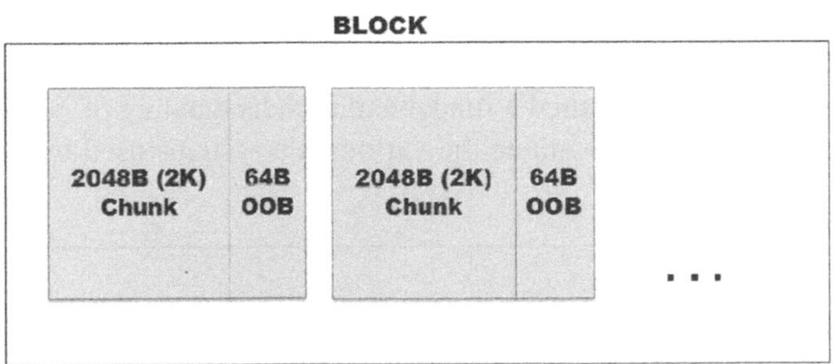

FIGURE 4.1

Block (128 KB = 64 × 2k chunks + OOB).

Table 4.5 MTD Partitions Size Conversions

Size (hex)	Name	Size (decimal, bytes)	Size (KB)	Size (MB)
0xa0000	misc	655,360	640	0.6
0x480000	recovery	4,718,592	4608	4.5
0x300000	boot	3,145,728	3072	3.0
0xf800000	system	260,046,848	253952	248.0
0xa0000	local	655,360	640	0.6
0x2800000	cache	41,943,040	40960	40.0
0x9500000	datadata	156,237,824	152576	149.0

```
ahoog@ubuntu:~$ adb shell cat /proc/mtd
dev:    size   erasesize  name
mtd0: 000a0000 00020000 "misc"
mtd1: 00480000 00020000 "recovery"
mtd2: 00300000 00020000 "boot"
mtd3: 0f800000 00020000 "system"
mtd4: 000a0000 00020000 "local"
mtd5: 02800000 00020000 "cache"
mtd6: 09500000 00020000 "datadata"
```

There are seven MTD partitions and the following section will examine where they are mounted, and provide a high-level overview of the directories and files found. In the previous listing, the size and erasesize are both hex values that provide important MTD/NAND flash properties. The erasesize specifies the size of each block which is 0x20000 or 131,072 bytes or 128 KB (128 × 1024) in decimal. This is consistent with the block figure, specifically 64 pages, each 2048 (2 KB) in size. The size column specifies the overall size of that partition. So, in this instance, we have the MTD partitions as shown in Table 4.5.

The values from Table 4.5 can also be verified using the df (disk free) command that provides a listing of mounted file systems and their total, used, and available space. Following is the df data for /system:

```
ahoog@ubuntu:~$ adb shell df /system
/system: 253952K total, 243724K used, 10228K available (block size 4096)
```

As you can tell, the size found in /proc/mtd is consistent in both our conversions and as displayed by the df command.

Now that we have established a fundamental understanding of NAND flash and MTD for Android, we will examine the various file systems used by Android.

FILE SYSTEMS

Like most Linux systems, there are several file systems in use on Android, many of which are used to boot and run the system. While we will touch on several of the file systems, the primary focus is on partitions where user data are stored, in particular the EXT, FAT32, and YAFFS2 file systems.

To determine what file systems a Linux kernel (and thus Android) supports, you can examine the contents of the file /proc/filesytem. On our reference HTC Incredible, it contains the following:

```
ahoog@ubuntu:~$ adb shell cat /proc/filesystems
nodev   sysfs
nodev   rootfs
nodev   bdev
nodev   proc
nodev   cgroup
nodev   tmpfs
nodev   debugfs
nodev   sockfs
nodev   pipefs
nodev   anon_inodefs
nodev   inotifyfs
nodev   devpts
        ext3
        ext2
nodev   ramfs
        vfat
        yaffs
        yaffs2
```

Of the 18 file systems supported by the HTC Incredible, only five are backed by a physical device such as NAND flash or the SD card. The remaining file systems have the "nodev" property, which means that they are essentially virtual file systems that are not written to any physical device. Furthermore, only six of the nodev file systems are actually used on the device:

1. rootfs
2. tmpfs
3. cgroup
4. proc
5. sysfs
6. devpts

And three of the device-backed file systems are used:

1. ext3
2. yaffs2
3. vfat

The following sections provide a brief overview of most file systems, and an in-depth analysis of YAFFS2, where significant user data are stored.

rootfs, devpts, sysfs, and cgroup File Systems

Many file systems in Linux are used to boot, operate, or manage the system and often will not contain information useful in a forensic investigation. However, security engineers and researchers may closely examine these file systems, and the kernel's inner-workings, in an attempt to identify security holes and other weaknesses. We will quickly highlight four of the more infrastructure-related file systems found in Android.

First, rootfs is where the kernel mounts the root file system (the top of the directory tree, noted with a forward slash) at startup. In order for the kernel to complete the boot process, it needs access to core files and libraries, thus the need to mount the root file system. As the kernel finalizes the boot process, subsequent file systems are mounted as directories off the root file system. For example (and more on this later in the chapter), the root file system would be mounted at / and contain key files. Then a more complete system directory would be mounted at /system. You can see the root file system and directories by running the "ls -l" command from a shell or typing "mount" to see which file systems are mounted and in what directory of the root file system.

The devpts file system is used to provide simulated terminal sessions on an Android device, similar to connecting to a traditional Unix server using telnet or ssh. Each time a virtual terminal connects, a new node under /dev/pts is created. For example, if you have a single adb shell connection to an Android device, /dev/pts would show the following:

```
ahoog@ubuntu:/dev/pts$ adb shell
$ ls -l /dev/pts
crw------- shell    shell    136,   0 2011-02-01 10:00 0
```

However, in the next example, there are two adb shell connections and one terminal app connection from an app installed on the device:

```
ahoog@ubuntu:~$ adb shell ls -l /dev/pts
crw------- shell    shell    136,   2 2011-02-01 10:02 2
crw------- app_105  app_105  136,   1 2011-02-01 10:02 1
crw------- shell    shell    136,   0 2011-02-01 10:00 0
```

As you can see, the original /dev/pts/0 connection exists. However, two additional connections are now present and the one from the terminal app is run under the app's unique user id (app_105).

Sysfs is another virtual file system that contains configuration and control files for the device. On the HTC Incredible, the following top-level directories exist:

```
ahoog@ubuntu:/dev/pts$ adb shell ls -l /sys
drwxr-xr-x root     root              2011-02-01 11:06 fs
drwxr-xr-x root     root              2011-01-31 15:42 devices
drwxr-xr-x root     root              2011-02-01 11:06 dev
drwxr-xr-x root     root              2011-02-01 11:06 bus
drwxr-xr-x root     root              2011-02-01 10:02 class
drwxr-xr-x root     root              2011-02-01 11:06 firmware
drwxr-xr-x root     root              2011-02-01 11:06 kernel
drwxr-xr-x root     root              2011-01-31 15:42 power
drwxr-xr-x root     root              2011-02-01 11:06 board_properties
drwxr-xr-x root     root              2011-02-01 11:06 module
drwxr-xr-x root     root              2011-02-01 11:06 block
drwxr-xr-x root     root              2011-02-01 11:06 android_touch
drwxr-xr-x root     root              2011-02-01 11:06 android_camera
drwxr-xr-x root     root              2011-02-01 11:06 camera_led_status
drwxr-xr-x root     root              2011-02-01 11:06 android_camera_awb_cal
```

For curiosity's sake, you can do an adb pull on /sys to your forensic workstation as the files can be read by any user. Execute the following:

```
ahoog@ubuntu:/dev/pts$ adb pull /sys sys
pull: building file list...
<snip>
pull: /sys/camera_led_status/led_hotspot_status -> ./camera_led_status/
       led_hotspot_status
pull: /sys/camera_led_status/led_wimax_status -> ./camera_led_status/
       led_wimax_status
pull: /sys/camera_led_status/led_ril_status -> ./camera_led_status/led_ril_status
pull: /sys/android_camera_awb_cal/awb_cal -> ./android_camera_awb_cal/awb_cal
3370 files pulled. 0 files skipped.
0 KB/s (33334 bytes in 233.611s)
```

As you can see, a large number of files were pulled, and you can now use the full suite of Linux tools to examine the data. While the forensic value of this information requires additional research, it clearly provides low-level information about the device that can assist in security research. For example, if you wanted to learn more about the NAND device, you could examine the following directory:

```
ahoog@ubuntu:~/sysfs$ ls -l ./module/msm_nand/parameters/
total 12
-rw-r--r-- 1 ahoog ahoog 123 2011-02-01 09:11 info
-rw-r--r-- 1 ahoog ahoog   5 2011-02-01 09:11 pagesize
-rw-r--r-- 1 ahoog ahoog   8 2011-02-01 09:11 vendor
```

And then each file:

```
ahoog@ubuntu:~/sysfs$ cat ./module/msm_nand/parameters/vendor
Samsung

ahoog@ubuntu:~/sysfs$ cat ./module/msm_nand/parameters/info
<<  NAND INFO  >>
flash id         =5500BCEC
vendor           =Samsung
width            =16 bits
size             =512 MB
block count      =4096
page count       =64

ahoog@ubuntu:~/sysfs$ cat ./module/msm_nand/parameters/pagesize
2048
```

Understanding the NAND device in detail is clearly an important step in forensic and security analysis. With nearly 3000 files, there is considerable data to examine. Here is a quick way to look at the file names, paths, and sizes that will allow you to then easily examine relevant files (try running two terminal sessions and listing the files in one terminal and use copy/paste to "cat" the file contents in the other terminal):

```
ahoog@ubuntu:~$ find sysfs  -type f -ls | less
933783    4 -rw-r--r--   1 ahoog    ahoog         91 Feb  1 09:11
sysfs/board_properties/virtualkeys.atmel-touchscreen
933855    4 -rw-r--r--   1 ahoog    ahoog          2 Feb  1 09:11
sysfs/android_camera/node
933857    4 -rw-r--r--   1 ahoog    ahoog         22 Feb  1 09:11
sysfs/android_camera/sensor
933856    4 -rw-r--r--   1 ahoog    ahoog          2 Feb  1 09:11
sysfs/android_camera/cam_mode
933863    4 -rw-r--r--   1 ahoog    ahoog         32 Feb  1 09:11
```

```
sysfs/android_camera_awb_cal/awb_cal
933782     4 -rw-r--r--   1 ahoog    ahoog         2 Feb  1 09:11
sysfs/power/pm_trace
933779     4 -rw-r--r--   1 ahoog    ahoog         5 Feb  1 09:10
sysfs/power/wait_for_fb_wake
933781     4 -rw-r--r--   1 ahoog    ahoog         2 Feb  1 09:11
sysfs/power/pm_trace_mask
<snip>
```

> **TIP**
>
> **Additional sysfs analysis**
>
> Beyond manually examining the sysfs file system, there are detailed resources on the Internet which provide additional background. One such resource is a paper by Patrick Mochel providing a helpful background (The sysfs filesystem, n.d.).

The final virtual file system is called cgroups and is used to track and aggregate tasks in the Linux file system. On the HTC Incredible, two cgroup file systems are created: one at /dev/cpuctl and the other at /acct. While additional analysis may yield results, the accounting data generally do not prove useful in forensic analysis.

proc

The proc file system provides detailed information about kernel, processes, and configuration parameters in a structured manner under the /proc directory. Some of the files can be examined by the shell user. However, many files prevent access unless you have root privileges. As before, one method for exploring the proc file system is to pull the files from the Android device onto your forensic workstation. It will take some time and could hang on certain files causing an incomplete copy.

```
ahoog@ubuntu:~$ adb pull /proc proc
pull: building file list...
```

On the HTC Incredible, the above process hung when trying to copy process 76 and had to be canceled with a Ctrl-C:

```
pull: /proc/76/task/5959/auxv -> proc/76/task/5959/auxv
failed to copy '/proc/76/task/5959/auxv' to 'proc/76/task/5959/auxv':
Permission denied
pull: /proc/76/task/5959/environ -> proc/76/task/5959/environ
failed to copy '/proc/76/task/5959/environ' to 'proc/76/task/5959/environ':
Permission denied
pull: /proc/76/task/6993/fd/16 -> proc/76/task/6993/fd/16
 ^C

ahoog@ubuntu:~/proc$ du -hs
25M     .
ahoog@ubuntu:~/proc$ find . -type f | wc -l
5998
```

Before canceling, we successfully pulled 25 MB of data and nearly 6000 files. As with the sysfs examination, you can manually examine the data using the find command to locate and list files:

```
ahoog@ubuntu:~/proc$ find .  -type f -ls | less
934618     4 -rw-r--r--   1 ahoog    ahoog        93 Feb  1 09:48 ./cpu/alignment
413065     4 -rw-r--r--   1 ahoog    ahoog         8 Feb  1 09:50 ./25/wchan
413062     4 -rw-r--r--   1 ahoog    ahoog         2 Feb  1 09:50 ./25/oom_score
413063     4 -rw-r--r--   1 ahoog    ahoog        20 Feb  1 09:50 ./25/cgroup
413069     0 -rw-r--r--   1 ahoog    ahoog         0 Feb  1 09:51 ./25/maps
566313     4 -rw-r--r--   1 ahoog    ahoog        85 Feb  1 09:50 ./25/net/sockstat6
566315     4 -rw-r--r--   1 ahoog    ahoog        108 Feb  1 09:50 ./25/net/if_inet6
<snip>
```

Alternatively, you can examine some files in /proc directly from the adb shell as follows:

```
ahoog@ubuntu:~$ adb shell
$ cd /proc
$ cat cpuinfo
Processor        : ARMv7 Processor rev 2 (v71)
BogoMIPS         : 162.54
Features         : swp half thumb fastmult vfp edsp thumbee neon
CPU implementer : 0x51
CPU architecture: 7
CPU variant      : 0x0
CPU part         : 0x00f
CPU revision     : 2

Hardware         : incrediblec
Revision         : 0002
Serial           : 0000000000000000
```

Valuable information about the device can be found in the proc file system. Examiners can audit these files and should start with files in the /proc directory instead of the subdirectories.

tmpfs

tmpfs is a file system that stores all files in virtual memory backed by RAM and, if present, the swap or cache file for the device. Most Android devices at this time do not have swap space. However, some aftermarket firmware enables this feature. The advantage of tmpfs is that by using RAM, the storage is very fast and also non-permanent and hence not saved on reboot.

Of course, for forensic examiners, this poses a challenge. If important data are located on a tmpfs mount point, it must be collected before the device is rebooted or loses power. It also presents a unique opportunity because the tmpfs is often readable by the shell user and forensic programs can be copied and executed in tmpfs without modifying the NAND flash or SD card. This may allow an examiner to acquire forensic data from an Android device without modifying the NAND flash or SD card in any way.

> **WARNING**
>
> **Investigating tmpfs**
>
> If your primary interest is in memory analysis of the device, making changes to tmpfs is not advised unless you first have a forensic copy of the parts of memory you are interested in.

On the HTC Incredible, the standard installation has four tmpfs mount points:

- /dev
- /mnt/asec
- /app-cache
- /mnt/sdcard/.android_secure

The /dev directory contains device files that allow the kernel to read and write to attached devices such as NAND flash, SD card, character devices, and more. The /mnt/asec and /mnt/sdcard/.android_secure directories are a relatively new addition to Android and allow apps to be stored on the SD card instead of /data/data, which provides more storage.

Interestingly, the /app-cache is also a new addition and appears to provide tmpfs space, which apps can use. On the HTC Incredible, the Web Browser (com.andrew.browser) created a directory in /app-cache and stores cache files from web browsing.

```
ahoog@ubuntu:~$ adb shell ls -l / | grep app-cache
drwxrwxrwt root     root              2011-01-31 15:42 app-cache

ahoog@ubuntu:~$ adb shell
$ ls -l /app-cache
drwxr-xr-x app_12   app_12            2011-01-31 15:42 com.android.browser
```

From the first listing, we can see that the app-cache directory has read, write, and browse permissions set for all users. In addition, the final "t" in the permissions "rwxrwxrwt" indicates that only root or the owner of the directory can delete or rename the directory.

The second listing shows the directory's inside app-cache, which only has com.android.browser. However, as we dig deeper into the directory, we discover the directory and files we are most interested in only allow the app itself (com.android.browser, user id of app_12) or root access to the files.

```
ahoog@ubuntu:~$ adb shell ls -l /app-cache/com.android.browser/cache
drwxrwx--x app_12   app_12            2011-01-31 15:57 webviewCache

ahoog@ubuntu:~$ adb shell ls -l /app-cache/com.android.browser/cache/webviewCache
opendir failed, Permission denied
```

As we have root access on the device, here is what the directory contained:

- 1.4 MB of data
- 64 files
- 18 ASCII files (mostly CSS and JavaScript)
- 1 empty file
- 9 GIF files
- 5 HTML files
- 11 JPEG files
- 17 PNG files
- 3 UTF-8 files

```
ahoog@ubuntu:~/app-cache/com.android.browser/cache/webviewCache$ du -hs
1.4M    .

ahoog@ubuntu:~/app-cache/com.android.browser/cache/webviewCache$ find . -type f  |
wc -l
64

ahoog@ubuntu:~/app-cache/com.android.browser/cache/webviewCache$ find . -type f |
xargs file
./1d15a326: ASCII text, with very long lines
./982785ed: HTML document text
./fe3f9f59: GIF image data, version 89a, 1 x 1
./1cdb9fc0: PNG image, 140 x 44, 8-bit colormap, non-interlaced
./1c32cdf6: JPEG image data, JFIF standard 1.01
./aacce58f: ASCII C program text
./ad01e1f2: PNG image, 100 x 66, 8-bit/color RGB, non-interlaced
./39c4b622: PNG image, 140 x 44, 8-bit colormap, non-interlaced
./fcf0e4eb: PNG image, 64 x 3, 8-bit colormap, non-interlaced
./9244746c: PNG image, 140 x 44, 8-bit colormap, non-interlaced
./13bf2ef2: ASCII C program text, with very long lines
./44e36c36: PNG image, 560 x 370, 8-bit/color RGB, non-interlaced
./ffbedd54: JPEG image data, JFIF standard 1.01
./c780272a: ASCII English text
<snip>
```

If you browse the webviewCache directory from your Ubuntu workstation, you can easily preview images and other files (Fig. 4.2).

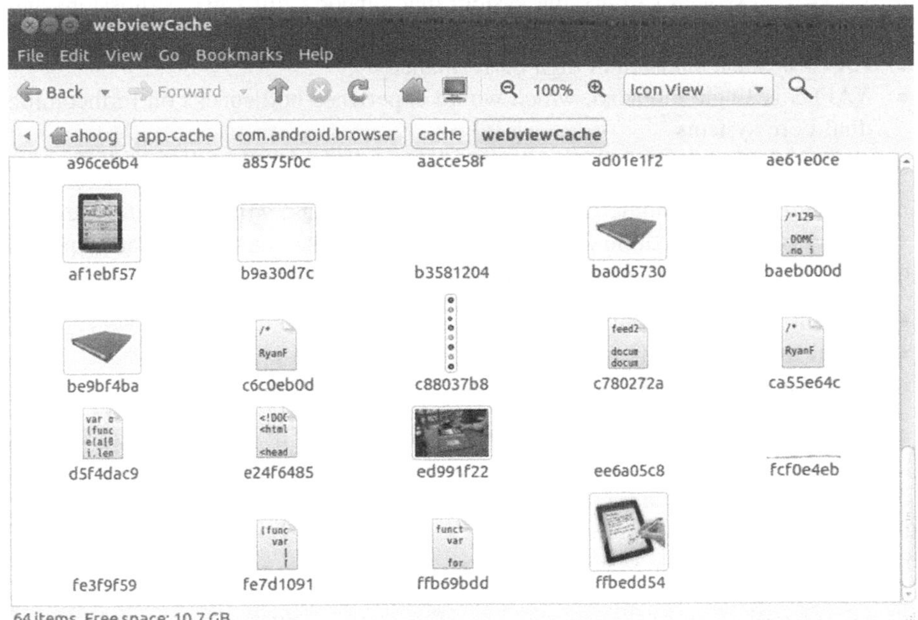

FIGURE 4.2

Browser webviewCache from Ubuntu workstation.

The /app-cache tmpfs directory contains information that would be important in a forensic investigation. This underscores the growing need to educate front-line responders to ensure that devices are properly handled to maximize the forensic investigation's effectiveness.

Extended File System (EXT)

The extended file system (EXT) is the de facto file system for Linux developed specifically for the operating system. As you already know, Linux supports a large number of file systems. However, the default is EXT. Since the original version of EXT was developed in 1992, there have been three additional releases: EXT2, EXT3, and EXT4.

Although EXT has been integral to most laptop, desktop, and server Linux distributions, it was not found in early Android devices. In 2010, however, EXT began to show up in devices, and on December 9, 2010, Google announced in their Android Developer blog that an increasing number of Android devices were going to move from YAFFS to the EXT (Android developers blog, n.d.). The move from YAFFS to EXT seems to be driven by several factors that were discussed online (Way, n.d.), including

- More Android devices are moving from raw NAND flash to regular block device (eMMC)
- EXT4 is a standard Linux file system that supports full Unix permissions and semantics
- EXT4 is stable and offers high performance
- YAFFS is single threaded, which would experience bottlenecks on forthcoming dual-core systems

The first Android device to use EXT4 is the Google Nexus S, and it is expected that many tablet devices running Android's Honeycomb release will also use this new file system. As only one Android device currently uses EXT4, many changes are expected over time. Currently, the Nexus uses EXT4 in the following mount points:

- System image (read-only, /system)
- Local user data (read–write, /data/data)
- Cache partitions (read–write, /cache and possible others)

From a forensics standpoint, EXT4 is simply another file system that examiners need to understand and forensic tools need to support. Of course, most forensic tools do not fully (or even nominally) support EXT4 so this presents a bit of a problem. File carving techniques do work and it is expected that more forensic software will begin to support the file system over time.

FAT32/VFAT

Android devices often have one or more Microsoft FAT32 partitions, generally on the SD card and eMMC. The reason for leveraging this venerable file system is not due to superior design but is due to sheer compatibility with other operating systems. Microsoft's FAT32 file system was widely supported in most operating systems including Mac OS X, all Windows versions (obviously), Linux, and more. This means that Android data stored on the FAT32 partitions can be easily read, modified, or even deleted on other file systems.

In Linux, the file system driver for a FAT32 partition is called VFAT, not to be confused with Microsoft's earlier Virtual FAT file system that bridged the FAT16 and FAT32 implementation by adding, among other features, long file name support. On the HTC Incredible, there are three mount points that use FAT32:

- /mnt/sdcard
- /mnt/secure/asec
- /mnt/emmc

As you may recall from Chapter 3's section on USB interfaces, when an Android device is connected to another computer, there is an option to expose the devices' USB mass storage (UMS) interfaces to enable file sharing. On the HTC Incredible, both the /mnt/sdcard and /mnt/emmc partitions can be presented to other operating systems over the USB connection as a UMS device.

The /mnt/secure/asec partition is an encrypted partition on the SD card where Android devices can store apps. When the ability to run apps from the SD card was introduced, the security engineers were understandably concerned that app data could easily be damaged or compromised because file permissions are not maintained in the VFAT/FAT32 partitions. As such, the app (.apk file) is encrypted on the physical device and when in use, it is decrypted and temporarily stored at /mnt/asec or another location specified by design.

As discussed previously, the removable SD card is mounted at /mnt/sdcard and generally contains photos, videos, thumbnails, downloaded files, text to speech temporary files, and Google Maps Navigation data as well as data from many Android Market applications. The newer /mnt/emmc is a FAT32 partition, not removable, and resides in storage architected into the device. In the devices examined thus far, the eMMC is formatted as FAT32, again for interoperability.

YAFFS2

When the first Android device was released, many people were surprised to see a relatively unknown file system play a key role in the system. YAFFS, which is an acronym for Yet Another Flash File System, is an open-source file system developed specifically for NAND flash and is licensed under both the GNU Public License (GPL) and a commercial license agreement for those who do not wish to follow the strict GPL guidelines (YAFFS licence FAQs, n.d.). Android devices use the latest release of YAFFS (YAFFS2) that follows more strict NAND flash guidelines meant to improve the endurance of the NAND flash while optimized to run on low-memory mobile or embedded devices.

YAFFS2 was developed by Aleph One Ltd, a company based in New Zealand. Driven by customer requests, Aleph One began YAFFS design in December 2001 and released the first publicly available source code in May 2002. The primary developer (or certainly the most visible) is Charles Manning who is described as "The Embedded Janitor" and has been developing and "mopping up" embedded systems for 20 years (YAFFS: the NAND-specific flash, n.d.). Charles is quite active on the YAFFS mailing list and is the de facto expert on YAFFS and YAFFS2.

> **TIP**
>
> **Additional YAFFS2 resources**
>
> Analysts and engineers interested in the internals of YAFFS2 are encouraged to read the full documentation (and source code, if that's your thing) from http://www.yaffs.net/ and sign up for the mailing list.

YAFFS2 was built specifically for the growing NAND flash devices and has a number of important features that address the stringent needs of this medium. YAFFS2 is

- a log-structured file system (which protects data even through unexpected power outages)
- provides built in wear-leveling and error correction
- capable of handling bad blocks
- fast and has a small footprint in RAM

However, since its usage was limited prior to Android, there are currently no forensic tools (commercial or open source) that support the file system. This leaves the forensic analysts with few options except to download the YAFFS2 source code, grab a forensic image of a partition, open it up in your favorite hex editor, and start digging. Although some utilities should develop over time, Android's move to EXT4 may reduce the motivation for commercial forensic companies to develop such support.

As covered in the NAND flash section, YAFFS2 addressed the memory in blocks through the MTD subsystem and each block contains a set number of pages (called chunks in YAFFS documentation and code). When YAFFS2 is ready to write data to the NAND flash, it passes both the data and metadata structures to the MTD. The MTD is then responsible for writing (as well as reading) both the data and the metadata to the NAND flash.

For most Android devices, the MTD subsystem addressed NAND flash in blocks that are divided into 64 chunks with each chunk containing 2048 bytes (so blocks are 128K) plus a 64-byte out-of-band/spare area (OOB) where various tags and metadata are stored. When a block is allocated for writing, it is assigned a sequence number that starts at 1 and increments with each new block.

All data structures stored in YAFFS2 are referred to as Objects and can be files, directories, symbolic links, and hard links. Each chunk either stores a yaffs_ObjectHeader (object metadata) or data for the object. The yaffs_ObjectHeader tracks various information including the Object type, the parent object, a checksum of the name to speed up searching, the object name, permissions and ownership, MAC information, and the size of the object if it is a file.

In the 64-byte OOB/spare area, YAFFS2 not only stores critical information about the chunk but also shares the area with the MTD subsystem. The critical YAFFS2 tags are as follows:

- 1 byte: block state (0xFF if block is good, any other value for a bad block)
- 4 bytes: 32-bit chunk ID (0 indicates that chunk is storing a yaffs_ObjectHeader, else data)
- 4 bytes: 32-bit Object ID (similar to traditional Unix inode)
- 2 bytes: number of data blocks in this chunk (all but final chunk will be fully allocated)
- 4 bytes: sequence number for this block
- 3 bytes: ECC for tags (in Android, handled by MTD)
- 12 bytes: ECC for data (in Android, handled by MTD)

If an object is changed, a new yaffs_ObjectHeader is written to flash because NAND memory can only be written once before erasing. The old data and headers still exist but are ignored in the file structure by examining the values of the sequence number. Using this process complies with the guideline that blocks in NAND flash can never be re-written (only written once and then erased when no longer needed). This, of course, can be of enormous benefit to the data-recovery process as modified or deleted data will still exist on the NAND flash unless the block went through the garbage collection process used to erase a block and prepare it to accept new data.

Similarly, when a file is deleted in YAFFS2, the parent directory for the ObjectHeader is moved to a special, hidden directory called unlinked. The file remains in this directory until all of the chunks in the file are erased. To achieve this, the file system tracks the number of chunks in the system for the file. When it reaches 0, the remnants of the file no longer exist. At that point, it will no longer track the object in the unlinked directory.

While the file system structure can be regenerated completely from the OOB area and ObjectHeader information, this is not efficient—especially as the size of NAND flash memory grows. The structure is thus loaded and maintained in RAM (with writes to the NAND flash as needed) using a tree-node structure (T-node) to track all allocated chunks. T-nodes are a fixed 32 bytes and, at their lowest level (level 0), store an index used to locate the first chunk ID. As the file size grows, additional levels are added, which consist of eight pointers to other T-nodes.

To regenerate, YAFFS2 reads each chunk in its block allocation order, starting from the end and working back, and populates the file system structures as T-nodes in RAM. This requires scanning the entire NAND—a time-consuming operation. To work around this issue, checkpointing was developed for YAFFS2, which prefers the RAM structure to NAND flash (using 10 blocks) when it is properly unmounted.

A few other key concepts are needed to round out your understanding on YAFFS2. First, garbage collection is queued up and, if needed, is done each time a write-to-the-system occurs. If all the chunks in a block are no longer in use, the block is a candidate for garbage collection. The system is also capable of taking the "dirtiest" block, copying allocated chunks to new blocks, thus making the block available for garbage collection. To make the block available again, it is erased by writing all 1's (0xFF).

On an Android device, we can find detailed information about the YAFFS2 file systems by examining the /proc/yaffs files:

```
ahoog@ubuntu:~$ adb shell cat /proc/yaffs
YAFFS built:Sep 30 2010 18:41:07
$Id$
$Id$

Device 0 "system"
startBlock......... 0
endBlock........... 1983
totalBytesPerChunk. 2048
nDataBytesPerChunk. 2048
chunkGroupBits..... 0
chunkGroupSize..... 1
nErasedBlocks...... 10
nReservedBlocks.... 5
blocksInCheckpoint. 3
nTnodesCreated..... 9600
nFreeTnodes........ 62
nObjectsCreated.... 1100
nFreeObjects....... 20
nFreeChunks........ 5690
nPageWrites........ 0
nPageReads......... 551024
nBlockErasures..... 0
nGCCopies.......... 0
garbageCollections. 0
passiveGCs......... 0
nRetriedWrites..... 0
nShortOpCaches..... 10
nRetireBlocks...... 0
eccFixed........... 0
eccUnfixed......... 0
tagsEccFixed....... 0
tagsEccUnfixed..... 0
cacheHits.......... 0
nDeletedFiles...... 0
nUnlinkedFiles..... 460
nBackgroundDeletions 0
useNANDECC......... 1
isYaffs2........... 1
inbandTags......... 0

Device 1 "datadata"
startBlock......... 0
endBlock........... 1191
totalBytesPerChunk. 2048
nDataBytesPerChunk. 2048
chunkGroupBits..... 0
chunkGroupSize..... 1
nErasedBlocks...... 11
nReservedBlocks.... 5
blocksInCheckpoint. 0
```

```
nTnodesCreated.....  3700
nFreeTnodes........  119
nObjectsCreated....  3000
nFreeObjects.......  84
nFreeChunks........  50903
nPageWrites........  2368440
nPageReads.........  1028358
nBlockErasures.....  38623
nGCCopies..........  323313
garbageCollections.  18186
passiveGCs.........  2454
nRetriedWrites.....  0
nShortOpCaches.....  10
nRetireBlocks......  0
eccFixed...........  0
eccUnfixed.........  0
tagsEccFixed.......  0
tagsEccUnfixed.....  0
cacheHits..........  1017819
nDeletedFiles......  0
nUnlinkedFiles.....  643647
nBackgroundDeletions 0
useNANDECC.........  1
isYaffs2...........  1
inbandTags.........  0
```

We can see many useful details, for example, on the "datadata" YAFFS2 partition mounted at /data/data. By examining the /proc/yaffs listing for this partition, we can learn the following:

1. There are 1192 blocks (0 through 1191) and we know there are 64 chunks (2048 bytes) per block. So, 128K × 1192 = 152,576K, which you can confirm by running the df command or examining /proc/mtd as we did above.
2. The number of Page Reads, Page Writes, and Block Erasures are shown. This will provide a general idea of how much the NAND flash is used.
3. One strategy in the garbage collection procedure is to find blocks that are nearly free, copy the remaining data out, and then mark the block available for collection. We can see this happening at a high rate (323,313).
4. We can see there are no ECC errors detected.
5. The YAFFS2 metadata reports over 643,000 unlinked files.
6. YAFFS2 is not using software ECC and instead relies on either MTD or the NAND flash.

If you compare the system partition that does not have the high read and write usage of the /data/data direction, you will notice significant differences. Inspecting the /proc/yaffs file may help provide necessary background information when explaining error-correcting code, fragmented data, and more.

The best way to gain a deeper understanding of YAFFS2 is to simply create, modify, and examine the file system directly. All of this is possible on the Ubuntu workstation created for other exercises throughout the book. Since we already have a Linux virtual machine and the build-essential package installed (which includes the necessary C compiler and supporting packages), we need to now install the mtd-utils package:

```
ahoog@ubuntu:~$ sudo apt-get install mtd-utils
```

Then, we download the latest YAFFS2 source code:

```
ahoog@ubuntu:~$ curl http://www.aleph1.co.uk/cgi-bin/viewvc.cgi/
yaffs2.tar.gz?view=tar > yaffs2.tar.gz
  % Total    % Received % Xferd  Average Speed   Time    Time     Time  Current
                                 Dload  Upload   Total   Spent    Left  Speed
100  391k    0  391k    0     0   242k      0 --:--:--  0:00:01 --:--:--  277k
```

And then extract yaffs2.tar.gz and compile so we can use the kernel module:

```
ahoog@ubuntu:~$ tar xzf yaffs2.tar.gz
ahoog@ubuntu:~$ cd yaffs2/
ahoog@ubuntu:~/yaffs2$ make
make -C /lib/modules/2.6.35-25-generic/build M=/home/ahoog/yaffs2 modules
make[1]: Entering directory `/usr/src/linux-headers-2.6.35-25-generic'
  CC [M]  /home/ahoog/yaffs2/yaffs_mtdif.o
<snip>
```

Next, we are going to load the needed kernel modules to simulate an MTD in RAM (unless you happen to have some NAND flash lying around which you can hook up directly) and then mount a YAFFS2 partition.

First, we'll create a place to mount the file system in our home directory:

```
ahoog@ubuntu:~$ cd; mkdir -p ~/mnt/yaffs2
```

Next we need to load a few kernel modules to enable MTD support:

```
ahoog@ubuntu:~$ sudo modprobe mtd
[sudo] password for ahoog:
ahoog@ubuntu:~$ sudo modprobe mtdblock
```

Next, we create the simulated NAND flash with the nandsim kernel module:

```
ahoog@ubuntu:~$ sudo modprobe nandsim first_id_byte=0x20 second_id_byte=0xa2
third_id_byte=0x00 fourth_id_byte=0x15
```

> **TIP**
>
> **Additional information on Linux MTD**
>
> The Linux MTD web page provides more details on nandsim. The web site provides deep background information and support for MTD so please visit it for full details.

Additional details on nandsim from the Linux MTD web site are provided here for direct reference (NAND FAQ, n.d.):

> *"NAND simulator (nandsim) is an extremely useful debugging and development tool which simulates NAND flashes in RAM or a file. To select the simulated flash type one should specify ID bytes of your flash—the ones which are returned by the*

"Read ID" command (0x90)—consult the flash manual. The following are examples of input parameters:

- *modprobe nandsim first_id_byte=0x20 second_id_byte=0x33—16MiB, 512 bytes page*
- *modprobe nandsim first_id_byte=0x20 second_id_byte=0x35—32MiB, 512 bytes page;*
- *modprobe nandsim first_id_byte=0x20 second_id_byte=0x36—64MiB, 512 bytes page;*
- *modprobe nandsim first_id_byte=0x20 second_id_byte=0x78—128MiB, 512 bytes page;*
- *modprobe nandsim first_id_byte=0x20 second_id_byte=0x71—256MiB, 512 bytes page;*
- *modprobe nandsim first_id_byte=0x20 second_id_byte=0xa2 third_id_byte=0x00 fourth_id_byte=0x15—64MiB, 2048 bytes page;*
- *modprobe nandsim first_id_byte=0xec second_id_byte=0xa1 third_id_byte=0x00 fourth_id_byte=0x15—128MiB, 2048 bytes page;*
- *modprobe nandsim first_id_byte=0x20 second_id_byte=0xaa third_id_byte=0x00 fourth_id_byte=0x15—256MiB, 2048 bytes page;*
- *modprobe nandsim first_id_byte=0x20 second_id_byte=0xac third_id_byte=0x00 fourth_id_byte=0x15—512MiB, 2048 bytes page;*
- *modprobe nandsim first_id_byte=0xec second_id_byte=0xd3 third_id_byte=0x51 fourth_id_byte=0x95—1GiB, 2048 bytes page;"*

Now that we have the simulated NAND flash, we can verify size and partition info by examining the /proc/mtd just as we did directly on the Android device:

```
ahoog@ubuntu:~$ cat /proc/mtd
dev:    size   erasesize  name
mtd0: 04000000 00020000 "NAND simulator partition 0"
```

The system shows that we have one MTD partition (mtd0), and erasesize in hex of 0x20000 bytes (128 KB), and a total size in hex of 0x4000000 (65,536 KB or 64 MB). Next, we need to load the YAFFS2 kernel module into memory:

```
ahoog@ubuntu:~$ sudo insmod ~/yaffs2/yaffs2.ko
```

Before we mount the YAFFS2 file system, let's take a look at the uninitialized simulated NAND flash in a hex editor. If you try to use tools like dd or simply xxd to view the NAND flash device, you will not see the OOB areas because they are not exposed to most tools. This is to prevent the intermixed 64 bits of metadata from confusing programs that do not expect OOB in their file (imagine trying to display a PDF that has 64 bytes of binary OOB data after each 2k chunk). To read the full NAND flash including the OOB, we use the program nanddump that is part of the previously installed mtd-utils package. This will read the data and return them in binary. There are several options to consider which can be easily viewed:

```
ahoog@ubuntu:~$ nanddump --help
Usage: nanddump [OPTIONS] MTD-device
Dumps the contents of a nand mtd partition.

           --help               Display this help and exit
           --version            Output version information and exit
-a         --forcebinary        Force printing of binary data to tty
-c         --canonicalprint     Print canonical Hex+ASCII dump
-f file    --file=file          Dump to file
-i         --ignoreerrors       Ignore errors
-l length  --length=length      Length
-n         --noecc              Read without error correction
-o         --omitoob            Omit oob data
-b         --omitbad            Omit bad blocks from the dump
-p         --prettyprint        Print nice (hexdump)
-q         --quiet              Don't display progress and status messages
-s addr    --startaddress=addr  Start address
```

For our purposes, we want to use nanddump to extract the full NAND with OOB and pipe the output to a hex editor (xxd) for viewing:

```
ahoog@ubuntu:~$ sudo nanddump -a /dev/mtd0ro | xxd | less
0000000: ffff ffff ffff ffff ffff ffff ffff ffff  ................
0000010: ffff ffff ffff ffff ffff ffff ffff ffff  ................
0000020: ffff ffff ffff ffff ffff ffff ffff ffff  ................
0000030: ffff ffff ffff ffff ffff ffff ffff ffff  ................
0000040: ffff ffff ffff ffff ffff ffff ffff ffff  ................
0000050: ffff ffff ffff ffff ffff ffff ffff ffff  ................
0000060: ffff ffff ffff ffff ffff ffff ffff ffff  ................
0000070: ffff ffff ffff ffff ffff ffff ffff ffff  ................
0000080: ffff ffff ffff ffff ffff ffff ffff ffff  ................
<snip>
```

Notice that the simulated NAND flash contains the expected 0xFF values that a blank or erased NAND flash should have. The above command will allow you to examine how the raw NAND flash is modified when we initialize and subsequently modify the file system.

So, finally, we are ready to mount a YAFFS2 file system:

```
ahoog@ubuntu:~$ sudo mount -t yaffs2 /dev/mtdblock0 ~/mnt/yaffs2/
```

You can verify the file system is mounted and accessible:

```
ahoog@ubuntu:~$ sudo mount -t yaffs2 /dev/mtdblock0 ~/mnt/yaffs2/
ahoog@ubuntu:~$ mount | grep yaffs2
/dev/mtdblock0 on /home/ahoog/mnt/yaffs2 type yaffs2 (rw)

ahoog@ubuntu:~$ ls -la ~/mnt/yaffs2/
total 8
drwxr-xr-x 1 root  root  2048 2011-02-03 11:37 .
drwxr-xr-x 3 ahoog ahoog 4096 2011-02-03 07:21 ..
drwx------ 1 root  root  2048 2011-02-03 11:37 lost+found
```

So, we can see a YAFFS2 file system is mounted with read/write permissions at ~/mnt/yaffs2. Even though we have not created any files, the directory contains a lost+found virtual directory where files and directories whose parent directory cannot be determined are stored. If you use the xxd hex editor again to examine the simulated NAND flash device, it will still contain 0xFF. However, if you write a single file with the following command:

```
ahoog@ubuntu:~$ nano -w ~/mnt/yaffs2/book.txt
```

and put the contents "Android Forensics and Mobile Security" in the file, then when we examine the raw NAND flash, we can clearly see the YAFFS2 structures including the ObjectHeaders, Objects, and file contents. Here's a portion of the hex content using nanddump and a slightly modified xxd command by adding the -a option that will skip 0x00 rows:

```
ahoog@ubuntu:~$ sudo nanddump -a /dev/mtd0ro | xxd -a | less
0000000: 0100 0000 0100 0000 ffff 626f 6f6b 2e74  .........book.t
0000010: 7874 0000 0000 0000 0000 0000 0000 0000  xt.............
0000020: 0000 0000 0000 0000 0000 0000 0000 0000  ................
*
00007e0: ffff ffff ffff ffff ffff ffff ffff ffff  ................
00007f0: ffff ffff ffff ffff ffff ffff ffff ffff  ................
0000800: ffff 0110 0000 0101 0010 0100 0080 0000  ................
0000810: 0000 2aaa aaaa 0400 0000 fbff ffff ffff  ..*............
0000820: ffff ffff ffff ffff fff0 cfaa 5567 ffff  ...........Ug..
0000830: ffff ffff ffff ffff ffff ffff ffff ffff  ................
0000840: 416e 6472 6f69 6420 466f 7265 6e73 6963  Android Forensic
0000850: 7320 616e 6420 4d6f 6269 6c65 2053 6563  s and Mobile Sec
0000860: 7572 6974 790a 0a00 0000 0000 0000 0000  urity...........
0000870: 0000 0000 0000 0000 0000 0000 0000 0000  ................
*
0001040: ffff 0110 0000 0101 0000 0100 0000 2700  .............'.
0001050: 0000 1900 0000 0800 0000 f7ff ffff ffff  ................
0001060: ffff ffff ffff ffff aa66 5bff ffff ffff  .........f[.....
0001070: ffff ffff ffff ffff ffff ffff ffff ffff  ................
0001080: 0100 0000 0100 0000 ffff 626f 6f6b 2e74  .........book.t
0001090: 7874 0000 0000 0000 0000 0000 0000 0000  xt.............
00010a0: 0000 0000 0000 0000 0000 0000 0000 0000  ................
```

Beginning at offset 0x0000000, we can see the blank ObjectHeader where we can easily see the file name in ASCII (book.txt). Beginning at 0x0000800 through 0x000083F, we can see the OOB data that is stored by YAFFS2 and then MTD as packed binary data and must be decided. The actual contents of the file are written to the NAND flash at 0x0000840. We see another OOB from 0x0001040 through 0x000107F and then the ObjectHeader is written to the NAND flash again at 0x0001080 because the original ObjectHeader represented the blank file. Once we added the content and saved the file, the data was written to the NAND flash and a *new ObjectHeader was written* to the NAND flash. The new ObjectHeader reflects the new metadata about the Object including what chunks hold the data, MAC (modified, accessed, changed) data, and more.

A key point to understand is that YAFFS2 could not simply update the first ObjectHeader with this information because it would first have to erase that entire block. So instead it writes a new ObjectHeader, generates a high sequence number for that header which makes it the most up-to-date ObjectHeader for the file. As you can imagine, the old ObjectHeader and data remain on the NAND flash unless they go through garbage collection and thus provide a great opportunity to recover file metadata and contents using forensic techniques.

YAFFS Example

In this final section about YAFFS2, a fictitious scenario is presented to illustrate how ObjectHeaders and Objects are written to the NAND flash. The example was presented by Charles Manning in his "*How Yaffs Works*" (How YAFFS works, n.d.). Anyone interested in the internals of YAFFS is encouraged to print, read, or re-read this document. In the example, we use a NAND flash which, for simplicity, has four chunks per block and is erased (0xFF). After each change is described, a table will show the contents of the NAND flash.

First, we create an empty file on the NAND flash as shown in Table 4.6.

Table 4.6 Blank File Created

Block	Chunk	ObjectId	ChunkId	Status (Live or Shrink/Delete)	Comment
0	0	500	0	Live	ObjectHeader for blank file, length of 0

The ObjectHeader points to an empty file. Next, we write three chunks of data to the file, as shown in Table 4.7.

So far, this may seem straightforward. The object is now taking up the entire first block.

> **NOTE**
>
> **Fictitious NAND flash**
>
> Remember, our fictitious NAND flash has four chucks per block, not the typical 64 chunks we see in commercial NAND flash.

Table 4.7 Write Three Chunks of Data

Block	Chunk	ObjectId	ChunkId	Status (Live or Shrink/Delete)	Comment
0	0	500	0	Live	ObjectHeader for blank file, length of 0
0	1	500	1	Live	First chunk of data
0	2	500	2	Live	Second chunk of data
0	3	500	3	Live	Third chunk of data

Table 4.8 Save the File's New ObjectHeader					
Block	**Chunk**	**ObjectId**	**ChunkId**	**Status (Live or Shrink/ Delete)**	**Comment**
0	0	500	0	Shrink/delete	Obsoleted ObjectHeader. Originally for blank file, length of 0
0	1	500	1	Live	First chunk of data
0	2	500	2	Live	Second chunk of data
0	3	500	3	Live	Third chunk of data
1	0	500	0	Live	New ObjectHeader, file length 3.

Next, we are going to save the file that will cause a new ObjectHeader to be written to the NAND flash as shown in Table 4.8.

The key point to understand here is that YAFFS2 is unable to go back and update the original ObjectHeader with the new size, chunks of data, and others. Instead, it must write a new ObjectHeader that will contain the metadata needed for the updated file. In YAFFS2, the new ObjectHeader is given a larger sequence number and thus it becomes the current ObjectHeader and YAFFS2 simply ignores the previous one (however, it remains on disk).

Next, the file will be opened with read/write access and the first chunk of data will be given a new value. Finally, the file is saved and closed, which results in additional data written to the NAND flash, as shown in Table 4.9.

Again, since we cannot simply change the original first chunk of data in the file, a new data chunk is written to the NAND flash and the previous data chunk is obsolete. This is achieved as yet another new ObjectHeader is written to the NAND flash, which points to the new first chunk of data for the file. Next, we are going to truncate the file to a zero length file and the resulting NAND flash changes are shown in Table 4.10.

As the file was truncated, none of the chunks in Block 0 are in use any longer. This makes the block available for garbage collection, which will occur on the next write cycle. This is referred to as lazy garbage collection because it uses an existing write cycle to perform any necessary garbage collection. As before, a new ObjectHeader is written to the NAND flash to account for the truncated file.

Finally, we rename the file and the NAND flash results are shown in Table 4.11.

During this cycle, Block 0 was garbage collected and is now available for writing data. As the file was renamed, a new ObjectHeader was written to the NAND flash. With all chunks in Block 1 now obsolete, they are available for garbage collection. However, bear in mind that due to the limited endurance of NAND flash, write/erase cycles are avoided.

Table 4.9 Save the New Data and ObjectHeader

Block	Chunk	ObjectId	ChunkId	Status (Live or Shrink/ Delete)	Comment
0	0	500	0	Shrink/delete	Obsoleted ObjectHeader. Originally for blank file, length of 0
0	1	500	1	Shrink/delete	Obsoleted first chunk of data
0	2	500	2	Live	Second chunk of data
0	3	500	3	Live	Third chunk of data
1	0	500	0	Shrink/delete	Obsoleted ObjectHeader, file length 3
1	1	500	1	Live	New first chunk of data
1	2	500	2	Live	New ObjectHeader, file length 3

Table 4.10 Truncate File and Write New ObjectHeader

Block	Chunk	ObjectId	ChunkId	Status (Live or Shrink/ Delete)	Comment
0	0	500	0	Shrink/delete	Obsoleted ObjectHeader. Originally for blank file, length of 0
0	1	500	1	Shrink/delete	Obsoleted first chunk of data
0	2	500	2	Shrink/delete	Second chunk of data
0	3	500	3	Shrink/delete	Third chunk of data
1	0	500	0	Shrink/delete	Obsoleted ObjectHeader, file length 3
1	1	500	1	Shrink/delete	New first chunk of data
1	2	500	2	Shrink/delete	New ObjectHeader, file length 3
1	3	500	3	Live	New ObjectHeader, file length 0

Table 4.11 Rename File and Write New ObjectHeader

Block	Chunk	ObjectId	ChunkId	Status (Live or Shrink/ Delete)	Comment
0	0				Erased
0	1				Erased
0	2				Erased
0	3				Erased
1	0	500	0	Shrink/delete	Obsoleted ObjectHeader, file length 3
1	1	500	1	Shrink/delete	New first chunk of data
1	2	500	2	Shrink/delete	New ObjectHeader, file length 3
1	2	500	2	Shrink/delete	New ObjectHeader, file length 0
2	0	500	0	Live	New ObjectHeader, file renamed, file length 0

The implications for forensics are that the entire history of ObjectHeader and Object data chunks, unless garbage collected, would remain on the NAND flash. With proper software, the NAND flash could be scanned and the entire history of the file system could essentially be rebuilt. Not only would the timeline contain the date/time of every edit, but it is possible to recover the actual state of the file. In practice, the state of the YAFFS2 partitions is not this simple. However, the general principle remains relevant.

MOUNTED FILE SYSTEMS

We have covered many components of Android's memory systems in detail. Not only have we explored RAM and the NAND flash, but we have also examined many of the file systems in great detail. This background information will assist in your forensic and security analysis of Android devices. To better understand this more academic information, we will now explore the mounted file systems found on an Android device.

Mounted File Systems

Let us start with the file systems mounted on the HTC Incredible:

```
ahoog@ubuntu:~$ adb shell mount
rootfs / rootfs ro,relatime 0 0
tmpfs /dev tmpfs rw,relatime,mode=755 0 0
devpts /dev/pts devpts rw,relatime,mode=600 0 0
proc /proc proc rw,relatime 0 0
sysfs /sys sysfs rw,relatime 0 0
none /acct cgroup rw,relatime,cpuacct 0 0
tmpfs /mnt/asec tmpfs rw,relatime,mode=755,gid=1000 0 0
none /dev/cpuctl cgroup rw,relatime,cpu 0 0
/dev/block/mtdblock3 /system yaffs2 rw,relatime 0 0
/dev/block/mmcblk0p1 /data ext3 rw,nosuid,noatime,nodiratime,
errors=continue,data=writeback 0 0
/dev/block/mtdblock6 /data/data yaffs2 rw,nosuid,nodev,relatime 0 0
/dev/block/mmcblk0p2 /cache ext3
rw,nosuid,nodev,noatime,nodiratime,errors=continue,data=writeback 0 0
tmpfs /app-cache tmpfs rw,relatime,size=8192k 0 0
/dev/block/vold/179:9 /mnt/sdcard vfat
rw,dirsync,nosuid,nodev,noexec,relatime,uid=1000,gid=1015,fmask=0702,dmask=0702,
allow_utime=0020,codepage=cp437,iocharset=iso8859-1,shortname=mixed,utf8,
errors=remount-ro 0 0
/dev/block/vold/179:9 /mnt/secure/asec vfat
rw,dirsync,nosuid,nodev,noexec,relatime,uid=1000,gid=1015,fmask=0702,dmask=0702,
allow_utime=0020,codepage=cp437,iocharset=iso8859-1,shortname=mixed,utf8,
errors=remount-ro 0 0
tmpfs /mnt/sdcard/.android_secure tmpfs ro,relatime,size=0k,mode=000 0 0
/dev/block/vold/179:3 /mnt/emmc vfat
rw,dirsync,nosuid,nodev,noexec,relatime,uid=1000,gid=1015,fmask=0702,dmask=0702,
allow_utime=0020,codepage=cp437,iocharset=iso8859-1,shortname=mixed,utf8,
errors=remount-ro 0 0
```

When you run the mount command without parameters, it returns the list of mounted file systems and their options. Table 4.12 is a description of the output using several entries. However, note that each entry above ends with "0 0" which is omitted from the table for space reasons. The "0 0" entry determines whether or not the file system is archived by the dump command and the pass number that determines the order in which the file system checker (fsck) checks the device/partition for errors at boot time. On most desktop or server Linux systems, the root file system has a pass number of 1 so it is checked prior to other file systems.

The /mnt/sdcard has many options. The options are:

1. rw: mounted to allow read/write
2. dirsync: all updates to directories are done synchronously
3. nosuid: does not allow setuid (which would allow other users to execute programs using the permission of file owner)
4. nodev: does not interpret any file as a special block device
5. noexec: does not let all files execute from the file system
6. relatime: updates the file access time if older than the modified time
7. uid=1000: sets the owner of all files to 1000
8. gid=1015: sets the group of all files to 1015

Table 4.12 Output of Mount Command Overview

Device Name	Mount Point	File System Type	Options	Notes
rootfs	/	rootfs	ro,relatime	This is the ro (read-only) root file system mount at /
tmpfs	/dev	tmpfs	rw,relatime, mode=755	The device directory is mounted as tmpfs and has permissions set to 755 that are read, write, and execute for root (rwx) and read/execute for everyone else
/dev/block/ mtdblock6	/data/ data	yaffs2	rw,nosuid, nodev,relatime	While the /data directory is an ext3, the /data/data where app data is stored is a YAFFS2 file system. It is mounted to allow read/ write access, does not allow setuid (which would allow other users to execute programs using the permission of file owner), does not interpret any file as a special block device, and updates the file access time if older than the modified time
/dev/block/ vold/179:9	/mnt/ sdcard	vfat	See SD card numbered list	See SD card numbered list

9. fmask=0702: sets the umask applied to regular files only (set permissions ---rwxr-x, or user=none, group=read/write/execute,other=read/execute)
10. dmask=0702: sets the umask applied to directories only (set permissions ---rwxr-x, or user=none, group=read/write/execute,other=read/execute)
11. allow_utime=0020: controls the permission check of mtime/atime.
12. codepage=cp437: sets the codepage for converting to shortname characters on FAT and VFAT file systems.
13. iocharset=iso8859-1: character set to use for converting between 8-bit characters and 16-bit Unicode characters. The default is iso8859-1. Long file names are stored on disk in Unicode format.
14. shortname=mixed: defines the behavior for creation and display of file names that fit into 8.3 characters. If a long name for a file exists, it will always be the preferred display. Mixed displays the short name as is and stores a long name when the short name is not all upper case.

15. utf8: converts 16-bit Unicode characters on CD to UTF-8.
16. errors=remount-ro: defines the behavior when an error is encountered; in this case, remounts the file system read-only.

All of the mount command options are explained in the manual page (man 8 mount). However, for most cases, a quick scan will reveal the information an examiner needs including the mount points, types, and permissions on the file systems.

The df command will provide information about the free space available on the mounted file systems:

```
ahoog@ubuntu:~$ adb shell df
/dev: 211600K total, 0K used, 211600K available (block size 4096)
/mnt/asec: 211600K total, 0K used, 211600K available (block size 4096)
/system: 253952K total, 243724K used, 10228K available (block size 4096)
/data: 765992K total, 129840K used, 636152K available (block size 4096)
/data/data: 152576K total, 52048K used, 100528K available (block size 4096)
/cache: 198337K total, 10790K used, 187547K available (block size 1024)
/app-cache: 8192K total, 7140K used, 1052K available (block size 4096)
/mnt/sdcard: 1955520K total, 245664K used, 1709856K available (block size 32768)
/mnt/secure/asec: Permission denied
/mnt/emmc: 6920512K total, 233152K used, 6687360K available (block size 32768)
```

As you can see, one of the mount points (/mnt/secure/asec) returned a permission denied when the shell user tried to determine how much disk space was free. By looking at the parent directory, we can see that only root has access to the directory:

```
ahoog@ubuntu:~$ adb shell ls -l /mnt
d---rwxr-x system   sdcard_rw          1969-12-31 18:00 emmc
drwxr-xr-x root     system             2011-01-31 15:42 asec
drwx------ root     root               2011-01-31 15:42 secure
d---rwxr-x system   sdcard_rw          2011-02-01 17:49 sdcard
```

Interestingly, two of these file systems/directories can be exposed through the USB mass storage (UMS) option and when that occurs, the permissions on the directories change. If the UMS option is not enabled, the file systems are fully accessible to the Android device as you can see for /mnt/emmc and /mnt/sdcard.

However, when UMS is active and the two file systems are available to the connected workstation, the permissions change:

```
ahoog@ubuntu:~$ adb shell ls -l /mnt
d--------- system   system            2011-01-23 10:08 emmc
drwxr-xr-x root     system            2011-01-23 10:08 asec
drwx------ root     root              2011-01-23 10:08 secure
d--------- system   system            2011-01-23 10:08 sdcard
```

As you can see, all permissions on /mnt/emmc and /mnt/sdcard are removed and thus the Android device cannot access /mnt/emmc or /mnt/sdcard from the phone directly (i.e., it is exclusively shared with the connected workstation).

SUMMARY

The physical memory, file systems, and data structures present on an Android device are the fundamental building blocks for data storage. Having a deep understanding of these structures will not only enable you to understand an Android device but to also perform your own research and development when presented with new file systems and data structures.

References

Android developers blog: Saving data safely. (n.d.). Retrieved February 2, 2011, from http://android-developers.blogspot.com/2010/12/saving-data-safely.html.

Android reverse engineering. (n.d.). thomascannon.net. Retrieved January 29, 2011, from http://thomascannon.net/projects/android-reversing/.

Data storage. (n.d.). Android Developers. Retrieved March 13, 2011, from http://developer.android.com/guide/topics/data/data-storage.html#netw.

How YAFFS works: the internals. (n.d.). YAFFS. Retrieved February 4, 2011, from http://www.yaffs.net/how-yaffs-works-internals.

Nand Faq. (n.d.). *Memory technology device (MTD) subsystem for Linux*, Retrieved March 13, 2011, from http://www.linux-mtd.infradead.org/faq/nand.html.

The sysfs filesystem. (n.d.), Retrieved February 1, 2011, from http://www.kernel.org/pub/linux/kernel/people/mochel/doc/papers/ols-2005/mochel.pdf.

Way, T. (n.d.). *Android will be using ext4 starting with Gingerbread. Thoughts by Ted. Welcome to thunk.org*, Retrieved February 2, 2011, from http://thunk.org/tytso/blog/2010/12/12/android-will-be-using-ext4-starting-with-gingerbread/.

Licence FAQs, Y. A. F. F. S. (n.d.). *YAFFS*, Retrieved February 4, 2011, from http://www.yaffs.net/yaffs-licence-faqs.

YAFFS: the NAND-specific flash file system—Introductory Article. (n.d.). Retrieved February 2, 2011, from http://www.yaffs.net/yaffs-nand-specific-flash-file-system-introductory-article.

CHAPTER

Android device, data, and app security

5

INFORMATION IN THIS CHAPTER

- Data theft targets and attack vectors
- Security considerations
- Individual security strategies
- Corporate security strategies
- App development security strategies

INTRODUCTION

There is a delicate balance in being both a forensic analyst and a privacy advocate. If a device were 100% secured, then forensic investigation of the device would fail to return any information. On the other hand, if a device's security measures were completely absent, forensic expertise would hardly be necessary to extract meaningful data from the device.

The primary consumers of mobile forensics are law enforcement and government agencies. They use and secure many types of sensitive data on mobile devices, and they have the mandate and authority to investigate crimes. They rely not only on digital forensic analysis, but can also exercise their authority through search warrants and subpoenas and compel most organizations to produce needed information such as financial records, e-mail, Internet service provider logs, and more.

Similarly, corporations need to protect their sensitive data, and at times launch internal investigations to ensure security. While their authority does not reach beyond their company, in the United States, corporations can exercise wide authority pertaining to searches on devices they own.

Finally, individuals have the right to access their own data. Whether they exercise this in the pursuit of civil litigation or for other matters, they have the authority to do so on devices they own.

In the cases of individuals and corporations, the parties generally have no need to recover sensitive information such as credit cards, banking information, or passwords on the device they have authority to investigate. Corporations would not seek an individual's credit card data in an internal investigation, and they have the means to access corporate e-mail systems and change passwords. In the case of individuals, they already have access to their own financial records, e-mail, and other such sensitive data. In the case of law enforcement and government agencies, they can use their subpoena and search warrant powers to acquire the data they seek.

So, in the end, the only people likely to benefit from highly sensitive data being stored insecurely on mobile devices are cyber criminals. In the course of many individual, corporate, and criminal investigations of mobile devices, we have encountered highly sensitive personal information that was not central to the case. However, if cyber criminals had access to that device—whether in their physical possession or through remote exploits—the data they could gather would represent a significant risk to the consumer.

Likewise, corporations are targets for commercial espionage, financial theft, intellectual property theft, and a wide variety of other attacks. As many corporations move to employee-owned devices, even more control and oversight of the device is lost, placing corporate data at great risk.

And finally, law enforcement and government agencies are negatively affected by mobile security issues. The agencies are comprised of individuals who share the same risk of data exposure as consumers. Like corporations, the agencies themselves may be the target of attacks, which seek not only sensitive data that could jeopardize investigations or embarrass the agency but also attacks with motives as serious as international espionage. And a challenge unique to law enforcement and government agencies is that many, many crimes involving mobile devices must be investigated, straining already overloaded criminal investigation units and digital forensic laboratories.

For these reasons, mobile device security is a rising concern for individuals, corporations, and law enforcement and government agencies.

DATA THEFT TARGETS AND ATTACK VECTORS

At this point anyone still reading is quite aware that smartphones, and Android devices in particular, contain an enormous amount of information, often blending both personal and corporate data. Android devices can be a target of data theft as well as a means by which theft can occur (attack vector). Understanding the various threats and scenarios will allow security engineers and developers to design appropriate controls to mitigate risk. While this chapter cannot possibly provide exhaustive coverage of such a broad topic, specific threats and mitigation strategies will be covered and should serve as a strong starting point for security professionals.

Android Devices as a Target

Primary focus of mobile security research, exploits, and articles has been on smartphones as a target of data theft—and rightfully so. The risks to consumers, corporations, and agencies are very real, and most security experts agree that malicious software targeting mobile devices is on the rise and will remain a focus of cyber criminals.

Mobile devices contain a wealth of personal and corporate data in a highly concentrated and portable form. Criminals are generally pragmatic and cyber criminals are no exception. If they can exploit one device that contains not only user names, passwords, and sensitive data about an individual, but also the same types of information about their employers, they will clearly target that opportunity. Furthermore, while the data from one mobile app may not provide sufficient information for the criminal to achieve their goal, combining the information found from the numerous installed applications typically yields an alarmingly complete profile of the owner.

Mobile devices are not only easy to lose and relatively easy to steal, but they also have a fairly short usage scenario before consumers want the latest model. Both of these situations result in a large number of smartphones available for purchase through venues such as eBay and Craigslist, and many of the devices are not properly wiped leaving personal data intact. Furthermore, malicious code, malware, and remote exploits increasingly target mobile devices, and history indicates they will result in significant data theft. The extent of their effectiveness will only be determined over time; but given the urgent pace of development of the operating systems (Android in this case), and the rapid proliferation of mobile apps, it is certainly reasonable to expect that many of these attacks will succeed.

Data at Rest

Data at rest is a term used to describe data that are stored in nonvolatile memory and thus are neither located in RAM nor in transit through networks (cellular, data, or other networks). The term data at rest is often used in laws and regulations and defines one key state where data must be secured.

Throughout this book, we highlight different examples of data that an Android device contains. Here, let's consider two fictitious scenarios: one focusing on corporate customers and one focusing on an individual.

For the individual, the Android device is used for personal communications, personal finance, entertainment, and general information surfing. Examining the phone might recover the following:

- SMS/MMS: All allocated (undeleted) SMS and MMS will be recoverable as well as much of the unallocated (deleted but still on the NAND flash). The information recovered will include not only the messages themselves, but any attachments including pictures, videos, audio files, phone contacts (.vcf file), calendar items, and more. There are also many third-party SMS/MMS apps that may include additional features.
- Call logs: While also available from the wireless carrier, the full call logs are recoverable. These could include call attempts that failed to make it to the carrier as well as other metadata that we can correlate, such as location (this can also be

generally estimated based on cell towers) and other activities happening on the device prior to the call being placed.

- Voice mail: In the case of installed voice-mail applications, such as Verizon's visual voice mail, allocated voice-mail messages are usually recoverable as audio files (.OGG). Some unallocated voice-mail messages may be recoverable as well.
- Financial apps: While they vary widely, most installed financial apps store some data locally or cache web pages. In some cases, the information recoverable can include user login, password, account numbers, and transaction details. In our testing, for example, the Mint.com app stored a user name, PIN for accessing the local app, and some bank account transaction information.
- Personal e-mail: Most installed e-mail apps store the contents of e-mail messages in plain text, including e-mail headers (To/From e-mail addresses). In some cases, the user credentials including user login and password are also recoverable. The standard Android mail app, for example, when used to connect to Hotmail via POP3, was found to store the password in plain text.
- Web history: Allocated web history including URLs visited, cookies, and cached pages are recoverable. Unallocated space may include additional web history information.
- Google search history: URLs from Google including search terms.
- YouTube: URLs of videos watched.
- Pictures and videos: Photos and videos taken by the user, stored on the device, related to applications, and others.
- Geo-location: GPS coordinates in pictures, other artifacts.
- Game history and interactions.

In this fictitious situation, a skilled forensic examiner can recover extensive information about an individual.

In our corporate example, it simply builds on the individual since most devices blend the individual's information with their corporate information. Here are some additional items typically recoverable from a corporate device:

- Corporate e-mail and attachments
- Voice mail and faxes sent via e-mail
- User names, passwords, and domain information
- Wi-Fi access points, information, and passwords
- Calendar items
- Instant Messenger or other communications with employees
- Corporate files stored on the device for convenience

As you can see, if an attacker was looking for an effective way to infiltrate a corporation, an employee's device (or better yet, several employees' devices) can provide many insights and avenues for an attack—not to mention recovering sensitive corporate information directly from the device.

One concrete example that may raise significant alarm with corporate security managers is how Android's built-in e-mail application stores credentials for an e-mail account that uses Microsoft's exchange ActiveSync (EAS) protocol. The credentials used to authenticate to EAS are a user's active directory domain user name and password. Many corporations centralize their authentication, authorization, and accounting (AAA) services into an active directory that enables single sign-on and simplified management. Overall, the simplification leads to more effective security. In the Android mail application (com.android.mail), the user's EAS is stored in plain text in a well-defined location. The database is stored in /data/data/com.android.email, Here is an overview of the folders and files:

```
ahoog@ubuntu:~$ tree com.android.email/
com.android.email/
├── cache
│   └── webviewCache
├── databases
│   ├── 1.db_att
│   │   ├── 1
│   │   ├── 2
│   │   └── 3
│   ├── EmailProviderBody.db
│   ├── EmailProvider.db
│   ├── webviewCache.db
│   └── webview.db
├── files
│   └── deviceName
├── lib
└── shared_prefs
    └── AndroidMail.Main.xml
```

The password is located in the EmailProvider.db in a table called HostAuth in a column conveniently named password:

```
ahoog@ubuntu:~$ sqlite3 com.android.email/databases/EmailProvider.db
SQLite version 3.6.22
Enter ".help" for instructions
Enter SQL statements terminated with a ";"
sqlite> .mode line
sqlite> select * from HostAuth;
        _id = 1
   protocol = eas
    address = owa.CorpExchangeServerExample.com
       port = 0
      flags = 5
      login = thisIsTheirUserNameInPlainText
   password = thisIsTheirPasswordInPlainText-Seriously
     domain = NeverHurtsToHaveTheDomainInfoToo
accountKey = 0
```

In addition to the account's user name, password, and domain, the full subject and body of e-mail are stored in the data directory, as well as attachments, preferences, and other information. All are stored in plain text (the term silver platter comes to mind).

There are two primary techniques attackers use to access data at rest. The first requires physical access to the device and will use a variety of techniques that are essentially the same techniques used by forensic examiners and which will be explored in Chapter 6. While physical access to a device is not necessarily easy to achieve, we mention plausible scenarios above, including lost or stolen phones as well as phones that are replaced with newer models but not securely wiped. In addition, people who travel internationally, especially executives at corporations, may find their phones are temporarily confiscated and examined by customs officials as they enter a country. In this scenario, the officials have unfettered physical access to the device.

The other primary techniques attackers use to access data at rest are remote exploits and malicious software. In these scenarios, the attackers are able to gain additional privileges by using programmatic and social engineering techniques. The techniques may include exploiting vulnerabilities found in the Linux kernel and core Android libraries, phishing attacks, or exploiting vulnerabilities in apps. In addition, users may inadvertently install apps and grant permissions beyond the access needed, thereby allowing malicious software access to data at rest. Finally, social engineering remains a highly effective way to compromise systems, and mobile devices are not immune from this. Users are accustomed to installing a variety of apps, often knowing little about the app provider and often trust and freely follow links presented to them in e-mail and SMS, opening avenues to social engineering-based attacks.

Data in Transit

Data in transit (sometimes called data in motion) is a term used to describe data that is in transit through networks (cellular, Wi-Fi, or other networks) or is located in RAM. The term data in transit is often used in laws and regulations and defines another key state where data must be secured.

In general, most of the information stored on a device (and described above) will, at some point, have traveled through the network. Beyond the data itself, quite a bit of information never persisted to the device is transmitted and must be protected. Some examples include the following:

- Passwords: Many applications do not store passwords on the device and require the user to authenticate each time the app is opened. The password is therefore only transmitted, not stored.
- Two-factor authentication
- Password reset security responses
- Data displayed in an application but not saved or cached to nonvolatile storage (e.g., account numbers and balances)

A good way to demonstrate the data traveling through the network is with an example. In this case, a computer running BackTrack 4 (a Linux-based penetration testing suite), was connected to a network hub, which also has a Wi-Fi access point connected to it. The network interface on the computer is set to promiscuous mode, which allows the device to see all traffic on the network hub, even if the traffic was not destined for the interface. The urlsnarf program is run which intercepts the traffic on the network interface (eth0) and inspects it for URLs. If a URL is found, it is printed to screen. Bear in mind, all network traffic is intercepted so any unencrypted data such as user names or passwords could be similarly captured and viewed.

```
root@bt:~# sudo urlsnarf
urlsnarf: listening on eth0 [tcp port 80 or port 8080 or port 3128]
10.1.10.11 - - [17/Mar/2011:09:26:19 -0500] "GET
http://api.twitter.com/1/statuses/mentions.json?include_entities=true&count=100&
since_id=45865608952295424 HTTP/1.1" - - "-" "TwitterAndroid/2.0.1 (122)
ADR6300/8 (HTC;inc;verizon_wwe;inc;)"
10.1.10.11 - - [17/Mar/2011:09:26:19 -0500] "GET
http://api.twitter.com/1/statuses/retweets_of_me.json?include_entities=true&
count=100&since_id=15855940804812800 HTTP/1.1" - - "-" "TwitterAndroid/2.0.1
(122) ADR6300/8 (HTC;inc;verizon_wwe;inc;)"
10.1.10.11 - - [17/Mar/2011:09:26:20 -0500] "GET
http://api.twitter.com/1/statuses/home_timeline.json?include_entities=true&
count=100&since_id=48383245812895746 HTTP/1.1" - - "-" "TwitterAndroid/2.0.1
(122) ADR6300/8 (HTC;inc;verizon_wwe;inc;)"
10.1.10.11 - - [17/Mar/2011:09:26:20 -0500] "GET
http://api.twitter.com/1/account/rate_limit_status.json HTTP/1.1" - - "-"
"TwitterAndroid/2.0.1 (122) ADR6300/8 (HTC;inc;verizon_wwe;inc;)"
10.1.10.11 - - [17/Mar/2011:09:26:20 -0500] "GET
http://api.twitter.com/1/direct_messages.json HTTP/1.1" - - "-"
"TwitterAndroid/2.0.1 (122) ADR6300/8 (HTC;inc;verizon_wwe;inc;)"
10.1.10.11 - - [17/Mar/2011:09:26:20 -0500] "GET
http://api.twitter.com/1/account/rate_limit_status.json HTTP/1.1" - - "-"
"TwitterAndroid/2.0.1 (122) ADR6300/8 (HTC;inc;verizon_wwe;inc;)"
10.1.10.11 - - [17/Mar/2011:09:26:21 -0500] "GET
http://api.twitter.com/1/direct_messages/sent.json HTTP/1.1" - - "-"
"TwitterAndroid/2.0.1 (122) ADR6300/8 (HTC;inc;verizon_wwe;inc;)"
10.1.10.11 - - [17/Mar/2011:09:27:35 -0500] "GET http://goo.gl/4G7Bx HTTP/1.1"
- - "-" "Mozilla/5.0 (Linux; U; Android 2.2; en-us; ADR6300 Build/FRF91)
AppleWebKit/533.1 (KHTML, like Gecko) Version/4.0 Mobile Safari/533.1"
10.1.10.11 - - [17/Mar/2011:09:28:51 -0500] "GET http://mrkl.it/ HTTP/1.1"
- - "-" "Mozilla/5.0 (Linux; U; Android 2.2; en-us; ADR6300 Build/FRF91)
AppleWebKit/533.1 (KHTML, like Gecko) Version/4.0 Mobile Safari/533.1"
10.1.10.11 - - [17/Mar/2011:09:28:51 -0500] "GET http://mrkl.it/
-/media/static/main.css HTTP/1.1" - - "http://mrkl.it/" "Mozilla/5.0 (Linux; U;
Android 2.2; en-us; ADR6300 Build/FRF91) AppleWebKit/533.1 (KHTML, like Gecko)
Version/4.0 Mobile Safari/533.1"
10.1.10.11 - - [17/Mar/2011:09:28:51 -0500] "GET http://mrkl.it/
-/media/static/fancybox/jquery.fancybox-1.3.4.pack.js HTTP/1.1"
- - "http://mrkl.it/" "Mozilla/5.0 (Linux; U; Android 2.2; en-us; ADR6300
Build/FRF91) AppleWebKit/533.1 (KHTML, like Gecko) Version/4.0 Mobile
Safari/533.1"
10.1.10.11 - - [17/Mar/2011:09:28:51 -0500] "GET
http://ajax.googleapis.com/ajax/libs/jquery/1.5.1/jquery.min.js HTTP/1.1"
- - "http://mrkl.it/" "Mozilla/5.0 (Linux; U; Android 2.2; en-us; ADR6300
Build/FRF91) AppleWebKit/533.1 (KHTML, like Gecko) Version/4.0 Mobile
Safari/533.1"
10.1.10.11 - - [17/Mar/2011:09:28:51 -0500] "GET http://mrkl.it/
-/media/static/fancybox/jquery.fancybox-1.3.4.css HTTP/1.1"
- - "http://mrkl.it/" "Mozilla/5.0 (Linux; U; Android 2.2; en-us; ADR6300
Build/FRF91) AppleWebKit/533.1 (KHTML, like Gecko) Version/4.0 Mobile
Safari/533.1"
10.1.10.11 - - [17/Mar/2011:09:28:52 -0500] "GET http://mrkl.it/
-/media/static/misc/screenshot-demo.png HTTP/1.1" - - "http://mrkl.it/"
"Mozilla/5.0 (Linux; U; Android 2.2; en-us; ADR6300 Build/FRF91)
AppleWebKit/533.1 (KHTML, like Gecko) Version/4.0 Mobile Safari/533.1"
10.1.10.11 - - [17/Mar/2011:09:28:52 -0500] "GET http://mrkl.it/
-/media/static/main.js HTTP/1.1" - - "http://mrkl.it/" "Mozilla/5.0 (Linux; U;
Android 2.2; en-us; ADR6300 Build/FRF91) AppleWebKit/533.1 (KHTML, like Gecko)
Version/4.0 Mobile Safari/533.1"
10.1.10.11 - - [17/Mar/2011:09:28:52 -0500] "GET http://mrkl.it/
-/media/static/sign-in-with-twitter-1.png HTTP/1.1" - - "http://mrkl.it/"
"Mozilla/5.0 (Linux; U; Android 2.2; en-us; ADR6300 Build/FRF91)
AppleWebKit/533.1 (KHTML, like Gecko) Version/4.0 Mobile Safari/533.1"
```

```
10.1.10.11 - - [17/Mar/2011:09:28:53 -0500] "GET
http://www.youtube.com/embed/ptq21VOfgfs?rel=0&hd=1 HTTP/1.1"
- - "http://mrkl.it/" "Mozilla/5.0 (Linux; U; Android 2.2; en-us; ADR6300
Build/FRF91) AppleWebKit/533.1 (KHTML, like Gecko) Version/4.0 Mobile
Safari/533.1"
10.1.10.11 - - [17/Mar/2011:09:28:53 -0500] "GET http://www.
google-analytics.com/__utm.gif?utmwv=4.8.9&utmn=722592738&utmhn=mrkl.it&
utmcs=UTF-8&utmsr=800x1183&utmsc=32
-bit&utmul=en&utmje=0&utmfl=10.1%20r92&utmdt=Welcome&utmhid=414400362&utmr=-&
utmp=%2F&utmac=UA-21535947
-2&utmcc=__utma%3D15198314.1123929794.1300372147.1300372147.1300372147.1%3B%2B
__utmz%3D15198314.1300372147.1.1.utmcsr%3D(direct)%7Cutmccn%3D(direct)%7Cutmcmd%
3D(none)%3B&utmu=q HTTP/1.1" - - "http://mrkl.it/" "Mozilla/5.0 (Linux; U;
Android 2.2; en-us; ADR6300 Build/FRF91) AppleWebKit/533.1 (KHTML, like Gecko)
Version/4.0 Mobile Safari/533.1"
10.1.10.11 - - [17/Mar/2011:09:28:54 -0500] "GET http://mrkl.it/
-/media/static/favicon.ico HTTP/1.1" - - "http://mrkl.it/" "Mozilla/5.0 (Linux;
U; Android 2.2; en-us; ADR6300 Build/FRF91) AppleWebKit/533.1 (KHTML, like
Gecko) Version/4.0 Mobile Safari/533.1"
10.1.10.11 - - [17/Mar/2011:09:28:54 -0500] "GET
http://s.ytimg.com/yt/swfbin/watch_as3-vflFkxRDW.swf HTTP/1.1"
- - "http://www.youtube.com/embed/ptq21VOfgfs?rel=0&hd=1" "Mozilla/5.0 (Linux;U;
Android 2.2; en-us; ADR6300 Build/FRF91) AppleWebKit/533.1 (KHTML, like Gecko)
Version/4.0 Mobile Safari/533.1"
10.1.10.11 - - [17/Mar/2011:09:28:57 -0500] "GET
http://i1.ytimg.com/crossdomain.xml HTTP/1.1"
- - "http://s.ytimg.com/yt/swfbin/watch_as3-vflFkxRDW.swf" "Mozilla/5.0 (Linux;
U; Android 2.2; en-us; ADR6300 Build/FRF91) AppleWebKit/533.1 (KHTML, like
Gecko) Version/4.0 Mobile Safari/533.1"
10.1.10.11 - - [17/Mar/2011:09:28:57 -0500] "GET
http://i1.ytimg.com/vi/ptq21VOfgfs/hqdefault.jpg HTTP/1.1"
- - "http://s.ytimg.com/yt/swfbin/watch_as3-vflFkxRDW.swf" "Mozilla/5.0 (Linux;
U; Android 2.2; en-us; ADR6300 Build/FRF91) AppleWebKit/533.1 (KHTML, like
Gecko) Version/4.0 Mobile Safari/533.1"
```

There are several well-known techniques that attackers use to compromise data in transit, along with new techniques that security researchers either discover themselves or practitioners uncover "in the wild." Some of the well-known techniques include:

- Man-in-the-middle (MITM) attacks
- MITM Secure Sockets Layer (SSL) attacks
- DNS spoofing attacks (including /etc/hosts)
- TMSI overflow baseband attacks

The baseband attacks are a very new technique focusing on the cellular modem (baseband) firmware. According to Ralf-Philipp Weinmann who presented his exploit at the DeepSec 2010 conference, the baseband firmware is code written in the 1990s. Until recently, the technologies behind the GSM networks were poorly understood. However, over time researchers have unraveled the protocols and hardware and today it is possible to create a rogue GSM station with readily available hardware powered by open source software. With control over the GSM network, an attacker can execute a TMSI overflow attack that causes a heap overflow in the GSM baseband stack of Apple iOS devices prior to 4.2. This attack can lead to remote code execution on the baseband processor (Ralf-Philipp Weinmann, n.d.).

While the baseband attack is cutting edge security work, the MITM attacks have been around much longer and are well understood and fairly easily executed. Generally, these techniques require the attacker to fully control a computer that is between the mobile device and the ultimate destination the device is trying to communicate with. In addition, the attacker may control key network services or devices such as a network switch, Wi-Fi access point, or DNS server, facilitating the attack.

Once the attacker is able to position their computer between the Android device and the ultimate destination, they can launch the attack. For this scenario, let us assume an Android device connects to a Wi-Fi network unaware that a malicious attacker controls the network. The user begins to surf the Internet and ultimately decides to check their Twitter account. To keep the example simple, let us assume the Twitter app they use does not implement SSL—most do not, although recently the official app began to move in this direction.

When they launch the app, it will connect to Twitter's web site, authenticate, and take the user to their account. Of course, in the interim, the attacker was capturing the web traffic and now has the Twitter user name and password. If the app did use SSL, but did not properly verify the SSL certificate, they would be susceptible to an MITM SSL attack, illustrated in Fig. 5.1.

Although such an attack may only capture one password, most users reuse user names and passwords for many different sites. Once the attacker has one user name

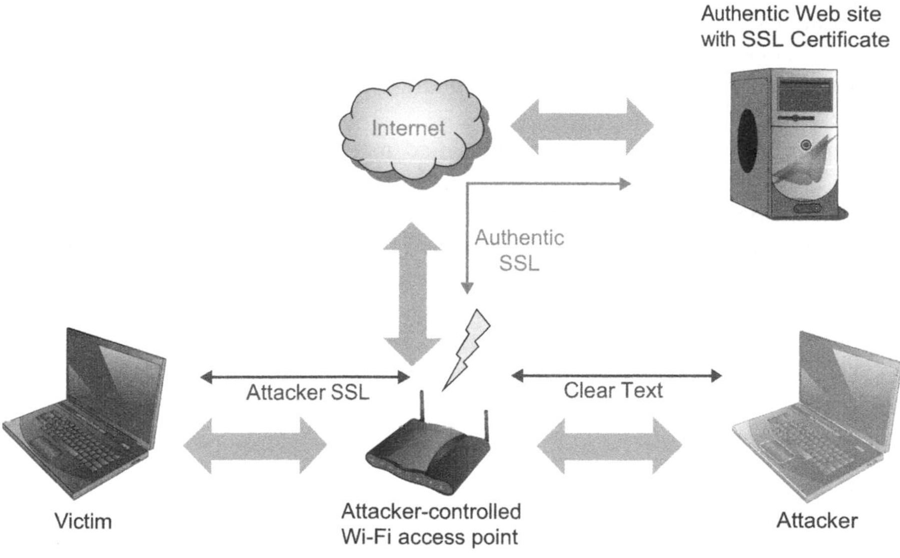

FIGURE 5.1

Man-in-the-middle SSL.

and password, they can begin to research more about the consumer and generally will be able to find additional systems they can access.

Another very well-known attack leverages interception of HTTP session cookies to hijack another user's authenticated session on a web site and begin acting as that user. Eric Butler's Firesheep extension for the Firefox browser (http://codebutler.com/firesheep) demonstrates how easy this type of attack can be. Although using strong encryption such as WPA on Wi-Fi and other local measures can make things more difficult, as long as web sites do not require HTTPS end-to-end this type of attack remains possible.

Android Devices as an Attack Vector

While the press and many security researchers largely focus on attacks directed at mobile devices, a growing concern is use of the Android device as an attack vector, particularly in environments where sensitive data are stored. The most common scenarios are found in corporations with trade secrets, intellectual property, or other data requiring protection. Corporations often implement sophisticated systems designed to prevent, or at least detect, the theft of data. These systems are not only expensive to purchase, but they generally require skilled staff to maintain, monitor, and then act on the information they provide.

Until recently, most data protection systems focused on securing the perimeter of the enterprise to keep attackers outside the protected areas. Over time, systems designed to protect against internal threats were also developed. The most recent systems delve even deeper into the network and infrastructure in an attempt to thwart attacks. These systems focus on areas such as data loss prevention (DLP), network access control (NAC), and network forensics. However, currently available solutions do not yet fully address the threat presented by mobile devices.

Smartphones are obviously popular, and most people use them as intended. Often, they are personally owned and heavily used devices, so asking someone to forfeit their device is an intrusive request. For these reasons, Android devices and other smartphones end up in locations which house sensitive information, and yet no one shows concern. If instead someone brought a digital camera, voice recording device, camcorder, external hard drive, or their own networking equipment, it might raise some eyebrows. Of course, an Android device essentially contains all of these features and more in a compact and innocent looking device.

Data Storage

Perhaps the simplest example of how an Android device can be used to steal information is to use it as a USB mass storage device. Until recently, smartphones had very little data storage. However, as NAND flash matured, manufacturers realized they could cost-effectively create devices that stored many gigabytes of data. Android devices today can easily store eight to 16 GB of data on the NAND flash, and many devices include an external SD card, which can store an additional 16 GB or more.

Recording Devices

Android devices are also well equipped to record nearly anything around them. They can easily take photographs of sensitive equipment or documents. They can also record video that captures a path through a building, including the sounds, security stations, windows, stairwells, and other items of interest along the way. Finally, Android devices can also passively record audio. All of this can be done without drawing any attention.

Circumventing Network Controls

Perhaps an even more dangerous feature is the ability of an Android device to provide a separate network connection for a computer or devices with wireless capabilities. There are several ways to achieve this. In one scenario, an attacker (perhaps a disgruntled employee) could connect their Android device to their workstation. Casual observation may not raise any alarm since many people do this to charge their phones while at work. However, by installing a small program on both the Android device and the computer, a new network connection is provided to the computer. In this case, the traffic routed from the computer and out the Android device is completely outside the control of the environment. This connection completely circumvents the firewall, network access control, data loss prevention, and other security controls in place at the company.

The newest Android devices do away with the USB cables and software packages needed in the above scenario. Instead, the Android device becomes a fully functional wireless access point through which the computer can connect. This scenario just as effectively circumvents the network security controls in place and can be performed with the device in a briefcase or pocket.

REALLY SNEAKY TECHNIQUES

If anyone believes cyber criminals or other attackers are not intelligent and creative, they are showing a serious lapse in judgment. So, let's think outside the box using some of the techniques described above.

For this scenario, the attacker is an employee who works at a company, which has significant trade secrets and intellectual property. (The attacker would not necessarily need to work there; however, it keeps the example simple.) Many of the executives who have access to this information also have laptops and smartphones. Many of these same executives drink coffee at a popular cafe, which offers free Wi-Fi. The wireless access point at the coffee shop is called "indigo" and since they do not want to require a password, the access point is open and unencrypted. While the executives are drinking, eating, or meeting at the cafe, they connect their smartphones and laptops to the Wi-Fi.

When they return to the office, they leave the wireless active on their smartphones and laptops. The disgruntled employee, of course, knows about the cafe's wireless access point and decides to enable the access point feature on his Android device. Naturally, he has root access on his device, so he also installs and runs software that allows him to capture the network traffic. When one of the executives gets close to his Android device, the smartphone or laptop associates with his access point. He is then able to intercept traffic and either capture sensitive files and communications or perhaps capture credentials he could then use to access key network resources.

While there are obstacles the attacker would have to overcome to implement this scenario, it is highly plausible and illustrates the unique risks Android devices present when used as an attack vector.

SECURITY CONSIDERATIONS

Security, like development, is an art. There might be some who do not agree with that statement but very few of those individuals are going to read a forensics and security book. Security is an artistic process in the sense that art is "the products of human creativity" and "a superior skill that you can learn by study and practice and observation" (WordNet Search, n.d.). So why is all of this relevant? Successful security strategies require the right mix and balance of experience, judgment, risk assessment, creativity, observation, skill, and maybe even a little bit of luck. This section aims to cover a few broad concepts related to Android and security.

Security Philosophy

Security is nearly always a compromise, weighing the risk of an attack against the costs (financial or other costs) of mitigating that risk. While in theory an entirely secure system is possible, in practice it is nearly impossible to achieve, especially when social engineering attacks are available. The task of securing a system is very difficult even when the security professional controls access to the device including physical and remote access.

Mobile devices are even more difficult to secure than traditional systems. Most of the control that a corporate security engineer would have over a computer system is not possible on an Android device. First, the device is comprised of hardware and software assembled and maintained by a large, complex, and diverse group of participants including the core Android team, software and hardware from the manufacturer, and software and hardware from the wireless carrier. Furthermore, the device owner has the ability to install custom apps and even modify the device significantly if they have sufficient privileges. Finally, the device travels through many networks, none of which can be fully trusted. Yes, securing mobile devices is a major challenge.

In spite of these challenges, certain security controls could be engineered into the device. To summarize an overall strategy and philosophy, the following meme is useful:

If you secure it, they won't come.

The concept—adapted from Universal Studio's 1989 film "Field of Dreams," where a voice is heard encouraging the lead character to build a baseball field on his Iowa farm—is simple. In the movie, the voice repeatedly says, "If you build it, he will come" (Ten, n.d.). Eventually, the lead character does build the field and, in fact, mysterious guests do show up. But you'll have to watch the movie for the complete story.

So, how does this apply to mobile security? There is a wide margin between the ideal cryptographically secure system and a system that stores all information in plain text in a well-organized and known structure as described in the previous com.android.email example. Since the mobile device is a risk from many different vectors, even encrypted data can be compromised. However, providing some level of obfuscation or encryption will complicate the process required for an attacker to compromise the data. While this approach is not 100% secure, attackers are pragmatic and tend to target the easily accessible data.

One argument against this approach is that obfuscation or encryption that can be compromised provides a false sense of security causing the user to act more carelessly with the device in the belief that the security of their data is impenetrable. Whereas if the data are stored as plain text and the users are aware of the risk, they will use significant caution with the device.

Ultimately, the individual and corporate consumers of mobile devices will steer the mobile security ecosystem in the direction they value through their purchasing decisions. This necessarily depends on education. Consumers must be sufficiently aware of the data security risks and possible solutions available.

There are a number of potential solutions which, while not providing a cryptographically secure system, do improve the security of the data by increasing the complexity of a successful attack. The list below illustrates several concepts:

1. Require the user to enter the password the first time an app is run after a reboot, and only store the password in memory. In this case, the password is not stored on the device in plain text. However, it is in memory and an attacker with sufficient privileges on the device could recover the password.
2. Further, secure the concept above by encrypting the password stored in memory with a key based on time, pseudo-random data, etc. In this fashion, the attacker now must have root on the device and instead of just dumping the processes' memory, they must locate the encryption key, the encrypted password, and the algorithm used to comprise the password.
3. Building further, the memory password could expire in time or the encryption key used in memory could be changed.
4. If the password is stored on the NAND flash, encrypt it with a pass phrase, which is entered after the device reboots.

Although none of the ideas provide a completely secure system, the level of effort and privilege needed to compromise the data are orders of magnitude higher than compromising sensitive data stored in plain text, and thus deters most attackers.

US Federal Computer Crime Laws and Regulations

There are a number of federal laws in the US that relate to the security of data at rest and in transit. The goal of this section is to simply enumerate several of the more relevant laws and provide a brief background on them. In total, more than 40 federal statues exist which can be used in the prosecution of computer-related crimes (Country, n.d.). In addition, each State typically has laws and regulations addressing computer crimes.

At the Federal level, the US Department of Justice (DoJ) divides computer crime into three distinct areas, two of which have broad application to the types of crimes involved when compromising a mobile device. The two areas are (Country, n.d.):

1. Crimes that target a computer network or device directly including hacking, viruses, worms, malware, sniffers, and others.
2. Crimes committed using computer networks or devices such as fraud, identity theft, corporate espionage, and so on.

The Computer Fraud and Abuse Act (CFAA) focuses on attacks against government and financial institution computers or computers involved in interstate or foreign commerce. The Act covers narrow areas, such as accessing computers without proper authorization to gain data related to national security issues, as well as more broad sections, such as accessing a computer without proper authorization in order to commit fraud or to gain something of value. The CFAA was amended by the National Information Infrastructure Protection Act to cover new abuses and to include those intending to commit the crime.

The Electronic Communications Privacy Act (ECPA) is another law covering computer crimes, which makes it illegal to intercept stored or transmitted electronic communication without authorization. The ECPA contains several key areas:

- Communication in transit including oral, wire, or electronic communications (Wiretap).
- Data at rest (Stored Communication Act) that protects data stored on nonvolatile memory.
- Collecting communication metadata such as phone numbers, IP addresses, and other data used to route communication (but not the message itself). This is called the "pen registers and trap and trace devices," which refers to the actual devices and techniques used to capture the information.

One final law worth pointing out is the Economic Espionage Act, which passed in 1996 and focused on the theft of trade secrets. Prior to the law's enactment, it was difficult to prosecute economic or corporate espionage. However, by defining trade secrets and requiring the owner of the information to have taken reasonable measures to protect the secret, it was now possible to criminalize the theft of intellectual property.

This section barely addresses the significant body of legal work which can be used to prosecute computer crimes. However, it should be clear that there are laws designed to protect data both in transit and at rest.

In addition to Federal and State laws that criminalize computer crimes, a host of regulatory bodies govern corporations who operate in industries which involve sensitive data. Many of the regulations provide not only specific guidelines and requirements the firms must follow, but also civil and criminal statues with both financial penalties and, in the most serious cases, may even involve incarceration. A list of the better known regulations include the following:

- Payment card industry data security standard (PCI)
- Health Insurance Portability and Accountability Act (HIPAA)
- HITECH Act Enforcement Interim Final Rule (additions to HIPAA)
- Federal Information Security Management Act (FISMA)
- Family Education Rights and Privacy Act of 1974 (FERPA)
- Gramm-Leach-Bliley Financial Services Modernization Act of 1999 (GLBA)
- Sarbanes Oxley (SOX)

Clearly the US Congress recognizes the importance of data and computer security and provides a wide array of laws, regulations, and other resources to compel and enforce the security measures necessary to successfully operate the systems critical to commerce.

Open Source Versus Closed Source

There is active debate discussed often on the Internet about whether open source software is more secure than closed source software. As with many long-standing debates, the main proponents of each side are committed to their conclusions and the debate continues on.

The basic reason behind the belief that open source software is more secure is that the code can be examined for flaws and quickly fixed. Implicit in this belief are two assumptions:

1. Developers will perform security code reviews on open source projects.
2. The software's maintainer will quickly patch the security flaws.

Of course, if both the steps are not taken, then clearly the open source software will contain security flaws and without the patch, attackers will have precisely the information they need to exploit the bug. However, if both of these steps are taken, then the security of the code will evolve with the benefit of many people examining the code and the resulting patches.

In contrast, the closed source model relies on a company developing secure code, scouring their code for security flaws, patching the flaws, and then distributing the updates in a timely manner to subscribers. For anyone tasked with securing desktops running Microsoft's Windows platforms, they are well aware of the continuous stream of patches released on the second Tuesday of each month, which has been dubbed "Patch Tuesday." Microsoft also releases patches for serious exploits outside of the scheduled Patch Tuesdays.

In a fairly high profile finding, Microsoft acknowledged (Microsoft Security Advisory, n.d.) that security researcher Tavis Ormandy discovered a 17-year-old security flaw in every 32-bit version of Microsoft Windows since 1993 (Windows NT through Windows 7) (Johnston, n.d.). Ormandy posted the full details of the exploit to the Full Disclosure mailing list nearly seven months after notifying Microsoft of the vulnerability on June 12, 2009 ([Full-disclosure] Microsoft, n.d.). It is noteworthy that the official advisory to Microsoft's clients only happened after Ormandy posted the disclosure and after that point, Microsoft acknowledged the security flaw within one day.

In another recent example, security firm Matta Consulting discovered numerous critical security flaws in Cisco System's Unified Videoconferencing platform. The flaws enable a malicious third party to gain full control of the device, harvest user passwords, and possibly launch an attack against other parts of the target infrastructure (Cisco Unified Video, n.d.). Cisco acknowledged the flaws in their advisory with the hard-coded passwords representing the most alarming flaw:

> *The Linux shadow password file contains three hard-coded user names and passwords. The passwords cannot be changed, and the accounts cannot be deleted. Attackers could leverage these accounts to obtain remote access to a device by using permitted remote access protocols.*
>
> **(Cisco Security Advisory, n.d.)**

In the end, software development is a creative endeavor which, despite all best efforts and intention, will likely contain flaws. The overall security of the software or system is directly related to how quickly the flaws are discovered and resolved. Although over eight years old (an eternity from a security standpoint), David A. Wheeler's "Secure Programming for Linux and Unix HOWTO" provides an excellent overview of the debate and represents both the sides. He quotes Elias Levy (also known as Aleph One and moderator of the Bugtraq full disclose list in addition to CTO and co-founder of SecurityFocus) as saying:

> *So does all this mean Open Source Software is no better than closed source software when it comes to security vulnerabilities? No. Open Source Software certainly does have the potential to be more secure than its closed source counterpart. But make no mistake, simply being open source is no guarantee of security.*
>
> **(Secure Programming, n.d.)**

At the end of his HOWTO, Wheeler concludes that open source software can be more secure if the following happens:

- If the code is first closed source and then opened, it will start as less secure but over time will improve.
- People must review the code.
- The reviewers and developers must know how to write secure code.
- Once flaws are found, they must be quickly fixed and distributed.

Ultimately, each individual will have to decide if they believe open source or closed source software is more secure. Since large parts of Android system are indeed open source, it is likely the software will initially have a number of flaws discovered, but over time they will be addressed resulting in a more secure system.

Encrypted NAND Flash

The techniques and strategies for secure data in transmission are, generally speaking, more mature, vetted, and secure than the technologies used to securely store data at rest. The reason data in transmission are easier to secure is because the duration of time in which the information must be protected is short and well defined. After the transmission of data in transit is complete, the keys protecting the data can be discarded. In contrast, data at rest are nonvolatile and must, at any time, be accessible to the user. That means that the keys for decryption must be available on the device (or the user must type them every time, which is impractical) and thus they are accessible to an attacker.

Bruce Schneier, a respected security technologist, cryptographer, and author, summarizes the difficulties of using encryption to protect data at rest:

> *Cryptography was invented to protect communications: data in motion. This is how cryptography was used throughout most of history, and this is how the militaries of the world developed the science. Alice was the sender, Bob the receiver, and Eve the eavesdropper. Even when cryptography was used to protect stored data—data at rest—it was viewed as a form of communication. In "Applied Cryptography," I described encrypting stored data in this way: "a stored message is a way for someone to communicate with himself through time." Data storage was just a subset of data communication.*
>
> *In modern networks, the difference is much more profound. Communications are immediate and instantaneous. Encryption keys can be ephemeral, and systems like the STU-III telephone can be designed such that encryption keys are created at the beginning of a call and destroyed as soon as the call is completed. Data storage, on the other hand, occurs over time. Any encryption keys must exist as long as the encrypted data exists. And storing those keys becomes as important as storing the unencrypted data was. In a way, encryption doesn't reduce the number of secrets that must be stored securely; it just makes them much smaller.*
>
> *Historically, the reason key management worked for stored data was that the key could be stored in a secure location: the human brain. People would remember keys and, barring physical and emotional attacks on the people themselves, would not divulge them. In a sense, the keys were stored in a "computer" that was not attached to any network. And there they were safe.*
>
> *This whole model falls apart on the Internet. Much of the data stored on the Internet is only peripherally intended for use by people; it's primarily intended*

for use by other computers. And therein lies the problem. Keys can no longer be stored in people's brains. They need to be stored on the same computer, or at least the network, that the data resides on. And that is much riskier.

(Schneier on, n.d.)

Several other platforms, notably later models of Apple's iPhones, implement encryption on the user portions of the NAND flash. However, in the case of the 3.x versions of Apple's iOS, the encryption was quickly defeated for the reasons highlighted previously. As of March 2011, the encryption of iOS 4.x has not yet been broken. However, it is likely that over time this will happen.

The forensic strategies for dealing with encrypted NAND flash differ from unencrypted ones. If the NAND flash is not encrypted, the memory could be physically read via a chip-off or JTAG process and then decoded. However, with an encrypted NAND flash, this technique will no longer work. Instead, to extract the unencrypted data, the process executes on the device while it is running. In forensics, this is referred to as a live acquisition and is used in other scenarios such as a workstation or server that encrypts the contents of the hard drive or other storage device.

Encryption will play a growing role in securing both data in transit and data at rest. However, the data at rest will nearly always be vulnerable to attack. In this instance, the security designers must find the balance between a cryptographically secure system and one that offers little protection. The compromise will result in a system that provides reasonable protection of the data at rest and in transit without encumbering the user to the point where device is no longer useful.

INDIVIDUAL SECURITY STRATEGIES

While the large part of this chapter has focused on issues with mobile devices and data security, there are user practices that can minimize the risk of compromise. As before, this list is not intended to be comprehensive. Rather, it provides a solid basis for securing the device.

1. Always use a data network you trust. For mobile devices, this may include your wireless carrier's data network or Wi-Fi access point at work, home, or other trusted locations. This ensures that the networks used to transmit sensitive data are not malicious or used by an attacker to compromise your sensitive data. Although a carrier's network can be compromised, there is far greater security in place at a large company than on a smaller data network. Furthermore, while it is easy to acquire, setup, and manage a rogue Wi-Fi access point, it is far more difficult to implement rogue cellular data connections. So, in general, the cellular data connections provided by the wireless carriers reduce the risk of attack.
2. Always place a pass code on the Android device to thwart a casual attacker from gaining access to your sensitive data. Ideally, the Android device should perform a full wipe of the user data if the pass code is input incorrectly more than a set

number of attempts. That way an attacker cannot compromise your pass code through brute force. Also, if possible use the option for an alphanumeric password over a four-digit numeric PIN or pattern lock. The alphanumeric codes provide far greater security by allowing more complex pass codes. Think of the pass code on your device as similar to a password on your computer. It is hard to imagine (perhaps just for security researchers) that anyone would have a computer that did not have a password.

3. Check the free appWatchdog service at http://viaforensics.com/appwatchdog/ to determine if the applications you use pass a basic security test. appWatchdog audits mobile apps to determine if they securely store your user name, password, and sensitive app data. The web site provides a result of pass, warn, or fail for each area tested and details of what information was recovered. Currently, a mobile app version of appWatchdog is being developed that will allow the user to install directly on an Android (or iPhone) device and determine the audit status of installed apps. It will also allow the user to directly contact the app developer to request resolution to an audit issue as well as other notification options.
4. Never click on links in SMS messages and ideally avoid links in e-mail messages, especially shortened links like bit.ly or goo.gl. Smartphone and computer tablet users are three times more susceptible to e-mail phishing scams than traditional PC and laptop users, according to research by security firm Trusteer (Donohue, n.d.). The research determined that it is more difficult to identify fraudulent web sites from a smartphone due to reduced screen sizes and lack of software protecting the user from phishing scams. The best way to ensure that you are visiting the valid web site is to either type it in manually, or (perhaps a better approach) allow a trusted search engine to locate the web site on your behalf. This allows the user to type (or mistype) the name of the company and allows the search engine to find the appropriate sites. Some search engines, such as Google, are now attempting to deter malicious or compromised web sites and this provides an additional layer of protection for smartphone users.
5. Consider using an alternate web browser on your Android device. As mentioned previously, cyber criminals are pragmatic, which is why for many years they focused on attacking Microsoft Windows and largely ignored operating systems such as Linux and Mac. In the mobile environment, many of the bundled browsers are based on the open source WebKit project. As such, it is likely that initial web attacks against Android and other smartphone devices will focus on browsers utilizing WebKit. By using an alternative browser, you may find far fewer attacks targeting your platform. However, this may only provide a nominal and temporary increase in security.
6. When installing apps from the Android Market, ensure that the app is only granted permissions necessary to operate. If you are installing an enhanced alarm clock application and it requests access to your SMS and web history data, you should not grant it permission. Although this will not protect you from all malicious apps, it is an important layer of Android's security and one the user must take responsibility for.

Over time, not only will this list grow and evolve but hopefully new security controls will be introduced, which will help secure the mobile device and sensitive data.

CORPORATE SECURITY STRATEGIES

Corporations typically have more complex security requirements than individuals because they are responsible for protecting the entire corporation from both internal and external attacks. In addition, they may belong to a regulated industry required to operate under some of the guidelines listed earlier in this chapter. For these reasons, more fine grained control over assets, including mobile devices, is required.

Policies

One important aspect of mobile device management in corporations is a close evaluation of current policies making sure to update them for the new situations presented by mobile devices. Most policies do not account for smartphone and tablet devices and the situations that might arise through their use. Although a complete review of corporate policies is warranted, there are at least a few which will certainly require attention. They include the following:

- Acceptable Use (for company resources, now including mobile devices)
- Data Security (obviously want to place policies around mobile devices)
- Backups and Data Retention (will likely be impacted, especially from an electronic discovery standpoint)

Although updating policies does not directly improve security through information technology, it provides critical direction not only to the employees but also to the security architects and those involved in internal investigations and disciplines. If you have an outdated policy in place, it can be used against you. For example, if your Acceptable Use policy simply adds mobile devices into the description of covered resources, then all of the policies in place that allow a corporation to investigate a device they own are now explicitly defined. Otherwise in a contentious legal battle, it is quite possible opposing counsel would make the case that the mobile devices were not covered by policy and thus the evidence found on the device (e.g., company confidential documents) is not admissible. While your legal team may refute the argument, it is far less expensive and more effective to simply update the policy to include mobile devices.

Password/Pattern/PIN Lock

Passwords, pattern, and PIN locks are neither consistently nor effectively implemented on Android devices. However, they do offer some protection. These features have improved since they first appeared and will likely continue to improve over time. With the exponential increase in processing power and a simultaneous reduction in cost, using brute force techniques to crack protection mechanisms is affordable and more common each year. However, if the device is lost or stolen, it provides a basic level of protection that would be effective against nontechnical criminals.

All pass codes are not created equal. The most effective pass code is the one that allows or requires an alphanumeric password. While entering these codes is far more cumbersome for the users, it greatly increases the effort needed to crack the password. The next most effective pass code is the pattern lock found in the first Android device and many since then. The pattern technique introduced a new way to approach locking the device and as such required the user to learn the new technique resulting in a more effective lock. Instead of reusing old approaches (such as the PIN), the user had to come up with a new pattern and thus it would be hard for an attacker to use information about the person to guess the pattern lock. Perhaps for familiarity, the venerable PIN was also included in many Android devices. While it would be better to use a PIN than leave the phone unlocked, the PIN is probably the easiest lock to defeat. They typically have a finite number of digits (four is the common number), which dangerously constrains the number of overall combinations. Furthermore, the PIN has been used to secure many other system, most well known are Automated Teller Machine (ATM) cards. People tend to reuse PINs and to base them on easily discoverable facts about them.

As suggested in the individual strategies in the previous section, the pass code lock should have a maximum number of attempts allowed after which the device should perform a factory reset and full wipe of the user data partitions. This will prevent a brute force attack against the easier-to-defeat pass codes (i.e., the four-digit PIN) and provide an additional layer of security.

Remote Wipe of Device

One of the most sought after security features for smartphones by corporate security managers is the ability to remotely wipe the device. The feature is, without a doubt, extremely important and powerful. However, it is a very fragile feature, and the confidence it instills in security managers might be too high.

The basic premise behind the remote wipe is that the company can issue a command to the device causing it to wipe all data and perform a factory reset. Many of the smartphone platforms are building hooks into their system to allow this control. However, the features were not designed from the beginning and do not yet provide enough reliability to ensure high security.

Even provided the remote wipe hooks are present and working effectively, it is quite easy to prevent the remote wipe command by simply not placing the device on the network using airplane mode, removing the SIM card, or other such techniques. In fact, some corporation might first disable a terminated employee's cellular account and then send the remote wipe command. In most cases, they will have inadvertently removed their ability to remotely wipe the device. While the device is no longer connected to the network, it will still have full access to the data. Savvy device owners who have root access on their device could also look into filtering such requests to simply ignore them. However, the largest issue is simply that the remote wipe feature is not sufficiently mature.

In Android 2.1 on the Motorola Droid, the remote wipe feature triggered using Microsoft's Exchange ActiveSync did not cause the device to wipe data. However, when the same feature was tested on Android 2.2 on the Motorola Droid, the remote wipe did occur. If you are relying on the remote wipe feature for data security, you need to ensure that the remote wipe ability works on each of the Android hardware platforms for each Android version installed. This, unfortunately, is a difficult undertaking for most IT departments because the devices are widely distributed and do not have a good central administrative tool (more on that later).

One fairly simple technique to overcome the limitations of remote wipe is to install an application on the device that will automatically wipe the device if it is unable to check in with the enterprise system after a specific amount of time. Using such a technique (often called a watchdog or countdown app), provides a significant improvement in data security because the device will automatically erase if unable to connect to the corporate system after a certain number of attempts. So, even if a device is offline, security managers can ensure all corporate data will be wiped within a specific time frame. Of course, if a user disconnects his or her phone from the network for a long time for legitimate reasons, it will result in an erased phone, so user education on this feature is important. At this time, very few (if any) applications exist that support this feature.

There is another technique that addresses data residing on the NAND flash. It is possible to develop an app (and a few do exist) that would routinely erase the unused (unallocated) space on the device's user data storage partition. The benefit of this being that (most) deleted data would no longer be recoverable, even with a physical image. This erasing can be accomplished by having the app simply write a file with 0xFF until the partition fills up. At that point, the file is deleted and thus the allocated space has been overwritten. Of course, there can be many repercussions to such a program, including shortening the life of the NAND flash, causing the device to become unresponsive while writing the file, wearing down the battery, or causing other apps to crash or lose data if they try to access the partition when it is completely full.

Upgrade to Latest Software

Although the smartphone market is innovating quickly, it is far more difficult for enterprises to upgrade core infrastructure such as their Microsoft Exchange environment. However, the last two versions of Microsoft Exchange offer enhanced mobile management and security mechanisms. When Exchange is upgraded to the latest version (currently Exchange 2010), additional options to securely manage your device are available. Ensuring that the corporate infrastructure is up-to-date will improve not only the manageability but the overall security of connected mobile devices.

Similarly, the mobile devices themselves should apply updates as they become available. While in some cases a new bug or security flaw could be introduced, in general the updated software will not only patch previously discovered flaws but also add additional management and security features. The example from the remote wipe section above illustrates this well as Android 2.1 on the Motorola Droid did not properly execute the remote wipe command whereas Android 2.2 did.

Remote Device Management Features

Corporate customers have a growing need to manage the mobile devices connected to their infrastructure. Although the list of features will vary between companies, a general list of requirements might include the following:

- remotely provision devices
- remotely wipe devices
- enforce IT policies such as pass code, encryption, minimum OS versions, upgrade policies, allowed/denied applications, and more
- remotely install/upgrade apps

As of Android 2.2, new device administration application programming interfaces (APIs) were introduced. They include the ability for apps to incorporate the types of policy management listed earlier. Specifically, they support (Device Administration, n.d.) the following abilities.

- Password enabled: Requires that devices ask for PIN or passwords.
- Minimum password length: Sets the required number of characters for the password. For example, you can require PIN or passwords to have at least six characters.
- Alphanumeric password required: Requires that passwords have a combination of letters and numbers. They may include symbolic characters.
- Maximum failed password attempts: Specifies how many times a user can enter the wrong password before the device wipes its data. The Device Administration API also allows administrators to remotely reset the device to factory defaults. This secures data in case the device is lost or stolen.
- Maximum inactivity time lock: Sets the length of time since the user last touched the screen or pressed a button before the device locks the screen. When this happens, users need to enter their PIN or passwords again before they can use their devices and access data. The value can be between 1 and 60 min.
- Prompt user to set a new password.
- Lock device immediately.
- Wipe the device's data (i.e., restore the device to its factory defaults).

On the Device Administration page on developer.android.com (Device Administration, n.d.), several examples of this API are demonstrated, as illustrated in Fig. 5.2.

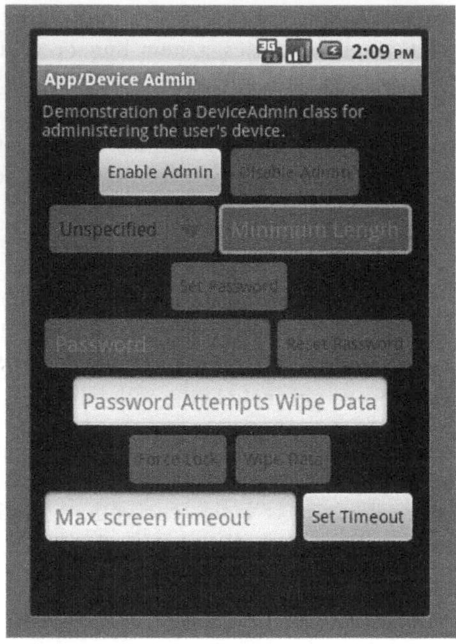

FIGURE 5.2

Device administration API sample.

When a user installs an app that uses the new administration APIs, they are presented with an Enable Device Admin screen, shown in Fig. 5.3.

Although this is an improvement over no device management, it falls well short of the needs and requirements of corporate customers. Also, though the APIs exist, developers must incorporate them into their apps.

Several companies are trying to fill the void in full feature device management. However, the solutions for smartphones are also still quite immature. Investing in a third-party solution may address a short-term need. However, over time, Android, the manufacturers, and device developers will develop more sophisticated management features and tools. Similarly, many corporate devices synchronize with the e-mail system using Microsoft's Exchange ActiveSync (EAS) protocol and management features continue to mature in this platform. So if immediate security concerns necessitate better remote management of devices, a corporation might consider implementing third-party tools for an incremental improvement in security. However, there is a risk that these tools will not meet or exceed the manufacturers' tools and thus the technology and personnel investment will not prove worthwhile.

As much of the corporate data found on mobile devices centers around e-mail, focusing security efforts in this area can yield good results. Several companies have recognized this need and have developed their own e-mail clients, which implement a variety of additional security mechanisms including two-factor authentication,

FIGURE 5.3

Enable device admin.

encrypted data stores, and additional management interfaces. However, security-conscious entities should audit the software to ensure they actually deliver on the functionality they claim to implement.

Clearly, remote device administration is important to corporate clients and while support for these features are still immature, expect significant improvements over the next few releases of Android.

Application and Device Audit

It is difficult to secure mobile devices and their data if you do not have a full understanding of what information is at risk. Corporations can initiate a mobile security and risk mitigation audit to evaluate the data exposed on mobile devices. By analyzing the actual devices and operating systems in use at their company, it is possible to determine what data are stored, where it might be at risk (on the device, in transit, in backups, etc.), and create specific policies, procedures, or even software implementation to minimize the risk.

A typical audit can include evaluation of many criteria including

- What type of corporate data might be stored on the device
- Where that data are stored

- What other applications can be installed, and access corporate data
- Effectiveness/capability of remote wiping and device administration
- Ability to implement corporate security policies
- Secure storage and transmission of passwords, authentication information, and other sensitive data
- Effectiveness of encryption

Once the supported devices are well understood, the task of securing the data at rest and in transit is less overwhelming, and specific strategies to minimize unacceptable risk can be developed.

As with other areas of information security, a strategy and ongoing process is necessary to maintain appropriate security measures and evaluate risk.

APP DEVELOPMENT SECURITY STRATEGIES

One final area extremely important to mobile security is the apps that are developed and installed. This includes not only third-party apps, but also apps distributed by the operating system developer (Android in this case), device manufacturers, and the wireless carriers. The apps are the primary mechanism by which users interact with their mobile device to access the information they are interested in. Often the information is sensitive and provides private details about the user.

Mobile App Security Testing

After discovering numerous mobile application security vulnerabilities in the course of performing forensic work, this author and colleagues at viaForensics began auditing the security of data in popular applications and disclosed their findings publicly on our web site. The goal of the free public service, called appWatchdog, is to improve mobile app data security and protect consumers. As consumer awareness of the data security risks rises, developers will be encouraged to thoroughly review their apps prior to release and achieve a higher level of security. The findings can be viewed at http://viaforensics.com/appwatchdog/. viaForensics plans to release a mobile app that will check the installed apps on an Android device and provide appWatchdog results for those already audited. It will also allow the consumer to suggest an app for review as well as contact the app developer if they have any concerns.

The appWatchdog service uses forensic and security assessment techniques to determine whether user names, passwords, credit card numbers, or other application data are being insecurely stored. The process involves installing the application and running it in the manner in which a consumer uses the app. The device is then forensically imaged and analyzed for personal information and application data. The findings are first communicated to the app developer and then publicly disclosed in order to provide this information directly to consumers. Users can then make an informed decision on whether or not they wish to continue use of that app, or perhaps wait for the developer to release a more secure version.

Each app is reviewed based on certain criteria that depend on the specific uses for the app. For example, with a mobile payment app, the app would be analyzed for user name, password, application data, and credit card numbers. However, for other applications, credit card numbers may not be relevant. The following criteria are explained in further detail, with the top three being the most applicable to most applications:

- *Securely stores passwords?* If any type of password is being stored unencrypted on the device, the application would get a "Fail."
- *Securely stores user names?* Application data are examined to determine whether user names are being stored unencrypted on the device.
- *Securely stores application data?* Each application is analyzed for app-related data. For example, financial apps are searched for account numbers, balances, and transfer information. Other applications might store additional personal user data, such as e-mail address, phone number, or address.
- *Securely stores credit card information?* For applications handling credit card information, data are examined to determine whether the full credit card number is stored unencrypted on the device as well as any supporting data associated with it, such as expiration date or security number on the back of the card.
- *Additional security tests:* These tests can include capturing wireless data sent from the mobile device and examining that traffic for user names, passwords, PINs, and any other relevant application data. Additional security tests are typically more time consuming and therefore only performed for an in-depth application security review.

The appWatchdog service only provides a basic indication of whether a mobile app implements security. By combining advanced mobile forensic and security techniques, a far deeper analysis of a mobile app is possible. The items listed below are some of the criteria that should be evaluated in order to determine whether a mobile application is secure.

- How does the application handle web history and caching?
- Does the application securely transmit login data?
- Does the application avoid MITM attacks?
- Does the application securely transmit sensitive data?
- Is the application protected from session hijacking?
- Is the application able to permanently delete data and prevent storage on the device?
- Does the application securely handle interruptions?
- Does the application properly secure data in backups?

A thorough application security audit leverages both advanced forensics and security tests to uncover security flaws, protecting both developers and users. via-Forensics provides these testing services and a certification, called appSecure. A similar testing methodology can be effectively applied by internal forensic and security teams provided they have the tools and expertise, as well as the budget and time, to execute the tests.

App Security Strategies

The results of appWatchdog and appSecure have led to some general guidelines that mobile app developers should consider as they design, develop, and test their apps. This list, as with others, is not necessarily exhaustive but provides some noteworthy concepts for consideration.

User Names

Avoid storing user names in plain text on the device. For obvious usability issues, you may decide to cache the user name on the device so the consumer does not have to type it in every time. However, consider masking a portion of the user name that would provide enough information for the consumer to identify their user name but not enough for an attacker to have the entire user name. The user name is one component needed to log into an account and the less an attacker knows, the less effective they will be.

For example, let us assume an application which accesses sensitive health information requires a user name. The consumer creates one called "andrewhoog." However, after the initial login, if the application only stores "andr****" and then displays that back to the user, it would be clear that they are logging into the correct account. However, an attacker might only get the first four characters. Furthermore, if the mask (using "*" in this case but could be presented in other ways) does not give away the overall length of the user name, it makes it even more difficult for the attacker to guess.

Finally, more online services are requiring more complex user names that must be of a certain length and be alphanumeric. So, whereas a user name "andrewhoog" might be fairly easy to guess, AndrewHoog6712 would be far more difficult. Some sites may even place further restrictions on the user name where it cannot contain any portion of your basic profile information such as your name.

Passwords

Perhaps far more concerning are applications that store the password in plain text. There are several strategies to avoid this serious problem. First, as discussed in the "Security philosophy" section, you could simply force the users to type their password in each time they run the app. If you think about logging into a banking web site from your home computer, you must log in every time. While you stay logged in for your current session, once a certain period of inactivity has passed (or you log out), you can no longer access the protected web site without re-entering your user name and password.

Another approach to consider is the use of security tokens to avoid storing the real password on the mobile device. If a user securely authenticates to a protected resource on the Internet, a security token can be generated, which not only expires after a certain period of time but is also unique to that device. While someone with physical access to the phone could access the protected resource, it would only last until the token expired, at which point they would need the user name and password again. Furthermore, if the security token was specific to the device and was compromised remotely, the token would not provide access to the restricted resource. Methodologies that use the security token approach also would not place any other protected resource on the Internet at risk, even if the account holder used the same user name and password (which is quite common).

Implementing a token-based authentication scheme is more complicated than a simple user name and password and is a methodology that is not as widely used or understood by developers. However, a number of APIs that provide this functionality are available and are maturing. One framework is called OAuth and is supported by many of Google's services. There are other APIs, but they tend to focus on a particular service. There are similarities and the OAuth web site describes the connection to other services this way:

> *OAuth is the standardization and combined wisdom of many well established industry protocols. It is similar to other protocols currently in use (Google AuthSub, AOL OpenAuth, Yahoo BBAuth, Upcoming API, Flickr API, Amazon Web Services API, etc). Each protocol provides a proprietary method for exchanging user credentials for an access token or ticker. OAuth was created by carefully studying each of these protocols and extracting the best practices and commonality that will allow new implementations as well as a smooth transition for existing services to support OAuth.*
>
> *An area where OAuth is more evolved than some of the other protocols and services is its direct handling of non-website services. OAuth has built in support for desktop applications, mobile devices, set-top boxes, and of course websites. Many of the protocols today use a shared secret hardcoded into your software to communicate, something which poses an issue when the service trying to access your private data is open source.*
>
> **(Introduction—OAuthn, n.d.)**

Since Google is moving toward OAuth, they provide detailed information about the APIs and how to use them. On the Google Code web site, they provide the following basic overview of the OAuth process (Default, n.d.):

1. Your application requests access and gets an unauthorized request token from Google's authorization server.
2. Google asks the user to grant you access to the required data.
3. Your application gets an authorized request token from the authorization server.
4. You exchange the authorized request token for an access token.
5. You use the access token to request data from Google's service access servers.

As you can tell from the steps, the actual user name and password are only sent to the authorization service (Google in this case) and are not stored nor shared with the requesting app. The requesting app is provided the various tokens used through the negotiation of the process and they will need to store the final access token, but the time and scope are both limited.

Although the typical scenario for OAuth allows a third-party service (i.e., a social media we bsite) time and scope limited, token-based authentication to the protected information (i.e., your Gmail contact list), it is interesting to point out that an app developer can use the OAuth service to authenticate to themselves. Using this approach, the app developers not only provide secure, token-based access to their service in a standardized fashion but they now have the infrastructure in place to allow approved third-party apps' access to the data, provided the account owner authorizes the access.

There are many different schemes and techniques that can be used to securely authenticate users who would not require a mobile app to store the user name and password in plain text on the mobile device. App developers must move to these more secure methodologies to better protect their customers.

Credit Card Data

Most people in the security industry are familiar with the Payment Card Industry (PCI) Data Security Standard (DSS), which provides standards for protecting credit card data. Prior to the formation of the PCI Security Standards Council (SSC), the major credit card vendors had their own standards for protecting credit card data. In 2006, the PCI SSC was launched by the following payment brands:

- American Express
- Discover Financial Services
- JCB International
- MasterCard Worldwide
- Visa Inc

These brands have a vested interested in reducing fraud in the payment card industry. In the version 2.0 document "Requirements and Security Assessment Procedures" published in October 2010, the specific requirements of the PCI DSS are listed. The following is a small sample of requirements that would cover situations where credit card data are used in a mobile app (Documents Library, n.d.).

- 3.2 Do not store sensitive authentication data after authorization (even if encrypted). Sensitive authentication data include the data as cited in Requirements 3.2.1 through 3.2.3
- 3.2.1 Do not store the full contents of any track (from the magnetic stripe located on the back of a card, equivalent data contained on a chip, or elsewhere). These data are alternatively called full track, track, track 1, track 2, and magnetic-stripe data.
- 3.2.2 Do not store the card verification code or value (three-digit or four-digit number printed on the front or back of a payment card) used to verify card-not present transactions.

- 3.2.3 Do not store the personal identification number (PIN) or the encrypted PIN block.
- 3.3 Mask PAN when displayed (the first six and last four digits are the maximum number of digits to be displayed).
- 3.4.1 If disk encryption is used (rather than file- or column-level database encryption), logical access must be managed independently of native operating system access control mechanisms (e.g., by not using local user account databases). Decryption keys must not be tied to user accounts.

The PCI DSS, while not without criticism, is a fairly mature standard with a goal of protecting a staggering volume of financial transactions. It is interesting to compare some of the standards the PCI DSS has developed over time such as requiring encryption, limiting the storage of sensitive information, and masking sensitive information when displayed to screen.

It should really go without saying that storing the credit card in plain text on a mobile device would not only violate the PCI DSS standard but would also place the card owner at great risk if the device was compromised. Perhaps not surprisingly, the appWatchdog service described above checks for credit card data stored in plain text and, unfortunately, uncovers this information in some applications.

If an app requires payment processing, it would be advisable to integrate with mature online services such as PayPal and Google Checkout, or work with a payment provider to implement a secure payment application. Be advised, this is a significant undertaking, not only from a development and testing perspective, but also requiring an ongoing security audit process.

Sensitive App Data

Many mobile apps contain sensitive data that the consumer would not want out of their control. There are various levels to the data. Here is a simplistic list designed to illustrate the levels:

1. No sensitive user data—for example, a calculator app would not contain any sensitive user data.
2. No sensitive user data but some potential metadata—for example, a weather application would not contain any sensitive user data; however, it might contain the GPS coordinates and date/time stamp when it was run.
3. Contains user data but not sensitive—some applications are intended for public consumption such as messages people share on Twitter. If a user was informed that all of his or her Twitter messages were readable by the world, most (except those which protect to their messages) would not be concerned.
4. Contains sensitive user data—many applications fall into this category and contain sensitive user data such as your full e-mail messages, SMS and MMS messages, voice mail, call logs, and more.
5. Highly sensitive user data—this is a special level that covers apps that contain financial information, health care information, password vaults, and other apps which place the consumers at great risk if their security is compromised.

It is helpful to differentiate the sensitivity of data an app contains in order to provide appropriate levels of security. If a calculator app required two-factor authentication and AES-256 encryption, users would obviously be annoyed and might try to calculate the 15% tip on paper (which once written down would place it at risk for a number of physical and social engineering attacks, but we digress).

However, the appWatchdog service regularly uncovers apps containing sensitive data of levels 4 and 5 which are stored in plain text on the NAND flash. If you develop an application with sensitive data at this level, you should protect the data with some level of security. There are a number of options including

1. Don't store the data—this is the simplest approach and mitigates any attack which grants access to the NAND flash. As discussed previously, the cryptographic algorithms used to protect data in transit are far more effective than any approach to securing data at rest (at least on a mobile device). Most mobile devices are highly connected to the Internet and thus caching the data is not necessary. Of course, there are advantages to caching the data, which include providing access even if the device is offline as well as improving app responsiveness.
2. Encrypt the data—as discussed previously, encrypting data at rest on a mobile device requires that the keys are also stored on the device and as such it cannot provide perfect security. However, if the keys are sufficiently difficult to locate, it provides a much higher level of protection than plain text. Also, as remote attacks against mobile devices increase, they may gain access to the NAND flash but not other areas where the encryption keys are stored, such as memory. If the data were in plain text, they would be at risk; whereas if the data were encrypted, the consumer would be protected in this instance.

Securing sensitive data is critical to protecting consumers and the industry must mature and consider this as a requirement for apps.

SSL/TLS

One final area to discuss is the implementation of Secure Sockets Layer (SSL) and Transport Layer Security (TLS) that protects data in transit. It is critical that app developers properly implement SSL/TLS, including a full validation of the digital certificates to prevent MITM attacks. Although SSL/TLS is effective in protecting data in transit, without proper implementation it leaves the users highly vulnerable to attack. While testing apps for the appWatchdog service, a test-attacking machine would regularly display the user name and password for apps not in scope as it would automatically execute (i.e., some apps log in on a schedule to check to new messages) and fall victim to the compromise.

Beyond ensuring SSL/TLS is properly implemented and validated in the mobile app, SSL/TLS must also be securely configured on the server. SSL has been available since the 1990s to secure data transmission on untrusted networks. Earlier implementation of SSL contained security flaws that had to be addressed to ensure secure transmission. And over time, the algorithms were improved to reduce the risk

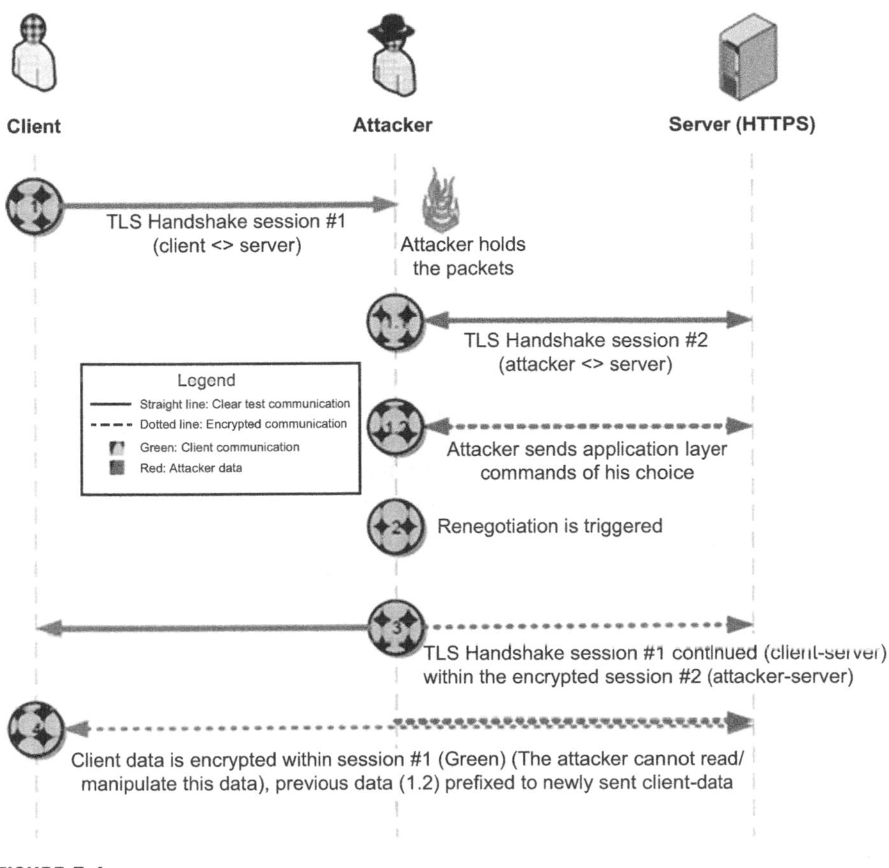

FIGURE 5.4

Generic TLS renegotiation prefix injection vulnerability.

of a brute force attack. The latest versions of the technology are known as TLS and generally work in the same way as SSL, so much so that many still simply use the term SSL for both.

A common problem is that the people responsible for implementing SSL/TLS on the server are not necessarily security engineers and hence tend to focus on server infrastructure. They might implement and test SSL/TLS and it would appear to be secure; but, there can be vulnerabilities. For example, MD5 is a common encryption algorithm that has been in wide use for more than 10 years. Although still considered useful for applications such as file integrity checking, authorities have designated it for retirement from use in securing communications. The US Department of Homeland Security CERT group states in Vulnerability Note #836068 "Software developers, Certification Authorities, web site owners, and users should avoid using the MD5 algorithm in any capacity. As previous research has demonstrated, it should be considered cryptographically broken and unsuitable for further use" (US-CERT Vulnerability Note VU#836068, n.d.). Real-time cracking of this encryption remains impractical, but stronger encryption is supported by all major Web browsers and mobile devices.

An even greater problem is the acceptance of the NULL cipher (no encryption) or weaker export-grade encryption in the server SSL/TLS settings. For a number of years the United States restricted the export of devices and software with cryptography technology, and so weaker encryption algorithms were implemented for use in exported software. The export ciphers use a short key length of only 40 bits and can be compromised much more easily than modern ciphers with longer keys of 128 or 256 bits.

Another issue in SSL/TLS use is the implemented version. TLSv1 is more than 10 years old and was found vulnerable to a "renegotiation attack" in 2009. In this attack, the server treats the client's initial TLS handshake as a renegotiation and thus believes that the initial data transmitted by the attacker are from the same entity as the subsequent client data (US-CERT Vulnerability Note VU#120541, n.d.). Thierry Zoller (November 2009), a security consultant, provided a well-written summary with visual depictions of the steps involved. Although many different attacks are explained, Fig. 5.4 is the first example provided in this summary that helps illustrate the attack.

Most servers using TLSv1 have been patched to close this vulnerability. However, the TLSv1 protocol has been updated and a more current TLSv1.2 offers the latest technology and strongest encryption ciphers. Older specifications including SSLv2 and SSLv3 are still widely in use and can be reasonably secure with adequate ciphers and key lengths, but they are not as secure as TLS.

Securing the transmission of sensitive data from a mobile device requires coordination, diligence, and a thorough understanding of SSL/TLS from not only the app developer but also from the team that maintains the server participating in the secure communication. Although SSL/TLS has been available for some time and may be taken for granted, it is important that a correct implementation and thorough security testing of the system be undertaken.

SUMMARY

Android devices can be both a target of malicious attacks and a tool used to carry out such attacks. Personal users as well as corporations must be aware of the risks and should take certain measures to protect against malicious misuse. Application developers must also increase their attention on security concerns and take responsibility for protecting user data. Implementing basic security measures discussed in this chapter, though not providing full protection, can at least serve as a deterrent against most attacks.

References

Country. (n.d.). Computer crime law—guide to computer crimes law. Retrieved February 10, 2011, from http://www.hg.org/computer-crime.html.

Cisco unified video conferencing multiple vulnerabilities. (n.d.). Matta Consulting. Retrieved February 11, 2011, from www.trustmatta.com/advisories/MATTA-2010-001.txt.

Cisco Security advisory: multiple vulnerabilities in Cisco unified video conferencing products—Cisco Systems. (n.d.). Retrieved February 10, 2011, from http://www.cisco.com/en/US/products/products_security_advisory09186a0080.

default. (n.d.). OAuth for installed applications—authentication and authorization for Google APIs—Google Code. Retrieved February 12, 2011, from http://code.google.com/apis/accounts/docs/OAuthForInstalledApps.htm.

Device administration. (n.d.). Android Developers. Retrieved February 11, 2011, from http://developer.android.com/guide/topics/admin/device-admin.html.

Donohue, B. (n.d.). Mobile device users more susceptible to phishing scams. Retrieved February 10, 2011, from http://threatpost.com/en_us/blogs/mobile-device-users-more-susceptible-phishing-scams-010511.

Documents Library. (n.d.). PCI security standards documents: PCI DSS, PA-DSS, PED standards, compliance guidelines and more. Retrieved February 12, 2011, from https://www.pcisecuritystandards.org/security_standards/documents.php?agreements=pcidss&association=PCI%20DSS.

[Full-disclosure] Microsoft Windows NT #GP trap handler allows users to switch kernel stack. (n.d.). Retrieved February 10, 2011, from http://lists.grok.org.uk/pipermail/full-disclosure/2010-January/072549.html.

Introduction—OAuthn. (n.d.). OAuth Community Site. Retrieved February 12, 2011, from http://oauth.net/about/.

Johnston, S. J. (n.d.). Microsoft warns about 17-year-old windows bug. Retrieved February 10, 2011, from http://www.esecurityplanet.com/features/article.php/3860131/article.htm.

Microsoft security advisory (979682) vulnerability in Windows kernel could allow elevation of privilege. (n.d.). Retrieved February 10, 2011, from http://www.microsoft.com/technet/security/advisory/979682.mspx.

Ralf-Philipp Weinmann. (n.d.). CryptoLUX. Retrieved February 10, 2011, from https://cryptolux.org/Ralf-Philipp_Weinmann.

Schneier on security: data at rest vs. data in motion. (n.d.). Retrieved February 9, 2011, from http://www.schneier.com/blog/archives/2010/06/data_at_rest_vs.html.

Secure programming for Linux and Unix HOWTO. (n.d.). David A. Wheeler's personal home page. Retrieved February 10, 2011, from http://www.dwheeler.com/secure-programs/Secure-Programs-HOWTO/open-source-security.html.

Ten, T. T. (n.d.). Field of dreams (1989)—Memorable quotes. The Internet movie database (IMDb). Retrieved February 10, 2011, from http://www.imdb.com/title/tt0097351/quotes?qt0314964.

US-CERT Vulnerability Note VU#836068. (n.d.). CERT Knowledgebase. Retrieved February 13, 2011, from http://www.kb.cert.org/vuls/id/836068.

US-CERT Vulnerability Note VU#120541. (n.d.). CERT Knowledgebase. Retrieved February 13, 2011, from http://www.kb.cert.org/vuls/id/120541.

WordNet search—3.0. (n.d.). Retrieved February 10, 2011, from wordnetweb.princeton.edu/perl/webwn?s=art.

Zoller, T. (2009, November 29). TLS & SSLv3 renegotiation vulnerability explained. SANS Internet Storm Center; Cooperative Network Security Community—Internet Security. Retrieved February 13, 2011, from http://isc.sans.edu/diary.html?storyid=7582.

CHAPTER

Android forensic techniques

INFORMATION IN THIS CHAPTER

- Procedures for handling an Android device
- Imaging Android USB mass storage devices
- Logical techniques
- Physical techniques

INTRODUCTION

Before we dive into the actual Android forensic techniques, there are a number of considerations that influence which technique forensic analysts should use. In this section, we will discuss the different types of investigations, the differences between logical and physical techniques, and how to limit or avoid modifications to the device.

Types of Investigations

There are a variety of situations that might benefit from the results of an Android forensic investigation. While the application of forensics is a commonality in all the situations, each one may require different procedures, documentation, and overall focus.

The first situation that people think of in general is investigations that will likely be adjudicated in a criminal or civil court of law. In these situations, there are a number of important considerations:

- Chain of custody
- Detailed contemporaneous notes and final reporting
- Possible validation of results using different tools or investigators
- Fact or opinion based testimony

Another common scenario is internal investigations in corporations. These investigations may end up litigated in court, but often they are used to determine the root cause of an issue (whether that is a system, external attack, or internal employee) and may result in disciplinary action against an employee.

Internal corporate investigations can cover many areas but the most common include:

- Intellectual property or data theft
- Inappropriate use of company resources
- Attempted or successful attack against computer systems
- Employment-related investigations including discrimination, sexual harassment, etc.
- Security audit (random or targeted)

There is also a need for forensics in cases involving family matters. The most common cases involve:

- Divorce
- Child custody
- Estate disputes

One final area where forensic investigation can yield significant value is for the security and operation of a government. Governments are usually the largest employer in a country and the United States is a good example. According to the US Census Bureau, data from the 2009 Annual Survey of Public Employment and Payroll revealed that the Federal government across all functions had over 3 million employees, while state and local governments has 16.6 million full-time equivalent employees (Government Employment & Payroll, n.d.).

Beyond employment-related matters, countries are also the potential target of attacks and foreign government intelligence gathering. Forensics can play a key role in thwarting attacks against a country, investigating successful attacks, counter intelligence scenarios, and in providing valuable intelligence needed for the governing of the country.

Difference Between Logical and Physical Techniques

Android forensic techniques are either logical or physical in nature. A logical technique extracts allocated data and is typically achieved by accessing the file system. Allocated data simply means that the data are not deleted and are accessible on the file system. One exception to this definition is that some files, such as an SQLite database, can be allocated and still contain deleted records in the database. While recovery of the deleted data requires special tools and techniques, it is possible to recover deleted data from a logical acquisition.

Physical techniques, on the other hand, target the physical storage medium directly and do not rely on the file system itself to access the data. There are advantages to this approach; the most significant is that physical techniques likely provide access to significant amounts of deleted data. As discussed in Chapter 4, file systems often only mark data as deleted or obsolete, and do not actually erase the storage medium unless needed. As physical forensic techniques provide direct access to the storage medium, it is possible to recover both the allocated and the unallocated (deleted or obsolete) data.

Of course, the analysis of an Android physical acquisition is generally far more difficult and time consuming. Also, the physical techniques are more difficult to execute and missteps could leave the device inaccessible.

In Android forensics, the most common logical technique does not provide direct access to the file system and operates at a more abstract and less-effective level than the traditional logical techniques, which can acquire all nondeleted data directly from the file system. This technique, which relies on the Content Providers built into the Android platform and software development kit (SDK), is effective in producing some important forensic data, but only a fraction of the data that are available on the system.

Modification of the Target Device

One of the guiding principles of any forensic investigation is to avoid modification of the target device in any manner. In many cases, this is achievable. For example, let's assume you are handed a desktop computer that is not powered on. You are informed it was seized from a suspect and that you need to launch a forensic investigation. The device is fairly easy to investigate without material changes to the data after you take custody. A typical investigation would fully document the computer, remove the hard drive, and connect it to a physical write blocker and acquire a bit-by-bit forensically sound image of the hard drive. The investigation would then take place on copies of the forensic image and the original device would remain unchanged.

As the power and functionality of computers has increased, this ideal situation has become more and more difficult to achieve. First, let's assume you are called to the scene of an investigation and there is a desktop computer, but this time the computer is in operation. Any interaction with the computer, whether you simply move it or even physically unplug the device, will modify the device in some way. While many examiners advocate simply unplugging the computer, unplugging the computer still changes the computer as the contents of RAM, open network connections, and more (all of which can be quite valuable in an investigation) are permanently lost.

If you instead decide to examine the device while it is running, all interactions change the device. To further complicate an investigation, it is possible that the computer is leveraging encryption and, while the device is running, that data may be accessible. However, if the device is powered off and you don't have the encryption keys, then you may permanently lose the ability to recover that data.

Another complicating factor can be the existence of servers that have special hardware, complex setups, or that simply cannot be powered down without significant impact to other systems or people. Some examples of complex service setups include complicated RAID setup, setups that rely on network-based storage area networks (SAN), and unsupported hardware. In such cases, the examiner must interact directly with the device while it is running even though those actions change the device.

Of course, mobile devices, and Android devices in particular, are nearly impossible to forensically analyze without any impact to the device. Unlike desktops, notebooks, and servers, there are portions of storage on an Android device that cannot be easily removed. And if the device is powered on, a shutdown of the device or pulling the battery again changes the device.

When mobile phones were first showing up in investigations, there was very little data stored in them that could be extracted from the device. Many investigations used traditional approaches, such as a search warrant on the wireless carrier to obtain call detail records. It was also possible to remove the subscriber identity module (SIM) card on GSM devices and extract some data. As phones began to store more data, there developed a deep divide between examiners who advocated the older methods (which had little impact on the device and subsequently retrieved only nominal data) and those who advocated exploiting the device more fully. The techniques used to exploit the devices did modify the device, leading to the ensuing debate.

As of 2011, much of the debate has subsided because the amount of data mobile devices now hold necessitates the more intrusive techniques. The Association of Chief Police Officers in the United Kingdom produces guidelines that address this issue quite clearly. The guide, *Good Practice Guide for Computer-Based Electronic Evidence* (ACPO Good Practice Guide, n.d.), establishes four principles of computer-based electronic evidence:

1. No action taken by law enforcement agencies or their agents should change data held on a computer or storage media, which may subsequently be relied upon in court.
2. In circumstances where a person finds it necessary to access original data held on a computer or on storage media, that person must be competent to do so and be able to give evidence explaining the relevance and the implications of their actions.
3. An audit trail or other record of all processes applied to computer-based electronic evidence should be created and preserved. An independent third party should be able to examine those processes and achieve the same result.
4. The person in charge of the investigation (the case officer) has overall responsibility for ensuring that the law and these principles are adhered to.

As mobile devices clearly present a circumstance where it is necessary to access the original device directly, then it is permissible provided the examiner is sufficiently trained, provides valid reasons for their approach and keeps a clear audit trail so that their actions are repeatable by a third party. This is certainly good advice and helps provide a solid framework for the forensic investigation of mobile devices.

PROCEDURES FOR HANDLING AN ANDROID DEVICE

One major challenge for forensic analysts is to devise a protocol for handling the device prior to the analyst taking direct custody. And this is certainly not a new issue for analysts as others involved in the investigation may also handle other digital devices such as computers or laptops. However, mobile devices are still relatively new and are often not handled properly by first responders. There is a tendency to immediately examine the device, which almost inevitably results in data modification and potential loss of access to the device.

Securing the Device

Many agencies and first responders have established a protocol for securing evidence. The following sections are meant to complement the existing procedures, not replace them. Of course, these represent special procedures, and educating first responders who have many other responsibilities can be quite challenging.

Pass Code Procedures

Pass code locked devices are becoming more common as a result of heightened security awareness in consumers and corporations. In the next section, we cover some specific techniques to circumvent pass codes. However, it is not always possible. The first consideration when obtaining information from a device is whether an opportunity exists to immediately disable or otherwise circumvent the pass code.

If you encounter an Android device and the screen is active, strong consideration should be given to checking and potentially changing its settings. For devices that have pass codes, there is a short period of time (from less than a minute up to about 15 min) where full access to the device is possible without re-entering the pass code. If a device is in this state, there are several steps to consider:

1. Increase the screen timeout to prevent or postpone the screen locking. The location for this setting is not consistent between Android versions and devices. For example, on a G1 running Android 1.5, the timeout can be set by pressing Menu (from the home screen), then Settings, Sound & display, Screen timeout, and then select "Never timeout." On an HTC Incredible running Android 2.2, press Menu (from the home screen), then Settings, Security, Lock phone after, and then finally "15 minutes." As long as the device has some nominal activity in the allotted timeout setting, it will remain accessible.
2. Enable USB debugging and "Stay awake" settings. The location for this setting has remained consistent in devices and can be accessed by pressing Menu (from the home screen), then Settings, Applications and Development. From there, you can check USB debugging and Stay awake. If you select the "Stay awake" setting and then connect it to a charge, the device will never go to sleep, which is effective in preventing the screen lock. By enabling USB debugging, the device can be accessed over USB enabling data extraction.

Of course, these steps are making changes to the device and should be thoroughly logged in the case notes describing the state of the device, the rationale for the attempted changes, and the outcome of each change. This will not only assist in future report writing but will likely be an important factor if your decision to change the device is challenged in court.

To make matters more difficult, it is also important to minimize touching the screen in case the screen lock becomes active. As we will discuss shortly, it is sometimes possible to determine the pattern lock of a device by enhancing photographs of the device's screen. The lesser the interaction a first responder has with the screen, the higher the success rate of this technique.

Network Isolation

As many examiners likely know, it is important to isolate the device from the network as soon as possible. In the worst-case scenario, a remote wipe could be initiated on the device which, if successful, would prevent the recovery of any data. While most remote wipes are done over the data network, some can be triggered over SMS, and hence ensure the device is fully isolated to prevent remote wipes. In other circumstances, additional messages on the device could be received or even removed by triggers outside your control. As the goal of a forensic image is to preserve the state of the device for additional analysis, any changes should be avoided.

There are a number of ways to isolate a device from the network and each of these methods have advantages and disadvantages. Table 6.1 summarizes the advantages and disadvantages of each technique.

As you can tell, isolating an Android device from the network is not an easy task and each option has advantages and disadvantages. While each examiner or their organization should determine the appropriate steps to undertake, the best option is probably placing the device in Airplane mode. This varies slightly between Android devices and versions but the general approach is the same:

1. Press and hold the Power off button and select Airplane mode.
2. Press Menu (from the home screen), then Settings, then the Wireless option which is generally near the top. Some examples are "Wireless controls" or "Wireless and networks." The next menu should present the Airplane mode option.

Fig. 6.1 is a screenshot from the Power off button approach. Fig. 6.2 shows the option via the Wireless settings.

Regardless of which technique you ultimately choose, the main goal should be to isolate the device from the network as soon as possible.

Power and Data Cables

While most forensic labs will have the cables necessary to charge and connect the device, it is always prudent to seize the cables directly from the scene. It's possible that a newer device is in use and the forensic toolkits do not yet have an appropriate cable. For example, a new specification for connecting media devices was developed called portable digital media interface (PDMI) and is integrated into two Android tablet devices, the Dell Streak and the Samsung Galaxy Tab. The PDMI interface

Table 6.1 Techniques for Device Isolation

Technique	Advantages	Disadvantages
Put the device in Airplane mode. This requires that you have full access to the Settings menu.	The device continues running and temporal data remains intact. Disables cellular data network as well as Wi-Fi.com.	You are modifying the device setting further. Only works if you have full access to the device.
If the phone is a GSM phone, remove the SIM card.	Easy to remove, effective in disabling all cellular voice, SMS, and data transmissions.	Does not disable Wi-Fi.com or other networks. Does not work on non-GSM phones including CDMA and iDEN phones.
Suspend account with wireless carrier.	Effective in disabling all cellular voice, SMS, and data transmissions for any phone.	Process may take some time and require a court order. Does not disable Wi-Fi.com or other networks.
Place device in a shielded bag, box, tent, or room.	Faraday shields prevent various types of network transmissions and can be an effective approach if you cannot utilize any of the previous options.	There is some debate about the effectiveness of portable Faraday shields, notably Faraday bags. Also, while the transmissions are blocked, the device attempts to contact the cellular network repeatedly thus draining the battery quickly. Cords cannot be inserted into the enclosure as they will transmit signals. A shielded room dedicated for mobile examinations is ideal. However, they are quite expensive to build and maintain.
Turn the device off.	Completely effective in preventing all network transmissions.	The device state is modified and temporal data is lost. Pass code on reboot could be enabled, thus restricting access to the device.

provides not only power and high-resolution video output, but also offers USB 3.0 support. Whereas the actual examination of one of these devices could be delayed while an appropriate cable is acquired, if it needed charging and you do not have the appropriate cable, the loss of power will result in the loss of temporal data.

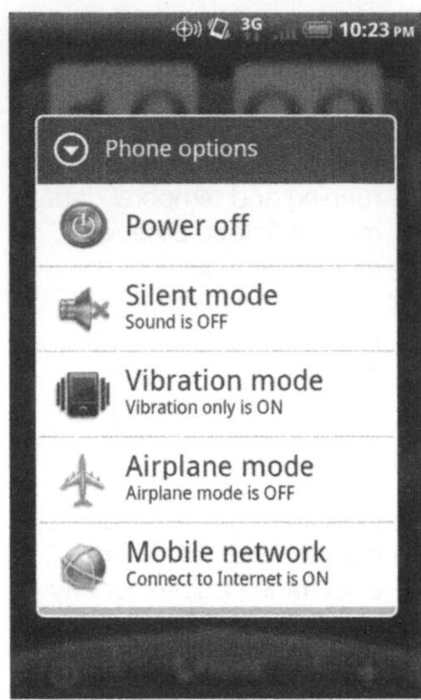

FIGURE 6.1

Airplane mode via the Power off button.

FIGURE 6.2

Airplane mode via the Wireless and networks settings.

Powered-off Devices

If a device is already powered off when you encounter it, the best option is to boot it into recovery mode to test for connectivity and root access. The owner may have already enabled USB debugging or have rooted the device, so you may have access to the data without booting into normal operational mode.

This approach is similar to performing forensics on a standard computer hard drive. The last thing any trained forensic analyst would do is boot the computer to determine what operating system is installed. Instead, the hard drive is removed and connected to a write blocker for imaging to prevent any changes to the evidence. Similarly, if a mobile device does not have to boot into normal mode, there is no need to do so as this may make changes to the device. Specific information on how to test a device in recovery mode for sufficient privileges is discussed later in this chapter.

How to Circumvent the Pass Code

The ability to circumvent the pass code on an Android device is becoming more important as they are utilized frequently and, in most cases, do not allow data extraction. While there is no guaranteed method, there are a number of techniques which have worked in certain situations.

As previously discussed, there are three types of pass codes Android devices currently support. The first is a pattern lock. This was the default on the initial Android devices. To access the device, the user draws a pattern on the locked phone and, if drawn properly, the device is unlocked. An example of a pattern lock on an HTC Incredible is shown in Fig. 6.3.

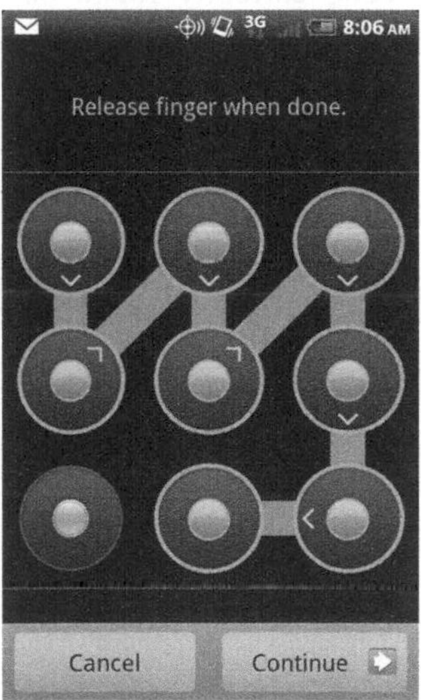

FIGURE 6.3

Android pattern lock.

FIGURE 6.4

Android PIN lock.

The second type of pass code is the simple personal identification number (PIN) which is commonly found on other mobile devices. Fig. 6.4 is an example of a PIN-enabled HTC Incredible.

The final type of pass code currently found on Android devices is a full, alphanumeric code, as shown in Fig. 6.5.

FIGURE 6.5

Android alphanumeric lock.

As discussed in Chapter 4, not all pass codes were created equal. The most effective pass code is one that allows or requires an alphanumeric password, as these are far more difficult to circumvent.

Utilize ADB if USB Debugging is Enabled

The first technique you should attempt, provided the phone is powered on, is to connect with the Android Debug Bridge (ADB) over USB, which was covered extensively in Chapter 3. Whereas only a fraction of Android devices will allow an ADB connection through the USB debugging setting, it is certainly worth trying as it easily provides sufficient access for data extraction. The most common reasons for which users enable USB debugging include:

- App development and testing
- Certain apps require this setting, such as PDAnet, which allows the device to provide Internet access to a tethered device over USB
- Custom ROMs
- Developer phones such as Google's Android developer phone (ADP1)
- Device hacking

It is quite simple to determine if USB debugging is enabled, provided you are using the Ubuntu virtual machine (VM) or have a forensic workstation with a properly installed and configured Software Development Kit. With the phone running in normal mode, plug it into the Ubuntu VM. From the command prompt type "adb devices." If USB debugging is enabled, the ADB daemon will return the device serial number along with the mode that the phone is presently in.

```
ahoog@ubuntu:~$ adb devices
List of devices attached
HT08XHJ00657    device
```

If it is disabled, it will not return anything when the "adb devices" command is entered.

```
ahoog@ubuntu:~$ adb devices
List of devices attached

ahoog@ubuntu:~$
```

Remember to pass the device through to your VM if you are running the command inside a virtual workstation. If the VM can't see the device, you will get the same result as if the USB debugging were not enabled. Once you verify that the USB connection is passed through to the Ubuntu VM, you can execute the lsusb command to verify that the operating system is aware of the connection:

```
ahoog@ubuntu:~$ sudo lsusb -v
[sudo] password for ahoog:

Bus 001 Device 005: ID 0bb4:0c9e High Tech Computer Corp.
Device Descriptor:
  bLength                18
  bDescriptorType         1
  bcdUSB               2.00
  bDeviceClass            0 (Defined at Interface level)
  bDeviceSubClass         0
  bDeviceProtocol         0
  bMaxPacketSize0        64
  idVendor           0x0bb4 High Tech Computer Corp.
  idProduct          0x0c9e
  bcdDevice            2.26
  iManufacturer           1 HTC
  iProduct                2 Android Phone
  iSerial                 3 HT08XHJ00657
  bNumConfigurations      1
<snip>
    Interface Descriptor:
      bLength                 9
      bDescriptorType         4
      bInterfaceNumber        1
      bAlternateSetting       0
      bNumEndpoints           2
      bInterfaceClass       255 Vendor Specific Class
      bInterfaceSubClass     66
      bInterfaceProtocol      1
      iInterface              4 ADB
<snip>
```

In this example, emphasis was placed on several areas that clearly show the Android device is connected and, in such cases, we can see an ADB interface is exposed. If the device is connected but you cannot connect via ADB, you should also kill your local ADB daemon and then start it again. This is easily accomplished as follows:

```
ahoog@ubuntu:~$ adb kill-server
ahoog@ubuntu:~$ adb devices
* daemon not running. starting it now on port 5037 *
* daemon started successfully *
List of devices attached
HT08XHJ00657    device
```

If the USB debugging is enabled, a forensic analyst can use the interface to gain access and perform a logical recovery of the device, which is covered in detail later in this chapter.

FIGURE 6.6

Enhanced photo showing smudge attack.

Smudge Attack

Initially, Android devices used the pattern lock for pass code protection instead of a numeric or alphanumeric code. A recent paper entitled "Smudge Attacks on Smartphone Touch Screens" by the University of Pennsylvania Department of Computer and Information Science demonstrated a technique for accessing pattern locked Android devices by enhancing photographs of the screen (Aviv, Gibson, Mossop, Blaze, Smith, n.d.). The paper's summary states:

> *Our photographic experiments suggest that a clean touch screen surface is primarily, but not entirely, reflective, while a smudge is primarily, but not entirely, diffuse. We found that virtually any directional lighting source that is not positioned exactly at a complementary angle to the camera will render a recoverable image of the smudge. Very little photo adjustment is required to view the pattern, but images generally rendered best when the photo capture was overexposed by two to three f-stops (4 to 8 times "correct" exposure).*

If care was taken by the first responders to minimize contact with the device's screen, this recovery technique may be viable. As an example of what is possible, Fig. 6.6 shows photos of the same Android device displayed side by side. The same original photo was used for both images but the image on the right was enhanced as part of the smudge attack process to highlight the contact points.

Recovery Mode

Some users install a custom ROM which usually enables root access to the device through a modified recovery mode. Most custom ROMs install a modified recovery partition which simplifies the process used to install the custom ROM. There are

Table 6.2 Key Combinations to Boot into Recovery Mode

Device	Key Combination
HTC G1	Hold home button and press power button. Use volume down to select RECOVERY and press power key.
Nexus One	Hold volume down and press power button.
Motorola Droid	Hold X key and press power button.
HTC Incredible	Hold volume down and press power button. Use volume down to select RECOVERY and press power key.

several popular recovery partitions that are primarily used with custom ROMs and both offer shell access with root privileges from within the recovery console itself. As the phone is not booted into normal mode, the pass code is circumvented and the user data partitions can be mounted read-only, thus preventing changes to that area.

Forensic analysts should attempt to boot into recovery mode if the device is powered off, when they take custody. If, instead, the device is running and a pass code is present, you should first attempt to connect via ADB and consider smudge attack. If neither of these is successful, you should then try to reboot into recovery mode. Like many other techniques, recovery mode is accessed in different ways depending on the device manufacturer and model. Table 6.2 covers the key combinations to access recovery mode on the phones referenced throughout this book. Each assumes the device is powered off already.

Once in recovery mode, you can connect the device to your Ubuntu workstation and attempt to connect using ADB. If the device is running a nonmodified recovery mode, the connection will fail. The screen generally shows a triangle with an exclamation point inside it and often a small Android device next to it. On other devices, you will be presented with the somewhat famous three Androids on a skateboard. Finally, other recovery modules clearly show they are in modified recovery code and provide a wide range of device options.

Flash a New Recovery Partition

There are a number of protocols, utilities, and devices that allow a skilled examiner to flash the recovery partition of a device with a modified image.

The first available protocol supporting this approach was fastboot. Fastboot is a NAND flash update protocol executed over USB while in bootloader mode. Most devices ship with bootloader protection enabled, which prohibits the use of this protocol. However, it is possible that the protection has been disabled. To determine if bootloader protection is enabled, you must access the bootloader and look at the signature information, which will indicate S-ON or S-OFF. The S represents security, and so S-ON, the default production build, has security enabled; S-OFF indicates security is not enabled. Some devices ship with S-OFF, such as the Google Nexus One, as it is preloaded with Google's Engineering SPL/Bootloader.

Other rooting techniques also disable this protection, so checking this on a pass code protected device may yield results. You can access the main bootloader using the first part of the key combinations in Table 6.2 in the previous section.

Fastboot does not require USB debugging to access the device. Hence, like recovery mode, it can be used to gain access to the device's data. Once the new recovery partition is available, the device should be rebooted into recovery mode and forensic imaging can take place.

Other techniques exist which allow the recovery partition to be flashed with a new image. Some examples include:

- Motorola's RSD Lite
- sbf_flash
- Samsung's Odin Multiloader

While these utilities and protocols may ultimately provide the privileges that a forensic analyst requires, there is considerable effort required to not only locate and test the techniques but to understand them sufficiently to use them in a forensic investigation.

Screen Lock Bypass App

Security researcher Thomas Cannon recently developed a technique that allows a screen lock bypass by installing an app through the new web-based Android Market (Cannon, T., n.d.). Cannon's technique utilizes a new feature in the web-based Android Market that allows apps to be installed directly from the web site. As such, you must have access to the Android Market using the primary Gmail user name and password for the device, which may be accessible from the primary computer of the user. Alternatively, you could access the Android Market if you knew the user name and password and had sufficient authority. Changing the user's Gmail password would not work in this instance.

Cannon explains the technique on this web site as in the following section (Cannon, T., n.d.).

How it Works

The procedure is quite simple really. Android sends out a number of broadcast messages which an application can receive, such as SMS received or Wi-Fi.com disconnected. An application has to register its receiver to receive broadcast messages and this can be done at run time, or for some messages, at install time. When a relevant message comes in, it is sent to the application and if the application is not running it will be started automatically.

After testing out various broadcast messages the best one I found for the purpose of this utility was android.intent.action.PACKAGE_ADDED. This exists in all APIs as version 1 and is triggered when an application is installed. Hence, to get the application to execute remotely, we first deploy it from the Android Market, then deploy any other application that will cause the first one to launch.

Once launched it is just a matter of calling the disableKeyguard() method in KeyguardManager. This is a legitimate API to enable applications to disable the screen lock when, say, an incoming phone call is detected. After finishing the call the app ought to enable the screen lock again, but we just keep it disabled.

This technique is certainly worth consideration if you have proper access to the Android Market.

Use Gmail User/Pass

On most Android phones, you can circumvent the pass code if you know the primary Gmail user name and password registered with the device. After a number of failed attempts (ten attempts on the G1), you will be presented with a screen that asks if you forgot your pass code. From there, you can enter the Gmail user name and password and you will then be prompted to reset the pass code. This technique does not require the phone to be online as it uses credential information cached on the phone.

If you do not have the current Gmail user name and password, but have sufficient authority (i.e., court order) to reset the password, you could attempt to compel Google to reset the account password. You would then have to connect the Android device to the network and gain access. This issue presents many challenges, including the need to place the device online, putting it at risk for remote wipe in addition to making changes to the device. Reports on various law enforcement mailing lists indicate this technique does not always work.

If this approach is attempted, additional research is warranted. In particular, it would be prudent to control the Internet connection the device uses, most likely a Wi-Fi.com access point. You could then limit the network access to only those which the Google server needed for authentication. In addition, a detailed network capture of test devices should be analyzed as well as the actual changes made to the device.

JTAG and Chip-off

At this time, most Android devices do not encrypt the contents of the NAND flash, which makes directly accessing and decoding the memory chips a potential work-around if a pass code is enabled. There are two primary techniques, which provide direct access to the chips. Both are technically challenging. The two techniques are:

- Joint test action group (JTAG)
- Physical extraction (chip-off)

Both techniques are not only technically challenging and require partial to full disassembly of the device, but they require substantial post-extraction analysis to reassemble the file system. For these reasons, JTAG and chip-off would likely be the very last choices to circumvent a locked device.

With JTAG, you connect directly to the device's CPU by soldering leads to certain JTAG pads on the printed circuit board (PCB). Then JTAG software can be used to perform a complete binary memory dump of the NAND flash, modify certain partitions to allow root access, or eliminate the pass code altogether.

In the chip-off procedure, the NAND flash chips are physically extracted from the PCB using heat and air. The chip, usually a small ball grid array (BGA) package, then needs to have the BGA connections regenerated and inserted into special hardware that connects to the chip and reads the NAND flash.

The advantages to these techniques are that they will work in any situation where the NAND flash is not encrypted. However, extensive research, development, testing, and practice are required to execute these techniques.

IMAGING ANDROID USB MASS STORAGE DEVICES

Every Android device to date has either an external Secure Digital (SD) card or an Embedded MultiMediaCard (eMMC) that provides the large storage space required by many users. These storage devices exist because the user's app data, typically stored in /data/data, is isolated for security and privacy reasons. However, users want to copy songs, pictures, videos, or other files between their Android device and a computer, and these large capacity FAT file system partitions solve that issue. The sensitive user data remains protected, yet the larger and more portable files are accessible to the user.

Initially, the approach to imaging the external storage was to simply remove it from the Android device and image using a USB write blocker. However, a number of challenges arose over time, including:

- Moving to eMMC storage meant that the mass storage was no longer removable.
- Apps can now run from the SD card and in this scenario, the .apk files are encrypted. If capturing an unencrypted copy of the app is critical to an investigation (for example, a case involving malware analysis or a Trojan horse defense), the SD card must remain in the Android device.
- Newer devices are using RAM disks (tmpfs) more frequently to store user data that might be helpful in an investigation. Often, removing the SD card requires the device to be shut down and the battery removed, thus losing the ability to recover the temporal data.

For these reasons, the recommended approach for imaging the USB Mass Storage (UMS) devices on Android no longer involves removing the SD card but instead imaging it via the UMS interface.

SD Card Versus eMMC

An SD card and eMMC are not all that different. The primary difference, of course, is that the SD cards are portable, easily moving from one device to the next. They use NAND flash, are based on the MultiMediaCard (MMC) specification, and have embedded storage controllers, so that systems MTD is not needed for guest operating systems to read them.

To date, Android devices accept microSD cards generally ranging from 2 GB up to 16 GB. However, larger cards are possible. Depending on the Android device, the SD card may be easily accessed and removed from a running device. However, many require that the device is shut down so that the battery can be removed.

For storage embedded on the device, several manufacturers have begun using eMMC, which consists of embedded storage with an MMC interface integrating directly onto the device's PCB. This standard simplifies accessing NAND flash with the standardized eMMC protocol and is capable of supporting file systems that are not NAND flash aware. This does not necessarily mean the file systems preserve the life of the NAND flash at the same level and sophistication that a NAND flash-aware file system like YAFFS2 does. However, the general lifespan of Android devices is certainly decreasing and is likely not an issue for most users.

How to Forensically Image the SD Card/eMMC

There are two primary methods to forensically acquire the SD card and eMMC without removing it from the device. The first method, covered here, exposes the UMS device interface to your forensic workstation and allows you to acquire the image with your forensic tool of choice. The second method does not expose the UMS to your forensic workstation and instead uses dd on the Android device. This requires adb port forwarding, which will be covered in the section on physical techniques later in this chapter.

Even though our Ubuntu VM has dd built in, we are going to download, compile, and install an updated version of dd maintained by the Department of Defense's Cyber Crime Center. The program, dc3dd, is a patched version of GNU dd and includes a number of features useful for computer forensics (dc3dd, n.d.), such as:

- Piecewise and overall hashing with multiple algorithms—Supports MD5, SHA-1, SHA-256, and SHA-512.
- Progress meter with automatic input/output file-size probing.
- Combined log for hashes and errors.
- Error grouping—Produces one error message for identical sequential errors.
- Verify mode—Able to hash output files and compare hashes to the acquisition hash.
- Ability to split the output into chunks with numerical or alphabetic extensions.
- Ability to write multiple output files simultaneously.

The program is open source software licensed under the GNU Public license version 3 (GPLv3) and is distributed online through SourceForge and was updated to version 7.0 in August 2010 (dc3dd, n.d.). At this point in the book, you should be fairly comfortable compiling programs and have all the tools needed, so here are the abbreviated steps.

```
mkdir -p ~/src
cd ~/src
curl http://cdnetworks-us-2.dl.sourceforge.net/project/dc3dd/
dc3dd/7.0.0/dc3dd-7.0.0.tar.gz
> dc3dd-7.0.0.tar.gz
tar xzf dc3dd-7.0.0.tar.gz
cd dc3dd-7.0.0/
./configure
make
sudo make install
```

At this point, you could proceed with imaging. However, typing out the entire dc3dd command each time is not only tedious but can result in typos that could cause irreparable damage. So create a shell script, which not only acquires the device but also records various system characteristics, date/time stamps, and creates log files, which can be helpful as you write your report at a later time.

We will place the acquire script in /usr/local/bin so you can easily run the script from any directory as /usr/local/bin is in your execution path by default:

```
ahoog@ubuntu:~$ sudo nano -w /usr/local/bin/acquire-disk.sh
```

Next, copy the following into the script, save by pressing Ctrl O, and exit with Ctrl-X:

```
#!/bin/bash

CLIENT="${1}"
CASE="${2}"
TAG="${3}"
SERIALNO="${4}"
SOURCEDEV="${5}"
DESTPATH="${6}"

OUTPUTPATH=$DESTPATH/$CLIENT/$CASE/$TAG-$SERIALNO
LOGFILE=$OUTPUTPATH/log/$TAG-$SERIALNO.log
STDERRLOG=$OUTPUTPATH/log/$TAG-$SERIALNO.stderr.log
SEPERATOR="-------------------------------------------\r"

if [ "$#" != 6 ]; then
        echo "Usage: acquire_disk.sh CLIENT CASE TAG SERIALNO SOURCEDEV
DESTPATH"
        exit 2
fi

# check directories, created if needed
if [ ! -d "$DESTPATH" ]; then
        echo "Destination path [$DESTPATH] does not exist, exiting"
        exit 1
fi

if [ -d "$DESTPATH/$CLIENT/$CASE/$TAG-$SERIALNO" ]; then
        echo "$DESTPATH/$CLIENT/$CASE/$TAG-$SERIALNO already exists, can't
overwrite evidence"
        exit 1
fi
```

```
GOTROOT=`whoami`

if [  "$GOTROOT" != "root" ]; then
       echo "must be root to execute"
       exit 1
fi

mkdir -p $OUTPUTPATH/log

echo -e "Start date/time" >> $LOGFILE
echo -e "$SEPERATOR" >> $LOGFILE
echo -e "`/bin/date`\n" >> $LOGFILE 2>> $STDERRLOG

echo -e "uname -a" >> $LOGFILE
echo -e "$SEPERATOR" >> $LOGFILE
echo -e "`uname -a`\n" >> $LOGFILE 2>> $STDERRLOG

echo -e "dmesg | tail -50" >> $LOGFILE
echo -e "$SEPERATOR" >> $LOGFILE
echo -e "`dmesg | tail -50`\n" >> $LOGFILE 2>> $STDERRLOG

echo -e "lshw" >> $LOGFILE
echo -e "$SEPERATOR" >> $LOGFILE
echo -e "`lshw`\n" >> $LOGFILE 2>> $STDERRLOG

VERSION=`fdisk -v`
echo -e "fdisk -l $SOURCEDEV [$VERSION]" >> $LOGFILE
echo -e "$SEPERATOR" >> $LOGFILE
echo -e "`fdisk -l $SOURCEDEV`\n" >> $LOGFILE 2>> $STDERRLOG

VERSION=`mmls -V`
echo -e "mmls $SOURCEDEV [$VERSION]" >> $LOGFILE
echo -e "$SEPERATOR" >> $LOGFILE
echo -e "`mmls $SOURCEDEV`\n" >> $LOGFILE 2>> $STDERRLOG

VERSION=`fsstat -V`
echo -e "fsstat $SOURCEDEV [$VERSION]" >> $LOGFILE
echo -e "$SEPERATOR" >> $LOGFILE
echo -e "`fsstat $SOURCEDEV`\n" >> $LOGFILE 2>> $STDERRLOG

VERSION=`dc3dd --version 2>&1 | grep dc3dd`
echo -e "dc3dd [$VERSION]" >> $LOGFILE
echo -e "$SEPERATOR" >> $LOGFILE
echo -e "dc3dd if=$SOURCEDEV of=$OUTPUTPATH/$TAG-$SERIALNO.dc3dd verb=on
hash=sha256 hlog=$OUTPUTPATH/log/$TAG-$SERIALNO.hashlog
log=$OUTPUTPATH/log/$TAG-$SERIALNO.log rec=off\n" >> $LOGFILE
dc3dd if=$SOURCEDEV of=$OUTPUTPATH/$TAG-$SERIALNO.dc3dd verb=on hash=sha256
hlog=$OUTPUTPATH/log/$TAG-$SERIALNO.hashlog log=$OUTPUTPATH/log/
$TAG-$SERIALNO.log rec=off

echo -e "ls -lR $DESTPATH/$CLIENT/$CASE/$TAG-$SERIALNO" >> $LOGFILE
echo -e "$SEPERATOR" >> $LOGFILE
echo -e "`ls -lR $DESTPATH/$CLIENT/$CASE/$TAG-$SERIALNO`\n" >> $LOGFILE

echo -e "End date/time" >> $LOGFILE
echo -e "$SEPERATOR" >> $LOGFILE
echo -e "`/bin/date`\n" >> $LOGFILE

#sha256sum all log files
cd $OUTPUTPATH/log/
sha256sum * > $TAG-$SERIALNO.sha256.log
```

Next, you have to change permissions, so that you can run the script and then run it without parameters to see the usage help:

```
ahoog@ubuntu:~$ sudo chmod 755 /usr/local/bin/acquire-disk.sh
ahoog@ubuntu:~$ sudo /usr/local/bin/acquire-disk.sh
Usage: acquire_disk.sh CLIENT CASE TAG SERIALNO SOURCEDEV DESTPATH
```

The great thing about this script, and open source in general, is that you can simply change it as you see fit. If you do not want to track client name, then simply remove it from the script.

Next, we have to mount the UMS device on your Ubuntu workstation. As covered in Chapter 1 in the Ubuntu VM setup, it is critical that you have disabled automount on your workstation. If you did not do this, please review the steps necessary and complete before presenting the UMS devices to the VM.

Additionally, the ideal situation would first connect the Android device to a hardware-based USB write blocker. However, some write blockers seem to have trouble when the connected device exposes more than one device ID. You should experiment with your USB write blocker and, ideally, have this working first.

> **NOTE**
>
> **Tableau UltraBlock USB**
>
> The Tableau UltraBlock USB model T8, running the latest firmware from August 9, 2009, was only able to pass through the first USB device found on the reference HTC Incredible, and so we were unable to use it when analyzing a device. Tableau has a new UltraBlock USB device which may work; however, we have not verified this. Examiners should test the various USB write blockers they have for compatibility.

Next, we need to determine to what devices the UMS is mapped. This information is displayed in the kernel logs and can be easily accessed with the "dmesg" command:

```
ahoog@ubuntu:~/$ dmesg
<snip>
[327202.720222] usb 1-1: new high speed USB device using ehci_hcd and address 12
[327203.032759] scsi11 : usb-storage 1-1:1.0
[327204.039549] scsi 11:0:0:0: Direct-Access     HTC      Android Phone    0100
PQ: 0 ANSI: 2
[327204.044572] scsi 11:0:0:1: Direct-Access     HTC      Android Phone    0100
PQ: 0 ANSI: 2
[327204.047208] scsi 11:0:0:2: CD-ROM            HTC      Android Phone    0100
PQ: 0 ANSI: 2
[327204.049854] sd 11:0:0:0: Attached scsi generic sg2 type 0
[327204.052640] sd 11:0:0:1: Attached scsi generic sg3 type 0
[327204.066738] sr1: scsi3-mmc drive: 0x/0x caddy
[327204.066817] sr 11:0:0:2: Attached scsi CD-ROM sr1
[327204.066892] sr 11:0:0:2: Attached scsi generic sg4 type 5
[327204.082001] sd 11:0:0:0: [sdb] Attached SCSI removable disk
[327204.091070] sd 11:0:0:1: [sdc] Attached SCSI removable disk
```

As discussed previously, the HTC Incredible exposes three USB interfaces in addition to ADB:

- CD-ROM for device driver install (sr1)
- eMMC UMS device (sdb)
- SD card UMS device (sdc)

However, the differences between /dev/sdb and /dev/sdc are not easily discernible until the UMS or Disk drive feature is enabled on the Android device. Once enabled, you should then examine the output of dmesg again.

> **WARNING**
>
> **Use hardware write blocker**
>
> Although the automount feature on the Ubuntu workstation has been disabled, it is critical that the forensic analyst connects only the Android device to the workstation through a hardware write blocker to ensure no changes are made to the device. All hardware should be thoroughly tested prior to active use in a case.

```
ahoog@ubuntu:~/$ dmesg
<snip>
[327520.269248] sd 11:0:0:1: [sdc] 3911680 512-byte logical blocks:
(2.00 GB/1.86 GiB)
[327520.298549] sd 11:0:0:1: [sdc] Assuming drive cache: write through
[327520.304747] sd 11:0:0:1: [sdc] Assuming drive cache: write through
[327520.304757]  sdc: sdc1
[327522.267959] sd 11:0:0:0: [sdb] 13844464 512-byte logical blocks:
(7.08 GB/6.60 GiB)
[327522.271097] sd 11:0:0:0: [sdb] Assuming drive cache: write through
[327522.277187] sd 11:0:0:0: [sdb] Assuming drive cache: write through
[327522.277202]  sdb:
```

It is now clearer that /dev/sdb is the 7 GB storage device (which is the eMMC) while the 2 GB SD card is mapped to /dev/sdc. We can now acquire the devices using our acquire script or any forensic imaging tool available on your forensic workstation. The script takes the following six parameters:

1. Client —This parameter creates the folder structure, examples might be "sheriffs-office" or a client name such as "viaforensics."
2. Case—This parameter provides a case name, such as af-book.
3. Tag—This parameter is tag number for the evidence you are forensically imaging, item001 in our example.
4. Serialno—This is the serial number of the device, disk, SD card, etc. If you do not have access to a serial number, you can type any text you choose such as unknown-serialno.
5. Sourcedev—This is the device you want to acquire such as /dev/sdb, /dev/sdc, etc. You can determine this using dmesg which is explained next.
6. Destpath—The top-level directory where the folders should be created. It could be your home directory (~) or perhaps a folder called clients (~/clients).

For this example, create a folder in your home directory called sd-emmc and then run the acquire script with sudo permissions.

```
ahoog@ubuntu:~$ sudo acquire-disk.sh viaforensics af-book item001
unknown-serialno /dev/sdc ~/sd-emmc
Cannot determine file system type

dc3dd 7.0.0 started at 2011-02-22 04:36:05 -0600
compiled options:
command line: dc3dd if=/dev/sdc of=/home/ahoog/sd-emmc/viaforensics/
af-book/item001-unknown-serialno/item001-unknown-serialno.dc3dd
verb=on hash=sha256 hlog=/home/ahoog/sd-emmc/viaforensics/af-book/
item001-unknown-serialno/log/item001-unknown-serialno.hashlog
log=/home/ahoog/sd-emmc/viaforensics/af-book/item001-unknown-serialno/
log/item001-unknown-serialno.log rec=off
device size: 3911680 sectors (probed)
sector size: 512 bytes (probed)
2002780160 bytes (1.9 G) copied (100%), 808.727 s, 2.4 M/s

input results for device '/dev/sdc':
   3911680 sectors in
   0 bad sectors replaced by zeros
   fc8f3d6dc7e659c3124a4113d2d0ebe87466b497038aedf9f7a1b89c44eda8b9 (sha256)

output results for file '/home/ahoog/sd-emmc/viaforensics/af-book/
item001-unknown-serialno/item001-unknown-serialno.dc3dd':
   3911680 sectors out

dc3dd completed at 2011-02-22 04:49:34 -0600
```

You can then use the same general command, but change the parameters to image the eMMC which, for the device, is located at /dev/sdb. After these commands complete, the forensic images and log files are in ~/sd-emmc and are structured as follows:

```
hoog@ubuntu:~$ tree -h sd-emmc/
sd-emmc/
└── [4.0K]  viaforensics
    └── [4.0K]  af-book
        ├── [4.0K]  item001-emmc-unknown-serialno
        │   ├── [6.6G]  item001-emmc-unknown-serialno.dc3dd
        │   └── [4.0K]  log
        │       ├── [ 686]  item001-emmc-unknown-serialno.hashlog
        │       ├── [ 39K]  item001-emmc-unknown-serialno.log
        │       ├── [ 374]  item001-emmc-unknown-serialno.sha256.log
        │       └── [   0]  item001-emmc-unknown-serialno.stderr.log
        └── [4.0K]  item001-sd-unknown-serialno
            ├── [1.9G]  item001-sd-unknown-serialno.dc3dd
            └── [4.0K]  log
                ├── [ 726]  item001-sd-unknown-serialno.hashlog
                ├── [ 39K]  item001-sd-unknown-serialno.log
                ├── [ 296]  item001-sd-unknown-serialno.sha256.log
                └── [   0]  item001-sd-unknown-serialno.stderr.log

6 directories, 10 files
```

For each UMS device forensically imaged, we not only have the verified image but also a hashlog for the dd image, log file with date, time, system info and commands run, an error log, and finally a listing of each log file and its sha256 hash. This ensures sufficient details are known about the imaging process.

> **TIP**
>
> **Encrypted apps on the SD card**
>
> If apps are installed on the SD card, they are encrypted and thus, if the files are examined from the SD card image, they will be unreadable. However, when the SD card is not mounted on your forensic workstation, the unencrypted .apk files are mounted in /mnt/asec. If an investigation relies on .apk app analysis, ensure you acquire a copy of the unencrypted files too.

LOGICAL TECHNIQUES

As discussed at the start of this chapter, logical forensic techniques extract data that is allocated. This is typically achieved by accessing the file system. Logical techniques are often the first type of examination a forensic analyst will run because they are not only easier to execute but often provide sufficient data for the case. Android forensics physical techniques can provide far more data. However, they are more difficult to successfully execute and take considerably more effort to analyze.

Logical techniques also have the advantage of working in far more scenarios as the only requirement is that USB debugging is enabled. In other words, Android forensics logical techniques do not require root access.

In this section, we first cover techniques that are freely available (although AFLogical is only free for active law enforcement and government agencies) followed by a review of available commercial software.

ADB Pull

In Chapter 4, the recursive adb pull command was demonstrated several times as various parts of the file system were copied to the Ubuntu workstation for further analysis. Unless an Android device has root access or is running a custom ROM, the adb daemon running on the device that proxies the recursive copy only runs with shell permissions. As such, some of the more forensically relevant files are not accessible. However, there are still files which can be accessed.

If you attempt to access files that the shell user does not have permissions to, it simply does not copy the files:

```
ahoog@ubuntu:~$ adb pull /data adbpull
pull: building file list...
0 files pulled. 0 files skipped.
```

However, if you have sufficient privileges (root in the next example), then this method is very simple and effective:

```
ahoog@ubuntu:~$ adb pull /data adbpull/
pull: building file list...
<snip>
pull: /data/miscrild_nitz_long_name_31026 -> data/misc/rild_nitz_long_name_31026
pull: /data/misc/akmd_set.txt -> data/misc/akmd_set.txt

712 files pulled. 0 files skipped.
963 KB/s (208943249 bytes in 211.671s)
```

As you can see from the output above, the entire "/data" partition was copied to a local directory in just over three and a half minutes. The directory structure is maintained during the copy so you can then simply browse or otherwise analyze the files of interest from the workstation.

As most phones will not have root access (at least by default), this technique may appear to be of little value. However, it is a powerful utility to understand and there are several scenarios ideal for this approach. These scenarios include:

- On nonrooted devices, an adb pull can still access useful files such as unencrypted apps, most of the tmpfs file systems that can include user data such as browser history, and system information found in "/proc," "/sys," and other readable directories.
- On rooted devices, a pull of nearly all directories is quite simple and certain files and directories from "/data" would be of interest.
- When utilizing the physical technique, it is not always possible to mount some acquired file systems such as YAFFS2. If adbd is running with root permissions, you can quickly extract a logical copy of the file system with adb pull.

As adb is not only a free utility in the Android SDK but also very versatile, it should be one of the primary logical tools used on a device.

WARNING

adb Pull issues

Some recursive pulls using adb can fail in the middle of the data transfer due to permission or other issues. You should closely monitor the results of the command to determine if any issues were encountered. Breaking the recursive pull of large directories into smaller data pulls may yield better results.

Backup Analysis

When Android was first released, it did not provide a mechanism for users to backup their personal data. As a result, a number of backup applications were developed and distributed on the Android Market. For users running custom ROMs, there was an even more powerful backup utility developed called nandroid.

Many of the backup utilities have a "Save to SD Card" option (which users found extremely convenient) as well as several options to save to "the cloud." Either way, users could take a backup of their devices, and if needed they could restore required data. This is not only a great way for users to protect themselves from data loss, but it can be a great source of information for forensic analysts.

One of the more popular backup apps is RerWare's My Backup Pro which can take a backup of device data using Content Provider and even the entire "/data/data" files if the device has root access. The user can choose between saving to the SD card and saving to RerWare's server. The app supports (RerWare, LLC, n.d.) the following:

- Application install files (if phone has root access, this includes APK + Data and Market Links)
- Contacts
- Call log
- Browser bookmarks
- SMS (text messages)
- MMS (attachments in messages)
- System settings
- Home screens (including HTC Sense UI)
- Alarms
- Dictionary
- Calendars
- Music playlists
- Integrated third-party applications

The last bullet, "integrated third-party applications," refers to companies who provide RerWare hooks for data backup. At least initially, RerWare would pay developers to include RerWare backup support in their apps.

Interestingly, the app runs not only on Android but also on Windows Mobile, Blackberry, and soon Symbian OS. The user can take a backup on one platform and restore on a completely different supported OS. RerWare saves a single SQLite file to the SD card when the device backup is stored locally.

In the more recent releases of Android, a new backup API is now available. Developers can simply integrate these APIs into their apps and the rest of the backup is handled by Android and Google. This provides the users with secure, cloud-based backups with consistency across apps, and will likely become the de facto standard. Unfortunately, current research has not yet discovered useful artifacts from the new backup APIs left on an Android device.

Regardless of the backup app, forensic analysts should determine if one was installed and, if so, where the backup data is stored. The SD card should be examined as well as other devices such as a computer or laptop. The data saved in a backup is obviously of significant value in an examination.

AFLogical

AFLogical is an Android forensics logical technique which is distributed free to law enforcement and government agencies. The app, developed by viaForensics, extracts data using Content Providers, which are a key feature of the Android platform. This is the same technique that commercial forensics tools use for logical forensics.

Recall that Android's security model is effective in limiting access to app data except in a few circumstances. Here is a quick recap of the key components of Android's security model:

- Each application is assigned a unique Linux user and group id.
- Apps execute using their specific user ID in a dedicated process and Dalvik VM.
- Each app has dedicated storage, generally in "/data/data," that only the app can access.

However, the Android framework does provide a mechanism by which apps can share data. An app developer can include support for Content Providers within their application, which allows them to share data with other apps. The developer controls what data is exposed to other apps. During the install of an app, the user controls whether or not an app should gain access to the requested Content Providers.

Some examples of Content Providers are:

- SMS/MMS
- Contacts
- Calendar
- Facebook
- Gmail

And there are many more.

The AFLogical app takes advantage of the Content Provider architecture to gain access to data stored on the device. Similar to commercial Android logical tools, USB debugging must be enabled on the device for AFLogical to extract the data. The current version, 1.5.1, extracts data from 41 Content Providers and provides the output information to the SD card in CSV format and as an info.xml file, which provides details about the device and installed apps. AFLogical supports devices running Android 1.5 and later, and has been specifically updated to support extraction of large data sets such as an SMS database with over 35,000 messages. The currently supported Content Providers are:

1. Browser Bookmarks
2. Browser Searches
3. Calendars
4. Calendar Attendees
5. Calendar Events
6. Calendar Extended Properties
7. Calendar Reminders
8. Call Log Calls
9. Contacts Contact Methods
10. Contacts Extensions
11. Contacts Groups
12. Contacts Organizations
13. Contacts Phones

14. Contacts Settings
15. External Media
16. External Image Media
17. External Image Thumb Media
18. External Videos
19. IM Account
20. IM Accounts
21. IM Chats
22. IM Contacts Provider (IM Contacts)
23. IM Invitations
24. IM Messages
25. IM Providers
26. IM Provider Settings
27. Internal Image Media
28. Internal Image Thumb Media
29. Internal Videos
30. Maps-Friends
31. Maps-Friends extra
32. Maps-Friends contacts
33. MMS
34. Mms Parts Provider (MMSParts)
35. Notes
36. People
37. People Deleted
38. Phone Storage (HTC Incredible)
39. Search History
40. SMS
41. Social Contracts Activities

Let's walk through the steps for running AFLogical on a device. First, ensure you have downloaded AFLogical, which requires registration and approval from viaForensics. (You can access the AFLogical page at http://viaforensics.com/products/tools/aflogical/.) Next, you need to replace the user's SD card with an SD card you control and ensure that USB debugging is enabled on the device. Then connect the Android device to your Ubuntu workstation and make sure you pass the USB connection through to the VM.

> **WARNING**
>
> **Replace user's SD card**
>
> This version of AFLogical writes content directly to the SD card and it is important that the user's SD card is removed and replaced with the examiner's SD card. Failure to do this will either write data to the user's SD card or AFLogical will fail as it cannot write to the SD card. The commercial version of this app will eventually replace the writing to the SD card in favor of port forwarding over adb.

From a terminal session, verify you can see the device:

```
$adb devices
List of devices attached
0403555511112222F           device
```

Assuming you saved the AFLogical app in your home directory, you can install it with the following command:

```
ahoog@ubuntu:~$ adb install ~/AndroidForensics.apk
523 KB/s (31558 bytes in 0.058s)
        pkg: /data/local/tmp/AndroidForensics.apk
Success
```

Note: If AFLogical is already installed on the device, an error will display and you must uninstall the existing app before you can install the new version. To uninstall, run the following command:

```
ahoog@ubuntu:~$ adb install /opt/via/AFLogical/AndroidForensics.apk
824 KB/s (31558 bytes in 0.037s)
        pkg: /data/local/tmp/AndroidForensics.apk
Failure [INSTALL_FAILED_ALREADY_EXISTS]

ahoog@ubuntu:~$ adb uninstall com.viaforensics.android
Success
```

After the application is successfully installed, you can run the program from either the Android device directly or via command line. If you run the app from command line, you can simply start the app and then complete using the device or have it run automated. To run the app and extraction automatically, execute the following:

```
ahoog@ubuntu:~$ adb shell am start -n
com.viaforensics.android/com.viaforensics.android.ExtractAllData
Starting: Intent { cmp=com.viaforensics.android/.ExtractAllData }
```

The program immediately starts and begins to extract data from all supported Content Providers. If you are viewing the screen, you would see an image similar to Fig. 6.7.

Or you can simply start the app with the following:

```
ahoog@ubuntu:~$ adb shell am start -n
com.viaforensics.android/com.viaforensics.android.ForensicsActivity
Starting: Intent { cmp=com.viaforensics.android/.ForensicsActivity }
```

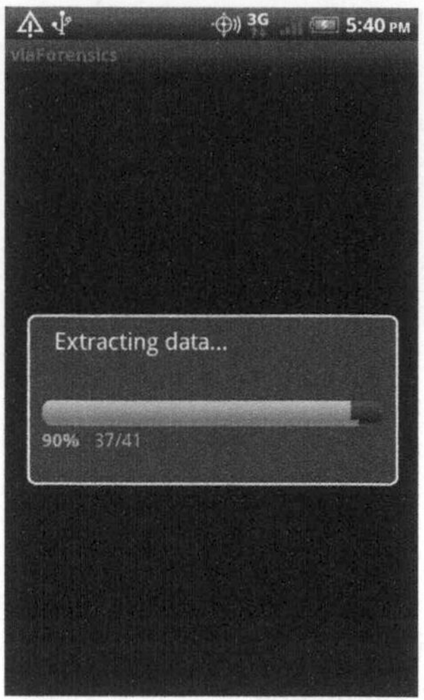

FIGURE 6.7

AFLogical, extract all from command line.

And then complete the acquisition using the screen presented on the device as shown in Fig. 6.8.

Otherwise, you can simply run the app directly from the All Apps screen on the device as shown in Fig. 6.9. First, access the Android app menu,

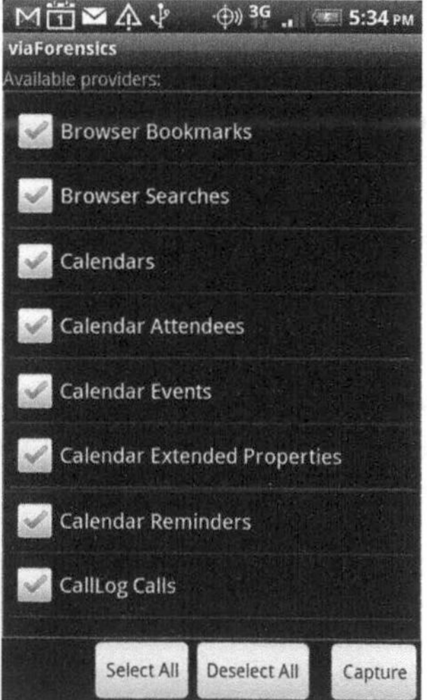

FIGURE 6.8

AFLogical, run from command line.

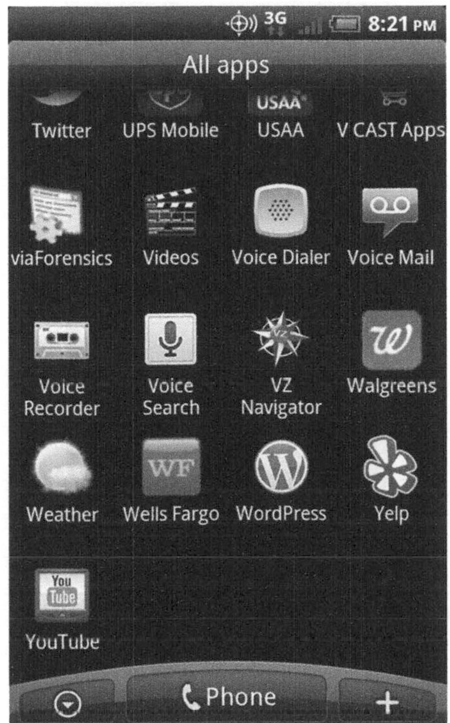

FIGURE 6.9

AFLogical in All Apps list.

look for a program called viaForensics and click on the icon to launch the app.

You will then be presented with the AFLogical data extraction screen. You can select or deselect individual Content Providers or leave all of them selected. Next, you hit Capture which will start the data collection process as illustrated in Fig. 6.10.

Once the data collection is complete, you will receive the corresponding message shown in Fig. 6.11.

The extracted data are saved to the SD card of the device in a directory called forensics and a subdirectory named after the date in YYYYMMDD.HHMM format. For this example, we moved the files from the SD card to an AFLogical directory on the local file system using adb pull. If you examine that folder, you see:

```
ahoog@ubuntu:~$ ls AFLogical/
20110221.1708
```

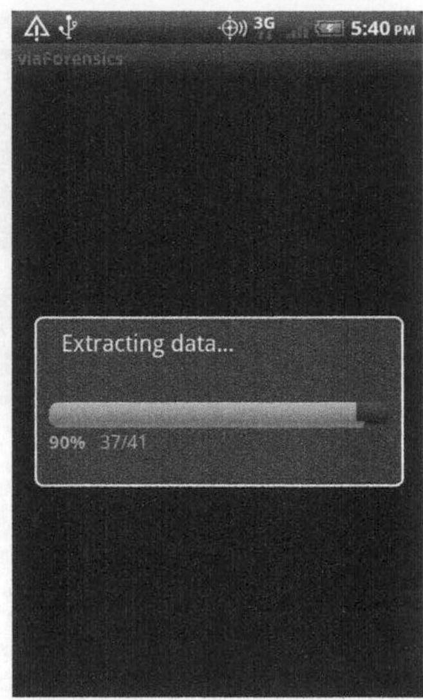

FIGURE 6.10

AFLogical capturing data.

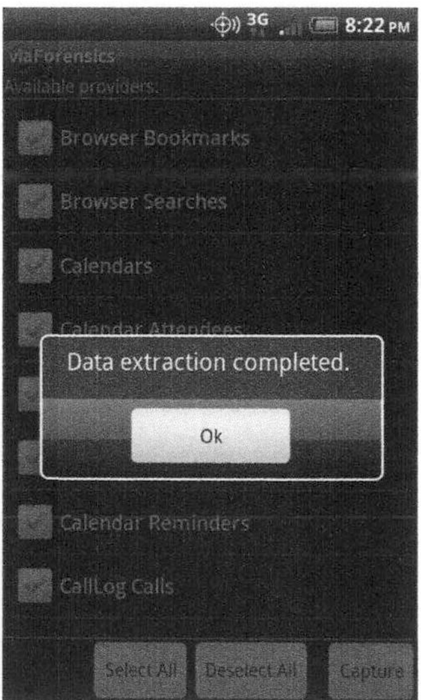

FIGURE 6.11

AFLogical, data extraction complete.

This then contains the extracted data:

```
ahoog@ubuntu:~$ ls AFLogical/20110221.1708/
Browser Bookmarks.csv          IM Providers.csv
Browser Searches.csv           IM ProviderSettings.csv
CallLog Calls.csv              info.xml
Contacts ContactMethods.csv    Internal Image Media.csv
Contacts Extensions.csv        Internal Image Thumb Media.csv
Contacts Groups.csv            Internal Videos.csv
Contacts Organizations.csv     Maps-Friends contacts.csv
Contacts Phones.csv            Maps-Friends.csv
Contacts Settings.csv          Maps-Friends extra .csv
External Image Media.csv       MMS.csv
External Image Thumb Media.csv MMSParts.csv
External Media.csv             People.csv
External Videos.csv            PhoneStorage (HTC Incredible).csv
IM Account.csv                 sanitize.sh
IM Accounts.csv                Search History.csv
IM Chats.csv                   SMS.csv
IM Contacts.csv                Social Contracts Activities.csv
IM Invitations.csv
```

The CSV files can be viewed using any editor or spreadsheet. There is also a file in the directory called info.xml, which contains information about the device including the IMSI, IMEI, Android version, network provider, and more, as well as the list of all installed apps.

```
ahoog@ubuntu:~$ less info.xml
<android-forensics>
<date-time>20110221.1708</date-time>
<IMSI>removed</IMSI>
<IMEI>removed</IMEI>
<build>
        <version.release>2.2</version.release>
        <version.sdk>8</version.sdk>
        <version.incremental>264707</version.incremental>
        <board>inc</board>
        <brand>verizon_wwe</brand>
        <device>inc</device>
        <display>FRF91</display>
        <fingerprint>verizon_wwe/inc/inc/inc:2.2/FRF91/264707:user/release-
keys</fingerprint>
        <host>HPA003</host>
        <id>FRF91</id>
        <model>ADR6300</model>
        <product>inc</product>
        <tags>release-keys</tags>
        <time>1285855309000</time>
        <type>user</type>
        <user>root</user>
</build>
<applications>
        <app>
                <label>Network Location</label>
                <className>null</className>
                <dataDir>/data/data/com.google.android.location</dataDir>
                <descriptionRes>0</descriptionRes>
                <flags>48709</flags>
                <manageSpaceActivityName>null</manageSpaceActivityName>
```

```
                <name>null</name>
                <packageName>com.google.android.location</packageName>
                <permission>null</permission>
                <processName>system</processName>
                <publicSourceDir>/system/app/NetworkLocation.apk
                </publicSourceDir>
                <sourceDir>/system/app/NetworkLocation.apk</sourceDir>
                <taskAffinity>com.google.android.location</taskAffinity>
                <uid>1000</uid>
                <enabled>true</enabled>
                <description>null</description>
                <packageinfo>                    <versionCode>8</versionCode>
                        <versionName>2.2</versionName>
                </packageinfo>  </app>
        <app>
                <label>IMDb</label>
                <className>null</className>
                <dataDir>/data/data/com.imdb.mobile</dataDir>
<snip>
```

The data can now be analyzed by the forensic examiner and easily shared with others.

> **WARNING**
>
> **Uninstall AFLogical**
>
> Do not forget to uninstall AFLogical. Failure to uninstall the app would mean that the Android device could potentially be returned to the owner with the forensic agent still accessible. To uninstall AFLogical, key in the following command:
>
> adb uninstall com.viaforensics.android
>
> This should return Success. Alternately, you can go to the home screen, press Menu, select Applications, Manage Applications, viaForensics, and finally Uninstall.

Commercial Providers

Many of the commercial mobile forensic software vendors now support Android. To date, the forensic software only supports a logical examination of an Android device using the same Content Provider technique used by AFLogical. It can be helpful for a forensic examiner to understand how each of the forensic software vendors implement Android support.

Each software company provided an evaluation copy of their software as well as an overview of their platform, which is included at the beginning of each section. A Motorola Droid running Android 2.2 was used for the examination. This section is not intended to evaluate each platform, but rather provide a helpful overview. The following forensic software packages were provided (reviewed in alphabetical order):

- Cellebrite UFED
- Compelson MOBILedit!
- EnCase Neutrino

- Micro Systemation XRY
- Paraben Device Seizure
- viaForensics' viaExtract

Two additional forensic software packages were tested. However, issues were encountered which prevented their inclusion at this time. These vendors do provide a forensic solution for Android and, if interested, you should review their offerings independently. The software packages omitted were Oxygen Forensic Suite 2010 and Logicube's CellDEK.

The challenge with any such overview is that the forensic software is updated frequently enough that a newer version likely already exists. Forensic examiners and security engineers interested in a particular software package should check the vendor's web site or contact them directly.

Cellebrite UFED

The following overview of Cellebrite was provided by the vendor:

The Cellebrite UFED Forensic system is a stand-alone device capable of acquiring data from approximately 1600 mobile devices and storing the information on a USB drive, SD card or PC. UFED also has a built-in SIM card reader and cloner. The ability to clone a SIM card is a powerful feature as you can create and insert a clone of the original SIM and the phone will function normally. However, it will not register on the mobile carrier's network, eliminating the need for Faraday bags and the possibility that the data on the phone will be updated (or erased). The UFED package ships with about 70 cables for connecting to most mobile devices available today. Connection protocols supported include serial, USB, infrared, and Bluetooth.

Cellebrite also distributes the UFED Report Manager, which provides an intuitive reporting interface and allows the user to export data/reports into Excel, MS Outlook, Outlook Express, and CSV or to simply print the report.

The UFED device fully supports Unicode and thus, can process phones with any language enabled. Also, the following data types are extracted:

- Phone Book
- Text Messages
- Call History (Received, Dialed, Missed)
- SIM ID Cloning
- Deleted Text Messages off SIM/USIM
- Audio Recordings
- Videos
- Pictures
- Phone Details (IMEI/ESN phone number)

Installation

The UFED system is a stand-alone unit and is packaged in a soft case containing the UFED device, user manual, software CD-ROM, USB Bluetooth radio (Cambridge

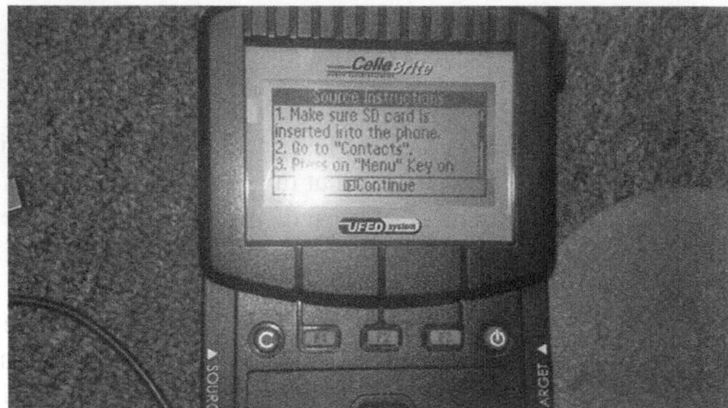

FIGURE 6.12

UFED instructions for Android device.

Silicon Radio Ltd), 250 MB USB drive, and roughly 72 cables for connecting to supported devices.

The UFED system provides several mechanisms by which the firmware and software can be updated. After setting the date and time, an examiner can simply connect the UFED system to the network via an Ethernet cable, provided DHCP and Internet access are available. Next, select Services, Upgrade, Upgrade Application Now, and select HTTP Server as the source. For this test, the latest Application software, version 1.1.0.5, was located and installed. As the UFED system is a stand-alone solution, no additional installs are necessary.

Acquisition

The acquisition of the Motorola Droid was quite fast and simple on the UFED system. After powering the device on, select Extract Phone Data, Motorola CDMA, Moto. A855 Droid (Android), USB disk drive (destination), and the desired Content types. The following instructions were then displayed by the UFED system (see Fig. 6.12):

```
Moto. A855 Droid (Android):
Before starting the transaction, prepare phonebook for transfer, as follows:
1. Make sure SD card is inserted into the phone.
2. Go to "Contacts".
3. Press on "Menu" Key on the phone.
4. Select "Import/Export".
5. Select "Export to SD card" and "OK".
6. Wait for completing of Export to .vcf file.

To enable phone USB Connectivity, set Connection settings as follows:
Menu -> Settings -> Applications -> Development -> Select the checkboxes: "USB
debugging" and "Stay awake".
```

It should be noted that the contacts list will be saved to the SD card if the suggested steps are followed. After performing these steps, you hit Continue and the acquisition proceeds. The UFED system next prompts:

```
Set USB to Mass Storage (Memory Card) mode on the SOURCE phone
```

And after this step is completed, the acquisition proceeds. You may be prompted to set UMS again before the acquisition is complete. The acquisition process took just over three minutes and provided the following prompt:

```
Moto. A855 Droid (Android):
Please return the Connection settings back: Menu -> Settings -> Applications ->
Development -> unmark the checkboxes: "USB debugging" & "Stay awake"
```

The results from the acquisition were stored on the flash drive that was plugged into the UFED. A 25 MB folder was created on this drive with folders for videos, audio, and images. There were also three files of interest created: PhoneBook 2010_11_23 (001).htm, SMSMessages 2010_11_23 (001).htm, and Report.htm. All these can be viewed in a web browser. The file Report.htm contains the entire report of the extraction. This contains sections for Phone Examination Report Properties, Phone Examination Report Index, Phone Contacts, Phone SMS—Text Messages, Phone Incoming Calls List, Phone Outgoing Calls List, Phone Missed Calls List, Images, Ringtones, Audio, and Video.

The entire acquisition process took approximately ten minutes. After the acquisition was completed, a quick examination of the SD card revealed a file named 00001.vcf that contained the contact information from the export process.

Phone information was well laid out and was quite accurate.

Data presentation and analysis

The acquisition data was stored on a flash drive connected to the UFED system and contained a folder that stored videos, audio files, and images as well as three HTML files, which contained the report data:

1. PhoneBook 2010_11_23 (001).htm
2. SMSMessages 2010_11_23 (001).htm
3. Report.htm

These files can be viewed in a web browser and samples from the report are displayed in Fig. 6.13, in which thorough phone information was captured.

Fig. 6.14 shows how the Phone Contacts are laid out.

Fig. 6.15 shows text messages displayed chronologically with detailed information on whether the message was sent or received.

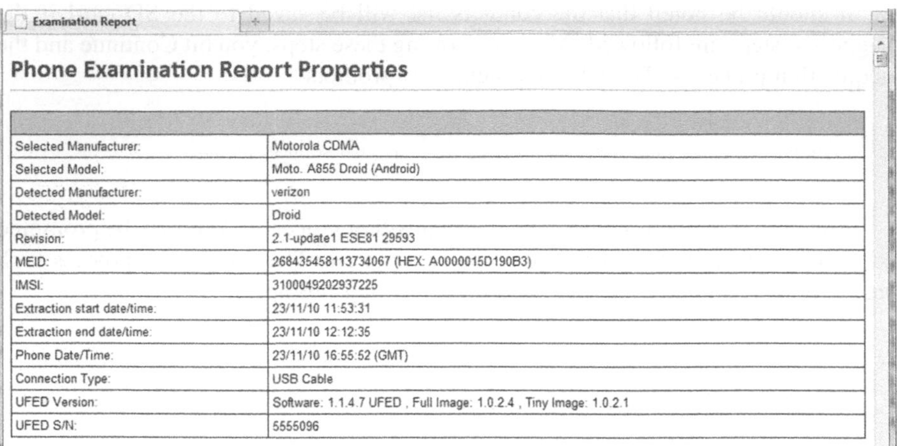

Examination Report

Phone Examination Report Properties

Selected Manufacturer:	Motorola CDMA
Selected Model:	Moto. A855 Droid (Android)
Detected Manufacturer:	verizon
Detected Model:	Droid
Revision:	2.1-update1 ESE81 29593
MEID:	268435458113734067 (HEX: A0000015D190B3)
IMSI:	3100049202937225
Extraction start date/time:	23/11/10 11:53:31
Extraction end date/time:	23/11/10 12:12:35
Phone Date/Time:	23/11/10 16:55:52 (GMT)
Connection Type:	USB Cable
UFED Version:	Software: 1.1.4.7 UFED , Full Image: 1.0.2.4 , Tiny Image: 1.0.2.1
UFED S/N:	5555096

FIGURE 6.13

UFED phone information reporting.

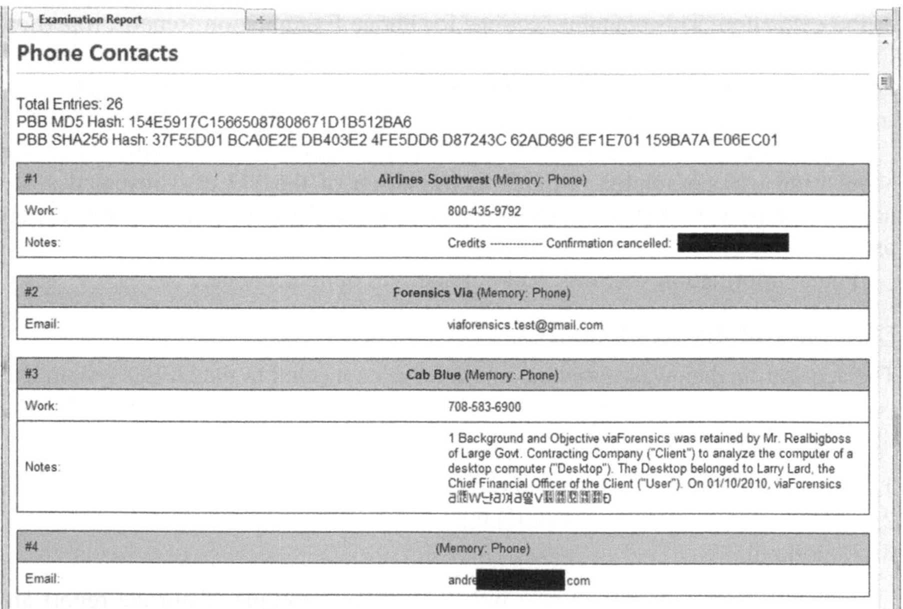

Examination Report

Phone Contacts

Total Entries: 26
PBB MD5 Hash: 154E5917C15665087808671D1B512BA6
PBB SHA256 Hash: 37F55D01 BCA0E2E DB403E2 4FE5DD6 D87243C 62AD696 EF1E701 159BA7A E06EC01

#1	**Airlines Southwest** (Memory: Phone)
Work:	800-435-9792
Notes:	Credits ------------ Confirmation cancelled:

#2	**Forensics Via** (Memory: Phone)
Email:	viaforensics.test@gmail.com

#3	**Cab Blue** (Memory: Phone)
Work:	708-583-6900
Notes:	1 Background and Objective viaForensics was retained by Mr. Realbigboss of Large Govt. Contracting Company ("Client") to analyze the computer of a desktop computer ("Desktop"). The Desktop belonged to Larry Lard, the Chief Financial Officer of the Client ("User"). On 01/10/2010, viaForensics

#4	(Memory: Phone)
Email:	andr com

FIGURE 6.14

UFED phone contacts reporting.

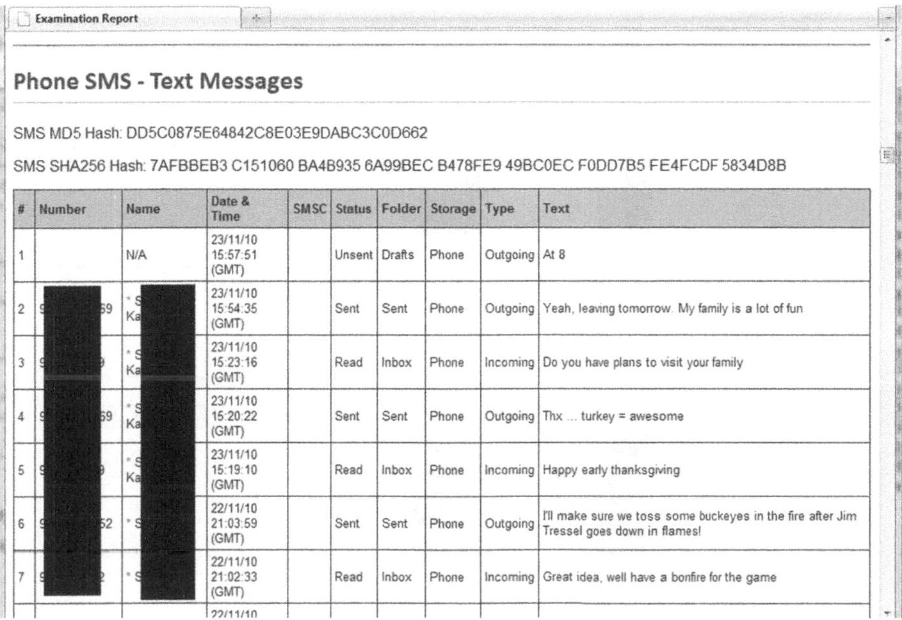

Examination Report

Phone SMS - Text Messages

SMS MD5 Hash: DD5C0875E64842C8E03E9DABC3C0D662

SMS SHA256 Hash: 7AFBBEB3 C151060 BA4B935 6A99BEC B478FE9 49BC0EC F0DD7B5 FE4FCDF 5834D8B

#	Number	Name	Date & Time	SMSC	Status	Folder	Storage	Type	Text
1		N/A	23/11/10 15:57:51 (GMT)		Unsent	Drafts	Phone	Outgoing	At 8
2	[illegible]	[illegible]	23/11/10 15:54:35 (GMT)		Sent	Sent	Phone	Outgoing	Yeah, leaving tomorrow. My family is a lot of fun
3	[illegible]	[illegible]	23/11/10 15:23:16 (GMT)		Read	Inbox	Phone	Incoming	Do you have plans to visit your family
4	[illegible]	[illegible]	23/11/10 15:20:22 (GMT)		Sent	Sent	Phone	Outgoing	Thx ... turkey = awesome
5	[illegible]	[illegible]	23/11/10 15:19:10 (GMT)		Read	Inbox	Phone	Incoming	Happy early thanksgiving
6	[illegible]	[illegible]	22/11/10 21:03:59 (GMT)		Sent	Sent	Phone	Outgoing	I'll make sure we toss some buckeyes in the fire after Jim Tressel goes down in flames!
7	[illegible]	[illegible]	22/11/10 21:02:33 (GMT)		Read	Inbox	Phone	Incoming	Great idea, well have a bonfire for the game
			22/11/10						

FIGURE 6.15

UFED SMS reporting.

However, deleted text messages are not displayed, nor are MMS messages.

Call logs are displayed chronologically as shown in Fig. 6.16, and include the length of the call. They are categorized into Incoming, Outgoing, and Missed sections.

Several calls were deleted from the call logs; however, UFED was able to extract and display the details.

All of the images found on the phone are reported, along with a thumbnail of the image and details, including file name, size, date and time created, and resolution, as shown in Fig. 6.17.

Deleted images did not appear, and it seemed as though a duplicate of each image was created. Both audio and video files are reported. The report includes file name, file size, date and time created, and a link to view or listen to the media, as shown in Fig. 6.18.

No deleted videos were returned and songs uploaded to the device did not appear in the report. The audio files that were reported were returned from Google Maps Navigation.

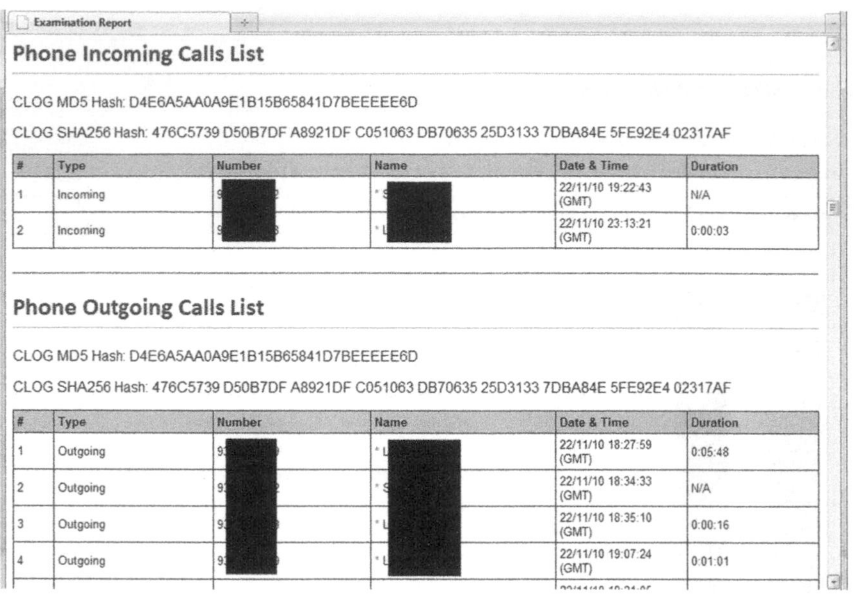

FIGURE 6.16

UFED phone calls reporting.

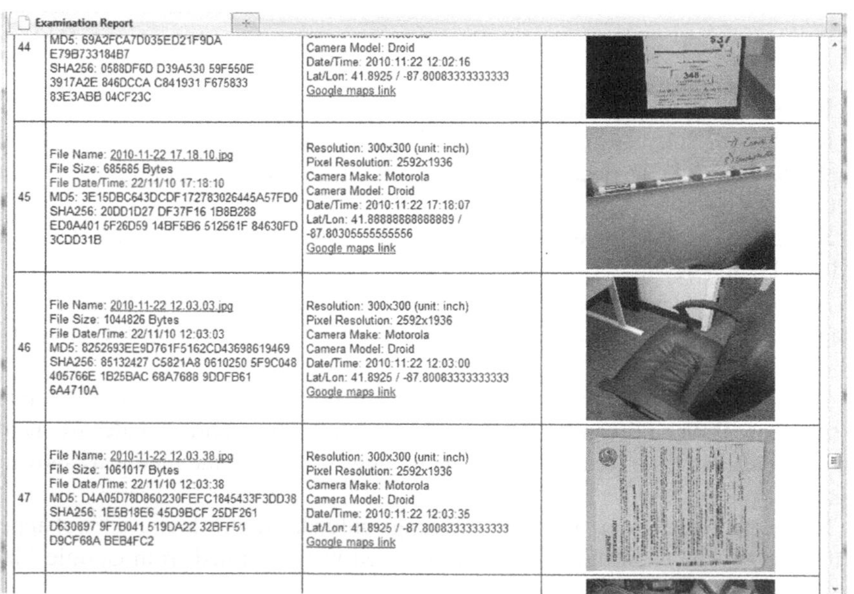

FIGURE 6.17

UFED images reporting.

Examination Report

Audio

#	File Name	File Size	File Date/Time	File Link
1	._speech_nav_6.wav MD5: 2BAA14778E75CC40819EB9CF62A36900 SHA256: 13D67661 C6C2711 8E898FC F6B0779 C564824 20E4A70 7805C5E C5CFD46 94CDE4A	141100 Bytes	22/11/10 17:47:24	._speech_nav_6.wav
2	._speech_nav_5.wav MD5: E8180DDA4FC4B1D906DBCB7B760C4E45 SHA256: CCF55A02 43F0CF4 6AB48C5 F4E892E F08D9FF D31F9E8 BE49DB9 9761569 BCF8F03	135084 Bytes	22/11/10 17:48:49	._speech_nav_5.wav
3	._speech_nav_4.wav MD5: 599B31EEB47624536F9132B9B9BA29B0 SHA256: A7A97428 67F8358 D0AC71F A1000EA A037FE9 0474E88 AFCDF0E C83BBB7 1A2913C	82604 Bytes	22/11/10 17:48:49	._speech_nav_4.wav

Video

#	File Name	File Size	File Date/Time	File Link
1	video-2010-11-22-12-11-26.3gp MD5: 1595E8179DB42491D418F085F6D9F87E SHA256: 453F6DB7 BF10E16 12DE98B A436B2F 9471873 613351C 0CF0448 6BF648B C13B9E1	7602947 Bytes	22/11/10 12:12:06	video-2010-11-22-12-11-26.3gp
2	bigTenNetworkCall.3gp MD5: 73D90D284FDC93E4F44140611306ABA0 SHA256: 3544FF97 D9AD4CA CF4274F D4B956D F1F6049 93410A0 3841D82 DD10CF5 FB6F207	3276388 Bytes	22/11/10 13:42:04	bigTenNetworkCall.3gp
	interceptionPlay.3gp MD5: 5859C0005DC4D3C82FF364A89E5D87C2			

FIGURE 6.18

UFED audio and video reporting.

Compelson MOBILedit!

The following overview of MOBILedit! was provided by the vendor:

With just a single click, MOBILedit! Forensic collects all possible data from mobile phones and generates extensive reports onto a PC that can be stored or printed. It is the most universal mobile phone solution with software supporting most GSM phones and open architecture allowing the support of any phone. The system allows you to customize the output making it completely adaptable to the needs of your judicial system.

MOBILedit! Forensic does a complete analysis of the phone including its phone book, last dialed numbers, missed calls, received calls, MMS messages, SMS messages, photos, videos, files, phone details, calendar, notes, tasks, and much more.

MOBILedit! Forensic caters to the entire world with reports that can be generated in any language. You are able to prepare creative templates according to your specific needs. You construct all the text that you would like to see appear in every final report. It also allows for XML export, so that you can connect the application with other systems. The XSL module exports and nicely formats all data in the package to an Internet browser. You can burn, send, and share the report as needed.

MOBILedit! Forensic reports can be created without the touch of a human hand. While there is no need to import or export stubs of data from SIMs or phones, it is possible in manual investigation mode in MOBILedit! Forensic. It is read-only and hence, it prevents changes in the device, which could mean the disappearance of evidence. All items are also protected against later modifications by MD5 hash codes used in digital signatures. It helps you to quickly locate the possible place of modification.

MOBILedit! Forensic also has frequent updates and upgrades so that you can be sure you are using the absolute latest in technology. Its detailed reports and user-friendly design make it a pleasure to work with.

Installation

The MOBILedit!4 Forensic application was downloaded from www.mobiledit.com and the install only took a few minutes. After the installation is completed and the application is run for the first time, you are presented with a prompt to check for updates.

To activate the software, Compelson sends an e-mail with an "activation card" attachment. This PDF file includes installation instructions as well as an activation key that worked without any issues.

Acquisition

To begin the acquisition, the examiner must first connect the Android device to the forensic workstation using USB and ensure USB debugging is enabled. MOBILedit! attempts to detect the device as shown in Fig. 6.19.

After clicking "Finish," there was a notification prompting the installation of the "Connector" app on the device, shown in Fig. 6.20.

Following the quick installation, you create a name for the investigation and select the type of data you want to extract. In the example shown in Fig. 6.21, the

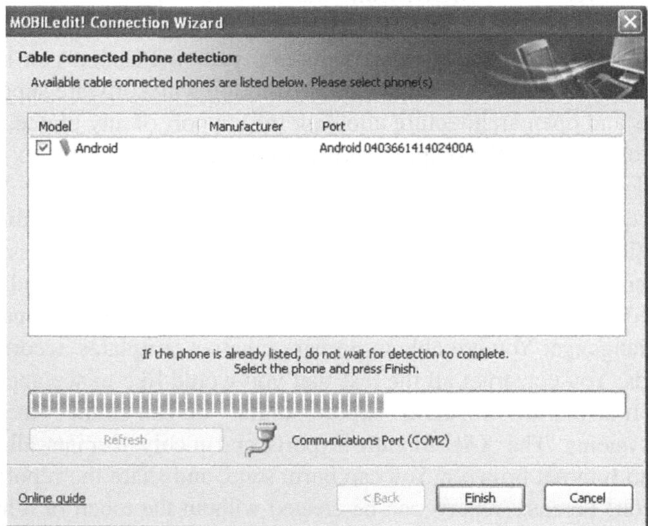

FIGURE 6.19

detect Android device.

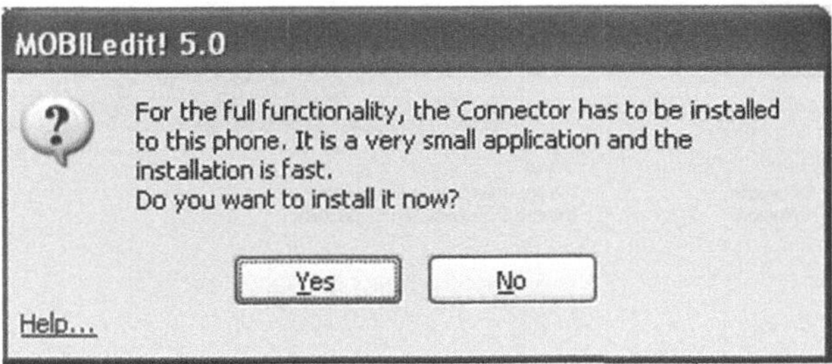

FIGURE 6.20

Install the connector.

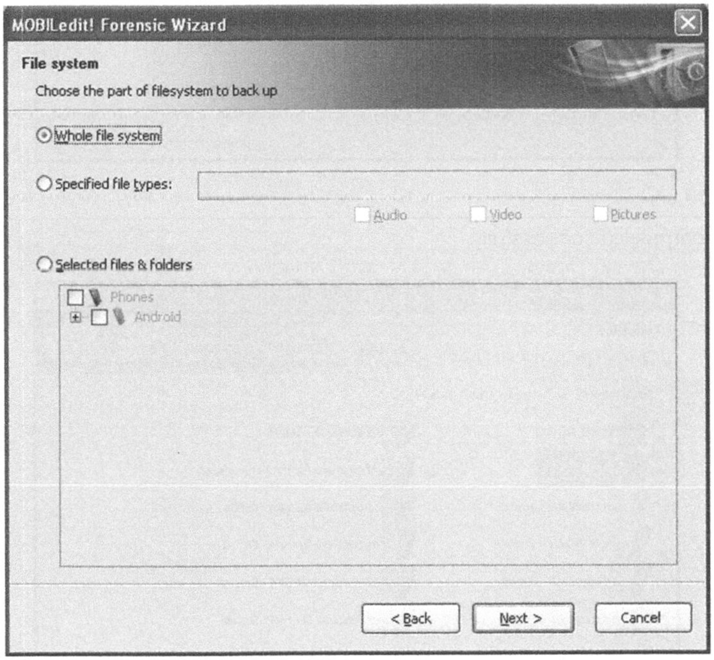

FIGURE 6.21

Take backup of the whole file system.

option to take a backup of the "Whole file system" was selected, which then executed without error and presented a success status as illustrated in Fig. 6.22.

You can then decide if you want to add this to an already existing case or create a new one. For this example, shown in Fig. 6.23, a new case was created and a data export format option of XLS was selected.

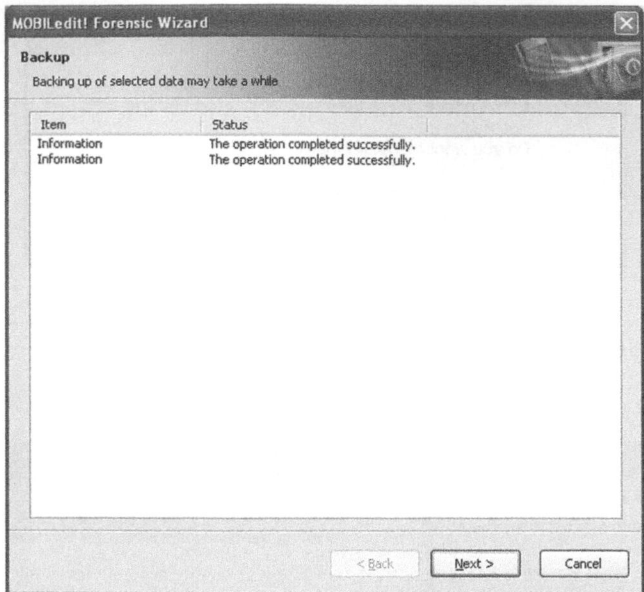

FIGURE 6.22

Operation completed successfully.

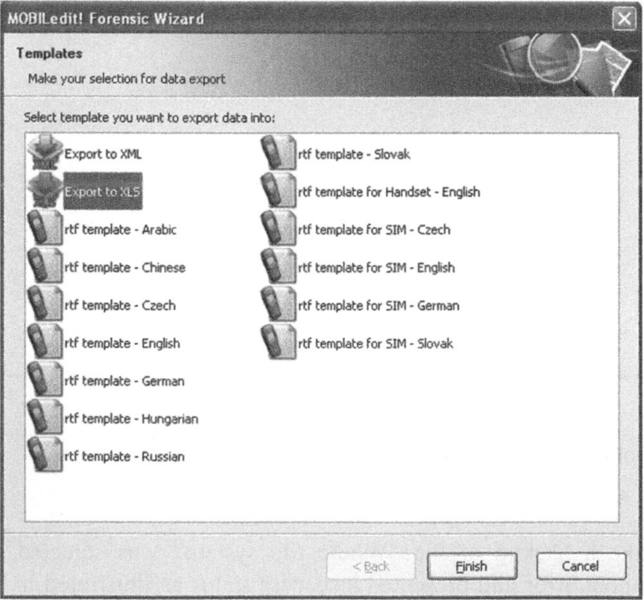

FIGURE 6.23

Data export format.

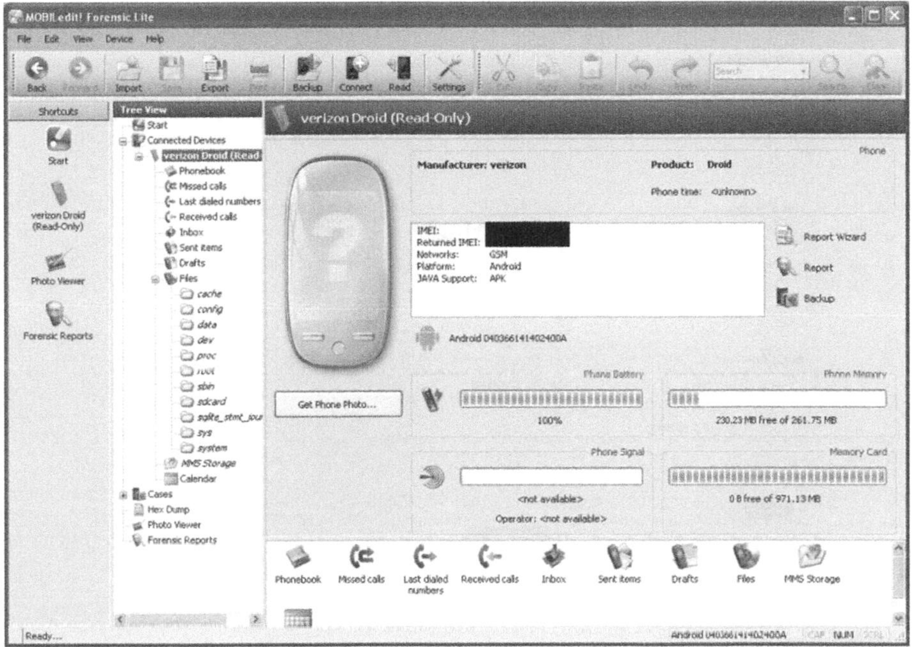

FIGURE 6.24

Main screen.

Data presentation and analysis

Immediately following the acquisition of the device, MOBILedit displays statistics on the devices that were acquired, as well as a view of the application data available for analysis. Fig. 6.24 shows the main screen where the examiner can see specific device information including the IMEI number, serial number, and details on the amount of Phone memory, Battery signal, Network signal, and Memory card space available on the device.

The next option in the Tree View is the Phonebook where the examiner can view all contacts stored within the Phonebook including e-mail address, phone numbers, nicknames, and any notes entered regarding the contact, as shown in Fig. 6.25.

Call logs are next and are separated into Missed calls, Last dialed numbers, and Received calls as shown in Fig. 6.26.

SMS messages are similarly separated into categories including Inbox, Sent items, and Drafts. Each section contains the date and time the message was received (or sent), the message content, and who the message was from. Contact names are linked to the Phonebook, so both name and phone numbers are displayed. Fig. 6.27 shows the SMS message inbox.

Any MMS messages are displayed within the "MMS Storage" folder, shown in Fig. 6.28. On the left-hand side, information about the message is displayed,

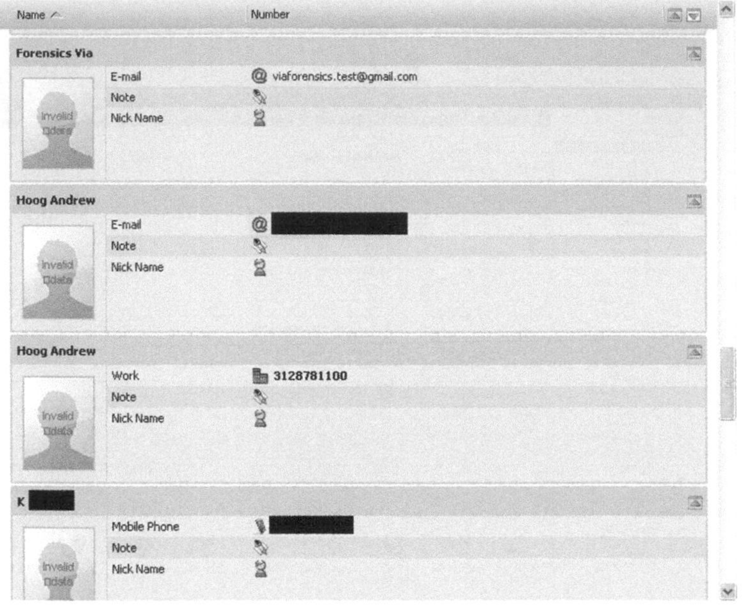

FIGURE 6.25

Phonebook.

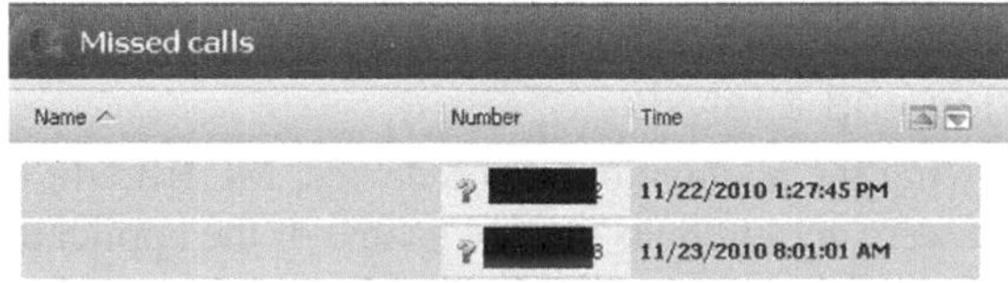

FIGURE 6.26

Call logs—Missed calls.

including the subject, number it was sent from, number it was sent to, and date and time. On the right-hand side is a preview of the actual image.

Selecting the Calendar option will literally pull up a calendar within the reporting tool as shown in Fig. 6.29.

Additional data extracted from the device or SD card is shown within the "files" directory. This directory contains a listing of the file system on the device. While some of these folders are empty (such as cache, config, and data), there are also some folders which contain raw files acquired from the device. For example, within the SD card folder, the subfolder "secret stuff" contained two files shown in Fig. 6.30.

Finally, the tool also provides a hex dump capability for specified files. After selecting "Hex Dump," and then a file (in this example, a .jpg file was selected),

Inbox

Received	From
11/23/2010 9:23:16 AM	9)
Do you have plans to visit your family	
11/23/2010 9:19:10 AM	9)
Happy early thanksgiving	
11/22/2010 3:02:33 PM	2)
Great idea, well have a bonfire for the game	
11/22/2010 3:00:20 PM	2)
Ohio St is...... wow, 17.5 pt favorites? Even I think thats a liiittle bit much	
11/22/2010 2:58:17 PM	)
Martin is a playmaker.... But were talking a D that allows 33 points a game!	
11/22/2010 2:51:27 PM	2)
Were talking about the same Denard that got benched a couple games ago? No WAY does he get through that D line. Heywards gonna eat the guy	

FIGURE 6.27

SMS messages—Inbox.

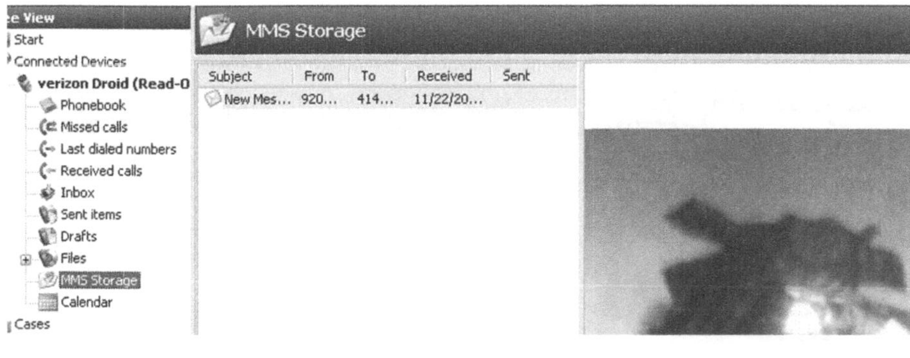

FIGURE 6.28

MMS storage.

the hex dump is viewed on the right-hand side using a hex editor as shown in Fig. 6.31.

Most of the raw user data files on the Android can be found within the "data" folder and, when MOBILedit created an entry in the Tree View for this folder (under the "Files" directory), it did not contain any files.

One thing to note is that when the acquisition and analysis was complete, the "MOBILedit! Connector" application was still installed on the device. Examiners should strongly consider manually uninstalling the software from the device after the investigation is complete.

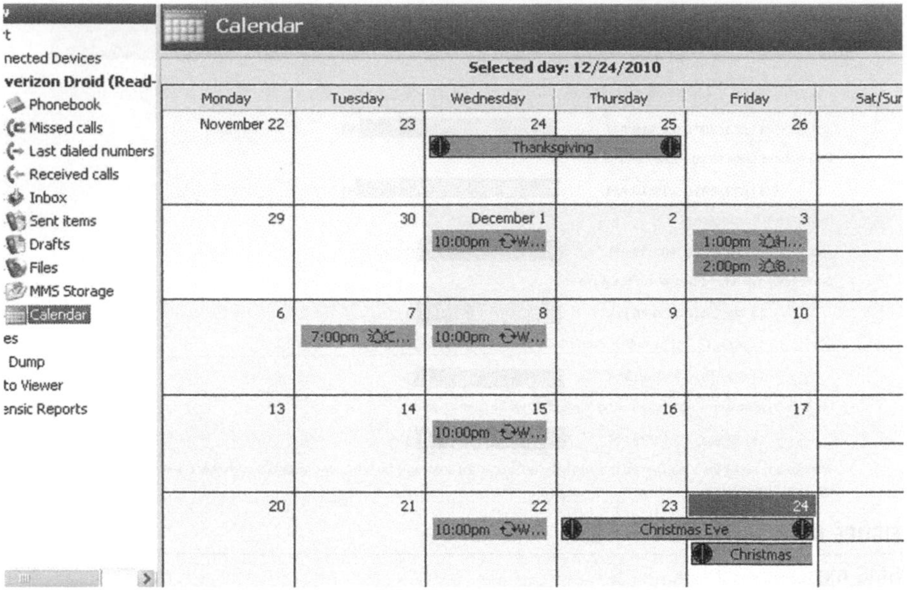

FIGURE 6.29

Calendar.

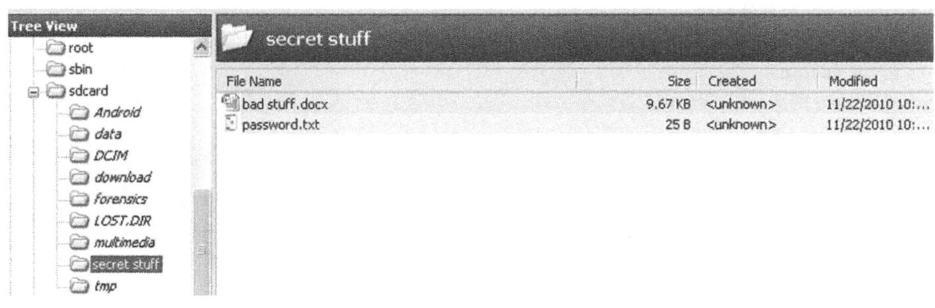

FIGURE 6.30

SD card files.

EnCase Neutrino

The following overview of Neutrino was provided by the vendor:

EnCase® Neutrino® is designed for law enforcement, security analysts, and eDiscovery specialists who need to forensically collect and review data from mobile devices. Investigators can process and analyze mobile device data alongside other types of digital evidence within any EnCase® product.

The solution features hardware support and parsing capabilities for the most common mobile devices and Smartphone operating systems including iPhone, Palm,

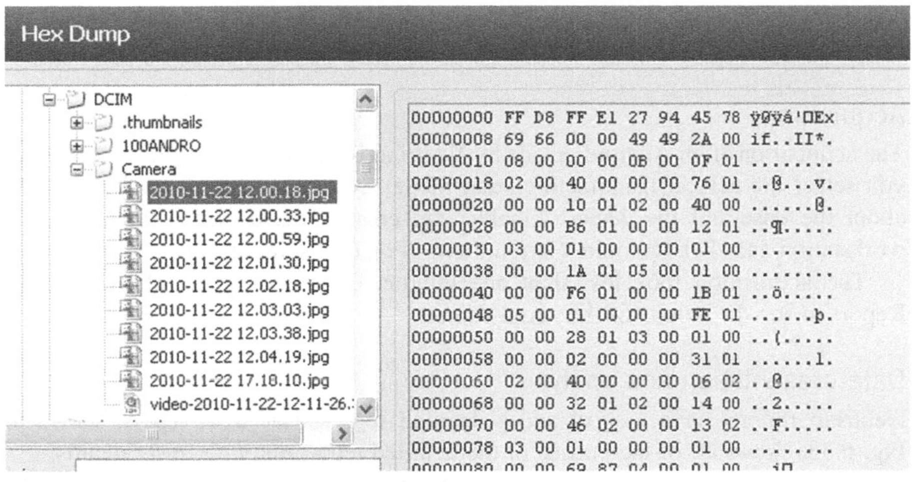

FIGURE 6.31

Hex dump.

BlackBerry®, Android, Windows Mobile, Motorola, Nokia, Samsung, and many more. Investigators can collect, analyze, and preserve all potentially relevant data including:

- Device Settings
- Contacts
- Call logs
- E-mail
- Images
- SMS/MMS
- Calendars
- Other files stored on the device

With EnCase Neutrino an investigator can:

- Collect data from a wide variety of devices, following an easy to use wizard
- Correlate data from multiple devices and computer media
- Seamlessly integrate collected data into EnCase Forensic or EnCase Enterprise for analysis
- Parse data quickly to improve speed of investigation process
- Access more data on selected devices in comparison to similar products

Installation

The installation of EnCase Neutrino first required installing EnCase, then Neutrino. The software installation proceeded without issue when following the on-screen instructions. To use the software, you must have a hardware USB dongle provided by EnCase.

Acquisition

The acquisition of an Android device by Neutrino is handled in a single screen. First, you select the device, manufacturer, and model. Next, you enter basic information about the case and the device. Finally, you connect the device to your forensic workstation and click "Acquire Current Item." Fig. 6.32 shows the acquisition screen.

The acquisition took less than one minute. Once completed, click Generate Report to see the results of the acquisition.

Data presentation and analysis

Neutrino reports have a short and a detailed report. The short report, shown in Fig. 6.33, shows all of the entries of the detailed report but with fewer details.

And the detailed view provides much greater detail about the contacts as shown in Fig. 6.34.

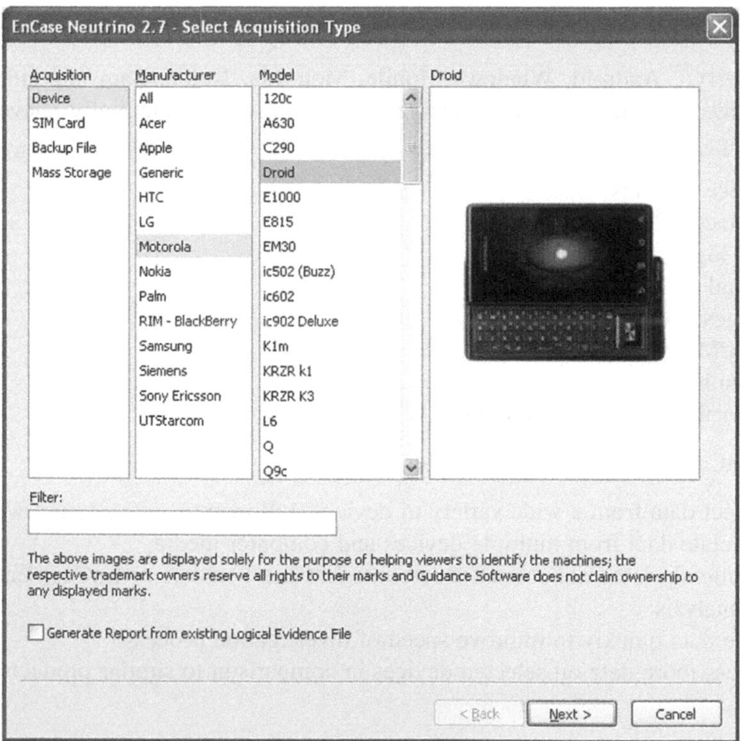

FIGURE 6.32

Neutrino acquisition screen.

Ma			m com
A			
E			
K a			
Andrew Hoog			
J			
J			
K			
R			

FIGURE 6.33

Neutrino contacts in short report.

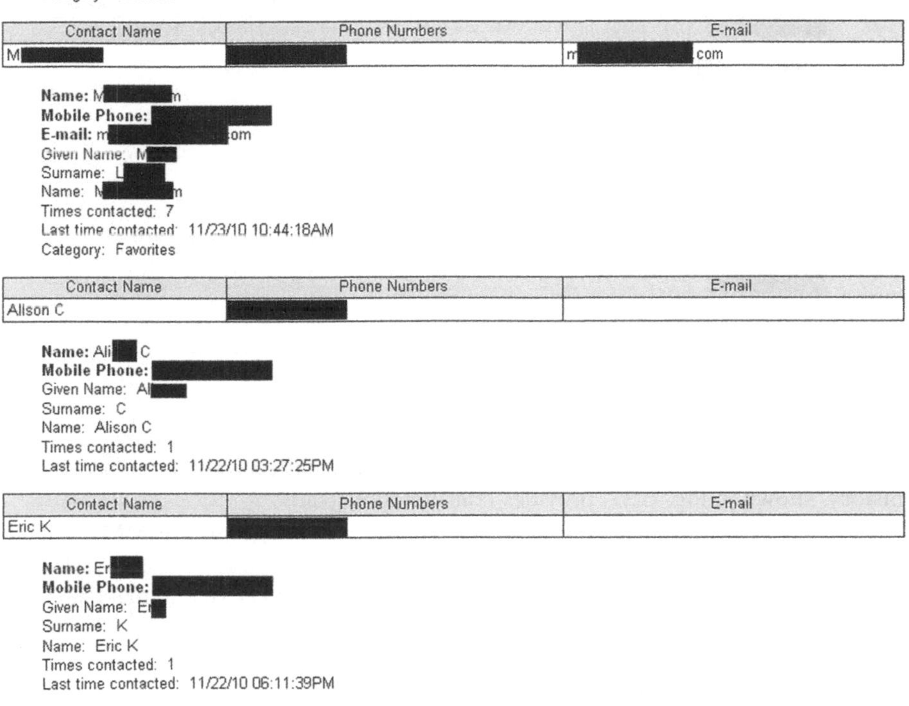

Last time contacted: 11/23/10 10:44:18AM
Category: Favorites

Contact Name	Phone Numbers	E-mail
M		m .com

Name: M m
Mobile Phone:
E-mail: m om
Given Name: M
Surname: L
Name: M m
Times contacted: 7
Last time contacted: 11/23/10 10:44:18AM
Category: Favorites

Contact Name	Phone Numbers	E-mail
Alison C		

Name: Ali C
Mobile Phone:
Given Name: Al
Surname: C
Name: Alison C
Times contacted: 1
Last time contacted: 11/22/10 03:27:25PM

Contact Name	Phone Numbers	E-mail
Eric K		

Name: Er
Mobile Phone:
Given Name: E
Surname: K
Name: Eric K
Times contacted: 1
Last time contacted: 11/22/10 06:11:39PM

FIGURE 6.34

Neutrino contacts in detailed report.

The SMS section also has a short and detailed view. The short view only shows the other phone number in the conversation, the date and time of the message, the message direction (sent or received), and the message contents. The detailed view, shown in Fig. 6.35, includes information such as the name associated with the phone number involved with the message and the status of the message.

Text:
I'll make sure we toss some buckeyes in the fire after Jim Tressel goes down in flames!
Type: sent
Folder: Outbox
Status: sent
Display Name: K
Status Text: read

Type	Remote Number	Date	Text
Read		11/22/10 04:02:33PM	Great idea, well have a bonfire for the game

Phone:
Date: 11/22/10 04:02:33PM
Text: Great idea, well have a bonfire for the game
Type: received
Folder: Inbox
Status: read
Display Name: K
Status Text: read

Type	Remote Number	Date	Text
Sent		11/22/10 04:01:15PM	Well, be ready Saturday evening for my Michigan flag to be planted ...

Phone:
Date: 11/22/10 04:01:15PM
Text:
Well, be ready Saturday evening for my Michigan flag to be planted in your front yard
Type: sent
Folder: Outbox
Status: sent
Display Name: K
Status Text: read

Type	Remote Number	Date	Text
Read		11/22/10 04:00:20PM	Ohio St is...... wow, 17.5 pt favorites? Even I think thats a liiii...

FIGURE 6.35

Neutrino SMS in detailed report.

MMS messages only appear in the detailed view, shown in Fig. 6.36.

No deleted SMS messages were recovered. The detailed view of the user's web history, shown in Fig. 6.37, provides considerable details.

The only photos recovered from the device were the images sent as MMS, not the photos or videos saved on the device's SD card.

The report can be exported in other formats, such as to HTML, so that the entire report can be viewed in one page, as illustrated in Fig. 6.38

Micro Systemation XRY

The following overview of XRY was provided by the vendor:

XRY is a dedicated mobile device forensic tool developed by Micro Systemation (MSAB) based in Stockholm.

XRY has been available since 2002 and "XRY Complete" is a package containing the software and hardware to allow logical and physical analysis of mobile devices. The product comes shipped in a handy portable case with bespoke interior and all the necessary hardware included, which are as follows:

- XRY Forensic Pack Software License Key
- Communication hub for USB, Bluetooth, and Infrared connectivity

MMS

Type	Date	Address	Subject
Read	11/22/10 06:21:41PM	4[redacted]0	New Message

From: 4143742520
Subject: New Message
Date: 11/22/10 06:21:41PM
Type: incoming
Status: read
Folder: Inbox
Attachments:
applicationsmil951.smil

imagejpeg952.jpg

Type: incoming
Status Text: read

FIGURE 6.36

Neutrino MMS in detailed report.

Page 39

Type: Visited URL
URL: http://ay-ziggy-zoomba.com/phpBB3
Title: http://ay-ziggy-zoomba.com/phpBB3
Date: 11/22/10 04:45:16PM
Visit Count: 1

Type	URL
Visited URL	http://ay-ziggy-zoomba.com/phpBB3/viewforum.php?f=3&sid=eb5246136c454119c448e51fde9ae2ca

Type: Visited URL
URL: http://ay-ziggy-zoomba.com/phpBB3/viewforum.php?f=3&sid=eb5246136c454119c448e51fde9ae2ca
Title: Ay-Ziggy-Zoomba.com • View forum - Football
Date: 11/22/10 04:46:03PM
Visit Count: 1

Type	URL
Visited URL	http://ay-ziggy-zoomba.com/phpBB3/viewforum.php?f=2&sid=eb5246136c454119c448e51fde9ae2ca

Type: Visited URL
URL: http://ay-ziggy-zoomba.com/phpBB3/viewforum.php?f=2&sid=eb5246136c454119c448e51fde9ae2ca
Title: Ay-Ziggy-Zoomba.com • View forum - Men's Hoops
Date: 11/22/10 04:46:17PM
Visit Count: 1

Type	URL
Visited URL	http://ay-ziggy-zoomba.com/phpBB3/viewtopic.php?f=2&t=27047

Type: Visited URL
URL: http://ay-ziggy-zoomba.com/phpBB3/viewtopic.php?f=2&t=27047
Title: Ay-Ziggy-Zoomba.com • View topic - Video about the bronze falcon
Date: 11/22/10 04:46:29PM
Visit Count: 1

Type	URL
Visited URL	http://yahoo.com/

FIGURE 6.37

Neutrino web history in detailed report.

- SIM ID cloner device
- Pack of SIM clone cards
- Write-protected universal memory card reader
- Complete set of cables for logical and physical acquisition
- XACT Hex Viewer software application
- XRY Reader Tool for distribution to third parties

XRY was designed and refined with the input of forensic investigators and a wizard guides you through the entire process to assist the examination. The new unified Logical/Physical extraction Wizard and the resulting reports help to show the examiner the full contents of the device in a neat, clean, and professional manner.

One of the unique features of XRY is the Device Manual with a complete and detailed list of available support for each device; identifying what data can be retrieved, and also what cannot be recovered which is sometimes just as relevant to investigators.

Examiner: [redacted]
Path: [redacted]
GUID: 90[redacted]322A6

Items included in the report

Contacts	Call logs	SMS	MMS	Messages	Calendar
•	•	•	•	•	•

Logical Evidence File: Droid
Case Number: 1
Evidence Number: 1
Examiner: [redacted]
Acquisition Start: 01/11/11 09:15:56AM
Acquisition Completed: 01/11/11 09:16:46AM
Location: Droid.L01
Encase version: 6.16.80
OS: Windows XP
Time Zone of the time data displayed: (GMT-05:00) Eastern Time (US & Canada)

Contacts	Call logs	SMS	MMS	Messages	Calendar
29	20	31	1	0	95

Phone Info

Model	Vendor	Serial No
		A[redacted]B3

Serial: A0[redacted]B3
Firmware: 0

FIGURE 6.38

Neutrino report exported as HTML.

All extractions, logical or physical, are saved in an XRY file which remains—for forensic security purposes. From the XRY file, you can create reports as required in Word, Excel, Open Office, or PDF. You can include case data, and references, choose what data is included in the report or not and then distribute it to other parties involved in the investigation; lawyers, prosecutors or other investigators. MSAB offer a free XRY reader and you can provide this to third parties to allow them to make notes on the report—while still maintaining the original forensic integrity of the data.

Within the package is the XACT Hex Viewer application to undertake more detailed examination of the raw data recovered and assist with searching and manual decoding to supplement the automatic decoding available in XRY Physical.

Version 5.1 of the XRY Forensic Pack was released on June 28, 2010 with additional support for the Apple iPad.

Installation

XRY is a Windows application that you install from a single setup program provided by the vendor. The setup includes an installation wizard, checks for software updates online, and takes approximately 15 minutes. The software requires the use of a hardware dongle to operate.

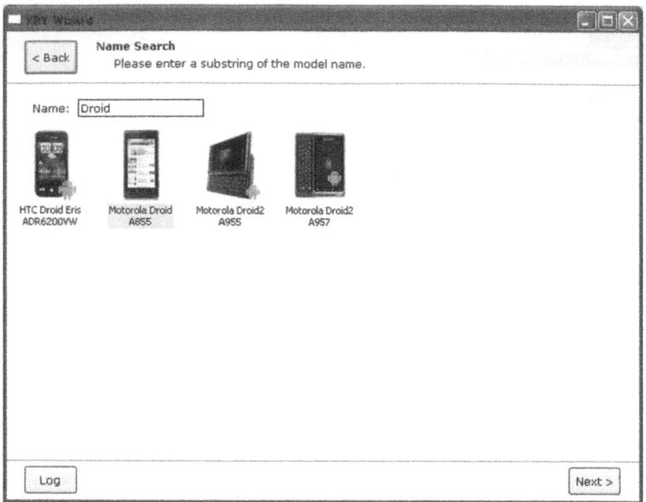

FIGURE 6.39

XRY—Search device type.

Acquisition

After the installation is complete, run the software, select Extract Data, and then choose to extract data from a phone. After that, you must identify the device type, which can be done in several ways. For this example, a search was executed by selecting Name Search, search for Droid, and select Motorola Droid A855, and then select Next. This is illustrated in Fig. 6.39.

Although the MSAB forensic suite supports physical extractions of some devices, only logical extraction is available for Android. After selecting logical acquisition, the software displays the data available for extraction as shown in Fig. 6.40.

Select Next and then the option to extract data by cable and a full read and finally click Next to start data extraction. When the extraction is complete, you see the extraction complete screen shown in Fig. 6.41.

Data presentation and analysis

After extraction, the application displays the data within the application and is easy to navigate. The contact list includes not only the details of a contact but where the contact was stored, as shown in Fig. 6.42.

The call logs provide the type of call (dialed or received), name, number, time, duration, and storage location, as shown in Fig. 6.43.

Fig. 6.44 shows the SMS messages including the number, name, message, time, status, storage, index, and the folder it is located in.

Fig. 6.45 shows that the only image extracted from the device was from an MMS.

FIGURE 6.40

XRY data types available for Droid extraction.

Other data was extracted. However, it is not displayed in a dedicated report section. For example, you can review the web browser history, web site bookmarks, and Google search history in the Log section of the report.

MSAB also has a tool called XACT, which provides a hex view of specific entries. For example, Fig. 6.46 shows the contents of an SMS message.

Paraben Device Seizure

The following overview of Device Seizure was provided by the vendor:

Paraben's Device Seizure (DS) is a handheld forensics tool that enables the investigator to perform logical and physical data acquisitions, deleted data recovery, and full data dumps, on approximately 2400 models of cell phones, PDAs/smart-phones, and portable GPS units. Physical data acquisition—often where deleted data is found—is possible from approximately two-thirds of the supported models. Furthermore, DS has been documented and verified as being 100% forensically

FIGURE 6.41

XRY extraction complete.

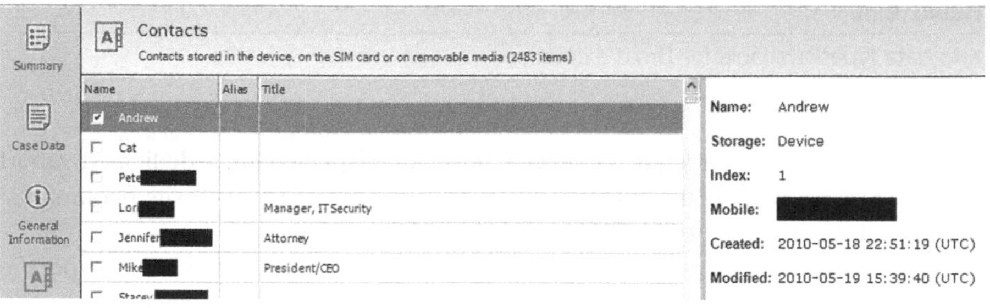

FIGURE 6.42

XRY contacts list.

sound, meaning the digital evidence is never altered in any way. These functions are all possible through a standard USB data cable connection with any PC.

Over the past two years Google's Android operating system for mobile devices has had a significant impact on the industry. Paraben focuses on staying in step with the latest innovations and has added support for the Android OS to DS. With the release of DS version 4.0, an investigator has the capabilities of acquiring the most commonly sought-after data such as call logs, address book, and SMS messages.

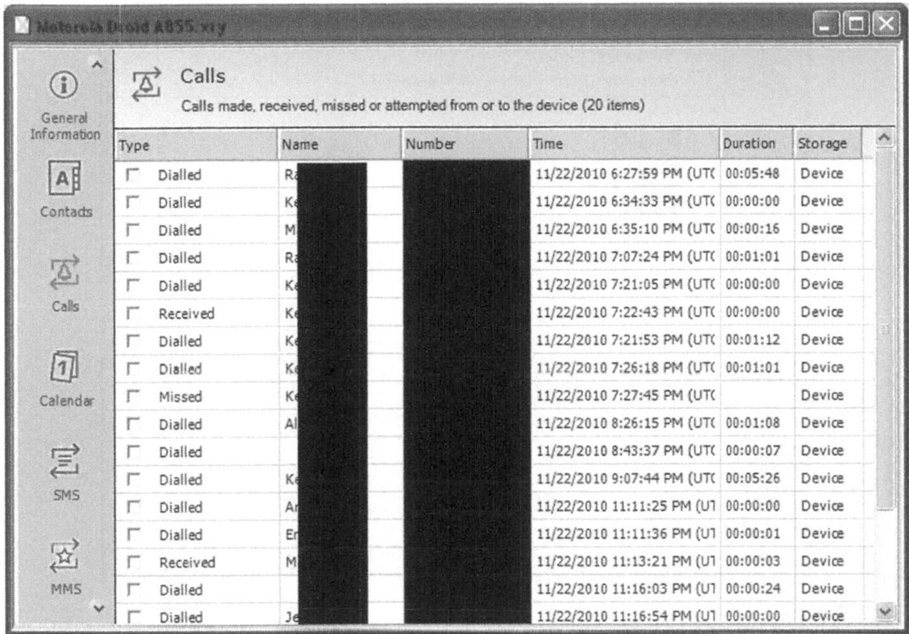

Type	Name	Number	Time	Duration	Storage
Dialled	R		11/22/2010 6:27:59 PM (UTC	00:05:48	Device
Dialled	K		11/22/2010 6:34:33 PM (UTC	00:00:00	Device
Dialled	M		11/22/2010 6:35:10 PM (UTC	00:00:16	Device
Dialled	R		11/22/2010 7:07:24 PM (UTC	00:01:01	Device
Dialled	K		11/22/2010 7:21:05 PM (UTC	00:00:00	Device
Received	K		11/22/2010 7:22:43 PM (UTC	00:00:00	Device
Dialled	K		11/22/2010 7:21:53 PM (UTC	00:01:12	Device
Dialled	K		11/22/2010 7:26:18 PM (UTC	00:01:01	Device
Missed	K		11/22/2010 7:27:45 PM (UTC		Device
Dialled	Al		11/22/2010 8:26:15 PM (UTC	00:01:08	Device
Dialled			11/22/2010 8:43:37 PM (UTC	00:00:07	Device
Dialled	K		11/22/2010 9:07:44 PM (UTC	00:05:26	Device
Dialled	A		11/22/2010 11:11:25 PM (UT	00:00:00	Device
Dialled	E		11/22/2010 11:11:36 PM (UT	00:00:01	Device
Received	M		11/22/2010 11:13:21 PM (UT	00:00:03	Device
Dialled			11/22/2010 11:16:03 PM (UT	00:00:24	Device
Dialled	J		11/22/2010 11:16:54 PM (UT	00:00:00	Device

FIGURE 6.43

XRY call log.

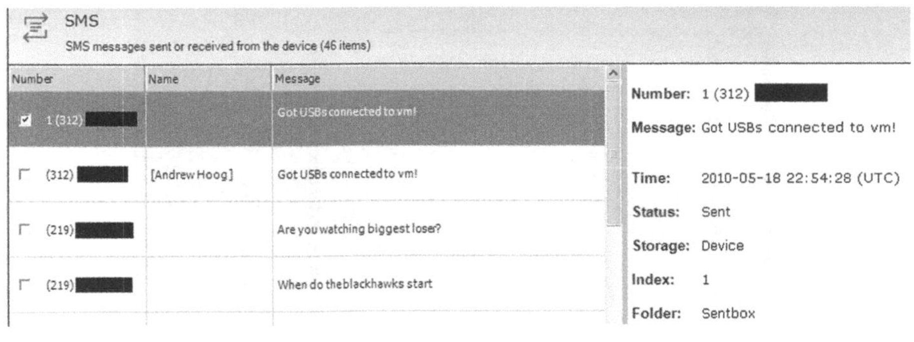

Number	Name	Message
1 (312)		Got USBs connected to vm!
(312)	[Andrew Hoog]	Got USBs connected to vm!
(219)		Are you watching biggest loser?
(219)		When do the blackhawks start

Number: 1 (312)
Message: Got USBs connected to vm!
Time: 2010-05-18 22:54:28 (UTC)
Status: Sent
Storage: Device
Index: 1
Folder: Sentbox

FIGURE 6.44

XRY SMS.

Beyond these data types, DS will also acquire multimedia files—MMS messages, images, video, and audio files. The full list of data types that can be acquired from Android models are as follows:

- Address Book including contacts groups, organizations, and address book settings, along with the standard name, phone number, and address
- SMS messages

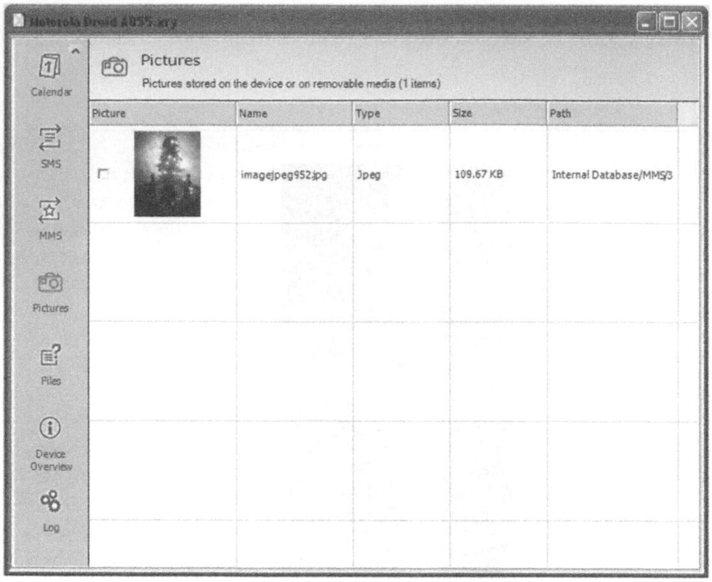

Motorola Droid A855.xry

Pictures

Pictures stored on the device or on removable media (1 items)

Picture	Name	Type	Size	Path
	imagejpeg952.jpg	Jpeg	109.67 KB	Internal Database/MMS/3

Calendar, SMS, MMS, Pictures, Files, Device Overview, Log

FIGURE 6.45

XRY images.

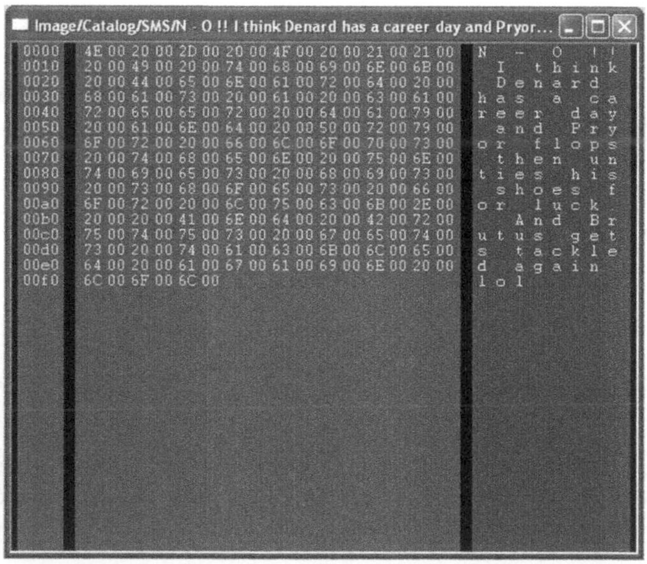

FIGURE 6.46

XACT—SMS message.

- MMS messages
- Call history
- Contact methods
- Browser history
- External image media (metadata)
- External image thumbnail media (metadata)
- External media, audio, and miscellaneous data (metadata)
- External videos (metadata)
- List of all applications installed and their version

Installation

Paraben DS version 4.1.3971.37683 was installed on the Windows forensic workstation. The setup process required the installation of many required drivers that took a considerable amount of time. The software must be registered prior to use, which is achieved either using a hardware dongle or through a registration key file provided by Paraben. To install the registration key file, you simply copy the file into the DS install directory, which is likely C:\Program Files\Paraben Corporation\Device Seizure.

Acquisition

To start the acquisition of a new Android device, you first open a new case and complete the required case information section. You then choose "Data Acquisition" and select Android at which point the following directions are provided:

```
Android based cell phones must be placed into "debugging" mode*. Follow the
instructions below:
1. On the cell phone, navigate to Settings>Application Settings and select the
Unknown Sources option.
2. On the cell phone, navigate to Settings>Application Settings>Development and
select the USB debugging option.
3. Install drivers for your cell phone. These drivers are provided in the
Device Seizure Drivers Pack that can be downloaded on www.paraben.com.
4. Connect the cell phone to the USB port on your computer.
* Please note that AT&T and Motorola have taken the "Unknown Sources", found on
step 1, out of Android devices. Device Seizure does not support these models.
```

According to these instructions, Motorola phones are not supported. However, the acquisition of the Motorola Droid was successful.

Follow the instructions, then click "Next" at which point DS attempts to identify the phone. Ensure the identified device information is accurate and click "Next" as shown in Fig. 6.47.

The next screen provides a list of supported data types that DS can extract from the device. All were selected, which includes acquiring the part of the file system it can read and the SD card, so the acquisition process is slow. Fig. 6.48 shows the DS acquisition timing.

The acquisition completed approximately two hours later and the prompt to sort files was accepted. The process of sorting the files took considerable time, but was

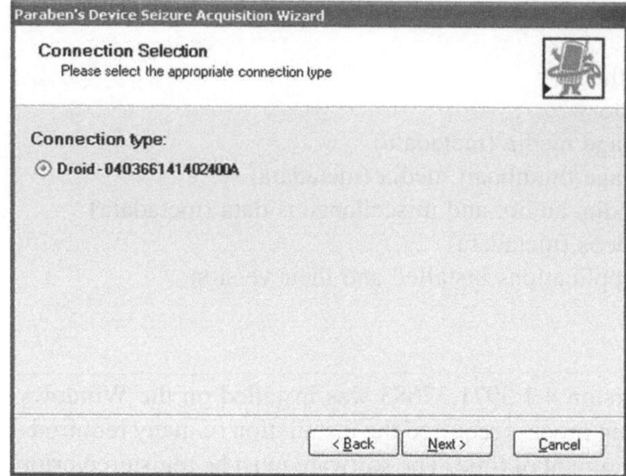

FIGURE 6.47

Device Seizure device identification.

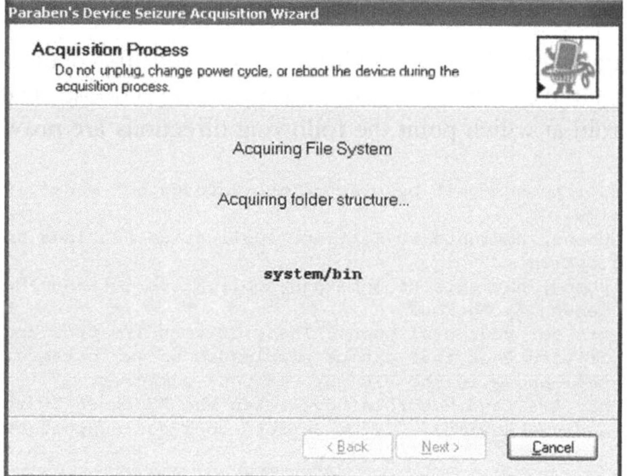

FIGURE 6.48

Device Seizure acquisition timing.

less than two hours. At that point, the acquisition process was complete. Fig. 6.49 shows the DS acquisition complete output.

Data presentation and analysis

Device Seizure displays the acquired data with the application in an easy to browse and navigate structure. The acquired directory structures are shown in Fig. 6.50.

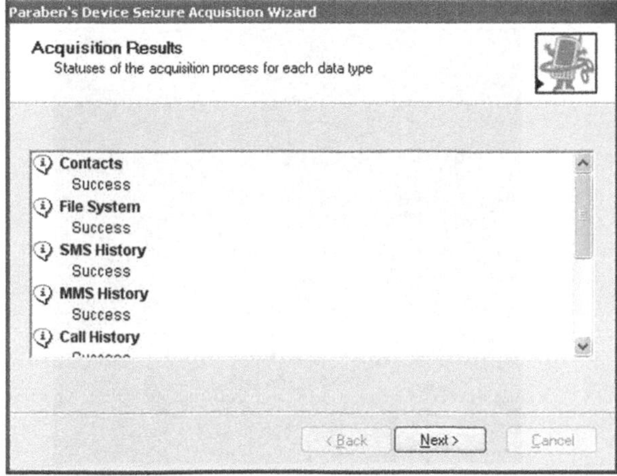

FIGURE 6.49

Device Seizure acquisition complete.

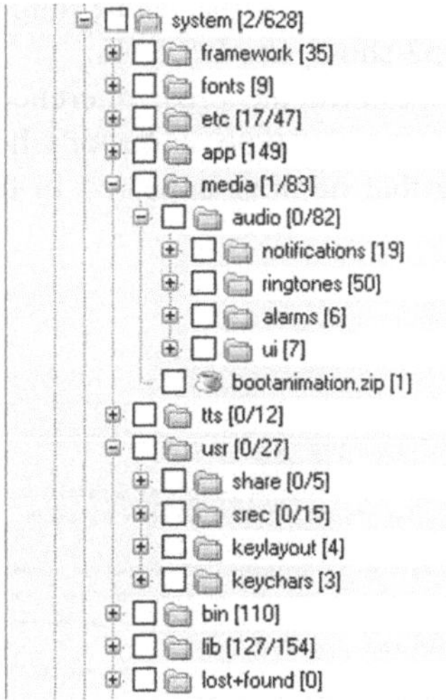

FIGURE 6.50

Device Seizure Droid directory structure.

Contacts provide not only the name, notes, phone numbers, and e-mail, but also helpful fields, such as number of times contacted, last time contacted, and a photo, if available, as shown in Fig. 6.51.

The SMS reporting provides the expected fields, but deleted messages were not included. The report does not cross-reference the contact data with the phone

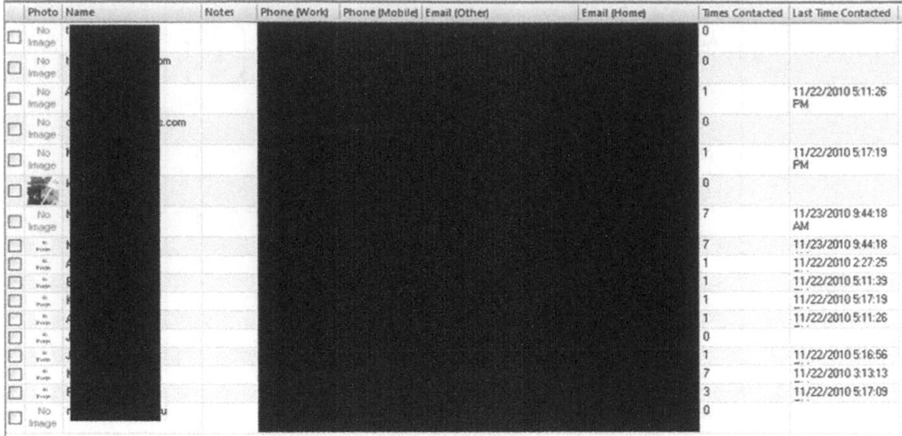

Photo	Name	Notes	Phone (Work)	Phone (Mobile)	Email (Other)	Email (Home)	Times Contacted	Last Time Contacted
No Image							0	
No Image							0	
No Image							1	11/22/2010 5:11:26 PM
No Image							0	
No Image							1	11/22/2010 5:17:19 PM
							0	
No Image							7	11/23/2010 9:44:18 AM
							7	11/23/2010 9:44:18
							1	11/22/2010 2:27:25
							1	11/22/2010 5:11:39
							1	11/22/2010 5:17:19
							1	11/22/2010 5:11:26
							0	
							1	11/22/2010 5:16:56
							7	11/22/2010 3:13:13
							3	11/22/2010 5:17:09
No Image							0	

FIGURE 6.51

Device Seizure contacts.

number, so the examiner must either know the phone number or handle the cross-referencing themselves. Fig. 6.52 shows the DS SMS.

However, the call logs do perform the cross-reference and display the date, message type, duration, number, number type, name, or whether the call was a new call (presumably the first time that number appeared in the call logs). Fig. 6.53 shows the call logs.

Date	Read	Address	Status	Type	Subject	Body
11/2	Yes		None	Inbox		Happy early thanksgiving
11/2	Yes		None	Sent		I'll make sure we toss some buckeyes in the fire after Jim Tressel goes down in flames!
11/2	Yes		None	Inbox		Great idea, well have a bonfire for the game
11/2	Yes		None	Sent		Well, be ready Saturday evening for my Michigan flag to be planted in your front yard
11/2	Yes		None	Inbox		Ohio St is...... wow, 17.5 pt favorites? Even I think thats a liittle bit much
11/2	Yes		None	Sent		What's the spread?
11/2	Yes		None	Inbox		Martin is a playmaker.... But were talking a D that allows 33 points a game!
11/2	Yes		None	Sent		Heyward ... the second best defenseman on the field to Mike Martin ... Hail to the Victors!
11/2	Yes		None	Inbox		Were talking about the same Denard that got benched a couple games ago? No WAY does he get through that D line. Heywards
11/2	Yes		None	Sent		And the Buckeye defense isn't really that good ...
11/2	Yes		None	Sent		N - O !! I think Denard has a career day and Pryor flops then unties his shoes for luck. And Brutus gets tackled again lol
11/2	Yes		None	Inbox		Sorry man, gave an FMA interview. Ill give em a chance at 2 good quarters of healthy competition. Maybe single digit turnovers. I
11/2	Yes		None	Sent		Go Blue! Do you think my Wolverines stand a chance Saturday?
11/2	Yes		None	Sent		Sometime Wednesday. My folks will never deep fry a turkey ... afraid they will torch the house lol
11/2	Yes		None	Inbox		Yup. I love thanksgiving! R u going to see ur family?
11/2	Yes		None	Inbox		Turkey ham mashed potatos corn bread! And u?
11/2	Yes		None	Sent		What are you having for dinner Thanksgiving?
11/2	Yes		None	Inbox		You have 1 unheard Visual Voice Mail messages. Please select the Visual VM icon to reinstall. Free Message from Verizon Wire
11/2	Yes		None	Sent		Great! I can drop it off tomorrow morning if u r ready
11/2	Yes		None	Inbox		Perfect. The members will be excited when the new equipment comes
11/2	Yes		None	Sent		325 for it all? Sounds good.
11/2	Yes		None	Inbox		75 for the bench and 250 for the smith
11/2	Yes		None	Sent		Yeah I know. Last time I used your bench press I noticed it couldn't do a lot of inclines. How is 75 for the bench and 275 for the S

FIGURE 6.52

Device Seizure SMS.

Date	Type	Duration	New	Number	Number Type (Cached)	Name (Cached)
11/22/2010 12:27:59 PM	Outgoing	05:48	Yes		Mobile	Rach L
11/22/2010 12:34:33 PM	Outgoing	00:00	Yes		Mobile	K
11/22/2010 12:35:10 PM	Outgoing	00:16	Yes		Mobile	M
11/22/2010 1:07:24 PM	Outgoing	01:01	Yes		Mobile	F
11/22/2010 1:21:05 PM	Outgoing	00:00	Yes		Mobile	K
11/22/2010 1:21:53 PM	Outgoing	01:12	Yes		Mobile	K
11/22/2010 1:22:43 PM	Incoming	00:00	Yes		Mobile	K
11/22/2010 1:26:18 PM	Outgoing	01:01	Yes		Mobile	K
11/22/2010 1:27:45 PM	Missed	00:00	No		Mobile	K
11/22/2010 2:26:15 PM	Outgoing	01:08	Yes		Mobile	A
11/22/2010 2:43:37 PM	Outgoing	00:07	Yes			
11/22/2010 3:07:44 PM	Outgoing	05:26	Yes		Mobile	K
11/22/2010 5:11:25 PM	Outgoing	00:00	Yes		Work	A
11/22/2010 5:11:36 PM	Outgoing	00:01	Yes		Mobile	E
11/22/2010 5:13:21 PM	Incoming	00:03	Yes		Mobile	M
11/22/2010 5:16:03 PM	Outgoing	00:24	Yes			
11/22/2010 5:16:54 PM	Outgoing	00:00	Yes		Mobile	J
11/22/2010 5:17:06 PM	Outgoing	00:00	Yes		Mobile	F
11/22/2010 5:17:17 PM	Outgoing	00:00	Yes		Mobile	K
11/23/2010 8:01:01 AM	Missed	00:00	No		Mobile	M

FIGURE 6.53

Device Seizure call logs.

A complete web history is available and parsed, including visit count and bookmarks. However, the data view is quite long and only the beginning information is displayed in Fig. 6.54.

Device Seizure allows the examiner to select any file and extract it to the forensic workstation for additional analysis. This is helpful for viewing or analyzing file types not supported natively in the DS environment. As the file sorting option was chosen during the acquisition stage, each extracted file was identified and grouped by type allowing quick access to files of interest. This is shown in Fig. 6.55.

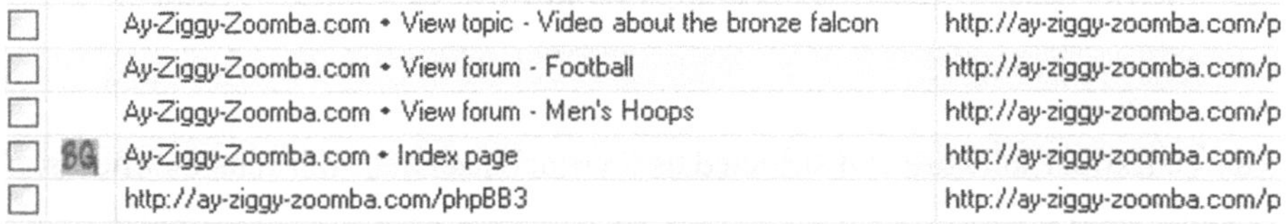

	Title	URL
	Ay-Ziggy-Zoomba.com • View topic - Video about the bronze falcon	http://ay-ziggy-zoomba.com/p
	Ay-Ziggy-Zoomba.com • View forum - Football	http://ay-ziggy-zoomba.com/p
	Ay-Ziggy-Zoomba.com • View forum - Men's Hoops	http://ay-ziggy-zoomba.com/p
	Ay-Ziggy-Zoomba.com • Index page	http://ay-ziggy-zoomba.com/p
	http://ay-ziggy-zoomba.com/phpBB3	http://ay-ziggy-zoomba.com/p

FIGURE 6.54

Device Seizure web history.

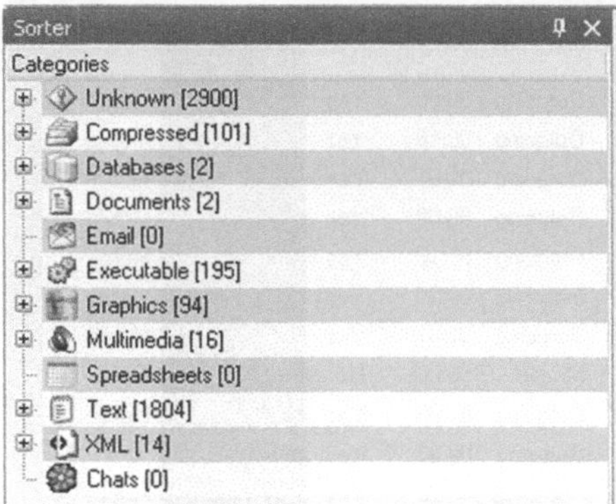

FIGURE 6.55

Device Seizure's file sorter.

viaForensics' ViaExtract

The following overview of viaExtract was provided by the vendor:

viaExtract is the latest Android forensic solution from viaForensics, a leader and innovator in the field. In addition to their mobile forensics white papers and book, viaForensics' provides a free Android forensics solution for law enforcement and government agencies called AFLogical.

Building on this experience, viaForensics developed viaExtract, which extracts, analyzes, and reports on data in Android devices. viaExtract is a modular solution and will next offer an Android forensic physical technique based on viaForensics' research and development. Up to date information on viaExtract is available online at http://viaforensics.com/products/viaextract/ including support for Android forensics physical techniques, additional supported mobile platforms, and advanced forensic recovery techniques.

viaForensics is a forensics and security firm that actively investigates mobile devices and traditional computers. Their direct experience as examiners has led to the development of a tool specifically tailored to forensic examiners. The tool was designed for frequent updates as the mobile forensic discipline is changing rapidly. A unique debug and reporting system integrated into viaExtract simplifies the process of sending debug and sanitized data to viaForensics to assist with the design and improvement of viaExtract operating on the diverse Android ecosystem.

Installation

The viaExtract software is distributed as a virtual machine, so it runs on Microsoft Windows, Apple OS X, Linux, or other operating systems that run supported virtualization software. The software is fully configured, as are necessary drivers and supporting libraries, which greatly simplifies the installation. There are several supported virtualization packages, which are free, including:

- Oracle's VirtualBox
- VMWare Player

A number of commercial packages are also available. The virtual machine is downloaded from viaForensics' web site and then imported into the supported software. Examiners can use features built into virtualization software, such as taking snapshots to restore the software to a pristine state after each case, or integrate it directly into their host operating system by sharing data storage and other valuable features.

Acquisition

After viaExtract is imported into the host system's virtualization software and is running, the forensic examiner logs into the Ubuntu virtual machine and runs viaExtract as shown in Fig. 6.56.

The examiner can then start a new case or open a previous one, as illustrated in Fig. 6.57.

After entering the case details, the examiner can then choose to extract data directly from an Android device or to load from a previous data extraction located on the file system. The latter feature is useful for cases where the examiner used via-Forensics' free AFLogical software to extract data from Android devices. It also allows the examiner to generate a new forensic report from a previous device's extracted data, which is quite useful as new reporting features are added.

For this example, we will extract data from an Android device by clicking Forward. We are then presented with the Load data screen, which provides

FIGURE 6.56

viaExtract software.

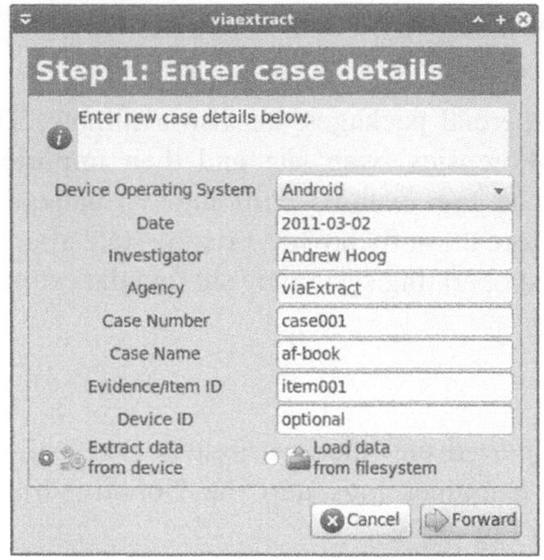

FIGURE 6.57

viaExtract—New case.

directions for enabling USB debugging. After you click OK the data extraction begins, as shown in Fig. 6.58.

After the data extraction is complete, the examiner is presented with a list of data extracts and has the ability to select what they want to include in the forensic analysis and report, as shown in Fig. 6.59.

After the selections are completed and the examiner clicks Apply, the report logic is executed and the data extraction is complete.

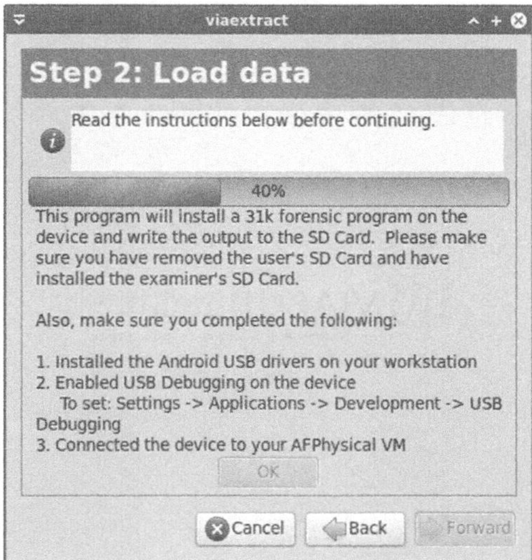

FIGURE 6.58

viaExtract—Data extraction.

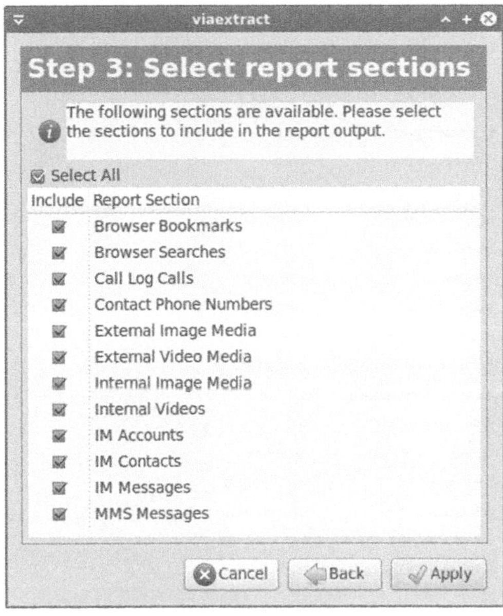

FIGURE 6.59

viaExtract—Forensic analysis and report.

Data presentation and analysis

After the data extraction is complete, viaExtract presents the analyzed data to the user. By navigating the selections on the left side of the application, the examiner can view different sections of the report. For example, the first section presented is the Device Information section as shown in Fig. 6.60.

Next, Fig. 6.61 shows browser history and bookmarks that are available in the report.

In this example, you can see several features of the report view, including:

- Ability to filter, on the fly, any section of the report
- Ability to sort ascending or descending on any column

In the next example, a filter of viaforensics.com was applied against 29 people records and 2 remained. However, many of the fields were displayed to the right of the screenshot as shown in Fig. 6.62.

In total, viaExtract currently supports just over 41 Content Providers. However, in the next release, roughly 100 Content Providers will be actively queried. If the device responds to the Content Provider, the extraction and subsequent reporting will succeed. Fig. 6.63 is an example of the Call Logs.

Fig. 6.64 shows the video media metadata.

Reports can also be exported to PDF format as shown in Fig. 6.65.

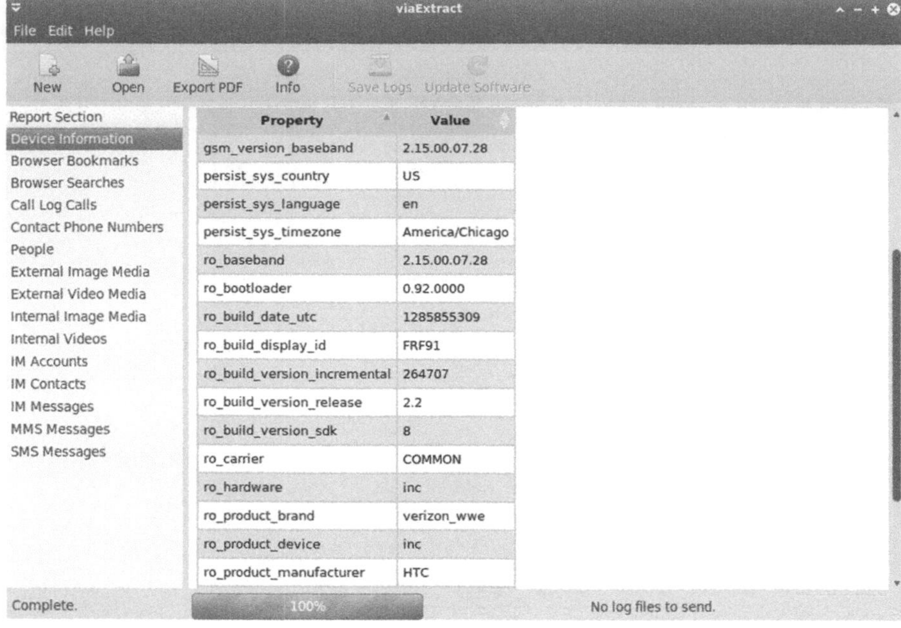

FIGURE 6.60

viaExtract—Device info.

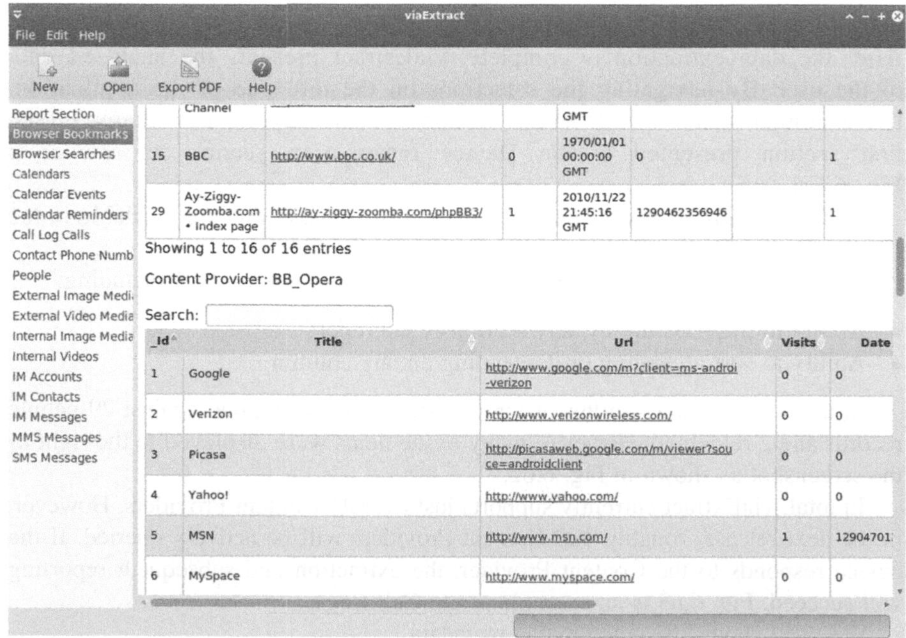

FIGURE 6.61

viaExtract—Browser history and bookmarks.

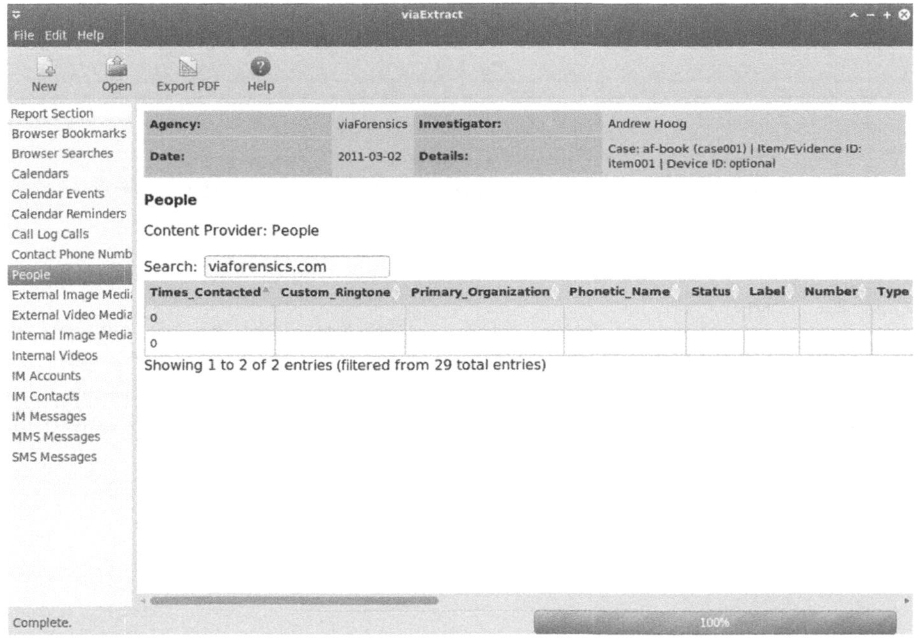

FIGURE 6.62

viaExtract—People records filtered.

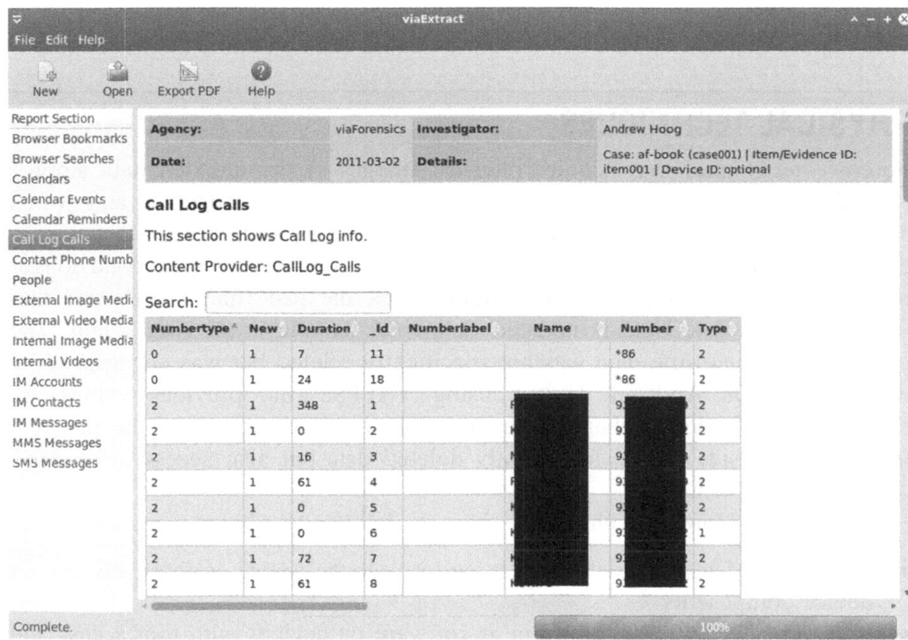

FIGURE 6.63

viaExtract—Call logs.

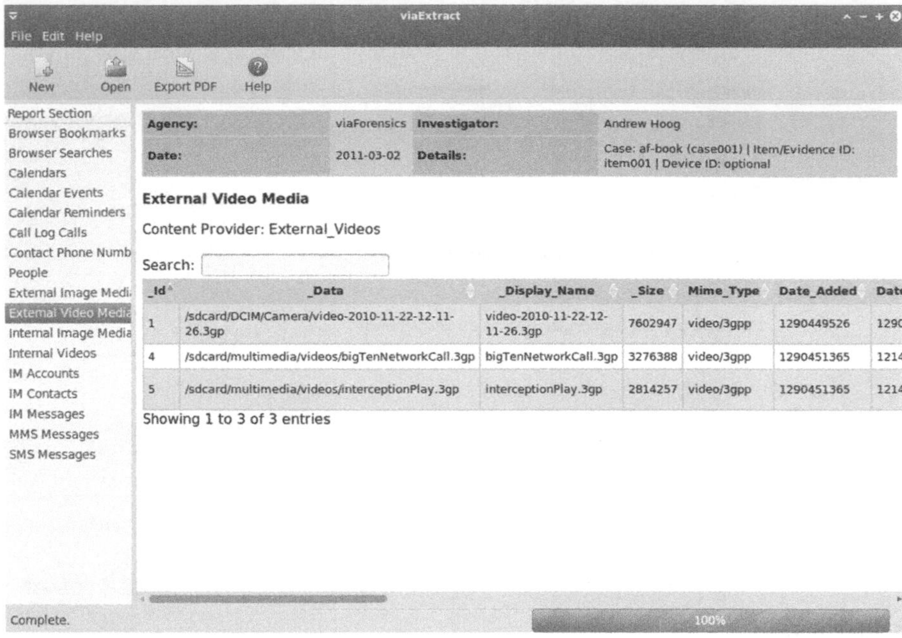

FIGURE 6.64

viaExtract—Video media metadata.

PHYSICAL TECHNIQUES

Forensic techniques that acquire physical images of the targeted data storage typically result in exponentially more data being recovered and often circumvent pass code protection. These techniques provide access to not only deleted data but also data that was simply discarded as the system no longer required it. For example, some systems track the last time a web site was visited and the date field is updated each time the site is accessed again. The previous date and time data was not specifically deleted but was not tracked by the system. On Android devices using YAFFS2, the previous values are recoverable provided garbage collection did not occur. As such, the physical techniques provide access to not only deleted data but also access to obsolete data on the system.

The Android forensics physical techniques fall into two broad categories:

- Hardware: Methods which connect hardware to the device or physically extract device components
- Software: Techniques which run as software on devices with root access and provide a full physical image of the data partitions

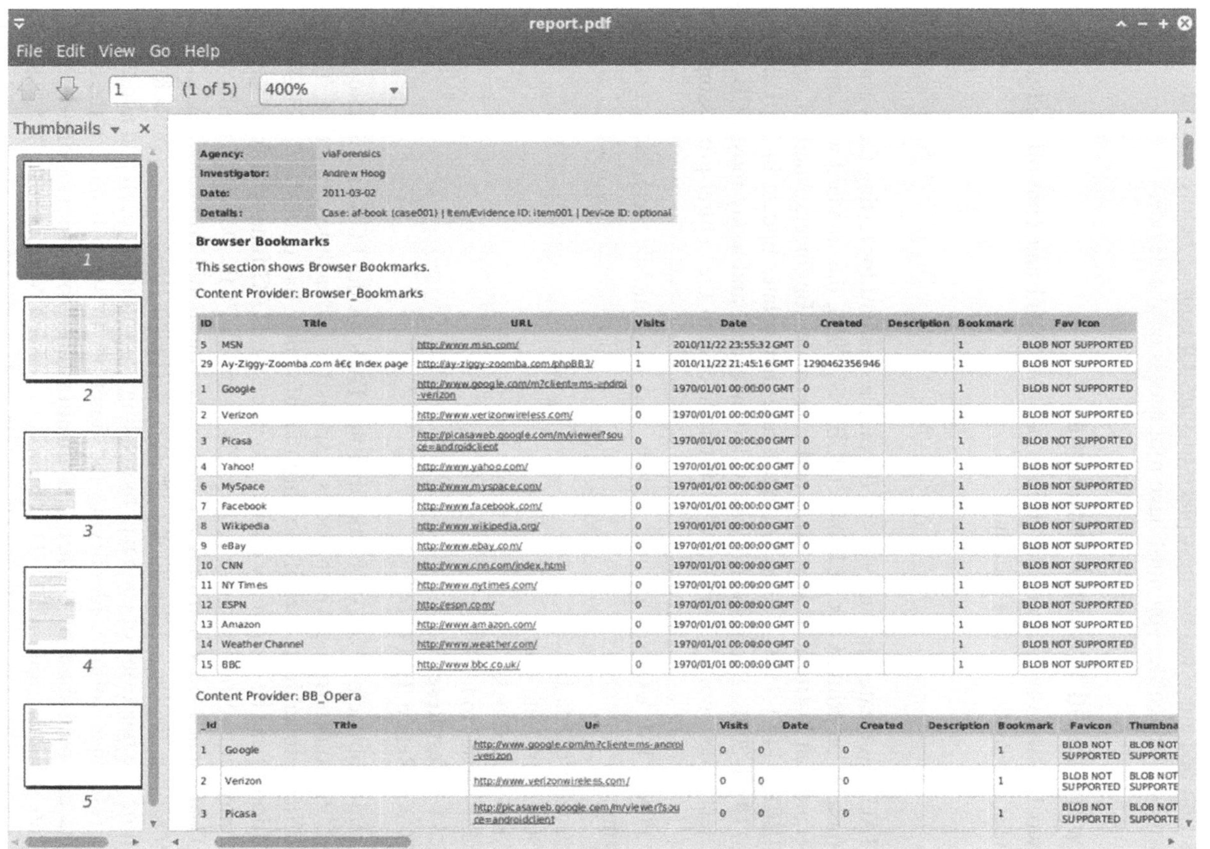

Agency:	viaForensics
Investigator:	Andrew Hoog
Date:	2011-03-02
Details:	Case: af-book (case001) | Item/Evidence ID: item001 | Device ID: optional

Browser Bookmarks

This section shows Browser Bookmarks.

Content Provider: Browser_Bookmarks

ID	Title	URL	Visits	Date	Created	Description	Bookmark	Fav Icon
5	MSN	http://www.msn.com/	1	2010/11/22 23:55:32 GMT	0		1	BLOB NOT SUPPORTED
29	Ay-Ziggy-Zoomba.com â€¢ Index page	http://ay-ziggy-zoomba.com/phpBB3/	1	2010/11/22 21:45:16 GMT	1290462356946		1	BLOB NOT SUPPORTED
1	Google	http://www.google.com/m?client=ms-android-verizon	0	1970/01/01 00:00:00 GMT	0		1	BLOB NOT SUPPORTED
2	Verizon	http://www.verizonwireless.com/	0	1970/01/01 00:00:00 GMT	0		1	BLOB NOT SUPPORTED
3	Picasa	http://picasaweb.google.com/m/viewer?source=androidclient	0	1970/01/01 00:00:00 GMT	0		1	BLOB NOT SUPPORTED
4	Yahoo!	http://www.yahoo.com/	0	1970/01/01 00:00:00 GMT	0		1	BLOB NOT SUPPORTED
6	MySpace	http://www.myspace.com/	0	1970/01/01 00:00:00 GMT	0		1	BLOB NOT SUPPORTED
7	Facebook	http://www.facebook.com/	0	1970/01/01 00:00:00 GMT	0		1	BLOB NOT SUPPORTED
8	Wikipedia	http://www.wikipedia.org/	0	1970/01/01 00:00:00 GMT	0		1	BLOB NOT SUPPORTED
9	eBay	http://www.ebay.com/	0	1970/01/01 00:00:00 GMT	0		1	BLOB NOT SUPPORTED
10	CNN	http://www.cnn.com/index.html	0	1970/01/01 00:00:00 GMT	0		1	BLOB NOT SUPPORTED
11	NY Times	http://www.nytimes.com/	0	1970/01/01 00:00:00 GMT	0		1	BLOB NOT SUPPORTED
12	ESPN	http://espn.com/	0	1970/01/01 00:00:00 GMT	0		1	BLOB NOT SUPPORTED
13	Amazon	http://www.amazon.com/	0	1970/01/01 00:00:00 GMT	0		1	BLOB NOT SUPPORTED
14	Weather Channel	http://www.weather.com/	0	1970/01/01 00:00:00 GMT	0		1	BLOB NOT SUPPORTED
15	BBC	http://www.bbc.co.uk/	0	1970/01/01 00:00:00 GMT	0		1	BLOB NOT SUPPORTED

Content Provider: BB_Opera

_id	Title	Url	Visits	Date	Created	Description	Bookmark	Favicon	Thumbna
1	Google	http://www.google.com/m?client=ms-android-verizon	0	0	0		1	BLOB NOT SUPPORTED	BLOB NOT SUPPORTE
2	Verizon	http://www.verizonwireless.com/	0	0	0		1	BLOB NOT SUPPORTED	BLOB NOT SUPPORTE
3	Picasa	http://picasaweb.google.com/m/viewer?source=androidclient	0	0	0		1	BLOB NOT SUPPORTED	BLOB NOT SUPPORTE

FIGURE 6.65

viaExtract—Export to PDF.

The hardware-based methods required specialized and often expensive equipment and training but can be very effective on devices where root access is unattainable. The software-based physical techniques are a more direct path to acquisition and are often the best place to start. Of course, before software-based techniques are possible, you must have root access on the device.

Hardware-Based Physical Techniques

The two hardware-based physical techniques are JTAG and chip-off and a brief overview is provided in this section.

JTAG

The JTAG was created in the 1980s to develop a standard for testing the wiring and interconnects on printed circuit boards (PCB). By 1990, the standard was complete and became an Institute of Electrical and Electronics Engineers standard, specifically IEEE 1149.1-1990 (IEEE SA, n.d.), and then a later update in 2001 named IEEE 1149.1-2001. The standard was widely accepted and today most PCBs have JTAG test access ports (TAPs) that facilitate access to the central processing unit (CPU).

A JTAG TAP exposes various signals and most mobile devices include the following:

1. TDI—Test Data In
2. TDO—Test Data Out
3. TCK—Test Clock
4. TMS—Test Mode Select
5. TRST—Test Reset
6. RTCK—Return Test Clock

A major obstacle to JTAG is locating the TAPs on the PCB and tracing them to the CPU to determine which pad is responsible for each test function. This is very difficult to achieve even if the chip manufacturer has published a CPU map. In addition, it can be extremely difficult to trace the JTAG functions from the chip and it may require first removing the CPU from the PCB. Device manufacturers have JTAG schematics, but they are generally considered company confidential and are only released to authorized service centers. Another approach is to determine the functions of each pad by reading the voltage at each pad and, based on the reference voltage, identifying the function. In some instances the JTAG pin-outs are published by flasher box manufacturers or various online groups. Fig. 6.66 is an example of the JTAG pin-outs for a T-Mobile HTC G1. The six pin-outs are indicated by the small white circles and the legend on the right provides the detailed information.

In most cases, your soldered wire leads to the pads on the PCB, and the other side is connected to a special device (flasher box) which, through software, will

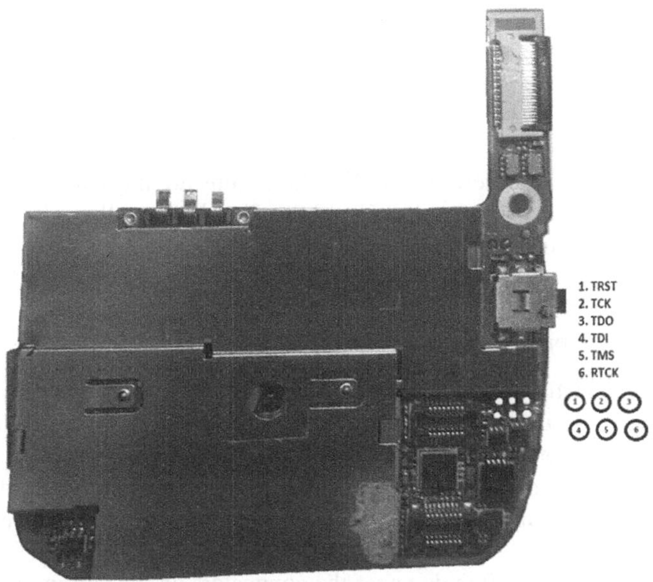

FIGURE 6.66

T-Mobile HTC G-1 PCB.

manage the CPU. Some companies make custom connectors which support a specific device and simplify the connection to the pads by placing the PCB between two jig boards with pogo pins. The pogo pins make contact with the JTAG pads on the PCB and can then easily connect to the flasher box. However, experienced engineers may find that soldering the leads directly to the PCB provides a more stable connection.

Once the leads are connected to the appropriate pads, power must be applied to the board to boot the CPU. Each CPU manufacturer publishes the reference voltage for their hardware and this voltage must not be exceeded. Some flasher boxes provide an option for managing the voltage but in general the power should be managed through an external power supply with a built-in digital voltmeter to ensure accuracy. Once the board is powered on, the flasher box software has the ability to perform a full binary memory dump of the NAND flash. However, the connection is serial and takes a considerable amount of time. Despite all of the complexities, if the JTAG technique is executed properly, the phone can be reassembled and will function normally with no data loss.

Though JTAG is an option for extracting data from an Android device's NAND flash, it is very difficult and should only be attempted by qualified personnel with sufficient training and specific experience in soldering small PCB connections. Errors in soldering to the JTAG pads or applying the wrong voltage to the board could not only disable JTAG but can also seriously damage the device. For these reasons, JTAG is not typically the first choice for a physical forensic image of an Android device.

Chip-off

Chip-off is a technique where the NAND flash chips are physically removed from the device and examined externally. The chip-off technique allows for the recovery of damaged devices and also circumvents pass code-protected devices. This removal process is generally destructive—it is quite difficult to reattach the NAND flash to the PCB and have the device operate.

There are three primary steps in the chip-off technique:

1. The NAND flash chip is physically removed from the device by either de-soldering it, or using special equipment that uses a blast of hot air and a vacuum to remove the chip. There are also techniques that heat the chip to a specified temperature. It is quite easy to damage the NAND flash in this process and specialized hardware, and even controlling software, exists for the extraction.
2. The removal process often damages the connectors on the bottom of the chip, so it must first be cleaned and then repaired. The process of repairing the conductive balls on the bottom of the chip is referred to as reballing.
3. The chip is then inserted into a specialized hardware device, so that it can be read. The devices generally must be programmed for a specific NAND flash chip and support a number of the more popular chips already.

At this point, you now have a physical image of the data stored on the NAND flash chip.

Although the chip-off process is quite effective, it also has a large barrier to entry. The cost of the equipment and tools is prohibitive and an examiner must again have very specialized training and skills. There is always the risk that the NAND flash chip will be damaged with chip-off, generally in its removal from the PCB. Finally, a clean room with protections from static electricity is also desirable. While local or even State law enforcement agencies and forensic firms may find the cost of chip-off too prohibitive, it is certainly a valid techniques that larger agencies would find useful in their suite of forensic techniques.

Software-Based Physical Techniques and Privileges

Software-based physical techniques have a number of advantages over the hardware-based techniques. Software-based techniques:

- Are easier to execute;
- Often provide direct access to file systems to allow a complete copy of all logical files (simplifies some analysis);
- Provide very little risk of damaging the device or data loss.

To execute the software-based physical techniques, you first must gain root privileges and then run the acquisition programs.

Unfortunately, root privileges on Android devices are not enabled by default. However, it is possible to gain root privileges in certain scenarios, several of which we will cover next. There are some major challenges to obtaining root privileges to keep in mind though:

1. Gaining root privileges changes the device in many situations.
2. The techniques for root privileges differ not only for each manufacturer and device but for each version of Android and even the Linux kernel in use. Just based on the Android devices and versions developed to date, there are literally thousands of possible permutations.
3. Many of the exploits used to gain root privileges are discussed online and often contain inaccurate information.

Given this, gaining root privileges can be quite difficult and is always very frustrating.

There are three primary types of root privileges:

1. Temporary root privileges attained by a root exploit, which does not survive a reboot. Typically the adb daemon is not running as root in this instance.
2. Full root access attained through a custom ROM or persistent root exploit. Custom ROMs often run the adb daemon as root while most of the persistent root exploits do not.
3. Recovery mode root attained by flashing a custom recovery partition or part of a custom ROM. Custom ROMs often run the adb daemon as root as do most of the modified recovery partitions.

Android enthusiasts who want root access are typically only interested in full, sustained root privileges. However, from a forensics standpoint, temporary root privileges or root access via a custom recovery mode are preferred.

If you need to gain access on a new device or Android version, you must have a separate device used for testing to ensure that the process works and no data are lost. Testing, although time consuming, is an important step in this situation.

The following sections cover each step in detail.

su

The first thing a forensic examiner should check is whether the device already has root privileges. This is the easiest of any technique discussed and is certainly worth the short time it takes to test. The device must have USB debugging enabled but even if the device is locked, you should still check. If the device is not pass code locked, make sure USB debugging is enabled, which was covered in Chapter 3.

Next, connect the device to your workstation and attempt to gain root privileges by requesting super user access with the "su" command as follows:

```
ahoog@ubuntu:~$ adb shell su
su: permission denied
```

In this instance, root privileges were not granted. This is the typical result of the command. However, the following was on a device that had root access:

```
ahoog@ubuntu:~$ adb shell su
#
```

Instead of receiving a permission denied error, root privileges were granted. This is indicated by the new # prompt. Sometimes a device will allow root access but require the user to grant the privileges by clicking OK on a prompt displayed on the device. If the device is not pass code protected, you should check to see if the prompt is displayed.

Researching Root Privilege Exploits

If the device does not already have root privileges, you can research possible techniques online. This process can be very frustrating as there are many inexperienced people who request help on the various discussion boards. However, while there are substantial amounts of inaccurate information, there are also very knowledgeable resources and techniques which do work.

Although there are many sites available that discuss Android root exploits, one truly stands above all others. The site, xda-developers, is an extremely popular and active site and is self-described as "the largest Internet community of smartphone enthusiasts and developers for the Android and Windows Mobile platforms" (Android & Windows Phone, n.d.). Many of the other web sites post various root exploits but generally link back to a discussion thread on xda-developers.

Often the best approach to researching root exploits is to simply search the Internet with your preferred search engine, have a test device, and a lot of patience.

Recovery Mode

Recovery mode is an operating mode for Android that was designed to apply updates, format the device, and perform other maintenance on the devices. The stock recovery mode on most devices is very basic, only provides a number of limited functions, and certainly does not provide root privileges in a shell.

Custom recovery partitions, on the other hand, nearly always allow root privileges through the shell. These new recovery partitions are typically installed by the user when the device is rooted and provide various functions that simplify the backup and update processes needed from the custom ROMS.

As with researching root exploits, examiners should use extreme caution when installing a custom recovery partition as the process often contains kernel and radio updates that could render the device unusable (often referred to as "bricked") if there are incompatibilities between the device, kernel, and radio firmware. Extensive testing must be performed on a lab device first to ensure no issues occur. And forensic examiners should understand what is being modified on the device during the installation of a custom recovery firmware.

The software that powers recovery mode is stored on a dedicated partition and is quite small. On many devices, you can see details of the recovery partition by examining /proc/mtd:

```
ahoog@ubuntu:~$ adb shell cat /proc/mtd
dev:    size   erasesize  name
mtd0: 00040000 00020000 "misc"
mtd1: 00500000 00020000 "recovery"
mtd2: 00280000 00020000 "boot"
mtd3: 04380000 00020000 "system"
mtd4: 04380000 00020000 "cache"
mtd5: 04ac0000 00020000 "userdata"
```

This list is from a T-Mobile HTC G1 and you can see that the recovery partition has a size of 0x500000 bytes, which is 5 MB (0x500000 = 5,242,880 then divide by 1024 twice to convert to KB and finally MB). Here are the sizes from other phones used throughout this book:

- T-Mobile HTC G1: 5 MB
- HTC Incredible: 4 MB
- Motorola Droid: 4 MB
- Google Nexus One: 4 MB

This is helpful to understand as we explore techniques to replace the small but important recovery partition in the next section.

In the previous section covering techniques for circumventing pass code-protected devices, accessing the recovery mode was one possible solution. In the same fashion, it is advisable to check the recovery partition for root privileges as it will enable the software-based physical techniques. First, boot the device into recovery mode as covered in Table 6.2, or simply search the Internet for the specific key combination for your device. Once the device is in recovery mode, connect it to your Ubuntu VM and run adb as follows:

```
ahoog@ubuntu:~$ adb devices
List of devices attached
0403555551222244F        recovery
```

In this case, adb discovered a device in recovery mode. However, many devices will simply not have adb access enabled in recovery mode, especially on stock devices. In such a case, you can then determine if the shell has root privileges as follows:

```
ahoog@ubuntu:~$ adb shell
#
```

As we discussed previously, if you are presented with a # prompt, this indicates root privileges. If instead you have a $ prompt, you do not have root privileges. However, you should at least try to gain them by running the su command.

Boot Loaders

As discussed in Chapter 2, the boot loader is a small program that is executed early in the Android boot process and is responsible for, among other details, selecting and loading the main kernel. On certain devices, special software exists, typically developed by the manufacturer, which can interact with the boot loader. This software is capable of writing new images to the NAND flash of a device. Manufacturers use this software to fix nonfunctional devices and likely in other situations such as development and testing. Forensic examiners can also use the software to flash a utility or exploit to a device's NAND flash, which will provide root privileges. However, the boot loaders of most devices are shipped from the factory in a locked state, which prevents such updates.

One example of software that interacts with Motorola Android devices is a program called RSD Lite developed by Motorola. RSD Lite is proprietary software and appears to only be distributed to Motorola Service Centers for device repair. It is assumed that anyone using this software has full authorization to do so, and this overview is only provided as a example of how some Android devices are flashed.

There are many web sites which discuss RSD Lite and provide guides for using the software. One such site, modmymobile.com, provides an article entitled "[Guide] Flashing Linux Motorola's with RSD Lite Versions," which offers step-by-step instructions for the software ([Guide] Flashing Linux, n.d.).

Provided the device is supported and the boot loader is unlocked, you connect the device to your workstation and then run the software, which detects the phone. You must then provide the appropriate .sbf file and then click Start to flash the device as shown in Fig. 6.67.

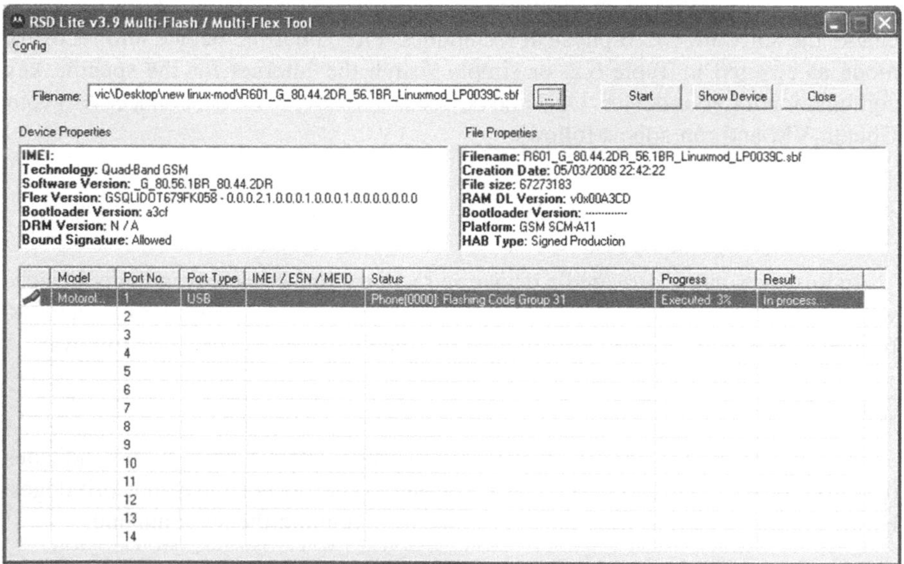

FIGURE 6.67

RSD Lite.

After the process is completed and the device is restarted, the new recovery partition (and any other areas modified by the .sbf file used) is ready. RSD Lite may provide a good option for forensic analysts who have proper authorization to use RSD Lite.

sbf_flash

Similar to Motorola's RSD Lite is a utility called sbf_flash that does not carry the license and usage restrictions of RSD Lite. The application was developed and posted online by an Android enthusiast and, while distributed in many places online, it is best to retrieve it from the author's blog OPTICALDELUSION, which is updated when new versions are available. This utility was developed on Linux, and now also runs on OS X, and thus, greatly simplifies the flashing of data to the NAND flash via an unlocked boot loader. The latest version of sbf_flash is 1.15 and it supports the following:

```
ahoog@ubuntu:~$ ./sbf_flash -h
SBF FLASH 1.15 (mbm)
http://opticaldelusion.org

Usage: ./sbf_flash <filename>

sbf_flash [options] [sbf file]
    -f                - force; attempt to continue on error
    -v                - verbose output (of CDT)
    -r                - read CDT information from the phone
    -x                - extract sbf file
    -d                - download cg from phone
    --cgname [file]   - upload/download cgname
                        matches any cgname shown with -r
                        optional file arg for contents
```

To use sbf_flash, you must first verify that the device is supported. For this example, we will cover the Motorola Droid; however, other devices are supported. The device must be placed in bootloader mode, which is accomplished by holding the up direction on the D pad while pressing the power button. The boot loader is easily recognized on the Motorola Droid by a solid black screen with the kernel version, USB status, and battery status in white text. Ensure the battery is fully charged before attempting this process as you could easily brick the device if the flashing process is interrupted with a power failure. Also, you must have the SBF file saved to your forensic workstation so you can flash it to the device. This is where extensive testing must occur prior to working on the target device to ensure compatibility and a detailed understanding of the process.

With the Droid in bootloader mode, we can query the device with sbf_flash as follows:

```
ahoog@ubuntu:~$ ./sbf_flash -r
SBF FLASH 1.15 (mbm)
http://opticaldelusion.org
```

```
 >> waiting for phone: Droid found.
 CG63 0xC0000000-0xC001FFFF mbmloader.img
 CG30 0xC0020000-0xC00BFFFF mbm.img
 CG55 0xC00C0000-0xC015FFFF mbmbackup.img
 CG31 0xC0160000-0xC01BFFFF cdt.bin
 CG38 0xD01CE000-0xD0359FFF pds
 CG34 0xC035A000-0xC03BCFFF lbl
 CG57 0xC03BD000-0xC041FFFF lbl_backup
 CG41 0xC0400000-0xC057FFFF sp
 CG42 0xC0580000-0xC061FFFF logo.bin
 CG44 0xC0620000-0xC067FFFF misc
 CG35 0xC0680000-0xC09FFFFF boot
 CG47 0xC0A00000-0xC0E7FFFF recovery
 CG39 0xD0EF4000-0xD9FB6FFF system
 CG40 0xD9FB7000-0xDFF3BFFF cache
 CG37 0xDFF3C000-0xF0D29FFF userdata
 CG53 0xDFD40000-0xDFF3FFFF kpanic
 CG54 0xDFF40000-0xDFFFFFFF rsv

Usage: ./sbf_flash <filename>
```

The sbf_flash utility looks for a device in bootloader mode and immediately flashes the image file to the NAND flash. The status of the update process is displayed on screen and afterwards the Droid is rebooted.

```
ahoog@ubuntu:~$ sbf_flash SPRecovery.sbf
=== SPRecovery.sbf ===
00: RDL03 0x80500000-0x8054CFFF DECE AP
01:  CG47 0xC0A00000-0xC0D5C7FF 02C0 AP

 >> waiting for phone: Droid found.
 >> uploading RDL03
Uploading: 100% OK
 >> verifying ramloader
 -- OK
 >> executing ramloader
Droid found.
 >> sending erase
 >> uploading CG47
Uploading: 100% OK
 >> verifying CG47
 -- OK
 >> rebooting
```

You should be prepared to immediately boot the device into recovery mode as later versions of the Motorola Droid's firmware implemented a routine that checks the hash signatures of the existing recovery partition against the stock recovery partition for that Android version. If there is a disparity, the system will rebuild the stock recovery partition during the boot process and thus overwrite the modified recovery image.

Once the new SBF file has been flashed, and the device is running in the modified recovery mode, you will have root access and can proceed with the software-based physical technique.

fastboot

Fastboot is another utility that flashes images to the NAND flash over USB. The source code for fastboot is contained in the AOSP and thus, the utility is built when you compile the AOSP code. Like sbf_flash, the boot loader must support fastboot, which not only requires a compatible boot loader but also one that has security turned off (S-OFF).

Fastboot was first used on the Google Android developer phone (ADP), which was manufactured by HTC. As such, much of the documentation and references for fastboot refer to the ADP, and HTC has a helpful reference page for the utility (HTC—Developer Center, n.d.). This page contains not only various stock NAND flash image files for the ADP device but also directions on using fastboot and accessing the appropriate mode on the device (HTC—Developer Center, n.d.):

To enter fastboot mode, power up the device (or reboot it) while holding down the BACK key. Hold the BACK key down until the boot loader screen is visible and displays "FASTBOOT." The device is now in fastboot mode and is ready to receive fastboot commands. If you want to exit fastboot mode at this point, you can hold down the keys MENU+SEND+END (on the ADP, SEND is the "Call" key and END is the "End call" key).

Note that the boot loader screen may vary across devices. For ADP devices, the boot loader screen shows an image of skateboarding robots. Other devices may show a different image or color pattern. In all cases, the boot loader screen shows the text "FASTBOOT" when in fastboot mode. The boot loader also shows the radio version.

Once in fastboot mode, verify fastboot detects the device with the following command:

```
ahoog@ubuntu:~$ ./fastboot devices
HT08XHJ00657    fastboot
```

Fastboot provides many options that are detailed when you execute fastboot with the help parameter as follows:

```
ahoog@ubuntu:~$ ./fastboot --help
usage: fastboot [ <option> ] <command>

commands:
  update <filename>                         reflash device from update.zip
  flashall                                  flash boot + recovery + system
  flash <partition> [ <filename> ]          write a file to a flash partition
  erase <partition>                         erase a flash partition
  getvar <variable>                         display a bootloader variable
  boot <kernel> [ <ramdisk> ]               download and boot kernel
  flash:raw boot <kernel> [ <ramdisk> ]     create bootimage and flash it
  devices                                   list all connected devices
  reboot                                    reboot device normally
  reboot-bootloader                         reboot device into bootloader

options:
  -w                                        erase userdata and cache
  -s <serial number>                        specify device serial number
  -p <product>                              specify product name
  -c <cmdline>                              override kernel commandline
  -i <vendor id>                            specify a custom USB vendor id
```

As you can see, once in flashboot mode, it is quite simple to flash the modified recovery partition:

```
ahoog@ubuntu:~$ fastboot flash recovery modified-recovery-image.img
```

After this process completes, you can reboot the phone into recovery mode and proceed with the software-based physical imaging technique.

AFPhysical Technique

The AFPhysical technique was developed by viaForensics to provide a physical disk image of Android NAND flash partitions. The technique requires root privileges on the device and should support any Android device. The technique, however, is not a simple process and the forensic analyst will have to adapt the technique for the specific device investigated. This is a direct result of the large variations in Android devices not only between manufacturers but between devices running different versions of Android.

The overall process for AFPhysical is quite simple:

1. Acquire root privileges on the target Android device.
2. Identify NAND flash partitions which need to be imaged.
3. Upload forensic binaries to the target Android device.
4. Acquire physical image of NAND flash partitions.
5. Remove forensic binaries if any were stored on nonvolatile storage.

Regardless of the technique, it is assumed you have root privileges on the device. For this example, we will use a Motorola Droid. As we are able to flash a modified recovery partition to a Motorola Droid, this technique will work on a device even if it is pass code locked.

After we have flashed the modified recovery partition and rebooted into recovery mode, connect the device to our Ubuntu VM and verify adb can locate the device by running adb devices.

```
ahoog@ubuntu:~$ adb devices
List of devices attached
040363260C006018        recovery
```

From there, access the shell to ensure you have root privileges:

```
ahoog@ubuntu:~$ adb shell
/ #
```

At this point, we need to understand more about the phone so we can decide what needs to be physically imaged. The first place to start is to examine the mounted file systems, if any:

```
/ # mount
rootfs on / type rootfs (rw)
tmpfs on /dev type tmpfs (rw,mode=755)
devpts on /dev/pts type devpts (rw,mode=600)
proc on /proc type proc (rw)
sysfs on /sys type sysfs (rw)
/dev/block/mtdblock7 on /cache type yaffs2 (rw,nodev,noatime,nodiratime)
```

Now, we know that the device uses MTD for NAND flash access as well as YAFFS2. To determine partitions exposed by MTD, we execute the following:

```
/ # cat /proc/mtd
dev:    size   erasesize  name
mtd0: 000a0000 00020000 "mbm"
mtd1: 00060000 00020000 "cdt"
mtd2: 00060000 00020000 "lbl"
mtd3: 00060000 00020000 "misc"
mtd4: 00380000 00020000 "boot"
mtd5: 00480000 00020000 "recovery"
mtd6: 08c60000 00020000 "system"
mtd7: 05ca0000 00020000 "cache"
mtd8: 105c0000 00020000 "userdata"
mtd9: 00200000 00020000 "kpanic"
```

An examiner should choose to image all of the MTD partitions. However, for this example we will focus on mtd8, the user data partition.

As we are now prepared to acquire the device, it may be helpful to refer back to the NAND flash and file system topics in Chapter 4 if some of the terminology or data structures are confusing. There are four Android physical acquisition strategies you can use once you have a device with root access:

1. Full nanddump of all partitions, including data and OOB (preferred)
2. A dd image of partitions, which only acquires the data, not the OOB
3. A logical acquisition of files using tar
4. A logical acquisition of files using adb

In addition, there are two primary ways to save the acquired data from the device:

1. Use adb port forward to create a network between the Ubuntu workstation and Android device over USB
2. Place an SD card into the device, mount, and save locally

There are advantages to both approaches. With adb port forwarding, you do not need to insert your own device and can immediately create the files on your workstation. When you save to the SD card, the acquisition is much faster. Both approaches are valid and will be demonstrated here.

We will start with the full nanddump of the user data partition as this provides the most complete forensic copy of the data. To achieve the nanddump, you must have a version of nanddump compiled for the ARM platform. Cross-compiling nanddump is beyond the scope of this book. However, you can either search for the program on the Internet or follow directions that are also posted online.

> **TIP**
>
> **Cross-compiling for ARM**
>
> Cross-compiling source code to run on the ARM platform can be quite difficult and there is sparse support for it online. One possible solution is to use Android's Native Development Kit (NDK) to build compatible binaries. Another option is to use Linux and install a cross-compiler such as Code Sourcery's G++ Lite 2009q3-67 for ARM GNU/Linux from http://www.codesourcery.com/sgpp/lite/arm/portal/release1039. Once a cross-compiler is installed, you must modify the source code's Makefile to indicate the cross-compiling option. Also check this book's web site at http://viaforensics.com/education/android-forensics-mobile-security-book/ for future updates.

To avoid writing any data to the NAND flash, we can again examine the output of the mount command and take note that the "/dev" directory is tmpfs and thus, is stored in RAM. We can therefore push the forensic utilities to "/dev":

```
ahoog@ubuntu:~$ adb push AFPhysical/ /dev/AFPhyiscal
push: AFPhysical/tar -> /dev/AFPhyiscal/tar
push: AFPhysical/md5sum -> /dev/AFPhyiscal/md5sum
push: AFPhysical/nanddump -> /dev/AFPhyiscal/nanddump
push: AFPhysical/nc -> /dev/AFPhyiscal/nc
4 files pushed. 0 files skipped.
1003 KB/s (2803303 bytes in 2.727s)
```

Next we need to make the programs executable on the device. To achieve this, we use the chmod command, which changes the permissions of a file including the execute flag. We will set all files to allow any user to read or execute the program:

```
ahoog@ubuntu:~$ adb shell
/ # cd /dev/AFPhyiscal
/dev/AFPhyiscal # ls -l
-rw-rw-rw-    1 0        0            711168 Jan 24  2011 md5sum
-rw-rw-rw-    1 0        0            669799 Jan 24  2011 nanddump
-rw-rw-rw-    1 0        0            711168 Jan 24  2011 nc
-rw-rw-rw-    1 0        0            711168 Jan 24  2011 tar
/dev/AFPhyiscal # chmod 755 *
/dev/AFPhyiscal # ls -l
-rwxr-xr-x    1 0        0            711168 Jan 24  2011 md5sum
-rwxr-xr-x    1 0        0            669799 Jan 24  2011 nanddump
-rwxr-xr-x    1 0        0            711168 Jan 24  2011 nc
-rwxr-xr-x    1 0        0            711168 Jan 24  2011 tar
```

As you can tell, after we execute the "chmod 755" command on the programs, they each have the execute bit now set, which is represented by the "x" in the file permissions.

If you decided to save the nanddump to the SD card, ensure you place a properly formatted SD card in the device and that it is mounted on the system. Then we can execute nanddump as follows:

```
/ # /dev/AFPhyiscal/nanddump /dev/mtd/mtd8ro > /sdcard/af-book-mtd8.nanddump
ECC failed: 0
ECC corrected: 0
Number of bad blocks: 1
Number of bbt blocks: 0
Block size 131072, page size 2048, OOB size 64
Dumping data starting at 0x00000000 and ending at 0x105c0000...

/ # ls -l /sdcard/af-book-mtd8.nanddump
-rwxrwxrwx    1 0        0       283041792 Jan  1 00:12 /sdcard/
af-book-mtd8.nanddump
```

And ultimately either transfer to your Ubuntu VM using adb pull or remove the SD card and copy via a direct USB connection, which is much faster.

> **NOTE**
>
> **MD5 hash**
>
> Although the user data partition was not mounted on the device during acquisition, the md5sum hash signature of "/dev/mtd/mtd8ro" will change even without any writes. This is due to the nature of NAND flash where the operating system and memory are in a nearly constant state of change from wear leveling, bad block management, and other mechanisms which occur despite the lack of changes to the user data. The best approach is to perform an md5sum of the resulting NAND flash file to ensure integrity from that point forward.

The second method for saving the NAND flash file or any other imaged data is to use netcat, which is a utility that allows you to redirect the output of a command to the network. For this approach, you will need two active terminal or ssh sessions. We will refer to them as Session0 and Session1. All of the Session0 commands will run on the Ubuntu VM and thus we will not go into the Android device shell from Session0. The commands which need to execute within the Android device's shell will all take place on Session1.

To begin, we first enable the network connection between the two endpoints using the adb port-forwarding capability:

```
SESSION0
--------------
ahoog@ubuntu:~$ adb forward tcp:31337 tcp:31337
```

This command essentially connects port 31337 on the Android device and the Ubuntu VM. Next, we execute nanddump on the Android device and pipe the output to netcat:

```
SESSION1
--------------
ahoog@ubuntu:~$ adb shell
/ # /dev/AFPhyiscal/nanddump /dev/mtd/mtd8ro | /dev/AFPhyiscal/nc -l -p 31337
ECC failed: 0
ECC corrected: 0
Number of bad blocks: 0
Number of bbt blocks: 0
Block size 131072, page size 2048, OOB size 64
Dumping data starting at 0x00000000 and ending at 0x105c0000...
```

Now that the Android device is sending the nanddump data over netcat, we need to receive it on the Ubuntu VM side:

```
SESSION0
--------------
ahoog@ubuntu:~$ nc 127.0.0.1 31337 > af-book-mtd8.nanddump
```

When nanddump completes, it simply exits without any additional output as does the netcat on the Ubuntu VM. We can verify that the nanddump was received on the workstation with ls:

```
SESSION0
--------------
ahoog@ubuntu:~$ ls -lh af-book-mtd8.nanddump
-rw-r--r-- 1 ahoog ahoog 270M 2011-02-26 20:58 af-book-mtd8.nanddump
```

At this point, you could continue to physically image the MTD partitions needed for the investigation, which should include at least the user data and the cache partitions.

In Chapter 7, we provide a program that will allow you to extract the OOB data from a nanddump to assist with forensic processing such as file carving. As you can generate the dd image in this manner, there is no need to acquire a dd image using the Android device. However, dd is built into Android and so we provide this example which is similar to the use of the nanddump example, except it uses the dd utility, and so does not capture OOB data. This example uses the reference HTC Incredible.

```
SESSION0
--------------
ahoog@ubuntu:~$ adb forward tcp:31337 tcp:31337

SESSION1
--------------
ahoog@ubuntu:~$ adb shell
$ su
# cat /proc/mtd
dev:    size   erasesize  name
mtd0: 000a0000 00020000 "misc"
mtd1: 00480000 00020000 "recovery"
mtd2: 00300000 00020000 "boot"
mtd3: 0f800000 00020000 "system"
mtd4: 000a0000 00020000 "local"
mtd5: 02800000 00020000 "cache"
mtd6: 09500000 00020000 "datadata"
# dd if=/dev/mtd/mtd6 bs=4096 | /dev/AFPhyiscal/nc -l -p 31337
38144+0 records in
38144+0 records out
156237824 bytes transferred in 182.898 secs (854234 bytes/sec)

SESSION0
--------------
ahoog@ubuntu:~$ nc 127.0.0.1 31337 > dd of=htc-datadata.dd bs=4096
```

Due to variations in Android devices, MTD, YAFFS2, and other nuisances, it is not always possible to mount the acquired nanddump image and extract the logical files. As you already have sufficient privileges, it is best to extract the desired logical data. This can be accomplished using a recursive adb pull because the adb daemon running on the device has root privileges. You can also use a utility such as tar to copy the data into a single archive file. In either instance, you must ensure the desired file system is mounted. Some of the modified recovery partitions provide a user interface for mounting the file systems. However, you can also do this on the command line and mount the file system read only. On the Motorola Droid referenced above, do the following:

```
SESSION1
--------------
/ # mount -o ro -t yaffs2 /dev/block/mtdblock8 /data
/ # mount -o ro,remount -t yaffs2 /dev/block/mtdblock7 /cache
/ # mount
rootfs on / type rootfs (rw)
tmpfs on /dev type tmpfs (rw,mode=755)
devpts on /dev/pts type devpts (rw,mode=600)
proc on /proc type proc (rw)
sysfs on /sys type sysfs (rw)
/dev/block/mtdblock7 on /cache type yaffs2 (ro)
/dev/block/mmcblk0p1 on /sdcard type vfat
(rw,nodev,noatime,nodiratime,fmask=0000,dmask=0000,allow_utime=0022,
codepage=cp437,iocharset=iso8859-1,errors=remount-ro)
/dev/block/mtdblock8 on /data type yaffs2 (ro)
```

The first command mounts the "/data" partition read only. The second command takes the already mounted "/cache" directory and remounts it read only. You can now perform the adb pull:

```
ahoog@ubuntu:~$ adb pull /data/data/com.android.providers.telephony sms
pull: building file list...
pull: /data/data/com.android.providers.telephony/databases/mmssms.db ->
sms/databases/mmssms.db
pull: /data/data/com.android.providers.telephony/databases/telephony.db ->
sms/databases/telephony.db
2 files pulled. 0 files skipped.
137 KB/s (44032 bytes in 0.311s)
```

The final option is to use the tar utility that places files and directories in a single archive often called a tarball.

```
SESSION1
--------------
ahoog@ubuntu:~$ adb shell
/ # /dev/AFPhyiscal/tar cpv -f - /data/data/com.android.providers.telephony
/cache | /dev/AFPhyiscal/nc -l -p 31337
tar: removing leading '/' from member names
data/data/com.android.providers.telephony/
data/data/com.android.providers.telephony/lib/
data/data/com.android.providers.telephony/databases/
data/data/com.android.providers.telephony/databases/telephony.db
data/data/com.android.providers.telephony/databases/mmssms.db
cache/
cache/recovery/
cache/recovery/log
cache/lost+found/

SESSION0
--------------
ahoog@ubuntu:~$ nc 127.0.0.1 31337 > af-book-droid-files.tar
```

In this example, we passed two directories to tar which we wanted archived: the directory containing SMS/MMS messages in "/data/data" and the "/cache" directory. We sent the archive over the network and received it on the Ubuntu VM. However, you could have also simply saved the archive to the SD card.

Once you have root privileges on an Android device and sufficient understanding of the device's architecture, you can use nanddump, dd, tar, netcat, and adb to create forensic images or simply copies of the data for analysis.

SUMMARY

There are several techniques that can be used to perform a forensic acquisition of an Android device. If the device is pass code protected, you must circumvent or bypass the protection to extract data. While a number of techniques to circumvent the pass code exist, it is not possible to achieve this in every circumstance. Once the device is accessible, the forensic analyst can choose from a logical acquisition which focuses primarily on undeleted data accessible through Content Providers or the more thorough but technically challenging physical acquisition. While the physical acquisition will produce more data, it generally requires more sophisticated analysis techniques which will be covered in Chapter 7.

References

ACPO Good Practice Guide for Computer-Based Electronic Evidence—7Safe Information Security. (n.d.). Retrieved February 19, 2011, from http://7safe.com/electronic_evidence/index.html#.

Android & Windows Phone: Tablets, Apps, & ROMs @ xda-developers. (n.d.). Retrieved February 23, 2011, from http://www.xda-developers.com/.

Aviv, Gibson, Mossop, Blaze, & Smith. (n.d.). Smudge attacks on smartphone touch screens. Retrieved February 21, 2011, from http://www.usenix.org/events/woot10/tech/full_papers/Aviv.pdf.

Cannon, T. (n.d.). Android lock screen bypass. Retrieved February 21, 2011, from http://thomascannon.net/blog/2011/02/android-lock-screen-bypass/.

dc3dd. (n.d.). Retrieved February 22, 2011, from http://dc3dd.sourceforge.net/.

Government Employment & Payroll. (n.d.). Retrieved February 19, 2011, from http://www.census.gov/govs/apes/.

[Guide] Flashing Linux Motorola's with RSD Lite Versions. (n.d.). Retrieved February 24, 2011, from modmymobile.com/forums/8-guides-downloads-forum-suggestions/218651-guide-flashing-linux-motorolas-rsd-lite-versions.html.

HTC—Developer Center. (n.d.). Retrieved February 28, 2011, from http://developer.htc.com/adp.html.

IEEE SA—1149.1—1990—IEEE Standard Test Access Port and Boundary-Scan Architecture. (n.d.). Retrieved February 23, 2011, from http://standards.ieee.org/findstds/standard/1149.1-1990.html.

RerWare, LLC: Android Backup and BlackBerry Backup—MyBackup Pro. (n.d.). Retrieved February 22, 2011, from http://www.rerware.com/.

CHAPTER

Android application and forensic analysis

7

INFORMATION IN THIS CHAPTER

- Analysis techniques
- FAT forensic analysis
- YAFFS2 forensic analysis
- Android app analysis and reference

INTRODUCTION

A lot of material has been discussed up to this point in the book covering not only the history and architecture of Android devices but also complete details on the file systems, ways to secure devices, and methodology to acquire data from them. But data without context and analysis is just noise. Many of the techniques used in traditional forensic investigations are applicable in Android forensics analysis.

ANALYSIS TECHNIQUES

This section will provide an overview of the analysis techniques followed by sections that demonstrate the procedures for specific file systems.

Timeline Analysis

Timeline analysis should be a key component to any investigation as the timing of events is nearly always relevant. There are many ways to build a forensic timeline. However, unless created with specialized software, the process can be quite tedious. Several software techniques will be covered in detail later in the chapter including free, open source forensic utilities from both The Sleuth Kit and log2timline. Other forensic tools can create timelines as well.

For supported file systems (for example, the FAT16/FAT32 file systems found on the SD cards and embedded MultiMediaCard [eMMC]), a number of tools are available which can create the timeline. However, YAFFS2 is not currently supported by any analysis tool and so creating a timeline requires significant manual analysis.

The primary source of timeline information is the file system metadata including the modified (file metadata), accessed, changed (file contents), and created. This metadata is often referred to as MAC times or sometimes MACB where the "B" represents when a file was created (born). File systems track different time stamps and have nuances that must be taken into account when performing forensic analysis.

For example, Microsoft's FAT file system has been the subject of many forensic investigations and analyses. The Microsoft Developers Network (MSDN) provides details on file times in FAT and NTFS file systems, stating:

> *Not all file systems can record creation and last access times, and not all file systems record them in the same manner. For example, the resolution of create time on FAT is 10 ms, while write time has a resolution of 2 s, and access time has a resolution of 1 day, and hence, it is really the access date. The NTFS file system delays updates to the last access time for a file by up to 1 h after the last access.*
>
> **(File Times, n.d.)**

Andre Ross created a useful graphical representation of this on his digfor (DIGital FORensics) blog (http://digfor.blogspot.com/2008/10/time-and-timestamps.html) shown in Fig. 7.1 (Ross, A., n.d.).

To further illustrate how FAT time stamps work, digital forensics and incident response firm cmdLab posted a blog entitled "Misinterpretation of File System Timestamps" (Casey, E., n.d.), which provides full details on FAT time stamps.

The confusion arises from the fact that FAT file systems represent create and last-write time stamps slightly differently. Last-write time stamps are 32-bit little-endian values, interpreted as follows:

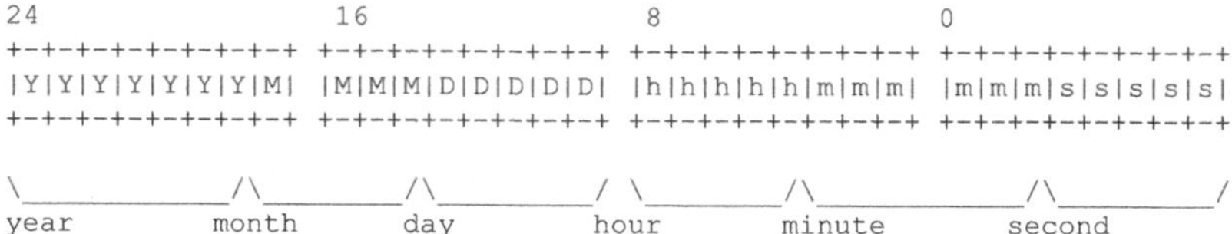

Take as an example the following FAT folder entry with the last-write date highlighted in bold:

```
$ icat /dev/sdb1 353884 | xxd
0000000: 2e20 2020 2020 2020 2020 2030 004f b079 . 0.O.y
0000010: 763a 763a 0000 b579 763a a502 0000 0000 v:v:...yv:......
0000020: 2e2e 2020 2020 2020 2020 2010 004f b079 .. ..O.y
0000030: 763a 763a 0000 b079 763a 6605 0000 0000 v:v:...yv:f.....
0000040: 4173 0061 006c 0076 0065 000f 009e 6e00 As.a.l.v.e....n.
0000050: 6500 7700 3400 2e00 6700 0000 6900 6600 e.w.4...g...i.f.
0000060: 5341 4c56 454e 7e31 4749 4620 0075 78b9 SALVEN~1GIF .ux.
0000070: 753a 763a 0000 78b9 753a 9212 c1d4 0000 u:v:..x.u:......
0000080: 4269 0066 0000 00ff ffff ff0f 0014 ffff Bi.f............
0000090: ffff ffff ffff ffff ffff 0000 ffff ffff ................
```

Converting to big endian gives 3a 75 b9 78, which has the following binary representation:

00111010 01110101 10111001 01111000

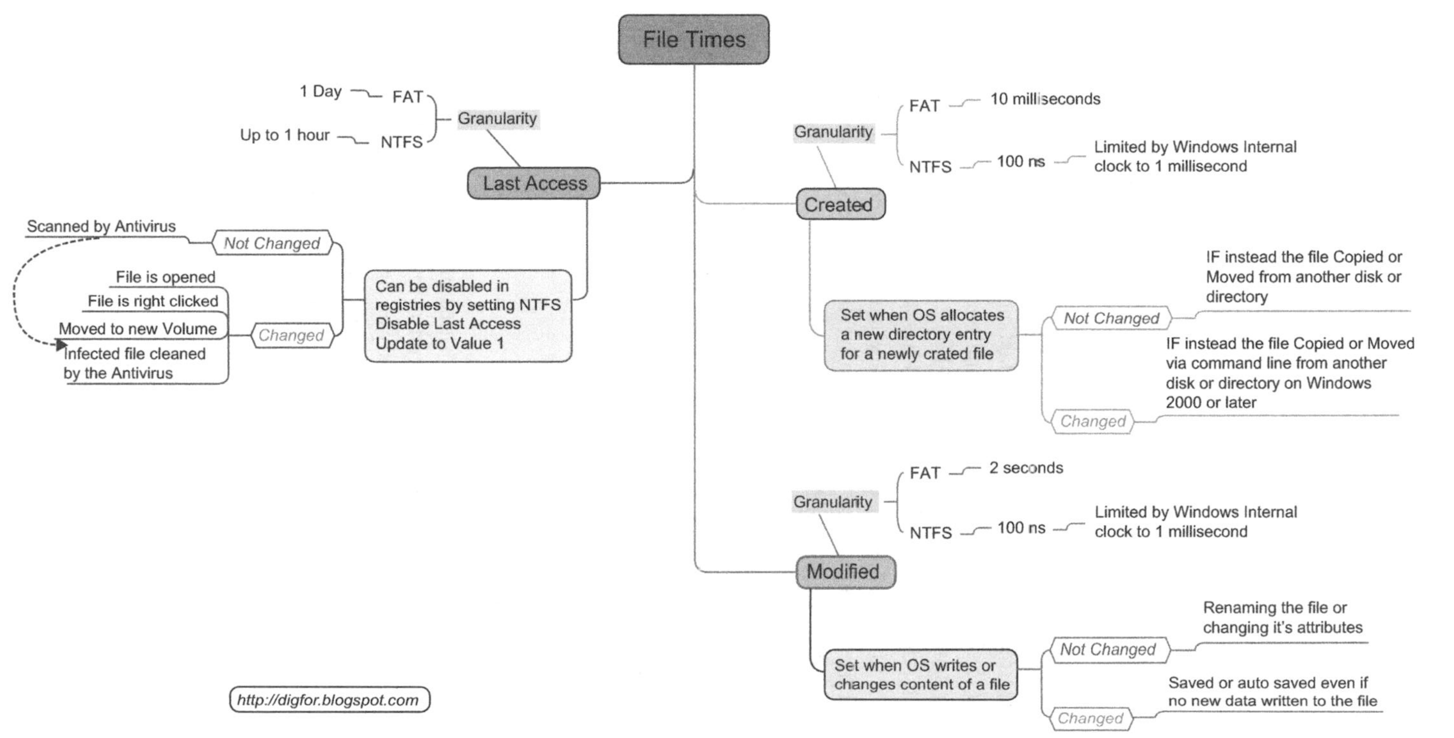

FIGURE 7.1

FAT and NTFS time and time stamps.

This translates to a time stamp of 2009.03.21 23:11:48 as follows:

- 7 bits = 0011101 = 29 years since 1980
- 4 bits = 0011 = 3 months
- 5 bits = 10101 = 21 days
- 5 bits = 10111 = 23 h
- 6 bits = 001011 = 11 min
- 5 bits = 11000 = 24 = 48 s

Note that 5 bits cannot store all 60 s, so last-write time stamps must be incremented in 2 s intervals, and are always an even number of seconds.

Although the create time follows a similar general calculation, it uses an additional 8 bits to represent one hundredths of a second. In the same directory listing above, the create time stamp is identical to the last modified time stamp except for an additional byte (75 78 b9 75 3a). The additional byte equates to 117 hundredths of a second, which brings the create time to 2009.03.21 23:11:49.17. Thus, the create time can have an odd number of seconds, and has a resolution of 10 ms.

One tool used in this book for timeline analysis is The Sleuth Kit (TSK), which supports several file systems. The TSK wiki provides the information presented in Table 7.1 to define the meaning of MACB time stamps for the supported file systems (Carrier, B., n.d.).

Unfortunately, TSK does not, as of version 3.2.1, fully support YAFFS2. However, there are some efforts to provide this information. For Android, TSK is effective in analyzing the FAT file systems as well as EXT3 which is found on some devices. TSK does not yet fully support EXT4 but the software is updated frequently and examiners should check the web site http://www.sleuthkit.org/ for the most recent changes.

File System Analysis

As discussed throughout this book, the directories and files in the Android file systems are obviously the primary focus of a forensic investigation. The final section of this chapter and book, "Android App Analysis and Reference," will provide a detailed analysis of Android apps. Combining this information with techniques demonstrated in Chapter 4 will provide the most significant results for an investigation.

Table 7.1 MAC Meaning by File System

File System	m	a	c	b
Ext 2/3	Modified	Accessed	Changed	N/A
FAT	Written	Accessed	N/A	Created
NTFS	File modified	Accessed	MFT modified	Created
UFS	Modified	Accessed	Changed	N/A

There are a number of directories that need to be examined for an investigation. Over time, examiners will need to expand the list to include new directories and files, as Android devices are changing rapidly. The best way to approach this problem is to first run the following command to determine which file systems are mounted on the system, where they are mounted, and what type they are. To demonstrate, let's look at four different Android phones including a T-Mobile/HTC G1, a Google Nexus One, a Motorola Droid, and an HTC Incredible.

To start, let's examine the output of the mount command on the G1 running Android 1.5:

```
ahoog@ubuntu:~$ adb shell mount
rootfs / rootfs ro 0 0
tmpfs /dev tmpfs rw,mode=755 0 0
devpts /dev/pts devpts rw,mode=600 0 0
proc /proc proc rw 0 0
sysfs /sys sysfs rw 0 0
tmpfs /sqlite_stmt_journals tmpfs rw,size=4096k 0 0
/dev/block/mtdblock3 /system yaffs2 ro 0 0
/dev/block/mtdblock5 /data yaffs2 rw,nosuid,nodev 0 0
/dev/block/mtdblock4 /cache yaffs2 rw,nosuid,nodev 0 0
```

This particular G1 was running a stock firmware and did not have an SD card inserted, so we are left with four file systems to examine, highlighted with emphasis.

Similarly, we examine the output of mount on the Nexus One running Android 2.1-update1:

```
ahoog@ubuntu:~$ adb shell mount
rootfs on / type rootfs (ro,relatime)
tmpfs on /dev type tmpfs (rw,relatime,mode=755)
devpts on /dev/pts type devpts (rw,relatime,mode=600)
proc on /proc type proc (rw,relatime)
sysfs on /sys type sysfs (rw,relatime)
tmpfs on /sqlite_stmt_journals type tmpfs (rw,relatime,size=4096k)
none on /dev/cpuctl type cgroup (rw,relatime,cpu)
/dev/block/mtdblock3 on /system type yaffs2 (ro,relatime)
/dev/block/mtdblock5 on /data type yaffs2 (rw,nosuid,nodev,relatime)
/dev/block/mtdblock4 on /cache type yaffs2 (rw,nosuid,nodev,relatime)
/sys/kernel/debug on /sys/kernel/debug type debugfs (rw,relatime)
/dev/block//vold/179:1 on /sdcard type vfat
(rw,dirsync,nosuid,nodev,noexec,relatime,uid=1000,gid=1015,fmask=0702,
dmask=0702,allow_utime=0020,codepage=cp437,iocharset=iso88591,shortname=mixed,
utf8,errors=remount-ro)
```

In this case, there are five file systems on the Nexus One, highlighted with emphasis, which should be the initial focus of an examination. The additional file system is the SD card mounted.

Next, we take a look at the Motorola Droid's mounted file systems when running Android 2.2.1:

```
ahoog@ubuntu:~$ adb shell mount
rootfs / rootfs ro,relatime 0 0
tmpfs /dev tmpfs rw,relatime,mode=755 0 0
```

```
devpts /dev/pts devpts rw,relatime,mode=600 0 0
proc /proc proc rw,relatime 0 0
sysfs /sys sysfs rw,relatime 0 0
none /acct cgroup rw,relatime,cpuacct 0 0
tmpfs /mnt/asec tmpfs rw,relatime,mode=755,gid=1000 0 0
none /dev/cpuctl cgroup rw,relatime,cpu 0 0
/dev/block/mtdblock4 /system yaffs2 ro,relatime 0 0
/dev/block/mtdblock6 /data yaffs2 rw,nosuid,nodev,relatime 0 0
/dev/block/mtdblock5 /cache yaffs2 rw,nosuid,nodev,relatime 0 0
/dev/block/mtdblock0 /config yaffs2 ro,relatime 0 0
/dev/block/vold/179:1 /mnt/sdcard vfat
rw,dirsync,nosuid,nodev,noexec,relatime,uid=1000,gid=1015,fmask=0702,dmask=
0702,allow_utime=0020,codepage=cp437,iocharset=iso8859-1,shortname=mixed,utf8,
errors=remount-ro 0 0
/dev/block/vold/179:1 /mnt/secure/asec vfat
rw,dirsync,nosuid,nodev,noexec,relatime,uid=1000,gid=1015,fmask=0702,dmask=
0702,allow_utime=0020,codepage=cp437,iocharset=iso8859-1,shortname=mixed,utf8,
errors=remount-ro 0 0
tmpfs /mnt/sdcard/.android_secure tmpfs ro,relatime,size=0k,mode=000 0 0
```

The Motorola Droid also has seven files systems of interest. However, they are slightly different from the Nexus One.

Finally, let's take a look at the HTC Incredible output previously discussed running Android 2.2:

```
ahoog@ubuntu:~$ adb shell mount
rootfs / rootfs ro,relatime 0 0
tmpfs /dev tmpfs rw,relatime,mode=755 0 0
devpts /dev/pts devpts rw,relatime,mode=600 0 0
proc /proc proc rw,relatime 0 0
sysfs /sys sysfs rw,relatime 0 0
none /acct cgroup rw,relatime,cpuacct 0 0
tmpfs /mnt/asec rw,relatime,mode=755,gid=1000 0 0
none /dev/cpuctl cgroup rw,relatime,cpu 0 0
/dev/block/mtdblock3 /system yaffs2 rw,relatime 0 0
/dev/block/mmcblk0p1 /data ext3
rw,nosuid,noatime,nodiratime,errors=continue,data=writeback 0 0
/dev/block/mtdblock6 /data/data yaffs2 rw,nosuid,nodev,relatime 0 0
/dev/block/mmcblk0p2 /cache ext3
rw,nosuid,nodev,noatime,nodiratime,errors=continue,data=writeback 0 0
tmpfs /app-cache tmpfs rw,relatime,size=8192k 0 0
/dev/block/vold/179:9 /mnt/sdcard vfat
rw,dirsync,nosuid,nodev,noexec,relatime,uid=1000,gid=1015,fmask=0702,dmask=070
2,allow_utime=0020,codepage=cp437,iocharset=iso8859-1,shortname=mixed,utf8,
errors=remount-ro 0 0
/dev/block/vold/179:9 /mnt/secure/asec vfat
rw,dirsync,nosuid,nodev,noexec,relatime,uid=1000,gid=1015,fmask=0702,dmask=070
2,allow_utime=0020,codepage=cp437,iocharset=iso8859-1,shortname=mixed,utf8,
errors=remount-ro 0 0
tmpfs /mnt/sdcard/.android_secure tmpfs ro,relatime,size=0k,mode=000 0 0
/dev/block/vold/179:3 /mnt/emmc vfat
rw,dirsync,nosuid,nodev,noexec,relatime,uid=1000,gid=1015,fmask=0702,dmask=070
2,allow_utime=0020,codepage=cp437,iocharset=iso8859-1,shortname=mixed,utf8,
errors=remount-ro 0 0
```

The HTC Incredible tops the list with nine file systems of interest. As you can tell, with different Android devices and different versions of Android, the file systems of interest change. However, from the above examination, we have created Table 7.2, which provides a strong starting point for file system examinations.

Table 7.2 File Systems to Include in an Investigation

Mount Point	File System Type	Relevance
/proc	proc	Examine on the phone with the "cat" command. Look for relevant metadata about the system such as file system statistics
/data/data (on older systems, entire /data is 1 partition/file system)	YAFFS2	Nearly all app data
/data (on newer phones /data can be further segemented)	EXT3/EXT4/YAFFS2	App and system data excluding the app data stores found in /data/data
/cache	YAFFS2/EXT3	Cache file system used by some apps and by the system
/mnt/asec	tmpfs	Unencrypted app .apk file, which is stored encrypted on the SD card but decrypted here for running systems to access and utilize
/app-cache	tmpfs	Temporary file system where com.android.browser (on HTC Incredible) stores cache. Other apps may also use this directory over time
/mnt/sdcard	vfat	FAT32 file system on removable SD card
/mnt/emmc	vfat	FAT32 file system on the Embedded MultiMediaCard (eMMC)

On a positive note, as these files are allocated, even for unsupported file systems such as YAFFS2, the files can be copied to another medium and examined with existing forensic tools and techniques an examiner owns and has knowledge of. For example, the contents of "/data/data" could be copied from an Android device onto your forensic workstation and then the content could be examined directly.

File Carving

File carving is a process in which specified file types are searched for and extracted across binary data, often resulting in a forensic image of an entire disk or partition. File carving works by examining the binary data and identifying files based on their known file headers. If the file format has a known footer, it will then scan from the header until it finds the footer (or hits a maximum file length set by the configuration file) and then save the carved file to disk for further examination.

Traditional file carving techniques require that the data are sequential in the image and this cannot produce the full file if it is fragmented. There are many reasons that files are fragmented as the process for saving the file to nonvolatile storage varies by file system type and is heavily influenced by the memory type such as NAND flash. This also means that files that are very large (such as videos) will be more difficult to recover.

Newer file carving techniques are being researched and developed to address the limitations experienced with file fragmentation. One such technique is developed by Digital Assembly, a digital forensics solutions company based in New York. Their technique, called SmartCarving, profiles the fragmentation characteristics of several popular file systems (except YAFFS2, unfortunately) and uses this information to carve even fragmented photos. Their product, Adroit Photo Forensics, can also carve images from unknown file systems (Digital Assembly, n.d.).

One popular tool used for carving data files is scalpel, an open source, high performance file carver written by Golden G. Richard III (Scalpel, n.d.). Scalpel reads a configuration file for desired file header and footer definitions in order to extract files from a raw image. It is file system independent and will work on FATx, NTFS, EXT2/3, HFS, or raw partitions. Scalpel is written in C and runs on Linux, Windows, OS X, and other operating systems which can compile the C code (Scalpel, n.d.).

There are two ways to acquire scalpel. First, on the forensic workstation, you can install via apt-get:

```
ahoog@ubuntu:~$ sudo apt-get install scalpel
```

This will install the latest version. Alternatively, you can compile from source, which will allow you to install the latest version on Linux or other platforms without waiting for the specific platform maintainer to update the prepackaged version.

```
cd ~
wget http://www.digitalforensicssolutions.com/Scalpel/scalpel-1.60.tar.gz
tar xzvf scalpel-1.60.tar.gz
cd scalpel-1.60/
make
```

The scalpel executable is now in "~/scalpel-1.60" and is simply called scalpel. In addition, there is a sample scalpel.conf in that same directory that is needed by scalpel to run and to extend the supported file definitions. Here's a starter scalpel.conf for an Android device:

```
#ext   case   size    header    footer
gif    y    5000000    \x47\x49\x46\x38\x37\x61    \x00\x3b
gif    y    5000000    \x47\x49\x46\x38\x39\x61    \x00\x3b
jpg    y    200000000    \xff\xd8\xff\xe0\x00\x10    \xff\xd9
jpg    y    5000000    \xff\xd8\xff\xe1    \x7f\xff\xd9

png    y    102400      \x50\x4e\x47?    \xff\xfc\xfd\xfe
png    y    102400      \x89PNG

db     y    409600    SQLite\x20format

email y    10240    From:

doc    y    10000000  \xd0\xcf\x11\xe0\xa1\xb1\x1a\xe1\x00\x00
```

```
\xd0\xcf\x11\xe0\xa1\xb1\x1a\xe1\x00\x00 NEXT
doc    y    10000000   \xd0\xcf\x11\xe0\xa1\xb1

htm    n    50000    <html          </html>

pdf    y    5000000    %PDF  %EOF\x0d    REVERSE
pdf    y    5000000    %PDF  %EOF\x0a    REVERSE

wav    y    200000    RIFF????WAVE
amr    y    200000    #!AMR

zip    y    10000000    PK\x03\x04    \x3c\xac

java    y    1000000    \xca\xfe\xba\xbe
```

As you can tell, the headers for this configuration file define the extension or file type (if it is case sensitive), the maximum size to carve, the header definition (in ASCII, hex, and other supported notations), and the footer (if it exists). A targeted file type for carving does not need to define each setting. For additional information, see the sample configuration file in the downloaded source files as there are many additional options that are quite powerful. Your Ubuntu workstation now has the software needed for file carving, which will be covered in the FAT32 and YAFFS2 sections.

It is worth pointing out that a large number of file signatures have already been assembled. Gary Kessler, an independent consultant and practitioner of digital forensics, actively maintains a table of file signatures on his web site (Kessler, G., n.d.). He references the "magic file," which is found on most Unix systems located at "/usr/share/file/magic" on the Ubuntu workstation. On the workstation, you can run the "file" command, which takes a file as an argument and attempts to determine the file type based on the signatures in the magic file.

A simple example is looking at an unknown file in "/mnt/emmc/.Trashes," called "._501," which cannot be easily identified by the file name (of course, some people might try to hide file types by changing the extension; however, by examining the file signature, this is easily discovered):

```
#ahoog@ubuntu:~/htc-inc/mnt/emmc$ file ./.Trashes/._501
./.Trashes/._501: AppleDouble encoded Macintosh file
```

Thus, the eMMC has an OS X file in the Trash, which might indicate that someone connected the Android device to a Mac computer.

Strings

The strings command on the Ubuntu workstation will extract, by default, ASCII printable strings—at least four characters long—from any file, text or binary. While this technique is not terribly elegant or sophisticated, it is quite effective at quickly examining binary data to determine if information of interest might be contained in the file.

There are several options that have a great impact on what strings output. First, let's take a look at the synopsis section of the command's man page (manual):

```
STRINGS(1)                    GNU Development Tools                    STRINGS(1)

NAME
       strings - print the strings of printable characters in files.

SYNOPSIS
       strings [-afovV] [-min-len]
               [-n min-len] [--bytes=min-len]
               [-t radix] [--radix=radix]
               [-e encoding] [--encoding=encoding]
               [-] [--all] [--print-file-name]
               [-T bfdname] [--target=bfdname]
               [--help] [--version] file
```

There are a few options you should always consider using when executing strings. First, the "—all" option tells strings to examine the entire file (on certain files, it only examines certain portions of the file). Second, the "--radix=" option instructs strings to print the offset within the file where the string was found. This is extremely helpful when you combine strings and a hex editor to examine possible evidence found in the file. The radix option can print the offset in octal (--radix=o), hex (--radix=x), or decimal (--radix=d). For most hex editors, you should consider hex or perhaps decimal offsets.

The other extremely important option controls the character encoding of the strings, which provides support for Unicode characters in both big-endian and little-endian formats:

```
       --encoding=encoding
           Select the character encoding of the strings that are to be found.
           Possible values for encoding are: s = single-7-bit-byte characters
           (ASCII, ISO 8859, etc., default), S = single-8-bit-byte characters,
           b = 16-bit bigendian, l = 16-bit littleendian, B = 32-bit
           bigendian, L = 32-bit littleendian.  Useful for finding wide
           character strings. (l and b apply to, for example, Unicode
           UTF-16/UCS-2 encodings).
```

This is important because not only does Android natively support Unicode but it also allows investigating a phone where the default language requires Unicode. Following are a few examples from the previous dd image:

```
ahoog@ubuntu:~$ strings --all --radix=x htc-datadata.dd | less
   880a htcchirp.db
   891d ^XMp4XM
   900a unlinked
   980a deleted
   a00a htcchirp.db-journal
```

In this example, the first lines of results were omitted. However, you can see the dd image is referencing the htcchirp.db at offset 0x880A and, shortly thereafter, we see unlinked (0x900A), deleted (0x980A), and finally htcchirp.db-journal (0xA00A). So what does all this mean? It seems likely that the htcchirp.db database was modified. During that time, it created a special file (htcchirp.db-journal, a journal file) that manages the update and allows the change to roll back if it was not successful. After the journal file was no longer needed, it was deleted. This is important information for understanding what occurred and where deleted data might exist (the journal file takes a complete snapshot of the SQLite page that is being updated and thus, the previous values are stored on the NAND flash).

Now, let's change the encoding parameter and look for the following:

```
ahoog@ubuntu:~$ strings --all --radix=x --encoding=b htc-datadata.dd | less
 c42404 xt=\"chicago tribune\"><b>chicago</b> tribune
</div>",259200,604800],["<div class=\"sg_g\"
       sg_text=\"chicago bears\"><b>chicago</b> bears
</div>",259200,604800],["<div class=\"sg_g\"
       sg_text=\"chicago weather\"><b>chicago</b> weather
</div>",259200,604800],["<div class=\"sg_g\"
       sg_text=\"chicago sun times\"><b>chicago</b> sun times
</div>",259200,604800],["<div class=\"sg_g\"
       sg_text=\"chicago public library\"><b>chicago</b> public library
</div>",259200,604800],
       ["<div class=\"sg_g\" sg_text=\"chicago bul

1943020 gt_bearsh[1295219345,["<div class=\"sg_n\"
sg_url=\"/url?ct=res&amp;oi=s
       uggest_nav&amp;q=http://www.bearshare.com/&amp;sa=X&amp;
source=suggest&amp;usg=AFQjCNGP71yyDMU
       jIhmvN-DN2Tm7yPYCAA\"><span style=\"display:inline;\">Free Music
Downloads - Download Free MP3
       Music - BearShare.com Music</span> <br/><span
style=\"display:inline;\">www.bearsha
```

In this example, we are looking for 16-bit big-endian characters. In this case, two examples were pulled from the results. In one example at offset 0xC42404, it's clear some sort of activity related to Chicago occurred. The examiner could simply open a hex edit, jump to offset 0xC42404, and look at the data around this entry in an attempt to understand the activity.

Equally interesting is the next entry at offset 0x1943020 that references the bearshare.com web site and has what appears to be a time stamp. If we convert the number 1295219345 into a date/time based on Unix Epoch, we get Sunday, 16 Jan 2011 23:09:05 GMT. Again, the examiner would need to examine the data more closely to validate any findings, but a good hypothesis is that some web-based activity took place on the Android device at that time.

One final example (and the other encodings can be left as an exercise for the reader) reveals the following:

```
ahoog@ubuntu:~$ strings --all --radix=x --encoding=l htc-datadata.dd | less
18451a8 rgc:0:lat41.8786
18451d2 rgc:0:lon-87.6359
18451fc rgc:1:last1288470018632
1845230 rgc:0:rgcOak Park, IL
1845260 rgc:1:acc912
```

This is a great example because it includes not only a (valid) longitude and latitude, but a time stamp (in milliseconds, not seconds, since 1970) that translates to GMT: Sat, 30 Oct 2010 20:20:18 GMT.

Strings is a very powerful command which, when combined with searching and filters, can quickly determine if phone numbers, names, locations, GPS coordinates, dates, and many more pieces of information are easily extractable in a data file.

Hex: A Forensic Analyst's Good Friend

In many forensic investigations, a logical acquisition or a logical file system analysis from a physical acquisition will provide more than enough data for the case. However, certain cases require a deeper analysis to find deleted data or unknown file structures. This is also necessary when the file system has little or no support in standard forensic tools, such as YAFFS2.

Understandably, many forensic analysts would prefer to not perform a deeper analysis because it requires significant time, is extremely tedious, and requires a fairly deep understanding and curiosity of data structures. However, the results from this type of analysis are often quite amazing. Important information about that individual case is learned, and this knowledge is generally applicable to many cases in the future.

For these reasons, every forensic analyst should be comfortable using a hex editor should the need arise. This allows the analysts to see exactly what data are being stored, look for patterns, and perhaps identify deleted or previously understood data structures.

Of course, let's explain this better with an example. First, make sure you install the following package on your Ubuntu workstation:

```
ahoog@ubuntu:~$ sudo apt-get install ncurses-hexedit
```

This is a very fast curses (terminal)-based hex editor. Of course, you can use any hex editor that is comfortable. Next, let's use the strings command to look at the mmssms.db file which is located in the /data/data/com.android.providers.telephony/databases directory to see if we can find some deleted text messages. In this sample case, it is known that text messages to 3128781100 were deleted from the device. First, let's use strings to see if we find that phone number in the SQLite file:

```
ahoog@ubuntu:~$ strings --all --radix=x mmssms.db | grep 3128781100 | wc -l
417
```

In this command, we use the pipe ("|") operator, which takes the output from one command and sends it to the next command. In this way we can link many commands together and get very powerful analysis techniques on the fly. Thus, the above command does the following:

1. Runs the strings command on the SQLite database.
2. Takes the output of the strings command and runs it through the grep program, which filters the output-based patterns provided. In this case, we provide the phone number in question. However, you can create very powerful search strings for grep including regular expressions.

3. Take the output from the grep command and see how many lines are returned by piping the output to the word count program ("wc") and instructing it to count by line instead of by word.

The result is that 417 entries for that phone number were found; obviously indicating that there was indeed communication with the phone number on that device. We next want to take a close look at the messages, so instead of piping the output to the wc program, let's look at the results directly and include one line of text after the phone number by adding the option "-A 1" to grep (also, we pipe the output to the "less" command to display it one page at a time):

```
ahoog@ubuntu:~$ strings --all --radix=x  mmssms.db   | grep -A 1 3128781100 |
less
  12108 3128781100
  1211b Activated my phone
--
  14080 3128781100
  14097 Have to meet CPA at 11:30.
--
  16116 3128781100
  16129 Can you try to refresh...
```

Thus, we know we have an SQLite database with the targeted number and messages. Let's use SQLite3 to better understand the database. Here we will use command line (covered in Chapter 4) but you can use a SQLite viewer with a graphical front end if you prefer.

> **TIP**
>
> **SQLite language reference**
>
> While we have mentioned several SQLite tools throughout this book, you may find the SQLite language reference at http://www.sqlite.org/lang.html to be a great resource. For those not familiar with SQL, it provides a thorough overview. If you already have an understanding of SQL, this language reference will help explain, as the page title reads, "SQL as Understood by SQLite."

```
ahoog@ubuntu:~$ sqlite3 mmssms.db
SQLite version 3.6.22
Enter ".help" for instructions
Enter SQL statements terminated with a ";"
sqlite> .tables
addr                  incoming_msg          sms
android_metadata      incoming_msg_v2       sr_pending
attachments           part                  threads
canonical_addresses   pdu                   threads_list
cbch                  pending_msgs          words
drm                   qtext                 words_content
htcmsgs               rate                  words_segdir
htcthreads            raw                   words_segments

sqlite> .schema sms
CREATE TABLE sms (_id INTEGER PRIMARY KEY,thread_id INTEGER,toa INTEGER
```

```
DEFAULT 0,address TEXT,person
INTEGER,date INTEGER,protocol INTEGER,read INTEGER DEFAULT 0,status INTEGER
DEFAULT -1,type
INTEGER,reply_path_present INTEGER,subject TEXT,body TEXT,sc_toa INTEGER
DEFAULT 0,report_date
INTEGER,service_center TEXT,locked INTEGER DEFAULT 0,index_on_sim INTEGER
DEFAULT -1,callback_number TEXT,
priority INTEGER DEFAULT 0,htc_category INTEGER DEFAULT 0,cs_timestamp LONG
DEFAULT -1, cs_id TEXT,
cs_synced INTEGER DEFAULT 0, error_code INTEGER DEFAULT 0,seen INTEGER
DEFAULT 0);
<snip>

sqlite> .mode line

sqlite> select * from sms limit 1;
                _id = 5
          thread_id = 3
                toa = 0
            address = 3121111111
             person = 901
               date = 1284137437259
           protocol = 0
               read = 1
             status = -1
               type = 1
reply_path_present = 0
            subject =
               body = Did you have a chance do upload the new classes to the
website?
             sc_toa = 0
        report_date =
     service_center =
             locked = 0
       index_on_sim = -1
    callback_number =
           priority = 0
       htc_category = 0
       cs_timestamp = -1
              cs_id =
          cs_synced = 0
         error_code = 0
               seen = 0

sqlite> .quit
```

In the above SQLite3 sessions, the following commands were run to better understand the data:

1. SQLite3 mmssms.db: Opens database for querying.
2. .tables: Lists the tables in the database.
3. .schema sms: Focuses on the sms table, asks database for the structure (schema) of the table. The schema was quite long and was truncated.
4. .mode line: Sets the display mode to line for easier viewing.
5. "select * from sms limit 1;": Instructs SQLite3 to display one record to the screen (limit one) from the sms table showing all columns.
6. .quit: Exits the program

Thus, we can now see that there are a number of fields in the sms table, but that after the phone number, there is a personal ID followed by the time stamp. Using a hex editor, let's see if we can determine the date/time stamp from the message about the phone being activated. First, let's open the mmssms.db in the hex editor we just installed:

```
ahoog@ubuntu:~$ hexeditor mmssms.db
```

This will then show you the beginning of the file in box hex as well as the printable ASCII strings in the right column:

```
File: mmssms.db                    ASCII Offset: 0x00000000 / 0x00077FFF (%00)
00000000  53 51 4C 69  74 65 20 66  6F 72 6D 61  74 20 33 00   SQLite format 3.
00000010  04 00 01 01  00 40 20 20  00 00 24 4A  00 00 00 00   .....@  ..$J....
00000020  00 00 00 00  00 00 00 00  00 00 00 3C  00 00 00 01   ...........<....
00000030  00 00 00 00  00 00 00 18  00 00 00 01  00 00 00 3C   ...............<
00000040  00 00 00 00  00 00 00 00  00 00 00 00  00 00 00 00   ................
00000050  00 00 00 00  00 00 00 00  00 00 00 00  00 00 00 00   ................
00000060  00 00 00 00  05 00 00 00  17 03 8D 00  00 00 00 45   ...............E
00000070  03 FB 03 F6  03 F1 03 EC  03 E7 03 E2  03 DD 03 D8   ................
00000080  03 D3 03 CE  03 C9 03 C4  03 BF 03 BA  03 B5 03 B0   ................
00000090  03 AB 03 A6  03 A1 03 9C  03 97 03 92  03 8D 00 00   ................
000000A0  00 00 00 00  00 00 00 00  00 00 00 00  00 00 00 00   ................
000000B0  00 00 00 00  00 00 00 00  00 00 00 00  00 04 81 0C   ................
000000C0  03 07 17 15  15 01 81 7B  74 61 62 6C  65 61 64 64   .......{tableadd
000000D0  72 61 64 64  72 05 43 52  45 41 54 45  20 54 41 42   raddr.CREATE TAB
000000E0  4C 45 20 61  64 64 72 20  28 5F 69 64  20 49 4E 54   LE addr (_id INT
000000F0  45 47 45 52  20 50 52 49  4D 41 52 59  20 4B 45 59   EGER PRIMARY KEY
00000100  2C 6D 73 67  5F 69 64 20  49 4E 54 45  47 45 52 2C   ,msq id INTEGER,
00000110  63 6F 6E 74  61 63 74 5F  69 64 20 49  4E 54 45 47   contact_id INTEG
00000120  45 52 2C 61  64 64 72 65  73 73 20 54  45 58 54 2C   ER,address TEXT,
00000130  74 79 70 65  20 49 4E 54  45 47 45 52  2C 63 68 61   type INTEGER,cha
00000140  72 73 65 74  20 49 4E 54  45 47 45 52  29 84 57 02   rset INTEGER).W.
00000150  07 17 13 13  01 89 15 74  61 62 6C 65  70 64 75 70   .......tablepdup
^G Help   ^C Exit (No Save)   ^T goTo Offset   ^X Exit and Save   ^W Search
```

We can press Control-T (^T) to jump to an offset in the file. In this case, the previous strings command included the "–radix=x," so we have the offset in hex (0x12108), so time to search:

```
File: mmssms.db                    ASCII Offset: 0x00000000 / 0x00077FFF (%00)
00000000  53 51 4C 69  74 65 20 66  6F 72 6D 61  74 20 33 00   SQLite format 3.
00000010  04 00 01 01  00 40 20 20  00 00 24 4A  00 00 00 00   .....@  ..$J....
00000020  00 00 00 00  00 00 00 00  00 00 00 3C  00 00 00 01   ...........<....
00000030  00 00 00 00  00 00 00 18  00 00 00 01  00 00 00 3C   ...............<
00000040  00 00 00 00  00 00 00 00  00 00 00 00  00 00 00 00   ................
00000050  00 00 00 00  00 00 00 00  00 00 00 00  00 00 00 00   ................
00000060  00 00 00 00  05 00 00 00  17 03 8D 00  00 00 00 45   ...............E
00000070  03 FB ┌──────────────────────────────────────────────┐ ...............
00000080  03 D3 │                 Goto Offset                  │ ...............
00000090  03 AB │                                              │ ...............
000000A0  00 00 │              Offset:  0x12108                │ ...............
000000B0  00 00 │                                              │ ...............
000000C0  03 07 │ Hint: Decimal 255 = Hex 0xFF = Octal 0377    │ ......{tableadd
000000D0  72 61 │                                              │ addr.CREATE TAB
000000E0  4C 45 └──────────────────────────────────────────────┘ E addr (_id INT
000000F0  45 47 45 52  20 50 52 49  4D 41 52 59  20 4B 45 59   EGER PRIMARY KEY
00000100  2C 6D 73 67  5F 69 64 20  49 4E 54 45  47 45 52 2C   ,msg_id INTEGER,
00000110  63 6F 6E 74  61 63 74 5F  69 64 20 49  4E 54 45 47   contact_id INTEG
00000120  45 52 2C 61  64 64 72 65  73 73 20 54  45 58 54 2C   ER,address TEXT,
00000130  74 79 70 65  20 49 4E 54  45 47 45 52  2C 63 68 61   type INTEGER,cha
00000140  72 73 65 74  20 49 4E 54  45 47 45 52  29 84 57 02   rset INTEGER).W.
00000150  07 17 13 13  01 89 15 74  61 62 6C 65  70 64 75 70   .......tablepdup
^G/^X/Escape Cancel   ^U Clear input
```

The hex editor is extremely responsive and jumps to the offset:

```
File: mmssms.db                                ASCII Offset: 0x00012108 / 0x00077FFF (%15)
00012100  01 01 00 01  01 01 01 00  33 31 32 31  31 31 31 31  ........31211122
00012110  32 32 01 2A  FC 97 C5 2C  01 FF 02 41  63 74 69 76  22.*...,...Activ
00012120  61 74 65 64  20 6D 79 20  70 68 6F 6E  65 00 00 FF  ated my phone...
00012130  33 31 32 34  34 34 33 33  33 33 00 00  FF 00 FF 00  3124443333......
00012140  7B 05 1C 00  01 01 21 00  05 01 01 01  01 01 00 81  {.....!.........
00012150  0B 01 00 00  01 01 0D 01  01 01 00 01  01 01 03 00  ................
00012160  33 33 33 35  35 35 37 37  37 37 01 2A  FC 8E 48 4B  3335557777.*..HK
00012170  00 01 FF 01  00 44 69 64  20 79 6F 75  20 68 61 76  .....Did you hav
00012180  65 20 61 20  63 68 61 6E  63 65 20 64  6F 20 75 70  e a chance do up
00012190  6C 6F 61 64  20 74 68 65  20 6E 65 77  20 63 6C 61  load the new cla
000121A0  73 73 65 73  20 74 6F 20  74 68 65 20  77 65 62 73  sses to the webs
000121B0  69 74 65 3F  00 00 FF 00  00 FF 00 00  00 81 25 04  ite?..........%.
000121C0  1C 00 01 01  3F 00 05 01  01 01 01 01  00 81 41 01  ....?.........A.
000121D0  00 00 01 01  0D 01 01 01  00 01 01 01  02 00 73 74  ..............st
```

Looking at the hex data above, we can see the phone number and it ends at 0x12111. After that, we should see a person field, as it is the next column as specified in the table design (also called the table schema). If the person field is set, it links to the contact table to provide details on the person involved. In this case, no person was set, so SQLite does not record anything. Finally, we look at the next six bytes and we get 0x012AFC97C52C. When translated to decimal, the resulting number is 1284138059052. Finally, we can use a number of techniques to convert this time (Unix Epoch in milliseconds) to a more easily read date/time. One quick technique for this is to use the built-in date command. However, it only handles Unix Epoch in seconds, not milliseconds, so you can simply divide by 1000 (that is, omit the last three digits):

```
ahoog@ubuntu:~$ date -d @1284138059
Fri Sep 10 12:00:59 CDT 2010
```

The date command automatically displays the date in the current system time zone. Another quick way to convert the time is to use the web site designed to convert Unix Epoch time at http://www.epochconverter.com/ that handles both Unix Epoch in seconds and milliseconds (Epoch Converter, n.d.). To convert, copy the entire time stamp (not necessary to divide by 1000) into the web site text box and click "Timestamp to Human date" as in Fig. 7.2.

One final time stamp conversion technique to mention is the free utility DCode by Digital Detective, a digital forensic software company based in the United Kingdom. DCode supports many formats (Digital Detective, n.d.) and can covert from milliseconds as shown in Fig. 7.3.

This example is simply intended to illustrate the importance of data that might only be accessible if the forensic analyst moves beyond the forensic software they use and also examines the data directly. With well-known file systems and perhaps "standard" cases, this is often not necessary. However, mobile forensics, and Android forensics in particular, is a challenging area as many of the file formats, file systems, hardware, and software are not only very new (and not well supported) but also change at an alarming rate. Forensic analysts who dive into hex will find they uncover far more data than simply relying on existing forensic software.

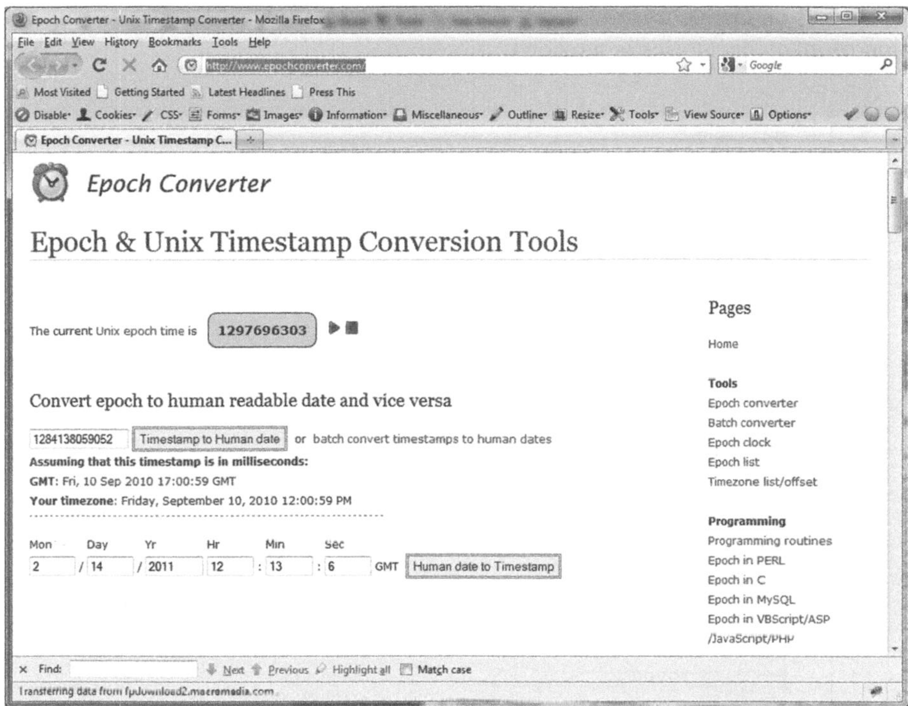

FIGURE 7.2

Time conversion on http://www.epochconverter.com/.

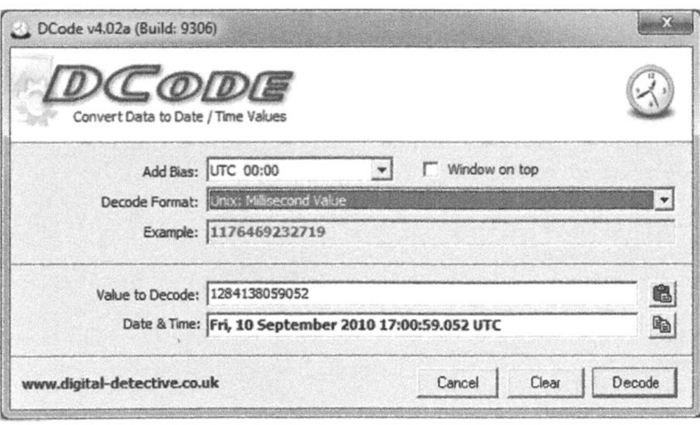

FIGURE 7.3

DCode time conversion utility by Digital Detective.

Android Directory Structures

A broad understanding of the Android directory structure is very helpful in the forensic analysis of a device. To perform this analysis, five important root level directories were copied from the HTC Incredible and then displayed with the tree command on the local workstation. Following the hierarchical layout, an explanation of many directories is provided.

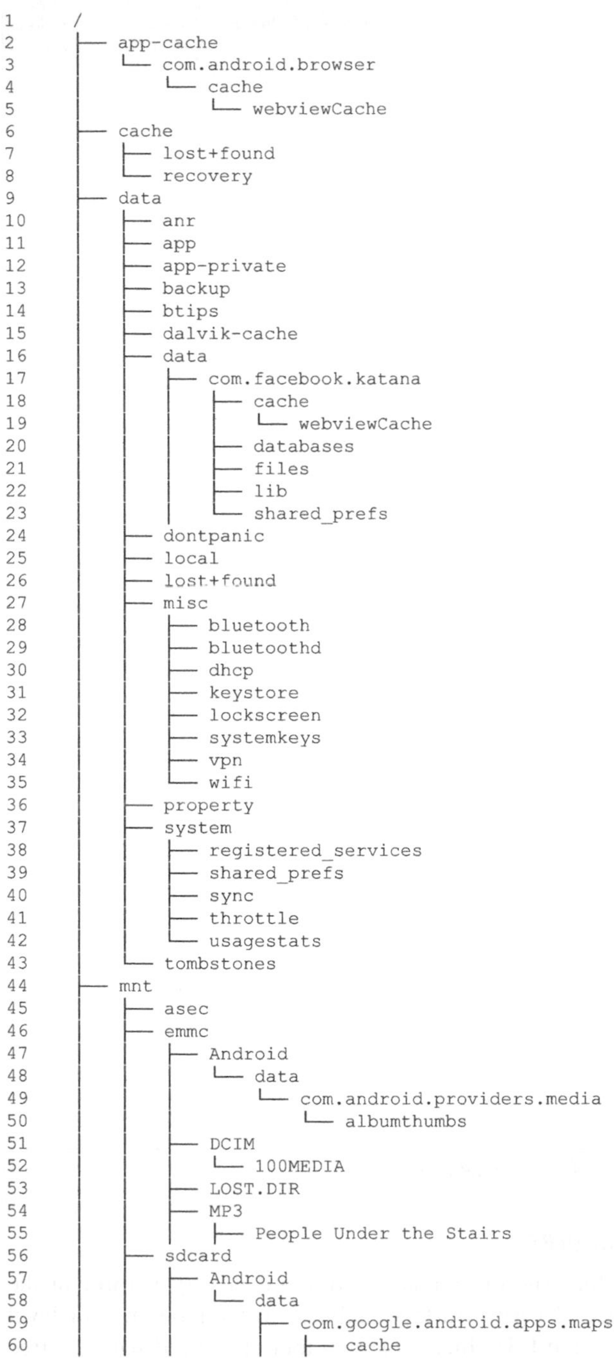

```
/
├── app-cache
│   └── com.android.browser
│       └── cache
│           └── webviewCache
├── cache
│   ├── lost+found
│   └── recovery
├── data
│   ├── anr
│   ├── app
│   ├── app-private
│   ├── backup
│   ├── btips
│   ├── dalvik-cache
│   ├── data
│   │   ├── com.facebook.katana
│   │   │   ├── cache
│   │   │   │   └── webviewCache
│   │   │   ├── databases
│   │   │   ├── files
│   │   │   ├── lib
│   │   │   └── shared_prefs
│   ├── dontpanic
│   ├── local
│   ├── lost+found
│   ├── misc
│   │   ├── bluetooth
│   │   ├── bluetoothd
│   │   ├── dhcp
│   │   ├── keystore
│   │   ├── lockscreen
│   │   ├── systemkeys
│   │   ├── vpn
│   │   └── wifi
│   ├── property
│   ├── system
│   │   ├── registered_services
│   │   ├── shared_prefs
│   │   ├── sync
│   │   ├── throttle
│   │   └── usagestats
│   └── tombstones
├── mnt
│   ├── asec
│   ├── emmc
│   │   ├── Android
│   │   │   └── data
│   │   │       └── com.android.providers.media
│   │   │           └── albumthumbs
│   │   ├── DCIM
│   │   │   └── 100MEDIA
│   │   ├── LOST.DIR
│   │   ├── MP3
│   │   │   ├── People Under the Stairs
│   ├── sdcard
│   │   ├── Android
│   │   │   └── data
│   │   │       ├── com.google.android.apps.maps
│   │   │       │   ├── cache
```

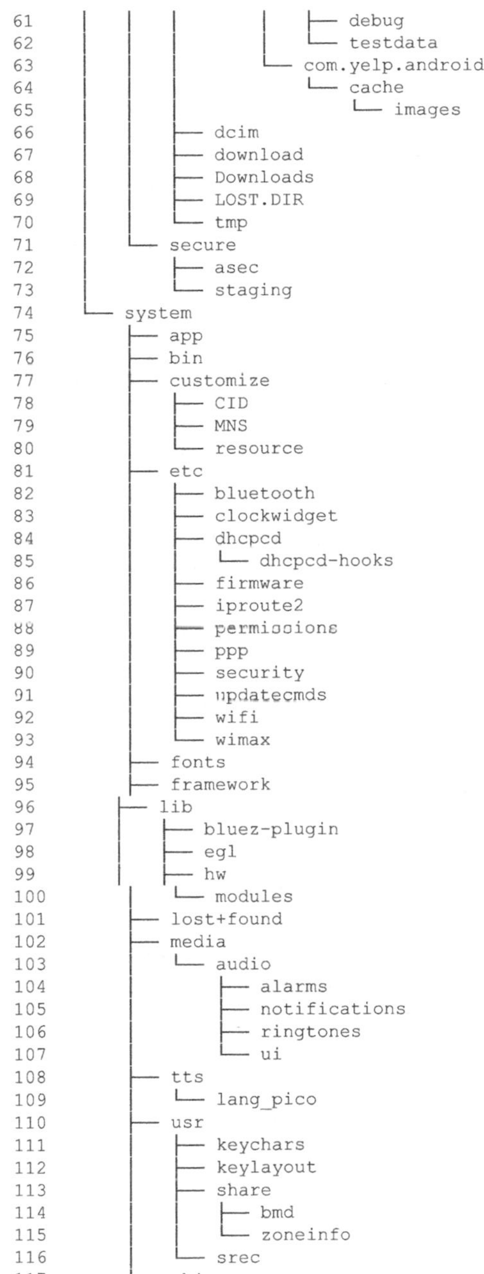

```
│   │   │       │   ├── debug
│   │   │       │   └── testdata
│   │   │       └── com.yelp.android
│   │   │           └── cache
│   │   │               └── images
│   │   ├── dcim
│   │   ├── download
│   │   ├── Downloads
│   │   ├── LOST.DIR
│   │   └── tmp
│   └── secure
│       ├── asec
│       └── staging
└── system
    ├── app
    ├── bin
    ├── customize
    │   ├── CID
    │   ├── MNS
    │   └── resource
    ├── etc
    │   ├── bluetooth
    │   ├── clockwidget
    │   ├── dhcpcd
    │   │   └── dhcpcd-hooks
    │   ├── firmware
    │   ├── iproute2
    │   ├── permissions
    │   ├── ppp
    │   ├── security
    │   ├── updatecmds
    │   ├── wifi
    │   └── wimax
    ├── fonts
    ├── framework
    ├── lib
    │   ├── bluez-plugin
    │   ├── egl
    │   ├── hw
    │   └── modules
    ├── lost+found
    ├── media
    │   └── audio
    │       ├── alarms
    │       ├── notifications
    │       ├── ringtones
    │       └── ui
    ├── tts
    │   └── lang_pico
    ├── usr
    │   ├── keychars
    │   ├── keylayout
    │   ├── share
    │   │   ├── bmd
    │   │   └── zoneinfo
    │   └── srec
    └── xbin
```

Line 1: At the top is the root directory, which creates the structure and mount points for the other file systems explored previously.
Line 2: As previously discussed, the HTC Incredible created an "/app-cache" directory of type tmpfs. You can see the browser cache structure. Presumably, over time, other apps may leverage this directory.
Lines 6–8: Android devices from the start had a dedicated "/cache" directory that originally appeared to be unused. However, this is certainly not the case and the "/cache" partition should be imaged for full analysis. Files including Gmail attachment previews, Browser DRM, some downloads (Market and other), as well as Over The Air (OTA) updates from the wireless carriers can be found here.
Line 9: The root level "/data" directory has a number of important subdirectories covered next. Note that some phones (such as the HTC Incredible) have a dedicated partition for the "/data/data" subdirectory.
Line 10: The "/data/anr" directory contains stack traces (debugging) from the system and is generally not accessible to the shell user. However, some of the adb debug commands appear to read this data.
Line 11: The "/data/app" directory contains the .apk files from the Android Market.
Line 12: The "/data/app-private" directory stores protected apps from the Android Market.
Line 13: More recent versions of Android have a secure cloud backup API that developers can integrate into their apps. The "/data/backup" directory is used to queue and manage these backups. However, thus far meaningful data has not been recovered from directory.
Line 14: The "/data/btips" (Texas Instrument's Bluetooth Protocol Stack) directory stores the log files if the associated app (com.ti.btips) crashes.
Line 15: The "/data/davlik-cache" directory contains the Davlik VM's cached dex files used to run apps.
Line 16: The "/data/data directory" contains the application specific data, easily the most important area to focus on in an investigation.
Lines 17–23: One app was kept in the directory hierarchy for demonstration purposes. The directory is named according to the package name and often clearly identifies the developer (Facebook in this case).
Line 24: For HHGTTG fans (famous advice to intergalactic travelers from the classic novel *The Hitchhiker's Guide to the Galaxy:* DON'T PANIC), there's a great directory named "/data/dontpanic," which is simply a place to store some error log files from the system. Again, a great benefit of an open system is the ability to examine code. Short of that, we would have simply had to guess the purpose or perform significant testing. From the AOSP:

```
# Create dump dir and collect dumps.
  # Do this before we mount cache so eventually we can use cache for
  # storing dumps on platforms which do not have a dedicated dump partition.

  mkdir /data/dontpanic
  chown root log /data/dontpanic
  chmod 0750 /data/dontpanic
```

```
# Collect apanic data, free resources and re-arm trigger
copy /proc/apanic_console /data/dontpanic/apanic_console
chown root log /data/dontpanic/apanic_console
chmod 0640 /data/dontpanic/apanic_console

copy /proc/apanic_threads /data/dontpanic/apanic_threads
chown root log /data/dontpanic/apanic_threads
chmod 0640 /data/dontpanic/apanic_threads

write /proc/apanic_console 1

# Collect ramconsole data
copy /proc/last_kmsg /data/dontpanic/last_kmsg
chown root log /data/dontpanic/last_kmsg
chmod 0640 /data/dontpanic/last_kmsg
```

Line 25: The "/data/local" directory is important as it allows shell (the user account nonrooted phones run adbd as) read/write access. When an app is installed, it is first copied to "/data/local." Also, some forensic techniques rely on this directory to upload important files, typically binaries.

Line 26: The "/data/lost+found" directory shows up in several places in YAFFS2 file systems. Again, a quick search (try "grep -R lost+found *.c" from the YAFFS2 source directory we downloaded) will explain that any files or directories found that do not have a path to the root directory will be placed in this folder.

```
/*
 * This code iterates through all the objects making sure that they are
rooted.
 * Any unrooted objects are re-rooted in lost+found.
 * An object needs to be in one of:
 * - Directly under deleted, unlinked
 * - Directly or indirectly under root.
 *
 * This fixes the problem where directories might have inadvertently been
deleted
 * leaving the object "hanging" without being rooted in the directory tree.
 */
```

Lines 27–35: The "/data/misc" directory contains files related to Bluetooth, dhcp, vpn, Wi-Fi, and more. One important file to point out is "/data/misc/wifi/wpa_supplicant.conf" that contains a list of Wi-Fi.com networks to which the device got connected. If the wireless access point required a password, it is stored in plain text in the file (have fun pen testers). Here's a partial listing:

```
ahoog@ubuntu:~/htc-inc/data/misc/wifi$ cat wpa_supplicant.conf
ctrl_interface=eth0
update_config=1

network={
        ssid="viaForensics"
        psk="s0rryN04cc3ss"
        priority=1
}
```

```
network={
        ssid="attwifi"
        key_mgmt=NONE
        priority=3
}

network={
        ssid="GoogleGuest"
        key_mgmt=NONE
        priority=4
}

network={
        ssid="sfo free wifi"
        key_mgmt=NONE
        priority=5
}
```

Line 36: The "/data/property" directory contains various system properties such as time zone, country, and language.
Line 37: Beyond the subdirectories you can see /data/system contains several key files. First, the accounts.db contains a list of accounts that require authentication and provides the name, type, password (encrypted), and authentication tokens (among other data). There are also two very important files related to the pass code or PIN for the device. The files are gesture.key and password.key and contain an encoded/encrypted hex value for the pass code.
Line 43: When a process crashes, a special tombstone file can be created. The file is ASCII and thus readable. More information can be found online such as one informative post on Crazydaks.com (Debugging in Android, n.d.).
Line 44: The "/mnt" directory is where the system mounts various file systems, including the SD card, the eMMC, and others.
Line 45: The "/mnt/asec" directory contains the unencrypted apps that are stored on the SD card. When Android introduced the ability to store apps on the SD card, they encrypted the contents for security reasons. However, when the system is up and running and unencrypted access to the files is necessary, they are decrypted and mounted in "/mnt/asec."
Line 46: The "/mnt/emmc" contains the FAT32 file system that resides on the NAND flash for some devices. Lines 47 through 55 are several examples of eMMC subdirectories.
Line 51: The "/mnt/emmc/DCIM directory," album thumbnails are stored here.
Line 52: The "/mnt/emmc/DCIM/100MEDIA" directory contains any pictures or videos taken by the HTC Incredible.
Line 53: The "/mnt/emmc/LOST.DIR" directories are found on FAT32 partitions and may contain files or fragments that the file system lost track of (similar to YAFFS2 lost+found directory). This directory should be examined.
Line 56: If a physical SD card is present, it is mounted at "/mnt/sdcard."
Line 66: As with the eMMC, the "/mnt/sdcard/dcim" directory would store pictures and videos from the device. On the HTC Incredible, they are stored in "/mnt/emmc/DCIM," so they are not present on the physical SD card.

Lines 67–68: The "/mnt/sdcard/download" and "/mnt/sdcard/Downloads" directories contain files downloaded by the browser, e-mail clients, and others.
Line 72: As mentioned previously, the "/mnt/sdcard/secure/asec" directory is encrypted and is where apps that reside on the SD card (instead of the NAND flash) store data.
Line 75: The "/system/app" directory contains .apk app files for apps that are provided with the system. This includes apps bundled by Google/Android, the manufacturer (HTC in this case), and the wireless carrier (Verizon in this case). In the case of the HTC Incredible, the directory contains a significant 152 .apk files. It's important to know this location in case app analysis is required for a case (which means you need access to the apk file). The .apk files present on the reference HTC Incredible were:

```
ahoog@ubuntu:~/htc-inc/system/app$ ls *.apk

AccountSyncManager.apk
AdobeReader.apk
amazonmp3.apk
ApplicationsProvider.apk
AppSharing.apk
Bluetooth.apk
BrcmBluetoothServices.apk
Browser.apk
Calculator.apk
Calendar.apk
CalendarProvider.apk
CertInstaller.apk
CheckinProvider.apk
CityID.apk
Clicker.apk
com.htc.FMRadioWidget.apk
com.htc.FriendStreamWidget.apk
com.htc.MusicWidget.apk
com.htc.NewsReaderWidget.apk
com.htc.StockWidget.apk
com.htc.TwitterWidget.apk
com.htc.WeatherWidget.apk
ContactsProvider.apk
CustomizationSettingsProvider.apk
CustomizationSetup.apk
DCSImpl.apk
DCSStock.apk
DCSUtility.apk
DebugTool.apk
DefaultContainerService.apk
DMPortRead.apk
DownloadProvider.apk
DrmProvider.apk
EPST.apk
Facebook.apk
FieldTest.apk
FieldTrial.apk
FilePicker.apk
Flashlight.apk
Flickr.apk
FriendStream.apk
GenieWidget.apk
Gmail.apk
GoogleCalendarSyncAdapter.apk
GoogleContactsSyncAdapter.apk
GoogleFeedback.apk
GooglePartnerSetup.apk
GoogleQuickSearchBox.apk
GoogleServicesFramework.apk
GSD.apk
HtcAddProgramWidget.apk
HTCAlbum.apk
htcbookmarkwidget.apk
HtcCalculatorWidget.apk
htccalendarwidgets.apk
HTCCamera.apk
HtcCarPanel.apk
HtcCdmaMccProvider.apk
HtcClockWidget.apk
HtcContacts.apk
htccontactwidgets.apk
HtcCopyright.apk
HtcDialer.apk
HtcFacebook.apk
HtcFMRadio.apk
HtcFootprints.apk
HtcFootprintsWidget.apk
HTC_IME.apk
HtcLocationPicker.apk
HtcLocationService.apk
HtcLockScreen.apk
htcmailwidgets.apk
HtcMessageUploader.apk
htcmsgwidgets.apk
HtcMusic.apk
HtcPhotoWidget.apk
HtcProfilesWidget.apk
HtcRingtoneTrimmer.apk
HtcRingtoneWidget.apk
HtcSettingsProvider.apk
htcsettingwidgets.apk
HTCSetupWizard.apk
HtcSoundRecorder.apk
HtcStreamPlayer.apk
HtcSyncwidget.apk
HtcTwitter.apk
HtcWeatherWallpaper.apk
HTMLViewer.apk
install_flash_player.apk
LbsProvider.apk
LiveWallpapers.apk
LiveWallpapersPicker.apk
MagicSmokeWallpapers.apk
Mail.apk
Maps.apk
MarketUpdater.apk
MediaProvider.apk
MediaUploader.apk
Mms.apk
Model0Wallpapers.apk
NetworkLocation.apk
NewsReader.apk
PackageInstaller.apk
PCSCII.apk
Phone.apk
PicoTts.apk
PluginManager.apk
QuickLookup.apk
Quickoffice.apk
QxdmLog.apk
restartapp.apk
Rosie.apk
RSS.apk
Settings.apk
SettingsProvider.apk
SetupWizard.apk
SlackerRadio.apk
SocialNetworkProvider.apk
Stock.apk
Street.apk
Superuser.apk
Talk.apk
teeter.apk
TelephonyProvider.apk
TtsService.apk
TVOUT.apk
Updater.apk
UpgradeSetup.apk
UploadProvider.apk
UserDictionaryProvider.apk
VCast.apk
Vending.apk
VisualizationWallpapers.apk
VoiceDialer.apk
VoiceSearch.apk
VpnServices.apk
VVM.apk
VzNav.apk
VzWBAClient.apk
VzWBAService.apk
VZWInstaller.apk
VzwLBSPerm.apk
VZW_MyVerizon.apk
VZW_Skype.apk
WeatherAgentService.apk
Weather.apk
WeatherProvider.apk
WeatherSyncProvider.apk
WidgetDownloadManager.apk
WifiRouter.apk
WorldClock.apk
YouTube.apk
```

Lines 76 and 117: The "/system/bin" and "/system/xbin" directories contain the Android binary files used on the system. Forensic analysts and security engineers (and most definitely Android researchers) can find many useful and undocumented commands by experimenting with files in these directories.
Lines 77–80: The "/system/customize" directories contain carrier-specific customizations for the phone, notably UI.
Line 81: The "/system/etc" directory is where Android stores the typical Linux/Unix configuration (/etc) directory. It contains numerous configuration files worthy of examination—too many to discuss in this book—but can vary from device to device.

There are far more directories and files to explore but the above overview provides a good starting point.

FAT FORENSIC ANALYSIS

The SD card can be a gold mine for forensic investigators. All the multimedia that has been synced with the phone, or taken with the phone's camera, is stored here. Items such as pictures, videos, voice recordings, application data, music, Google Map data, and potentially complete backup files from backup apps that use the SD card for storage are recoverable. In addition, investigators can also find cached mms image thumbnails, trash information relating to deleted objects, and downloaded application APKs.

For example, a typical user might use Google Maps to obtain driving directions to a local shopping center. Through forensic examination of the "com.google.android.apps.maps/cache" directory on the SD card, we are able to recover map image tiles and navigation voice prompts. These voice prompts are also stamped with a date and time, so a forensic investigator can literally retrace the location of that device for a given time and date.

Here's what it looks like after a short trip within a Chicago suburb:

```
ahoog@ubuntu:/mnt/readonly-fs/google_maps_navigation/cache$ ls -la
total 1184
dr-xr-xr-x 2 root root 32768 2010-11-16 15:32 .
dr-xr-xr-x 4 root root 32768 2010-11-16 13:31 ..
-r-xr-xr-x 1 root root 66476 2010-11-16 15:20 ._speech_nav_0.wav
-r-xr-xr-x 1 root root 142252 2010-11-16 15:19 ._speech_nav_1.wav
-r-xr-xr-x 1 root root 142380 2010-11-16 15:18 ._speech_nav_2.wav
-r-xr-xr-x 1 root root 73644 2010-11-16 15:15 ._speech_nav_3.wav
-r-xr-xr-x 1 root root 60460 2010-11-16 15:15 ._speech_nav_4.wav
-r-xr-xr-x 1 root root 107948 2010-11-16 15:15 ._speech_nav_5.wav
-r-xr-xr-x 1 root root 96300 2010-11-16 15:20 ._speech_nav_6.wav
-r-xr-xr-x 1 root root 6144 2010-11-16 13:31 tilecache_ImageTileStore.db
-r-xr-xr-x 1 root root 281600 2010-11-16 15:32 tilecache_VectorTileStore.db
```

It is also important to remember that SD cards can be mounted through Android as an external mass storage device. This allows the user to transfer any files between the SD card and his or her personal computer.

In Chapter 6, we demonstrated how to acquire the two current FAT32 partitions on Android devices that contain data. There are many books and articles which cover the analysis of FAT32 file systems and this section will not attempt to cover those again in detail. However, this section will demonstrate some techniques for examining the FAT32 partitions found on Android devices using the Ubuntu workstation.

FAT Timeline Analysis

To build a file system timeline of a FAT32 image, we utilize both The Sleuth Kit (TSK) and another great open source forensic tool called log2timeline. The log2timeline utility, written by Kristinn Gudjonsson, is a framework for automatic creation of a timeline that encompasses various log files and artifacts found on the system. log2timeline can be utilized on many systems and does an excellent job at extracting time stamp information for many file formats for analysis.

As we already have TSK setup, we need to take a few steps to install log2timeline. First, it has probably been a while since you first built the Ubuntu workstation so it is a good idea to update any packages which have newer versions and often contain security patches or bug fixes.

```
sudo apt-get update
sudo apt-get upgrade -u
```

The first step updates your software list and the second will actually perform the upgrade. Next, we'll install log2timeline, which Kristinn has greatly simplified by creating a Ubuntu package for his software.

```
sudo add-apt-repository "deb http://log2timeline.net/pub/ maverick main"
wget -q http://log2timeline.net/gpg.asc -O- | sudo apt-key add -
sudo apt-get update
sudo apt-get install log2timeline-perl
```

The four commands do the following:

1. Add the log2timeline custom software repository to the Ubuntu workstations overall list.
2. Download the public key used to validate the software and add to the list of accepted keys.
3. Update the software packages list.
4. Install log2timeline.

For this analysis, we are going to use the forensic image of the 2 GB SD card we imaged in Chapter 6. First, the examiner should always ensure that the hash signature of the image matches with the hash taken during forensic imaging to ensure the image is valid.

```
ahoog@ubuntu:~/sd-emmc/viaforensics/af-book/sdcard2-113serialno$ sha256sum
sdcard2-113serialno.dc3dd
e5dcc0af1d8a09c9af4d2db98f5f684d20a561666b9ff8df7c8b90a0b9d78770  sdcard2-
113serialno.dc3dd
```

If you recall, the hash of the input device (/dev/sdc in this case) was e5dcc0af1 d8a09c9af4d2db98f5f684d20a561666b9ff8df7c8b90a0b9d78770. The forensic image is now validated. Next, let's take a quick look at the file first with the file command:

```
ahoog@ubuntu:/home/ahoog$ file /home/ahoog/sd-emmc/viaforensics/af-book/
sdcard2-113serialno/sdcard2-113serialno.dc3dd
/home/ahoog/sd-emmc/viaforensics/af-book/sdcard2-
113serialno/sdcard2-113serialno.dc3dd: x86 boot sector; partition 1: ID=0x6,
starthead 2, startsector 129, 3911551 sectors, extended partition table
(last)\011, code offset 0x0
```

So we are, in fact, dealing with a disk image with a valid partition. Next, we can examine the disk image further with TSK's mmls:

```
ahoog@ubuntu:~/sd-emmc/viaforensics/af-book/sdcard2-113serialno$ mmls sdcard2-
113serialno.dc3dd
DOS Partition Table
Offset Sector: 0
Units are in 512-byte sectors

     Slot    Start        End          Length       Description
00:  Meta    0000000000   0000000000   0000000001   Primary Table (#0)
01:  -----   0000000000   0000000128   0000000129   Unallocated
02:  00:00   0000000129   0003911679   0003911551   DOS FAT16 (0x06)
```

And finally TSK's fsstat, but note that you have to provide a sector offset of 129 as the FAT partition starts there:

```
ahoog@ubuntu:~/sd-emmc/viaforensics/af-book/sdcard2-113serialno$ fsstat -o 129
sdcard2-113serialno.dc3dd
FILE SYSTEM INFORMATION
--------------------------------------------
File System Type: FAT16

OEM Name:
Volume ID: 0xe0fd1813
Volume Label (Boot Sector): NO NAME
Volume Label (Root Directory):
File System Type Label: FAT16

Sectors before file system: 129

File System Layout (in sectors)
Total Range: 0 - 3911550
* Reserved: 0 - 0
** Boot Sector: 0
* FAT 0: 1 - 239
* FAT 1: 240 - 478
* Data Area: 479 - 3911550
** Root Directory: 479 - 510
** Cluster Area: 511 - 3911550

METADATA INFORMATION
--------------------------------------------
Range: 2 - 62577158
Root Directory: 2
```

```
CONTENT INFORMATION
--------------------------------------------
Sector Size: 512
Cluster Size: 32768
Total Cluster Range: 2 - 61111

FAT CONTENTS (in sectors)
--------------------------------------------
511-574 (64) -> EOF
575-638 (64) -> EOF
639-702 (64) -> EOF
703-766 (64) -> EOF
767-830 (64) -> EOF
831-894 (64) -> EOF
895-958 (64) -> EOF
959-1022 (64) -> EOF
1023-1086 (64) -> EOF
<snip>
```

In this case, the partition is a FAT16 partition with data on it. So, we are going to first build the timeline with TSK's fls command:

```
ahoog@ubuntu:/home/ahoog$ time fls -z CST6CDT -s 0 -m /mnt/sdcard -f fat16 -r
-o 129 -i raw ~/sd-emmc/viaforensics/af-book/sdcard2-113serialno/sdcard2-
113serialno.dc3dd > ~/sdcard.body

real    0m55.765s
user    0m0.820s
sys     0m12.850s
```

The options set have the following meaning:

- -z CST6CDT—Sets time zone to CST6CDT for US Central Time
- -s 0—Sets the time skew if one is known
- -m /mnt/sdcard—Prefaces the path with this value when writing out the body file
- -f fat16—Sets file system to FAT16
- -r—Recursively traverses all directories to build the timeline
- -o 129—Sets the offset to 129 (a sector size of 512 bytes is assumed but can be changed with the -b option)
- -i raw—Sets the image type, in this case a raw image and not another forensic image format
- ~/sd-emmc/viaforensics/af-book/sdcard2-113serialno/sdcard2-113serial-no.dc3dd—Image file
- > ~/sdcard.body—Redirects the command's output to a file instead of displaying on the screen

Often it is helpful to know how long a command takes (if nothing else, over time you learn when it's best to go grab that coffee warmer). So, we preface fls with the time command, which will tell us how long the program took to run (real) and the various system time it took (user, sys). You can view the contents of the body file, but in a later step we will convert it to a more readable format. If you want to verify fls-returned results, you can always determine the total lines in the file:

```
ahoog@ubuntu:~$ wc -l sdcard.body
24399 sdcard.body
```

So, we have just over 24,000 entries. Next, we need to mount the file system read-only and then we can run log2timeline against it. To mount the file system using the dd image, you use the mount command and a special device called the loopback device. The full command is as follows:

```
ahoog@ubuntu:~$ mkdir -p ~/mnt/sdcard
ahoog@ubuntu:~$ sudo mount -t vfat -o loop,ro,offset=66048 ~/sd-emmc/
viaforensics/af-book/sdcard2-113serialno/sdcard2-113serialno.dc3dd ~/mnt/sdcard
```

Again, let's look at each of the options set. First, this command requires administrator rights so we run with sudo. The options are then:

- -t vfat
- -o loop,ro,offset=66068—This tells mount to use the loopback device as we are using a physical file instead of an actual device. The ro mounts the e-mail as read-only. Finally, we have to tell mount where to find the partition. From the mmls command, you recall that the offset was a sector 129. Mount does not know the sector size, so we calculate 129 × 512, which is equal to 66,048
- ~/sd-emmc/viaforensics/af-book/sdcard2-113serialno/sdcard2-113serialno.dc3dd—The dd images
- ~/mnt/sdcard—Where to mount the image

We can validate that the file system is mounted by executing the mount command with no options, which returns the list of all mounted file systems. We pipe this through grep to isolate the file system we are looking for:

```
ahoog@ubuntu:~$ mount | grep vfat
/dev/loop0 on /home/ahoog/mnt/sdcard type vfat (ro,offset=66048)
```

So, we can see the vfat file system is mounted read-only using loopback device "/dev/loop0" and located at "/home/ahoog/mnt/sdcard." You can see the total size with the df command:

```
ahoog@ubuntu:~$ df -h
Filesystem            Size  Used Avail Use% Mounted on
/dev/sda1              19G   18G  570M  97% /
none                  366M  208K  366M   1% /dev
none                  373M  256K  373M   1% /dev/shm
none                  373M  100K  373M   1% /var/run
none                  373M     0  373M   0% /var/lock
/dev/mtdblock0         64M  1.2M   63M   2% /home/ahoog/mnt/yaffs2
/dev/loop0            1.9G  244M  1.7G  13% /home/ahoog/mnt/sdcard
```

So, only 244 M of the 1.7 G available is in use. Now we are ready to use the time-scanner program that comes with log2timeline to extract additional timeline information from the files. We will append the command output to the same body file as fls:

```
ahoog@ubuntu:~$ time timescanner -d /home/ahoog/mnt/sdcard -z CST6CDT >>
sdcard.body
Loading output file: mactime
[timescanner] Recursive scan completed.  Successfully extracted timestamps from
410 artifacts (either files or directories).
Run time of the script 62 seconds.

real    1m2.241s
user    0m31.810s
sys     0m13.760s
```

The options for timescanner are as follows:

- -d /home/ahoog/mnt/sdcard—Specify the directory to scan for time stamp artifacts
- -z CST6CDT—Again set the time zone to U.S. Central Time
- >> sdcard.body—Append the output to the existing sdcard.body. Please note the double greater than sign (">>"), which instructs the shell to append to the file (and if it does not exist, creates it). If you forget and use a single ">", then you will overwrite the fls output.

Timescanner only extracted 410 artifacts, which is far less than the number you would extract on a scan of an entire hard drive. However, the 410 artifacts will certainly help build the overall timeline for the device.

Finally, we can create an easy-to-read (and easy-to-share) comma separated values (csv) file of the timeline with TSK's mactime command:

```
ahoog@ubuntu:~$ mactime -b sdcard.body -z CST6CDT -d > sdcard-timeline.csv
```

The following options were passed to mactime:

- -b sdcard.body—Specifies the body file to convert
- -z CST6CDT—Time zone
- -d—Output of the file in csv format

This only takes a few seconds for just under 25,000 entries but yields over 73,000 lines in the csv file.

```
ahoog@ubuntu:~$ wc -l sdcard-timeline.csv
73739 sdcard-timeline.csv
```

You can now easily browse the timeline in a spreadsheet program or even import it into a database for additional analysis. There are several interesting items to point out.

First, you will likely see many dates near January 1, 1970. This is caused by time stamps that were set to 0 or not set at all. As Unix Epoch is based on the number of seconds since 01/01/1970 00:00:00 UTC, then an offset would be that exact time. In the above examples, we set the time zone to CST6CDT which, in January, is GMT −6 hours. So, there are many artifacts with a time stamp of "Wed Dec 31 1969 18:00:00." While we are unable to glean specific timeline data on these artifacts, they may nonetheless contain important information.

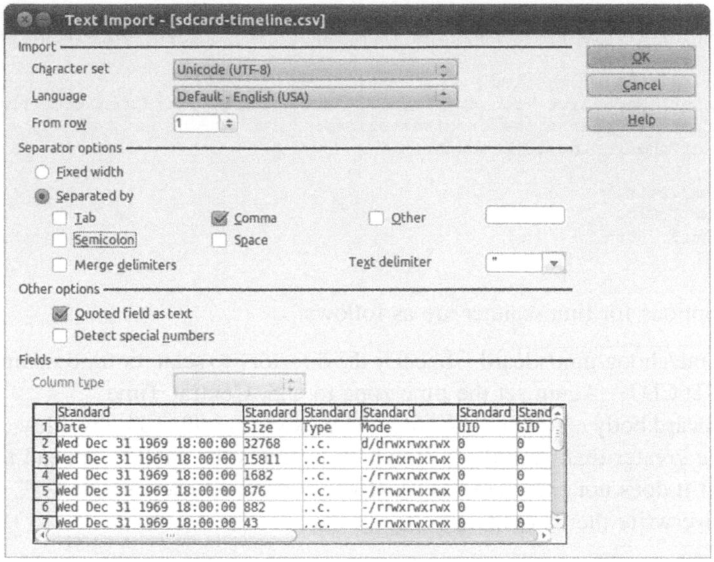

FIGURE 7.4

Text import of sdcard-timeline.csv into OO Calc.

If you double-click the sdcard-timeline.csv file from your Ubuntu workstation, Open Office's Calc program will present a Text Import screen as shown in Fig. 7.4. Make sure the "Separated by" is set to comma, then press OK.

The Calc program will then open and you can browse the timeline, illustrated in Fig. 7.5.

As you can see, most of the files are deleted. However, TSK and other programs can still recover them. One interesting event to examine is when an app was moved to the SD card for testing purposes. The app, Angry Birds, supports running from the SD card, which was tested at 06:17:28 on 02/15/2011, shown in Fig. 7.6.

The timeline clearly shows that a new file is created and modified at 06:17:28 in "/mnt/sdcard/.android_secure."

One final entry to point out is from log2timeline. As it came across a PDF, the metadata was extracted. We can see the following:

- Mon Nov 29 2010 04:44:47
- 23,159 bytes
- File modified
- Title: (Scanned Document)
- Author: [michelle]
- Creator: [HardCopy]
- Produced by: [Lexmark X543]
- File: /mnt/sdcard/.easc/Attachment/ATT_1291219677612.pdf

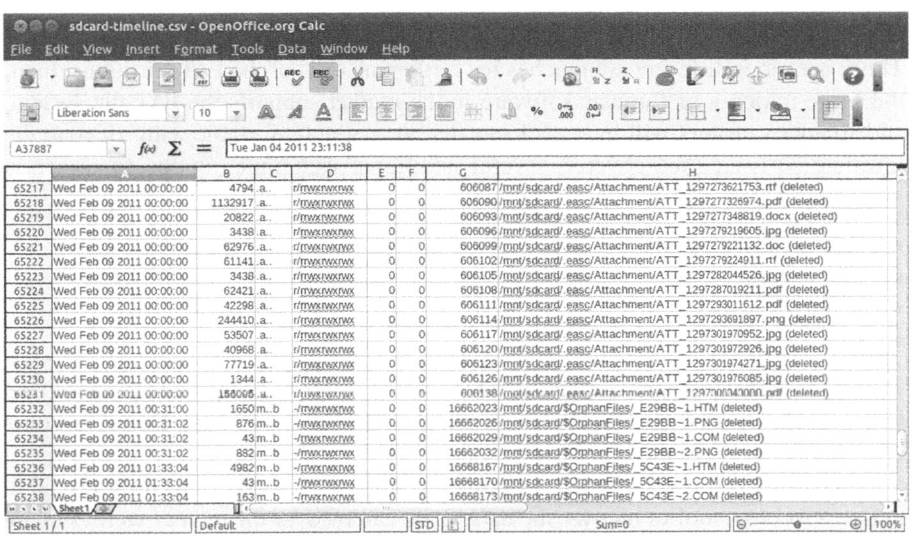

	A	B	C	D	E	F	G	H
65217	Wed Feb 09 2011 00:00:00	4794	.a..	r/rrwxrwxrwx	0	0	606087	/mnt/sdcard/.easc/Attachment/ATT_1297273621753.rtf (deleted)
65218	Wed Feb 09 2011 00:00:00	1132917	.a..	r/rrwxrwxrwx	0	0	606090	/mnt/sdcard/.easc/Attachment/ATT_1297277326974.pdf (deleted)
65219	Wed Feb 09 2011 00:00:00	20822	.a..	r/rrwxrwxrwx	0	0	606093	/mnt/sdcard/.easc/Attachment/ATT_1297277348819.docx (deleted)
65220	Wed Feb 09 2011 00:00:00	3438	.a..	r/rrwxrwxrwx	0	0	606096	/mnt/sdcard/.easc/Attachment/ATT_1297279219605.jpg (deleted)
65221	Wed Feb 09 2011 00:00:00	62976	.a..	r/rrwxrwxrwx	0	0	606099	/mnt/sdcard/.easc/Attachment/ATT_1297279221132.doc (deleted)
65222	Wed Feb 09 2011 00:00:00	61141	.a..	r/rrwxrwxrwx	0	0	606102	/mnt/sdcard/.easc/Attachment/ATT_1297279224911.rtf (deleted)
65223	Wed Feb 09 2011 00:00:00	3438	.a..	r/rrwxrwxrwx	0	0	606105	/mnt/sdcard/.easc/Attachment/ATT_1297282044526.jpg (deleted)
65224	Wed Feb 09 2011 00:00:00	62421	.a..	r/rrwxrwxrwx	0	0	606108	/mnt/sdcard/.easc/Attachment/ATT_1297287019211.pdf (deleted)
65225	Wed Feb 09 2011 00:00:00	42298	.a..	r/rrwxrwxrwx	0	0	606111	/mnt/sdcard/.easc/Attachment/ATT_1297293011612.pdf (deleted)
65226	Wed Feb 09 2011 00:00:00	244410	.a..	r/rrwxrwxrwx	0	0	606114	/mnt/sdcard/.easc/Attachment/ATT_1297293691897.png (deleted)
65227	Wed Feb 09 2011 00:00:00	53507	.a..	r/rrwxrwxrwx	0	0	606117	/mnt/sdcard/.easc/Attachment/ATT_1297301970952.jpg (deleted)
65228	Wed Feb 09 2011 00:00:00	40968	.a..	r/rrwxrwxrwx	0	0	606120	/mnt/sdcard/.easc/Attachment/ATT_1297301972926.jpg (deleted)
65229	Wed Feb 09 2011 00:00:00	77719	.a..	r/rrwxrwxrwx	0	0	606123	/mnt/sdcard/.easc/Attachment/ATT_1297301974271.jpg (deleted)
65230	Wed Feb 09 2011 00:00:00	1344	.a..	r/rrwxrwxrwx	0	0	606126	/mnt/sdcard/.easc/Attachment/ATT_1297301976085.jpg (deleted)
65231	Wed Feb 09 2011 00:00:00	156006	.a..	r/rrwxrwxrwx	0	0	606138	/mnt/sdcard/.easc/Attachment/ATT_[illegible].pdf (deleted)
65232	Wed Feb 09 2011 00:31:00	1650	m..b	-/rrwxrwxrwx	0	0	16662023	/mnt/sdcard/$OrphanFiles/_E29BB~1.HTM (deleted)
65233	Wed Feb 09 2011 00:31:02	876	m..b	-/rrwxrwxrwx	0	0	16662026	/mnt/sdcard/$OrphanFiles/_E29BB~1.PNG (deleted)
65234	Wed Feb 09 2011 00:31:02	43	m..b	-/rrwxrwxrwx	0	0	16662029	/mnt/sdcard/$OrphanFiles/_E29BB~1.COM (deleted)
65235	Wed Feb 09 2011 00:31:02	882	m..b	-/rrwxrwxrwx	0	0	16662032	/mnt/sdcard/$OrphanFiles/_E29BB~2.PNG (deleted)
65236	Wed Feb 09 2011 01:33:04	4982	m..b	-/rrwxrwxrwx	0	0	16668167	/mnt/sdcard/$OrphanFiles/_5C43E~1.HTM (deleted)
65237	Wed Feb 09 2011 01:33:04	43	m..b	-/rrwxrwxrwx	0	0	16668170	/mnt/sdcard/$OrphanFiles/_5C43E~1.COM (deleted)
65238	Wed Feb 09 2011 01:33:04	163	m..b	-/rrwxrwxrwx	0	0	16668173	/mnt/sdcard/$OrphanFiles/_5C43E~2.COM (deleted)

FIGURE 7.5

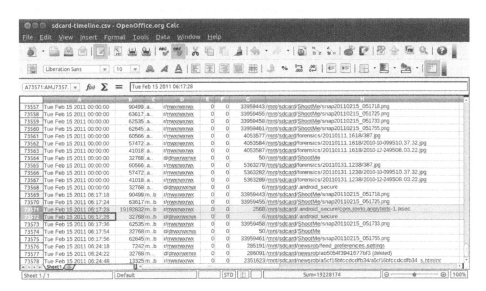

Viewing timeline in OO Calc.

	A	B	C	D	E	F	G	H
73557	Tue Feb 15 2011 00:00:00	90499	.a..	r/rrwxrwxrwx	0	0	33959443	/mnt/sdcard/ShootMe/snap20110215_051718.png
73558	Tue Feb 15 2011 00:00:00	63617	.a..	r/rrwxrwxrwx	0	0	33959455	/mnt/sdcard/ShootMe/snap20110215_051725.png
73559	Tue Feb 15 2011 00:00:00	62535	.a..	r/rrwxrwxrwx	0	0	33959458	/mnt/sdcard/ShootMe/snap20110215_051733.png
73560	Tue Feb 15 2011 00:00:00	62645	.a..	r/rrwxrwxrwx	0	0	33959461	/mnt/sdcard/ShootMe/snap20110215_051755.png
73561	Tue Feb 15 2011 00:00:00	60566	.a..	r/rrwxrwxrwx	0	0	4053577	/mnt/sdcard/forensics/20110111.1618/387.jpg
73562	Tue Feb 15 2011 00:00:00	57472	.a..	r/rrwxrwxrwx	0	0	4053584	/mnt/sdcard/forensics/20110111.1618/2010-10-099510.37.32.jpg
73563	Tue Feb 15 2011 00:00:00	41018	.a..	r/rrwxrwxrwx	0	0	4053587	/mnt/sdcard/forensics/20110111.1618/2010-12-249508.03.22.jpg
73564	Tue Feb 15 2011 00:00:00	32768	.a..	d/drwxrwxrwx	0	0	50	/mnt/sdcard/ShootMe
73565	Tue Feb 15 2011 00:00:00	60566	.a..	r/rrwxrwxrwx	0	0	5363279	/mnt/sdcard/forensics/20110131.1238/387.jpg
73566	Tue Feb 15 2011 00:00:00	57472	.a..	r/rrwxrwxrwx	0	0	5363282	/mnt/sdcard/forensics/20110131.1238/2010-10-099510.37.32.jpg
73567	Tue Feb 15 2011 00:00:00	41018	.a..	r/rrwxrwxrwx	0	0	5363289	/mnt/sdcard/forensics/20110131.1238/2010-12-249508.03.22.jpg
73568	Tue Feb 15 2011 00:00:00	32768	.a..	d/drwxrwxrwx	0	0	6	/mnt/sdcard/.android_secure
73569	Tue Feb 15 2011 06:17:18	90499	m..b	r/rrwxrwxrwx	0	0	33959443	/mnt/sdcard/ShootMe/snap20110215_051718.png
73570	Tue Feb 15 2011 06:17:24	63617	m..b	r/rrwxrwxrwx	0	0	33959455	/mnt/sdcard/ShootMe/snap20110215_051725.png
73571	Tue Feb 15 2011 06:17:28	19192832	m..b	r/rrwxrwxrwx	0	0	2568	/mnt/sdcard/.android_secure/com.rovio.angrybirds-1.asec
73572	Tue Feb 15 2011 06:17:28	32768	m..b	d/drwxrwxrwx	0	0	6	/mnt/sdcard/.android_secure
73573	Tue Feb 15 2011 06:17:36	62535	m..b	r/rrwxrwxrwx	0	0	33959458	/mnt/sdcard/ShootMe/snap20110215_051733.png
73574	Tue Feb 15 2011 06:17:54	32768	m..b	d/drwxrwxrwx	0	0	50	/mnt/sdcard/ShootMe
73575	Tue Feb 15 2011 06:17:56	62645	m..b	r/rrwxrwxrwx	0	0	33959461	/mnt/sdcard/ShootMe/snap20110215_051755.png
73576	Tue Feb 15 2011 06:24:18	7242	m..b	r/rrwxrwxrwx	0	0	285191	/mnt/sdcard/newsrob/feed_preferences.settings
73577	Tue Feb 15 2011 06:24:22	32768	m...	d/drwxrwxrwx	0	0	286091	/mnt/sdcard/newsrob/ab5054f3941677bf3 (deleted)
73578	Tue Feb 15 2011 06:24:48	13325	m..b	r/rrwxrwxrwx	0	0	2351623	/mnt/sdcard/newsrob/a5cf16bfccdcdfb34/a5cf16bfccdcdfb34_s.htmlnr

FIGURE 7.6

Timeline when app moved to SD card.

Timeline analysis is extremely powerful, especially if the forensic analyst combines traditional file system time stamped artifacts from Kristinn Gudjonsson's log2timeline.

FAT Additional Analysis

There are many different approaches for further analysis of the FAT partitions. First, the large majority of forensic software in the market supports the FAT file system, and many examiners will have tool sets that they are comfortable with. Beyond the forensic software, we covered several additional techniques in the first section including:

- File system analysis
- File carving
- Strings
- Hex analysis

These techniques are similar even when the file system type is different, so we will provide detailed coverage of them in the YAFFS2 section next. However, some brief concepts are highlighted below.

First, the SD card clearly has a significant amount of deleted files. It is advisable to use a forensic tool to recover the data. TSK can recover the data as well as many other forensic software packages. In addition, file-carving techniques should be used to recover files that are not referenced in the File Allocation Table of the partition. Strings and hex analysis are again great ways to quickly locate data of interest.

There is one more quick technique to mention if the Ubuntu workstation is used for file system analysis. Using the find and file commands, you can list all allocated files by name, path, and file type. You can easily sort them on the fly or import them into a spreadsheet or database for additional analysis. This technique only lists allocated (undeleted) files, but is quite effective.

The command is as follows:

```
ahoog@ubuntu:~$ find ~/mnt/sdcard -type f -print0 | xargs -0 file
/home/ahoog/mnt/sdcard/.android_secure/com.rovio.angrybirds-1.asec:
data
/home/ahoog/mnt/sdcard/.footprints/footprints.db:
SQLite 3.x database
/home/ahoog/mnt/sdcard/download/Swype-Installer.apk:
Zip archive data, at least v2.0 to extract
/home/ahoog/mnt/sdcard/download/Swype-Installer-1.apk:
Zip archive data, at least v2.0 to extract
/home/ahoog/mnt/sdcard/download/Swype-Installer-2.apk:
Zip archive data, at least v2.0 to extract
/home/ahoog/mnt/sdcard/download/Download.apk:
Zip archive data, at least v1.0 to extract
/home/ahoog/mnt/sdcard/download/PdaNetA242.pkg:
xar archive - version 1
/home/ahoog/mnt/sdcard/download/hotwatch-powerpoint.pdf:
PDF document, version 1.5
/home/ahoog/mnt/sdcard/download/dinner.pdf:
PDF document, version 1.3
/home/ahoog/mnt/sdcard/download/dinner-1.pdf:
PDF document, version 1.3
/home/ahoog/mnt/sdcard/download/Swype-Installer-3.apk:
Zip archive data, at least v2.0 to extract
/home/ahoog/mnt/sdcard/download/subpoena.pdf:
PDF document, version 1.3
```

```
/home/ahoog/mnt/sdcard/Android/data/com.google.android.apps.genie.geniewidget.
news-content-cache/.nomedia: empty
/home/ahoog/mnt/sdcard/Android/data/com.google.android.apps.maps/cache/
cache_vts.m:data
/home/ahoog/mnt/sdcard/Android/data/com.google.android.apps.maps/cache/
cache_rgts.m:data
/home/ahoog/mnt/sdcard/Android/data/com.google.android.apps.maps/cache/
cache_rgts.0:Microsoft Document Imaging Format
/home/ahoog/mnt/sdcard/Android/data/com.google.android.apps.maps/cache/
cache_vts.0:data
/home/ahoog/mnt/sdcard/Android/data/com.google.android.apps.maps/cache/
._speech_nav_5.wav: RIFF (little-endian) data, WAVE audio,
Microsoft PCM, 16 bit, mono 16000 Hz
```

In total, this command found and categorized 4352 allocated files on the SD card. Here's what each part of the command accomplished:

- find ~/mnt/sdcard—Finds files in the directory where we mounted the SD card image ~/mnt/sdcard
- -type f—Only examines regular files (i.e., doesn't list directories)
- -print0—Terminates each file name with a NULL character instead of the default new line which causes issues when file names have spaces
- "|"—Pipes the output of find to the next program
- xargs—This program builds and executes command lines using data from standard input (i.e., other programs' output)
- -0—Tells xargs that the data being piped is terminated by NULL character (matches the -print0 from find)
- file—This is the command xargs runs against each line returned by the find command

The find and xargs commands are very powerful ways to examine, interact, or otherwise manipulate a large set of files. By combining timeline and file system analysis, file carving, strings, and hex analysis, an investigator is armed with powerful tools to uncover information critical to the case.

FAT Analysts Notes

There are a few remaining notes for the FAT file systems on Android.

Apps on the SD Card

First, as mentioned in Chapter 6, as of Android 2.2, users can move supported applications to the SD card to save space in the "/data/data" directory where user data are stored. The app must explicitly support this capability, and typical candidates for this feature are apps that use a lot of storage such as a game. To test this feature, the popular Angry Birds game by Rovio Mobile (Rovio - Angry Birds, n.d.) was installed on the reference HTC Incredible. The app was briefly run and then closed. To move the app to the SD card, you select Settings from the home screen, then Applications, and finally Manage Applications as illustrated in Fig. 7.7.

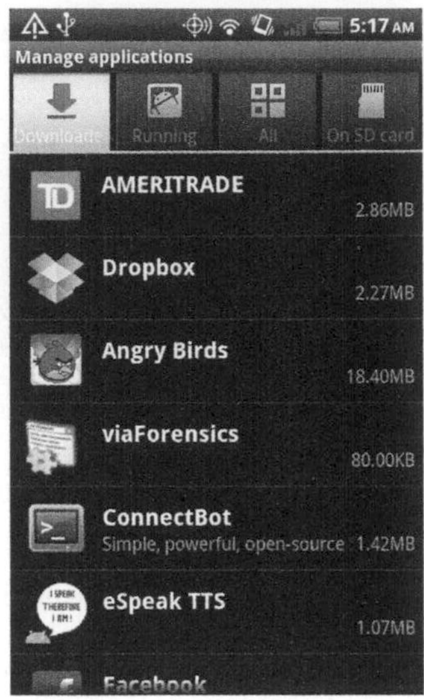

FIGURE 7.7

Manage applications screen.

As you can tell, the Angry Birds uses 18.40 MB of space on "/data/data," which is very precious space. So, the app developer included the necessary support to move the .apk to the SD card. The user can then select the app (Angry birds, in this case) and is then presented with a screen that has information and options about the app, including "Move to SD card" as shown in Fig. 7.8.

From this screen, you can see that the app itself uses 18.39 MB while user data is only 12.00 KB, a clear candidate for moving the .apk to the SD card. And, as illustrated in Fig. 7.9, it's as simple as clicking the "Move to SD card" button and waiting for the task to complete.

This is great from the user's perspective. But what does this mean for the forensic examiner or security analyst? A number of steps are taken that are described next and then highlighted in the code listing.

1. The .apk file is moved from "/data/app" (or "/data/app-private") to the SD card in an encrypted partition at /mnt/secure/asec (see highlighted parts of next listing) which can only be accessed via the root directory.
2. A new device mapper file system is mounted read-only and the app from "/mnt/secure/asec" is decrypted and accessible to the system at "/mnt/asec/com.rovio.angrybirds-1." The system must be able to access the unencrypted .apk file to run the app.
3. The user data remains in "/data/data" (in this case "/data/data/com.rovio.angrybirds").
4. If the SD card becomes inaccessible (whether it is removed, damaged, or simply mounted on a host computer for file sharing), the unencrypted volume is unmounted and no longer accessible to the system. This is why the core apps are currently unable to run from the SD card.

FIGURE 7.8

Move to SD card.

FIGURE 7.9

App move to SD card complete.

The .apk file is encrypted on the SD card to ensure that other apps (or processes) cannot corrupt or maliciously modify the app. However, app developers should not rely on the encryption to prevent people from accessing the .apk file as it is simply a matter of copying it from the unencrypted "/mnt/asec/<app-name>." The mount and ls commands in the following code illustrate the structure.

```
ahoog@ubuntu:~/sd-emmc$ adb shell mount
rootfs / rootfs ro,relatime 0 0
tmpfs /dev tmpfs rw,relatime,mode=755 0 0
devpts /dev/pts devpts rw,relatime,mode=600 0 0
proc /proc proc rw,relatime 0 0
sysfs /sys sysfs rw,relatime 0 0
none /acct cgroup rw,relatime,cpuacct 0 0
tmpfs /mnt/asec tmpfs rw,relatime,mode=755,gid=1000 0 0
none /dev/cpuctl cgroup rw,relatime,cpu 0 0
/dev/block/mtdblock3 /system yaffs2 ro,relatime 0 0
/dev/block/mmcblk0p1 /data ext3
rw,nosuid,noatime,nodiratime,errors=continue,data=writeback 0 0
/dev/block/mtdblock6 /data/data yaffs2 rw,nosuid,nodev,relatime 0 0
/dev/block/mmcblk0p2 /cache ext3
rw,nosuid,nodev,noatime,nodiratime,errors=continue,data=writeback 0 0
tmpfs /app-cache tmpfs rw,relatime,size=8192k 0 0
/dev/block/vold/179:3 /mnt/emmc vfat
rw,dirsync,nosuid,nodev,noexec,relatime,uid=1000,gid=1015,fmask=0702,
dmask=0702,allow_utime=0020,codepage=cp437,iocharset=iso8859-1,shortname=mixed,
utf8,errors=remount-ro 0 0
/dev/block/vold/179:9 /mnt/sdcard vfat
rw,dirsync,nosuid,nodev,noexec,relatime,uid=1000,gid=1015,fmask=0702,
dmask=0702,allow_utime=0020,codepage=cp437,iocharset=iso8859-1,shortname=mixed,
utf8,errors=remount-ro 0 0
/dev/block/vold/179:9 /mnt/secure/asec vfat
rw,dirsync,nosuid,nodev,noexec,relatime,uid=1000,gid=1015,fmask=0702,
dmask=0702,allow_utime=0020,codepage=cp437,iocharset=iso8859-1,shortname=mixed,
utf8,errors=remount-ro 0 0
tmpfs /mnt/sdcard/.android_secure tmpfs ro,relatime,size=0k,mode=000 0 0
/dev/block/dm-0 /mnt/asec/com.rovio.angrybirds-1 vfat
ro,dirsync,nosuid,nodev,noexec,relatime,uid=1000,fmask=0222,dmask=0222,
codepage=cp437,iocharset=iso8859-1,shortname=mixed,utf8,errors=remount-ro 0 0


ahoog@ubuntu:~/sd-emmc$ adb shell ls -l /mnt
d---rwxr-x system   sdcard_rw          1969-12-31 18:00 emmc
drwxr-xr-x root     system             2011-02-15 05:17 asec
drwx------ root     root               2011-02-14 07:59 secure
d---rwxr-x system   sdcard_rw          1969-12-31 18:00 sdcard

ahoog@ubuntu:~/sd-emmc$ adb shell ls -l /mnt/asec
dr-xr-xr-x system   root              1969-12-31 18:00 com.rovio.angrybirds-1

ahoog@ubuntu:~/sd-emmc$ adb shell ls -l /mnt/asec/com.rovio.angrybirds-1
-r-xr-xr-x system   root     17235931 2011-02-15 05:17 pkg.apk

# ls -l /mnt/secure/asec
----rwxr-x system   sdcard_rw 19192832 2011-02-15 05:17 com.rovio.angrybirds-1.
asec

# ls -l /data/data/com.rovio.angrybirds
drwxrwx--x app_106  app_106           2011-02-15 05:14 cache
drwxrwx--x app_106  app_106           2011-02-15 05:15 files
drwxr-xr-x system   system            2011-02-15 05:14 lib
```

If you need the .apk for analysis (for example, investigating malware), then it is critical to copy the "/mnt/asec" subdirectories during the acquisition process while the SD card is inserted and active on the Android device (that is, not mounted on the forensic workstation for physical acquisition).

nomedia

One other common item found on the SD card and eMMC partitions is an empty file named .nomedia that will instruct Android's media scanner to skip the directory, so that it does not include any of the media files in apps such as Gallery or Music. If a directory does not contain this file, then it is quite possible that images which were previously deleted might have thumbnails which can be found in the media scanner's directory. This will be covered further in the section on Android App Analysis and Reference.

YAFFS2 FORENSIC ANALYSIS

As discussed in Chapter 4, YAFFS2 is an open source, log-structured file system developed specifically for NAND flash, including support for wear-leveling and error-correcting code algorithms. This is great news not only for the phone owners, as YAFFS2 works very well on Android, but also for forensic analysts since a significant amount of old (deleted or updated) data is recoverable. But the good news stops there. As YAFFS2 is a relatively new file system, at this time no commercial forensic software solution supports it.

However, all is not lost. Using the power of Linux, the openness of YAFFS2, an effective acquisition strategy, and the techniques already discussed including file system analysis, file carving, strings, and hex analysis, a forensic examiner can extract significant amounts of relevant data from the file system.

As we dive into the analysis of YAFFS2, it's quite helpful to remember how it is structured. One important concept to recall is how the data are structured physically on the NAND flash via MTD. Generally, YAFFS2 and MTD organize the NAND flash into 128 KB blocks, which consist of 2048 KB chunks of data followed by 64 bytes of Out-Of-Band (OOB) data (making the total size on the NAND flash 132 KB), which is used to store disk and some file system metadata, as shown in Fig. 7.10.

Of course, it is not required that the Android device structure the NAND flash and MTD this way and the best way to verify is to examine the contents of the "/proc/mtd" file, which contains configuration information. Here is the file again from the reference HTC Incredible.

```
ahoog@ubuntu:~$ adb shell cat /proc/mtd
dev:    size   erasesize  name
mtd0: 000a0000 00020000 "misc"
mtd1: 00480000 00020000 "recovery"
mtd2: 00300000 00020000 "boot"
mtd3: 0f800000 00020000 "system"
mtd4: 000a0000 00020000 "local"
mtd5: 02800000 00020000 "cache"
mtd6: 09500000 00020000 "datadata"
```

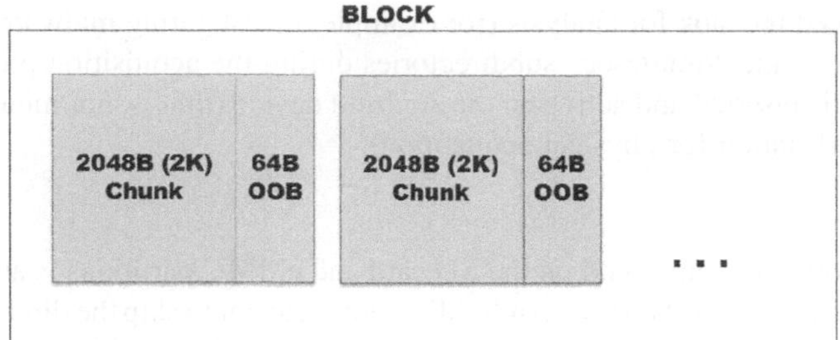

FIGURE 7.10

Block (128 KB = 64 × 2k chunks + OOB).

While we need the OOB data if we want to attempt to mount the YAFFS2 nanddump on the Ubuntu workstation, the 64-byte OOB data will definitely cause problems for most forensic techniques, notably file carving. To alleviate this problem, you can simply remove the OOB with a simple program. The program is written in Python and can be easily adapted to different block and OOB configurations.

First, let's open a new file for editing with sudo permissions, so that we can place the program in "/usr/local/bin" which is the best place to save custom scripts and programs.

```
ahoog@ubuntu:~$ sudo nano -w /usr/local/bin/removeOOB.py
```

Next, copy the following contents into the editor:

```
#!/usr/bin/env python

# Author: Andrew Hoog [ahoog at viaforensics dot com]
# Name: removeOOB.py
#

import subprocess, os, csv, getopt, sys

def usage():
   print """
Written by Andrew Hoog, remove the recurring 64 bytes of OOB data from
nanddump file with 2k chunks.  Resulting dd file in saved in current directory

Usage: removeOOB.py [-h] -o nanddump file

   -h|--help: prints this help function and exits
   -o|--oobFile: name of nanddump file to parse
   """

def main():
   try:
      opts, args = getopt.getopt(sys.argv[1:], "ho:", ["help", "oobFile="])
   except getopt.GetoptError, err:
      # print help information and exit:
      print str(err) # will print something like "option -a not recognized"
      usage()
      sys.exit(2)
```

```
    oobFile = None
    for o, a in opts:
        if o in ("-o", "--oobFile"):
            oobFile = a
        elif o in ("-h", "--help"):
            usage()
            sys.exit()
        else:
            assert False, "unhandled option"

    #open OOB file binary, read-only
    print "opening %s readonly" % oobFile
    try:
        yaffs2File = open(oobFile, 'rb')
    except:
        print "Unable to open file source file %s" % oobFile
        usage()
        sys.exit()

    #open .dd file binary, writable
    print "opening %s.dd r/w" % oobFile
    try:
        ddFile = open(oobFile + '.dd', 'wb')
    except:
        print "Unable to file %s" % oobFile + '.dd for output'
        usage()
        sys.exit()

    chunks=0

    data = yaffs2File.read(2048)
    oob = yaffs2File.read(64)

    print "Processing..."
    while data != "":
        ddFile.write(data)
        chunks += 1
        data = yaffs2File.read(2048)
        oob = yaffs2File.read(64)

    print "Complete.  Read %d chunks" % chunks
    yaffs2File.close()
    ddFile.close()

if __name__ == "__main__":
    main()
```

Then save with Ctrl-O and exit with Ctrl-X. Next, you have to make the Python file executable, so type in the following:

```
ahoog@ubuntu:~$ sudo chmod 755 /usr/local/bin/removeOOB.py
```

And finally we can run the program against a nanddump file:

```
ahoog@ubuntu:~$ removeOOB.py -o htcinc-mtd6-datadata.nanddump
opening htcinc-mtd6-datadata.nanddump readonly
opening htcinc-mtd6-datadata.nanddump.dd r/w
Processing...
Complete.  Read 76288 chunks
```

Let's make sure the removeOOB.py results are what we expect. According to "/proc/mtd," the "/dev/mtd/mtd6" partition has a size of 0x9500000 bytes and an erase size (block size) of 0x20000. The overall size in bytes is 156,237,824 (simply convert the size from hex to decimal) or roughly 154 MB. Similarly, the erase size is 2048 bytes, so if we divide 156,237,824 by 2048, we get 76,288 blocks in the data. This corresponds to the results from removeOOB.py. But there is one more thing we can check. As we know the nanddump has 64 bytes of OOB data after each 2k chunk, the total nanddump size on disk should be (76,288 × 64) + 156,237,824. The total should then be 161,120,256, which would represent the data chunks and their corresponding OOB. We can see what the size on disk is with a simple "ls −l":

```
ahoog@ubuntu:~$ ls -ltr htcinc-mtd6-datadata*
-rw-r--r-- 1 ahoog ahoog 161120256 2011-02-13 19:34 htcinc-mtd6-datadata.
nanddump
-rw-r--r-- 1 ahoog ahoog 156237824 2011-02-13 19:36 htcinc-mtd6-datadata.
nanddump.dd
```

As you can see, both the full nanddump and the .dd image (the nanddump with the OOB removed) correspond to the expected sizes.

As we now have the YAFFS2 nanddump file, dd image, and the logical files (either from tar, adb pull, or by mounting the YAFFS2 partition), we are ready to perform various techniques against the data.

YAFFS2 Timeline Analysis

Ideally, this section would detail the use of already-built forensic software that would build YAFFS2 timelines. Unfortunately, YAFFS2 is not yet supported by any forensic timeline tools, so examiners in need of this information must take a more difficult path.

Over the next few years, the forensics industry needs to perform far more research into YAFFS2. However, with Android moving towards EXT4, it is possible that most of the YAFFS2 research will not occur. Hopefully, this will not be the case.

Here, we will present some research that is intended to provide a basic framework to begin YAFFS2 research. This research was done on the simulated NAND flash initially covered in Chapter 4. While this approach provides the researcher with the control and privileges needed for effective research, it does not necessarily mimic production environments.

As discussed in Chapter 4, both YAFFS2 and MTD are involved in writing data to the NAND flash. The YAFFS2 module is responsible for all aspects of the file system. However, the writing of the data to the NAND flash is managed by MTD. Unfortunately, this adds considerable complexity to the analysis as MTD can accept the data from YAFFS2, which needs to be written to the NAND flash and then has the autonomy to write not only the YAFFS2 data but additional MTD data in the manner it sees fit. Some research into the data as it has persisted must take into account not only the YAFFS2 code but the MTD code. Additionally, there can be subtle differences in the YAFFS2 and MTD modules used on different Android devices, which adds yet another layer of complexity.

This does not mean understanding the YAFFS2 data found in a nanddump is impossible. To get started, we are going to setup a 64 MB simulated NAND flash device on our Ubuntu workstation.

```
sudo modprobe mtd
sudo modprobe mtdblock
sudo insmod ~/yaffs2/yaffs2.ko
sudo modprobe nandsim first_id_byte=0x20 second_id_byte=0xa2 third_id_byte=0x00
fourth_id_byte=0x15
```

You can verify the nandsim is properly setup:

```
ahoog@ubuntu:~$ cat /proc/mtd
dev:    size   erasesize  name
mtd0: 04000000 00020000 "NAND simulator partition 0"
```

Before we mount the YAFFS2 file system, we are going to enable various debugging features built into YAFFS2. There are many debugging options that YAFFS2 supports (YAFFS Debugging, n.d.), but we are only going to enable three of them. To do this, we first need to have full root permissions and then we will echo the debugging flags into "/proc/yaffs":

```
ahoog@ubuntu:~$ sudo -s
root@ubuntu:~# echo =none+os+write+mtd > /proc/yaffs
```

The value after echo command first removes any exiting debugging (none) and then enables the os, write, and mtd debugging options. You can view the results of the debugging in the system log located at "/var/log/syslog." Ideally, open a second terminal window or ssh session and use the tail command to continuously output the tail end of the syslog:

```
ahoog@ubuntu:~$ tail -f /var/log/syslog
Feb 17 18:29:34 ubuntu kernel: [ 4474.970406] new trace = 0xF0004082
```

Next, we create the mount point and mount a YAFFS2 file system:

```
mkdir -p ~/mnt/yaffs2
sudo mount -t yaffs2 /dev/mtdblock0 ~/mnt/yaffs2
```

At this point, the examiner should create a series of test cases, so that the expected controlled data can be examined on the simulated NAND flash to ultimately determine the structure. For this test, the following steps were taken:

1. Create a directory called test in "~/mnt/yaffs2" (mkdir ~/mnt/yaffs2/test)
2. Create "~/mnt/yaffs2/test/file1.txt" with the contents "viaforensics" (nano -w ~/mnt/yaffs2/test/file1.txt)
3. Update "~/mnt/yaffs2/test" and append "updated" to file (echo "updated" >> ~/mnt/yaffs2/test/file1.txt)
4. Read "~/mnt/yaffs2/test/file1.txt" (cat ~/mnt/yaffs2/test/file1.txt)

5. Change the user and group owner for the directory and file (chown -R pulse.rtkit ~/mnt/yaffs2/test)
6. Change the permission of the directory and file (chmod -R 777 ~/mnt/yaffs2/test)

As these tests are being executed, not only is the file system being updated but the debugging information is written to the syslog. The debugging is very verbose (and we only enabled three of the debugging options), so only two examples are provided here, which correspond to the following:

1. Creating the "~/mnt/yafs2/test" directory
2. Change the permission of file1.txt (chmod -R 777 ~/mnt/yaffs2/test)

```
mkdir ~/mnt/yafs2/test
----------------------------------
Feb 17 15:53:33 ubuntu kernel: [26704.104072] yaffs_lookup for 1:test
Feb 17 15:53:33 ubuntu kernel: [26704.104076] yaffs_lookup not found
Feb 17 15:53:33 ubuntu kernel: [26704.104078] yaffs_mkdir
Feb 17 15:53:33 ubuntu kernel: [26704.104080] yaffs_mknod: parent object 1 type 3
Feb 17 15:53:33 ubuntu kernel: [26704.104082] yaffs_mknod: making oject for test, mode 41ed dev 0
Feb 17 15:53:33 ubuntu kernel: [26704.104083] yaffs_mknod: making directory
Feb 17 15:53:33 ubuntu kernel: [26704.104191] yaffs_MarkSuperBlockDirty() sb = ffff88001bf74800
Feb 17 15:53:33 ubuntu kernel: [26704.104194] nandmtd2_ReadChunkWithTagsFromNAND chunk 0 data ffff88000d30c000 tags ffff880019f479f8
Feb 17 15:53:33 ubuntu kernel: [26704.104233] packed tags obj -1 chunk -1 byte -1 seq -1
Feb 17 15:53:33 ubuntu kernel: [26704.104235] ext.tags eccres 0 blkbad 0 chused 0 obj 0 chunk0 byte 0 del 0 ser 0 seq 0
Feb 17 15:53:33 ubuntu kernel: [26704.104237] packed tags obj -1 chunk -1 byte -1 seq -1
Feb 17 15:53:33 ubuntu kernel: [26704.104239] ext.tags eccres 1 blkbad 0 chused 0 obj 0 chunk0 byte 0 del 0 ser 0 seq 0
Feb 17 15:53:33 ubuntu kernel: [26704.104243] Writing chunk 0 tags 257 0
Feb 17 15:53:33 ubuntu kernel: [26704.104244] nandmtd2_WriteChunkWithTagsToNAND chunk 0 data ffff88000d30c800 tags ffff880019f47ba8
Feb 17 15:53:33 ubuntu kernel: [26704.104247] packed tags obj 805306625 chunk -2147483647 byte 0 seq 4097
Feb 17 15:53:33 ubuntu kernel: [26704.104249] ext.tags eccres 0 blkbad 0 chused 1 obj 257 chunk0 byte 0 del 0 ser 1 seq 4097
Feb 17 15:53:33 ubuntu kernel: [26704.104466] nandmtd2_ReadChunkWithTagsFromNAND chunk 0 data ffff88000d30c000 tags ffff880019f47aa8
Feb 17 15:53:33 ubuntu kernel: [26704.104471] packed tags obj 805306625 chunk -2147483647 byte 0 seq 4097
Feb 17 15:53:33 ubuntu kernel: [26704.104474] ext.tags eccres 0 blkbad 0 chused 1 obj 257 chunk0 byte 0 del 0 ser 0 seq 4097
Feb 17 15:53:33 ubuntu kernel: [26704.104476] packed tags obj 805306625 chunk -2147483647 byte 0 seq 4097
Feb 17 15:53:33 ubuntu kernel: [26704.104478] ext.tags eccres 1 blkbad 0 chused 1 obj 257 chunk0 byte 0 del 0 ser 0 seq 4097
Feb 17 15:53:33 ubuntu kernel: [26704.104487] yaffs_get_inode for object 257
Feb 17 15:53:33 ubuntu kernel: [26704.104488] yaffs_iget for 257
Feb 17 15:53:33 ubuntu kernel: [26704.104492] yaffs_FillInode mode 41ed uid 0 gid 0 size 2048 count 1
Feb 17 15:53:33 ubuntu kernel: [26704.104494] yaffs_mknod created object 257 count = 1
Feb 17 15:53:33 ubuntu kernel: [26704.330210] yaffs_MarkSuperBlockDirty() sb = ffff88001bf74800
Feb 17 15:53:33 ubuntu kernel: [26704.330214] Writing chunk 1 tags 1 0
Feb 17 15:53:33 ubuntu kernel: [26704.330217] nandmtd2_WriteChunkWithTagsToNAND chunk 1 data ffff88000d30c800 tags ffff880011c3dd00
Feb 17 15:53:33 ubuntu kernel: [26704.330219] packed tags obj 805306369 chunk -2147483648 byte 0 seq 4097
Feb 17 15:53:33 ubuntu kernel: [26704.330221] ext.tags eccres 0 blkbad 0 chused 1 obj 1 chunk0 byte 0 del 0 ser 1 seq 4097
Feb 17 15:53:37 ubuntu kernel: [26708.060113] yaffs_write_super
Feb 17 15:53:37 ubuntu kernel: [26708.060118] yaffs_do_sync_fs: dirty no checkpoint
Feb 17 15:53:37 ubuntu kernel: [26708.060121] flushing obj 257
Feb 17 15:53:37 ubuntu kernel: [26708.060122] flushing obj 2
Feb 17 15:53:37 ubuntu kernel: [26708.060123] flushing obj 1

chmod -R 777 ~/mnt/yaffs2/test
----------------------------------
Feb 17 15:59:00 ubuntu kernel: [27030.833325] yaffs_setattr of object 257
Feb 17 15:59:00 ubuntu kernel: [27030.833331] inode_setattr called
Feb 17 15:59:00 ubuntu kernel: [27030.833338] nandmtd2_ReadChunkWithTagsFromNAND chunk 11 data ffff88000d30c800 tags ffff88002e2efc38
Feb 17 15:59:00 ubuntu kernel: [27030.833356] packed tags obj 805306625 chunk -2147483647 byte 0 seq 4097
Feb 17 15:59:00 ubuntu kernel: [27030.833358] ext.tags eccres 0 blkbad 0 chused 1 obj 257 chunk0 byte 0 del 0 ser 0 seq 4097
Feb 17 15:59:00 ubuntu kernel: [27030.833360] packed tags obj 805306625 chunk -2147483647 byte 0 seq 4097
Feb 17 15:59:00 ubuntu kernel: [27030.833362] ext.tags eccres 1 blkbad 0 chused 1 obj 257 chunk0 byte 0 del 0 ser 0 seq 4097
Feb 17 15:59:00 ubuntu kernel: [27030.833366] yaffs_MarkSuperBlockDirty() sb = ffff88001bf74800
Feb 17 15:59:00 ubuntu kernel: [27030.833368] Writing chunk 12 tags 257 0
Feb 17 15:59:00 ubuntu kernel: [27030.833369] nandmtd2_WriteChunkWithTagsToNAND chunk 12 data ffff88000d30c800 tags ffff88002e2efc88
Feb 17 15:59:00 ubuntu kernel: [27030.833372] packed tags obj 805306625 chunk -2147483647 byte 0 seq 4097
Feb 17 15:59:00 ubuntu kernel: [27030.833378] ext.tags eccres 0 blkbad 0 chused 1 obj 257 chunk0 byte 0 del 0 ser 4 seq 4097
```

```
Feb 17 15:59:00 ubuntu kernel: [27030.833390] yaffs_setattr done returning 0
Feb 17 15:59:00 ubuntu kernel: [27030.833485] yaffs_readdir: starting at 0
Feb 17 15:59:00 ubuntu kernel: [27030.833486] yaffs_readdir: entry . ino 257
Feb 17 15:59:00 ubuntu kernel: [27030.833488] yaffs_readdir: entry .. ino 1
Feb 17 15:59:00 ubuntu kernel: [27030.833490] yaffs_readdir: file1.txt inode 258
Feb 17 15:59:00 ubuntu kernel: [27030.833493] yaffs_readdir: starting at 3
Feb 17 15:59:00 ubuntu kernel: [27030.833500] yaffs_setattr of object 258
Feb 17 15:59:00 ubuntu kernel: [27030.833501] inode_setattr called
Feb 17 15:59:00 ubuntu kernel: [27030.833504] nandmtd2_ReadChunkWithTagsFromNAND chunk 10 data ffff88000d30c800 tags ffff88002e2efc38
Feb 17 15:59:00 ubuntu kernel: [27030.833510] packed tags obj 268435714 chunk -2147483391 byte 21 seq 4097
Feb 17 15:59:00 ubuntu kernel: [27030.833512] ext.tags eccres 0 blkbad 0 chused 1 obj 258 chunk0 byte 0 del 0 ser 0 seq 4097
Feb 17 15:59:00 ubuntu kernel: [27030.833514] packed tags obj 268435714 chunk -2147483391 byte 21 seq 4097
Feb 17 15:59:00 ubuntu kernel: [27030.833517] ext.tags eccres 1 blkbad 0 chused 1 obj 258 chunk0 byte 0 del 0 ser 0 seq 4097
Feb 17 15:59:00 ubuntu kernel: [27030.833519] yaffs_MarkSuperBlockDirty() sb = ffff88001bf74800
Feb 17 15:59:00 ubuntu kernel: [27030.833520] Writing chunk 13 tags 258 0
Feb 17 15:59:00 ubuntu kernel: [27030.833522] nandmtd2_WriteChunkWithTagsToNAND chunk 13 data ffff88000d30c800 tags ffff88002e2efc88
Feb 17 15:59:00 ubuntu kernel: [27030.833524] packed tags obj 268435714 chunk -2147483391 byte 21 seq 4097
Feb 17 15:59:00 ubuntu kernel: [27030.833526] ext.tags eccres 0 blkbad 0 chused 1 obj 258 chunk0 byte 0 del 0 ser 7 seq 4097
Feb 17 15:59:00 ubuntu kernel: [27030.833533] yaffs_setattr done returning 0
Feb 17 15:59:01 ubuntu kernel: [27032.060195] yaffs_write_super
Feb 17 15:59:01 ubuntu kernel: [27032.060205] yaffs_do_sync_fs: dirty no checkpoint
Feb 17 15:59:01 ubuntu kernel: [27032.060208] flushing obj 258
Feb 17 15:59:01 ubuntu kernel: [27032.060209] flushing obj 257
Feb 17 15:59:01 ubuntu kernel: [27032.060210] flushing obj 2
Feb 17 15:59:01 ubuntu kernel: [27032.060212] flushing obj 1
```

The debugging provides valuable information including object id, sequence number, chunk id, and the detailed process YAFFS2 follows to create the file. If you enable additional debugging you will have even more data to correlate and use in your understanding of YAFFS2.

Before we examine the actual nanddump, there is one other helpful command worth pointing out. The stat command will provide detailed information about a file, directory, or other file system objects. For example, we can run stat against "~/mnt/yaffs2/test" and "~/mnt/yaffs2/test/file1.txt" and use the information in our research:

```
root@ubuntu:~/mnt/yaffs2# stat test
  File: `test'
  Size: 2048          Blocks: 4          IO Block: 4096   directory
Device: 1f00h/7936d   Inode: 257         Links: 1
Access: (0777/drwxrwxrwx)  Uid: (  109/   pulse)   Gid: (  117/   rtkit)
Access: 2011-02-17 15:53:33.000000000 -0600
Modify: 2011-02-17 15:55:02.000000000 -0600
Change: 2011-02-17 15:59:00.000000000 -0600

root@ubuntu:~/mnt/yaffs2# stat test/file1.txt
  File: `test/file1.txt'
  Size: 21            Blocks: 1          IO Block: 4096   regular file
Device: 1f00h/7936d   Inode: 258         Links: 1
Access: (0777/-rwxrwxrwx)  Uid: (  109/   pulse)   Gid: (  117/   rtkit)
Access: 2011-02-17 15:55:02.000000000 -0600
Modify: 2011-02-17 15:56:13.000000000 -0600
Change: 2011-02-17 15:59:00.000000000 -0600
```

We now have the Modified, Access, and Change properties of the file and directory and, combined with the actions we took to create the data, we have enough information to start our research.

It's time to look at the NAND flash, which requires root access. The following command will skip the rows of the NAND flash, which are all 0xFF and 0x00 making it easier to see trends. Also, only a small portion of the NAND flash is displayed here in hex for space reasons:

```
nanddump -c /dev/mtd0ro | grep -v "00 00 00 00 00 00 00 00 00 00 00 00 00 00 00
00" |
grep -v "ff ff ff ff ff ff ff ff ff ff ff ff ff ff ff ff" | less
0x00000000: 30 00 00 00 10 00 00 00 ff ff 47 56 37 47 00 00  |..........test..|
0x00000100: 00 00 00 00 00 00 00 00 00 00 ff ff de 14 00 00  |.............A..|
0x00000110: 00 00 00 00 00 00 00 00 dd 89 d5 d4 dd 89 d5 d4  |..........]M..]M|
0x00000120: dd 89 d5 d4 ff ff ff ff ff ff ff ff ff ff ff ff  |..]M............|
0x000001c0: ff ff ff ff ff ff ff ff ff ff ff ff 00 00 00 00  |................|
0x000001e0: ff ff ff ff ff ff ff ff 00 00 00 00 ff ff ff ff  |................|
0x000001f0: ff ff ff ff ff ff ff ff 00 00 00 00 00 00 00 00  |................|
  OOB Data: ff ff 10 01 00 00 10 10 00 03 10 00 00 08 00 00  |.........0......|
  OOB Data: 00 00 c0 a7 4f 91 30 00 00 00 30 00 00 00 ff ff  |...z............|
  OOB Data: ff ff ff ff ff ff ff ff ff f3 f0 ff 0f 3c ff ff  |.........?......|
  OOB Data: ff ff ff ff ff ff ff ff ff ff ff ff ff ff ff ff  |................|
<snip>
0x00006800: 10 00 00 00 10 10 00 00 ff ff 66 96 c6 56 13 e2  |..........file1.|
0x00006810: 47 87 47 00 00 00 00 00 00 00 00 00 00 00 00 00  |txt.............|
0x00006900: 00 00 00 00 00 00 00 00 00 00 ff ff ff 18 00 00  |................|
0x00006910: d6 00 00 00 57 00 00 00 63 99 d5 d4 d7 99 d5 d4  |m...u...6.]M}.]M|
0x00006920: 42 a9 d5 d4 51 00 00 00 ff ff ff ff ff ff ff ff  |$.]M............|
0x000069c0: ff ff ff ff ff ff ff ff ff ff ff ff 00 00 00 00  |................|
0x000069e0: ff ff ff ff ff ff ff ff 00 00 00 00 ff ff ff ff  |................|
0x000069f0: ff ff ff ff ff ff ff ff 00 00 00 00 00 00 00 00  |................|
  OOB Data: ff ff 10 01 00 00 20 10 00 01 10 10 00 08 51 00  |................|
  OOB Data: 00 00 51 af e2 e2 10 00 00 00 ef ff ff ff ff ff  |................|
  OOB Data: ff ff ff ff ff ff ff ff ff 00 3c ff 3c ff ff ff  |................|
  OOB Data: ff ff ff ff ff ff ff ff ff ff ff ff ff ff ff ff  |................|
```

The portion of the NAND flash included covers the following:

1. Create "~/mnt/yaffs2/test" directory
2. Permissions change on file1.txt (chmod -R 777 ~/mnt/yaffs2/test)

The data displayed are part of YAFFS2 ObjectHeaders and contain the metadata for the file system. The names of the files are clearly visible as are the 64-byte OOB areas. One key characteristic about this data is that the integers which represent Unix Epoch time stamps are in little-endian order, which means that you must read the data from right to left.

- Number as written to NAND flash: 63 99 d5 d4 (0x6399d5d4)
- Converted from little endian to big endian: 4d 5d 99 36 (0x4d5d9936, which is the hex read from right to left)
- Converting 0x4d5d9936 (hex) to base 10 is 1297979702
- Unix time stamp 1297979702 in human date/time format is Thu Feb 17 15:55:02 CST 2011 (date -d @1297979702)

Using this information, we can isolate a number of important artifacts in the nanddump as shown in Table 7.3.

Quite satisfyingly, the data from the debug logs, stat command, and the nanddump of the simulated NAND flash device all correspond. With additional analysis, it would be quite possible to create the MAC times for each file and directory on the NAND flash, which would provide obvious benefit to an examiner. It is also possible to gather full metadata information from ObjectHeaders still found on the NAND flash and—provided garbage collection did not occur on the block—the full content of the time at each point in time.

Table 7.3 Artifacts from YAFFS2 Nanddump

Offset	Hex	Decimal	Converted	Description
0x00000118 - 11B	dd 89 d5 d4	1297979613	Thu Feb 17 15:53:33 CST 2011	This is the *atime* (accessed time) for the directory created, which is the same as the modified and changed time as it was just created. This corresponds with the date/time from debugging statements
0x0000011C - 11F	dd 89 d5 d4	1297979613	Thu Feb 17 15:53:33 CST 2011	This is the *mtime* (modified time) of the directory, which is the same as the *atime* as it was just created
0x00000120 - 123	dd 89 d5 d4	1297979613	Thu Feb 17 15:53:33 CST 2011	This is the *ctime* (metadata changed time) of the directory, which is the same as the *atime* as it was just created
Bytes 3–6 in OOB	10 01 00 00	4097	N/A	Sequence number for the block
Bytes 7–10 in OOB	10 10 00 03	805306625	N/A	Object ID for directory test, consistent with debugging data
0x00006918 - 691B	63 99 d5 d4	1297979702	Thu Feb 17 15:55:02 CST 2011	File *atime*, not updated as file was created despite file being accessed
0x0000691C - 691F	d7 99 d5 d4	1297979773	Thu Feb 17 15:56:13 CST 2011	File *mtime*, consistent with update of file contents
0x00006920 - 6923	42 a9 d5 d4	1297979940	Thu Feb 17 15:59:00 CST 2011	File *ctime*, consistent with the permission change detailed in debug logs
Bytes 3–6 in OOB	10 01 00 00	4097	N/A	Sequence number for the block, same as previous as all data fit in 128 KB block and thus, a new sequence number was not allocated
Bytes 7–10 in OOB	20 10 00 01	268435714	N/A	Object ID for file1.txt, consistent with debugging data

It is worth pointing out that in the very limited testing and analysis demonstrated here, it appears the *atime* (accessed time) for the file is not updated every time the file is accessed. This is not really surprising as it would mean that any time a program accesses the file, a new ObjectHeader would have to be written to NAND flash. This would result in a far greater number of writes to the NAND flash and would not only use precious battery power, but would also wear out the NAND flash with metadata updates most users do not really care about. This practice is also not terribly unusual as Microsoft, by default, disabled *atime* update in Microsoft Windows Vista and Windows 7.

To be sure, this analysis is not trivial. It can provide valuable information and is a basis for forensic research on the YAFFS2 file system.

YAFFS2 File System Analysis

Hex analysis of the YAFFS2 file system is quite time consuming, so let's move on to techniques for analyzing the allocated files. Unfortunately, there are again challenges, as it can be quite difficult to mount a YAFFS2 nanddump after it is extracted from an Android device.

For this reason, as highlighted in Chapter 6, if you have root access on an Android device, it is best to not only acquire the appropriate YAFFS2 nanddump files, but to also logically copy important directories from the systems using adb pull, tar, or other method. That way, if you are unable to mount the YAFFS2 nanddump, you still have a logical copy of the files. The nanddump can then be used for timeline creation, other hex analysis, and file carving.

However, it is possible to mount some YAFFS2 nanddumps in Linux and, over time, expect more nanddump files to successfully mount. For this section though, we will focus on a nanddump from a Motorola Droid as they can be successfully mounted in Linux with nandsim and the YAFFS2 kernel module.

First, we need to load the appropriate kernel modules and create a 1 GB nandsim device.

```
sudo modprobe mtd
sudo modprobe mtdblock
sudo insmod ~/yaffs2/yaffs2.ko
sudo modprobe nandsim first_id_byte=0xec second_id_byte=0xd3 third_id_byte=0x51
fourth_id_byte=0x95
```

We now have a 1 GB nandsim device that is capable of housing the Droid's "/data" partition. The next step is to use nandwrite to copy both the data and OOB to the simulated NAND flash.

```
ahoog@ubuntu:~$ sudo nandwrite --autoplace --oob /dev/mtd0 droid_userdata.
nanddump
Writing data to block 0 at offset 0x0
Writing data to block 1 at offset 0x20000
Writing data to block 2 at offset 0x40000
Writing data to block 3 at offset 0x60000
Writing data to block 4 at offset 0x80000
Writing data to block 5 at offset 0xa0000
<snip>
```

The parameters instruct nandwrite to do the following:

- sudo nandwrite—Nandwrite requires root permission
- --autoplace—Use auto oob layout
- --oob—Image contains oob data
- /dev/mtd0—The mtd device to write the nanddump to
- droid_userdata.nanddump—The name of the nanddump file

If everything went as expected, we should now be able to mount the file system with the following commands:

```
ahoog@ubuntu:~$ mkdir -p ~/mnt/yaffs2
ahoog@ubuntu:~$ sudo mount -t yaffs2 /dev/mtdblock0 ~/mnt/yaffs2
```

There are two primary problems you can encounter during this process. First, YAFFS2 and MTD may not successfully mount the file system and will display this message:

```
ahoog@ubuntu:~$ sudo mount -t yaffs2 /dev/mtdblock0 ~/mnt/yaffs2
mount: wrong fs type, bad option, bad superblock on /dev/mtdblock0,
       missing codepage or helper program, or other error
       In some cases useful info is found in syslog - try
       dmesg | tail  or so
```

There can be many causes for this such as:

- Differences between device's YAFFS2 and MTD implementation and your workstation
- Corrupt or invalid nanddump
- File system issues

The second most common issue is that the file system mounts, but there are no files:

```
ahoog@ubuntu:~/mnt/yaffs2$ ls
lost+found
```

This is most likely due to differences between the device's YAFFS2 and MTD implementation and your workstation, and again can be difficult to debug. There are a few things you can try to resolve the issues. First, if you have a version of mtu-utils greater than 20090606-1, try installing the older version. Here's how to check your current version and optionally install:

```
ahoog@ubuntu:~$ dpkg -l | grep mtd-utils
ii  mtd-utils                           20100706-1
Memory Technology Device Utilities

ahoog@ubuntu:~$ sudo apt-get remove mtd-utils
ahoog@ubuntu:~$ wget http://mirror.pnl.gov/ubuntu//pool/universe/m/mtd-
utils/mtd-utils_20090606-1ubuntu0.10.04.1_amd64.deb
ahoog@ubuntu:~$ sudo dpkg -i mtd-utils_20090606-1ubuntu0.10.04.1_amd64.deb

ahoog@ubuntu:~$ dpkg -l | grep mtd-utils
ii  mtd-utils                           20090606-1ubuntu0.10.04.1
Memory Technology Device Utilities
```

Now that we downgraded the version of MTD, you could try the steps to mount a YAFFS2 nanddump again.

The other potential option is that your version of YAFFS2 is not consistent enough with the version used on the Android device. In order to get different versions of YAFFS2, you will need to use the source control system of either the YAFFS2 or the Android Open Source Project. You would then compile that source code, remove the existing YAFFS2 kernel module, insert the new one, and try again.

If these steps work, here is what you will see:

```
ahoog@ubuntu:~$ ls -l ~/mnt/yaffs2/
total 25
drwxrwx--x 1 ahoog ahoog 2048 2010-10-11 15:21 app
drwxrwx--x 1 ahoog ahoog 2048 2010-10-07 13:53 app-private
drwx------ 1 ahoog ahoog 2048 2010-10-11 20:16 backup
-rw-rw-rw- 1 root  root     8 2010-10-11 20:18 cc_data
drwxrwx--x 1 ahoog ahoog 2048 2010-10-11 15:21 dalvik-cache
drwxrwx--x 1 ahoog ahoog 2048 2010-10-11 15:21 data
drwxr-x--- 1 root   1007 2048 2010-10-07 13:53 dontpanic
drwxrwx--x 1  2000  2000 2048 2010-10-07 13:53 local
drwxrwx--- 1 root  root  2048 2010-10-07 13:53 lost+found
drwxrwx--t 1 ahoog  9998 2048 2010-10-11 19:02 misc
drwx------ 1 root  root  2048 2010-10-11 19:38 property
drwxrwxr-x 1 ahoog ahoog 2048 2010-10-11 20:20 system
drwxr-xr-x 1 ahoog ahoog 2048 2010-10-11 14:55 tombstones

ahoog@ubuntu:~$ df -h
Filesystem            Size  Used Avail Use% Mounted on
/dev/mtdblock0        1.0G   65M  960M   7% /home/ahoog/mnt/yaffs2
```

So we now have the full "/data" file system from a Motorola Droid accessible on our Ubuntu workstation, which you can then explore and analyze with the forensic tools of your choice. Ultimately, if you are unable to mount the nanddump on the Ubuntu workstation, you should still have the full set of logical files from the acquisition process, so it should not inhibit the analysis of the device.

YAFFS2 File Carving

The next technique useful for analyzing YAFFS2 file systems is file carving. Previously in this chapter, we installed and configured scalpel on our Ubuntu workstation. For this example, let's assume there is a file called htc-datadata.dd in the home directory of the logged-in user on the Ubuntu virtual machine. In that same directory (which you can reference with a ~ in your commands), there is a scalpel configuration containing the entries from the section 1.3 named scalpel-android.conf.

Please note that we are using the **dd image** for file carving, not the nanddump. This is necessary as the OOB data found after each 2k chunk of YAFFS2 data would significantly impact the ability of scalpel to carve valid files. The following command would run scalpel against the dd image and output the files in a folder called htc-scalpel-test in your home directory:

```
ahoog@ubuntu:~$ scalpel -c ~/scalpel-android.conf ~/htc-datadata.dd -o
~/htc-scalpel-test
Scalpel version 1.60
Written by Golden G. Richard III, based on Foremost 0.69.

Opening target "/home/ahoog/htc-datadata.dd"

Image file pass 1/2.
/home/ahoog/htc-datadata.dd: 100.0%
|************************************************************|  149.0 MB
Allocating work queues...
Work queues allocation complete. Building carve lists...
Carve lists built.  Workload:
gif with header "\x47\x49\x46\x38\x37\x61" and footer "\x00\x3b" --> 16 files
gif with header "\x47\x49\x46\x38\x39\x61" and footer "\x00\x3b" --> 385 files
jpg with header "\xff\xd8\xff\xe0\x00\x10" and footer "\xff\xd9" --> 2140 files
jpg with header "\xff\xd8\xff\xe1" and footer "\x7f\xff\xd9" --> 18 files
png with header "\x50\x4e\x47\x3f" and footer "\xff\xfc\xfd\xfe" --> 0 files
png with header "\x89\x50\x4e\x47" and footer "" --> 1442 files
db with header "\x53\x51\x4c\x69\x74\x65\x20\x66\x6f\x72\x6d\x61\x74" and
footer "" --> 5453 files
email with header "\x46\x72\x6f\x6d\x3a" and footer "" --> 1183 files
doc with header "\xd0\xcf\x11\xe0\xa1\xb1\x1a\xe1\x00\x00" and footer
"\xd0\xcf\x11\xe0\xa1\xb1\x1a\xe1\x00\x00" --> 0 files
doc with header "\xd0\xcf\x11\xe0\xa1\xb1" and footer "" --> 0 files
htm with header "\x3c\x68\x74\x6d\x6c" and footer
"\x3c\x2f\x68\x74\x6d\x6c\x3e" --> 732 files
pdf with header "\x25\x50\x44\x46" and footer "\x25\x45\x4f\x46\x0d" -->
1 files
pdf with header "\x25\x50\x44\x46" and footer "\x25\x45\x4f\x46\x0a" -->
0 files
wav with header "\x52\x49\x46\x46\x3f\x3f\x3f\x3f\x57\x41\x56\x45" and
footer "" --> 0 files
amr with header "\x23\x21\x41\x4d\x52" and footer "" --> 0 files
zip with header "\x50\x4b\x03\x04" and footer "\x3c\xac" --> 0 files
java with header "\xca\xfe\xba\xbe" and footer "" --> 0 files
Carving files from image.
Image file pass 2/2.
/home/ahoog/htc-datadata.dd: 100.0%
|************************************************************|  149.0 MB
Processing of image file complete. Cleaning up...
Done.
Scalpel is done, files carved = 11370, elapsed = 4 seconds.
```

In this instance, scalpel was able to recover 11,370 files and the output provides specifics on the file types and counts that were recovered. Fig. 7.11 is a screen shot from the Ubuntu workstation looking at one of the JPG directories.

The images do not have a high resolution but, especially when viewed directly on the workstation, you can discern the contents. Here are a few things that this small fraction of images shows:

- The top three pictures are the opening frames from YouTube movies, dragon cartoons in this case.
- The next picture is a fragment of a Facebook message asking about lunch and recommending sushi.
- The remaining pictures appear to be from various news articles.

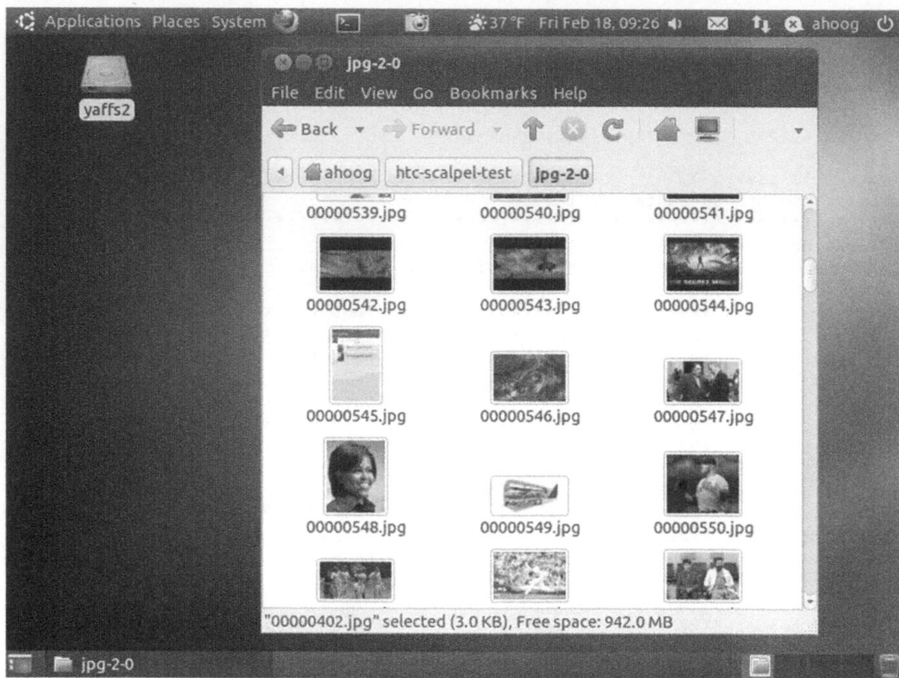

FIGURE 7.11

Viewing images recovered using scalpel.

As this demonstrates, file carving can recover important artifacts from YAFFS2 and is a valuable tool for forensic analysis.

YAFFS2 Strings Analysis

We have already demonstrated one example of using strings to find data on an Android device. However, let's work through another exercise to demonstrate not only the technique but the power of this type of analysis.

For this example, the examiner needs to find location information on the Android device. One term to search for, especially on an Android device, is maps.google.com as the Google Maps service is tightly integrated into the operating system. An extremely powerful utility for search is called grep and is used so extensively it is now a verb in technical vernacular ("Did you grep the device for map references?"). It is not only built into the Ubuntu virtual machine but it also supports very powerful regular expressions (often shortened to regex or regexp), which allow sophisticated pattern matching. There are many online resources which introduce both grep and regex with good examples.

For our example, we are going to use grep for its most basic functionality where we simply search for a string:

```
ahoog@ubuntu:~$ strings --all --radix=x htcinc-mtd6-datadata.nanddump | grep
maps.google.com | less
691e6 Nhttp://maps.google.com/?q=Naperville+Crime+Prevention&
cid=14683103809248498655 8d2e7cc
Vhttp://maps.google.com/?q=Kennedy+Space+Center+Visitor+Complex&
cid=3639318623825085463 8d30fce
http://maps.google.com/maps/gen_204?oi=miwd&sa=X&ct=miw_details&cd=1&ei=3oVUTdC
aNZn2iwPg2dyOBQ&q=Kennedy+near+Space+Center,+FL&cad=ip:174.253.2.53,client:
maps-mobile,cid:3639318623825085463,src:link
```

The query returned 775 examples—only a few are displayed here for brevity and privacy reasons. However, it is quite easy to determine some of the activity that took place on the device. Specifically:

- A search (the q= in the URL stands for query) for Naperville Crime Prevention was conducted and the URL is valid complete with address, phone number, pictures, directions, and more.
- A search for Kennedy Space Center Visitor Complex was also performed.
- The Kennedy Space Center query was then viewed by the mobile maps application and we can even see the IP address.

If we take a look at the IP address, which is part of the last query (174.253.2.53), we can use either command line tools or an online IP lookup service (What Is My IP Address, n.d.) to find out additional information. The results are shown in Fig. 7.12.

The information from the IP lookup service reveals several important pieces of information:

1. The device is using the Verizon Wireless network.
2. The device was located in the Chicago, IL area (it is possible to spoof and fake IP addresses but this is nontrivial and unlikely in most scenarios).

As we have the hex offset for the strings recovered, we could then look at data surrounding this search to determine the general time frame the search took place.

YAFFS2 Analyst Notes

The manual analysis required for much of the YAFFS2 forensics is certainly time consuming and a bit daunting, which makes the barrier of entry much higher than the analysis of well-understood and supported file systems. However, there are many resources that are easily accessible to assist an analyst new to this approach.

First, hopefully this book provided a good introduction to using Linux for forensic analysis (please recommend that all of your friends and colleagues should have a copy for their bookshelf).

Perhaps a bit more helpful is that a simple Google search will often result in many helpful posts on blogs, discussion boards, mailing lists, and other such

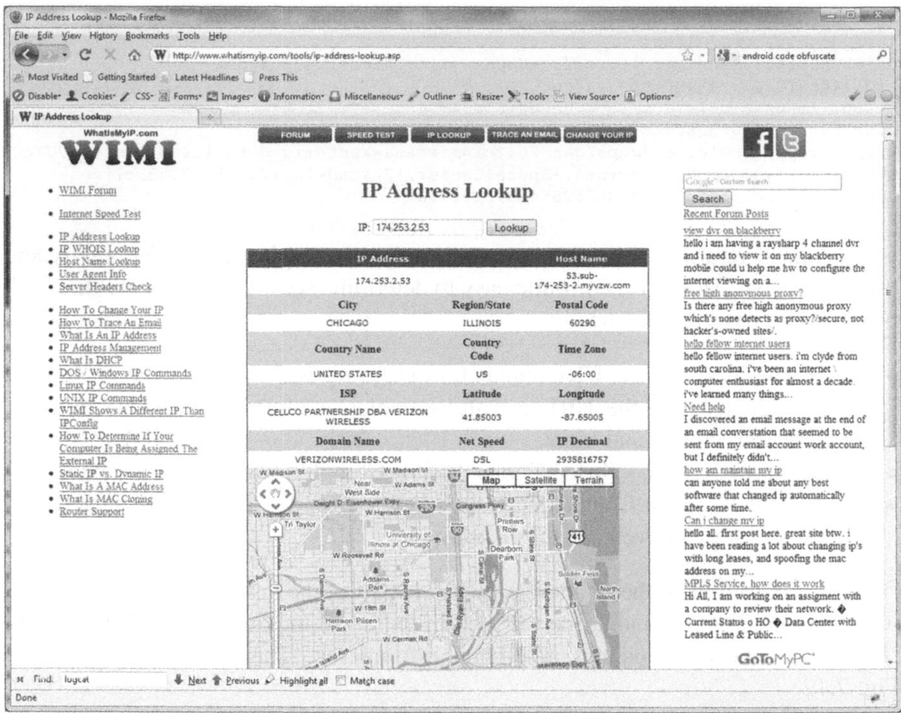

FIGURE 7.12

Results of IP address lookup.

resources. While there is certainly inaccurate information on the Internet, many of the technical people working in these areas post quite accurate and precise information. And, as a bonus, many of the authors are very responsive to inquiries and clarifications.

Next, there is an excellent introduction to Linux for law enforcement and forensic analysts, which is available online and at no cost. The web site, Linux LEO: The Law Enforcement and Forensic Examiner's Introduction to Linux, provides the guide in PDF format and introduces the reader to Linux concepts needed to use the operating system as a forensic tool (Grundy, B., n.d.).

As you use Linux further, you will find that it is quite easy to automate many of the manual tasks. This not only allows you to have great control over how the system works, but the automation can save considerable time. This is a great combination as the busy examiner can process more forensic data with cutting edge tools and at the same time explain exactly what the system did instead of just being able to say that a button was clicked and a report was produced.

The easiest way to start automating common Linux tasks is to simply write a shell script, which is very easy to write and essentially mimic the commands you would type in a terminal session.

For example, let's say you have a series of .csv files, which contain the results from running the AFLogical forensic technique on an Android device. You need to send the top row of each file to someone, but it should not contain any data from the device. You could open each file manually, delete the data rows, save the updated file to a new directory, and finally send the information. However, this could take quite some time. Instead, you could write a simple shell script.

First, let's open a new file for editing:

```
ahoog@ubuntu:~$ nano -w ~/sanitize-csv.sh
```

Then place the following into the file:

```
#!/bin/bash

# create a new directory to store the sanitized files
mkdir sanitized

#for each file ending with .csv
for f in *.csv
do
        #read the top 1 row of the file and save it to the sanitized directory
        #with the same filename followed by -1strowonly
        head -1 "$f" > sanitized/"$f"-1strowonly
done

#create a "tar gzip" archive of the file so it is easier share
tar czvf AFlogical-sanitized.tgz sanitized/*
```

Then save the file by pressing Ctrl-O and exit with Ctrl-X. Next, we have to make the script executable:

```
ahoog@ubuntu:~$ chmod 755 ~/sanitize-csv.sh
```

The files we want to sanitize are in a directory called AFLogical on the home directory of the user and, as you can tell, processing these by hand would be quite time consuming:

```
ahoog@ubuntu:~/AFLogical$ ls
Browser Bookmarks.csv            IM Providers.csv
Browser Searches.csv             IM ProviderSettings.csv
CallLog Calls.csv                info.xml
Contacts ContactMethods.csv      Internal Image Media.csv
Contacts Extensions.csv          Internal Image Thumb Media.csv
Contacts Groups.csv              Internal Videos.csv
Contacts Organizations.csv       Maps-Friends contacts.csv
Contacts Phones.csv              Maps-Friends.csv
Contacts Settings.csv            Maps-Friends extra .csv
External Image Media.csv         MMS.csv
External Image Thumb Media.csv   MMSParts.csv
External Media.csv               People.csv
External Videos.csv              PhoneStorage (HTC Incredible).csv
IM Account.csv                   sanitize.sh
IM Accounts.csv                  Search History.csv
IM Chats.csv                     SMS.csv
IM Contacts.csv                  Social Contracts Activities.csv
IM Invitations.csv
```

We can easily process these files simply now:

```
ahoog@ubuntu:~/AFLogical$ cd ~/AFLogical
ahoog@ubuntu:~/AFLogical$ ~/sanitize-csv.sh
sanitized/Browser Bookmarks.csv-1strowonly
sanitized/Browser Searches.csv-1strowonly
sanitized/CallLog Calls.csv-1strowonly
<snip>
```

Now, the AFLogical directory not only has a new subdirectory called sanitized with each of the updated files in it, but also a single file containing the data:

```
ahoog@ubuntu:~/AFLogical$ ls -lh *.tgz
-rw-r--r-- 1 ahoog ahoog 2.1K 2011-02-19 03:44 AFlogical-sanitized.tgz
```

This data can be easily e-mailed or copied to another drive.

Here's a more complex example, which will create a nandsim device, mount a blank YAFFS2 file system, generate several files, and then allow the user to unmount the file system. This is a quick way to automate the steps involved in testing YAFFS2.

```
#!/bin/bash

read -p "Load kernel modules? (y/n)?"
if [ "$REPLY" == "y" ] ; then
      sudo modprobe mtd
      sudo modprobe mtdblock
      sudo insmod ~/yaffs2/yaffs2.ko
else
      exit
fi
echo ""
echo "Choose nandsim size in MiB [64, 128, 256, 512, 1024]"
echo "1) 64 MiB"
echo "2) 128 MiB"
echo "3) 256 MiB"
echo "4) 512 MiB"
echo "5) 1024 MiB"
read size
case $size in
      1) sudo modprobe nandsim first_id_byte=0x20 second_id_byte=0xa2
third_id_byte=0x00 fourth_id_byte=0x15 ;;
      2) sudo modprobe nandsim first_id_byte=0x20 second_id_byte=0xa1
third_id_byte=0x00 fourth_id_byte=0x15 ;;
      3) sudo modprobe nandsim first_id_byte=0x20 second_id_byte=0xaa
third_id_byte=0x00 fourth_id_byte=0x15 ;;
      4) sudo modprobe nandsim first_id_byte=0x20 second_id_byte=0xac
third_id_byte=0x00 fourth_id_byte=0x15 ;;
      5) sudo modprobe nandsim first_id_byte=0xec second_id_byte=0xd3
third_id_byte=0x51 fourth_id_byte=0x15 ;;
      *)
      echo "invalid nandsim size"
      exit
      ;;
esac
```

```
read -p "Mount yaffs2 in ~/mnt/y? (y/n)?"
if [ "$REPLY" == "y" ] ; then
     echo ""
     echo "Mounting with sudo mount -t yaffs2 /dev/mtdblock0 ~/mnt/y"
     sudo mount -t yaffs2 /dev/mtdblock0 ~/mnt/y
else
     exit
fi

echo ""
read -p "Write viafile.txt with contents of viaforensics? (y/n)?"
if [ "$REPLY" == "y" ] ; then
     sudo echo "viaforensics" > ~/mnt/y/viafile.txt
else
     exit
fi

echo ""
read -p "Append .com to contents of viafile.txt? (y/n)?"
if [ "$REPLY" == "y" ] ; then
     sudo echo ".com" >> ~/mnt/y/viafile.txt
else
     exit
fi

echo ""
read -p "Rename viafile.txt to renamed.txt? (y/n)?"
if [ "$REPLY" == "y" ] ; then
     sudo mv ~/mnt/y/viafile.txt ~/mnt/y/renamed.txt
else
     exit
fi

echo ""
read -p "Delete renamed.txt? (y/n)?"
if [ "$REPLY" == "y" ] ; then
     sudo rm ~/mnt/y/renamed.txt
else
     exit
fi

echo ""
read -p "Create last.txt with afphysical? (y/n)?"
if [ "$REPLY" == "y" ] ; then
     sudo echo  "afphysical" > ~/mnt/y/last.txt
else
     exit
fi

echo ""
read -p "Unmount and remove modules? (y/n)?"
if [ "$REPLY" == "y" ] ; then
     sudo umount ~/mnt/y
     sudo rmmod yaffs2
     sudo rmmod nandsim
     sudo rmmod mtdblock
     sudo rmmod nand
     sudo rmmod mtd_blkdevs
     sudo rmmod mtd
     echo "Done"
else
     exit
fi
```

Hopefully, the absence of commercial tools which support the YAFFS2 file system is not viewed by the examiner as a situation where no additional data can be recovered. Using free, open source tools available on an Ubuntu workstation clearly provides a powerful means to further the investigation. When combining these techniques with the hex analysis outlined in this chapter, an examiner should find they are well prepared to extract evidence from YAFFS2 partitions on Android devices. When a case involving a medical device that runs embedded Linux with the YAFFS2 file system is placed on your desk you can confidently dive in and figure it out.

ANDROID APP ANALYSIS AND REFERENCE

While this chapter described many techniques useful for the forensic and security investigation of Android devices, it is helpful to have a reference of where data is stored for key applications. Of course, maintaining a complete reference would be nearly impossible not only due to the sheer number of applications but also due to the variation between specific devices and Android versions.

In the following sections, we analyze 10 important applications from the reference phones used throughout this book and provide the following data:

1. App information
2. Files and directories (including /data/data, SD card, and eMMC)
3. Important database tables
4. Analyst notes

Through the app analysis, all time stamps are in Unix Epoch milliseconds, the number of milliseconds since January 1, 1970, unless otherwise noted.

The apps tested were installed and used on the device and then analyzed with a custom Python program to automate some of the techniques described previously in this chapter. While significant information is provided, be advised that this is only a reference and likely incomplete. Analysts should use the forensic and security tools as well as the techniques described above for a full analysis of the device they are examining.

Messaging (sms and mms)

App Info

This is the default app shipped with Android that handles SMS and MMS messages.

- App Name: Messaging
- Package name: com.android.providers.telephony
- Version: 2.2
- Device: HTC Incredible
- App developer: Android

Directories, Files, and File Types

In /data/data/com.android.providers.telephony:

```
com.android.providers.telephony/     directory
├── app_parts                        directory
│   ├── PART_1285875367786           JPEG image data, JFIF standard 1.01
│   ├── PART_1287901591761           JPEG image data, JFIF standard 1.01
│   └── PART_1293199567316           JPEG image data, JFIF standard 1.01
├── databases                        directory
│   ├── mmssms.db                    SQLite 3.x database, user version 60
│   └── telephony.db                 SQLite 3.x database, user version 524296
└── lib                              directory
```

Important Database Tables and Files

Important database tables and files for mms and sms are shown in Table 7.4.

Table 7.4 Important Database Tables and Files from /data/data/com.android.providers.telephony/databases/mmssms.db

Database Tables/Files	Description
words_content	Content of messages
part	MMS attachment details including type, name, location on file system if binary (i.e., images), and content of attachment if plain text
sms	Full SMS messages including to, from, person, time stamp, read status, send/receive status, and message content

Analyst Notes

Analyst notes for /data/data/com.android.providers.telephony:

- The app_parts folder will contain the MMS attachments and can include images, video, or any other supported data. File types are not maintained, so use the file command or other file signature analysis tools to identify.
- The telephony database is usually of little interest as it only contains service information for the wireless carrier(s).
- The sms table contains all the messages and should be the primary focus.
- Several other tables seem to replicate parts of the sms table's content, so look at words_content and other tables to aid in your analysis.
- See also: com.android.mms.

MMS Helper Application

App Info

This app stores some MMS data and appears to be a helper application for the main Messaging app.

- App Name: com.android.mm
- Package name: com.android.mms
- Version: 2.2
- Device: HTC Incredible
- App developer: Android

Directories, Files, and File Types

In /data/data/com.android.mms:

```
com.android.mms                                       directory
├── bufferFileForMms                                  data
├── cache                                             directory
│   ├── PART_1285875367786                            PNG image, 80 x 60,
8-bit/color RGB, non-interlaced
│   ├── PART_1287901591761                            PNG image, 80 x 60,
8-bit/color RGB, non-interlaced
│   └── PART_1293199567316                            PNG image, 80 x 60,
8-bit/color RGB, non-interlaced
├── lib                                               directory
└── shared_prefs                                      directory
    ├── com.android.mms.customizationBySIM.xml        XML  document text
    ├── com.android.mms_preferences.xml               XML  document text
    ├── FIRST_EXECUTE.xml                             XML  document text
    ├── _has_set_default_values.xml                   XML  document text
    └── VERY_FIRST_EXECUTE.xml                        XML  document text
```

Important Database Tables and Files

- PART files in /data/data/com.android.mms/cache

Analyst Notes

Analyst notes for /data/data/com.android.mms:

- File "bufferFileForMms" might contain buffer data at the time of sending. However, it usually only contains 0x00.
- The PART files in cache are small PNG versions of the images found in the Messaging app at /data/data/com.android.providers.telephony/app_parts.

Browser

App Info

This is the built-in web browser for Android, based on the open source WebKit project.

- App Name: Internet
- Package name: com.android.browser
- Version: 2.2

- Device: HTC Incredible
- App developer: Android

Directories, Files, and File Types

In /data/data/com.android.browser:

```
com.android.browser/directory
├── app_appcache directory
│   └── ApplicationCache.db SQLite 3.x database, user version 5
├── app_databases directory
│   ├── Databases.db SQLite 3.x database
│   ├── http_a.ringleaderdigital.com_0 directory
│   │   └── 0000000000000002.db SQLite 3.x database
│   ├── http_blogs.techrepublic.com.com_0.localstorage SQLite 3.x database
│   ├── http_b.scorecardresearch.com_0.localstorage SQLite 3.x database
│   ├── http_forumlogr.disqus.com_0.localstorage SQLite 3.x database
│   ├── http_mashable.com_0.localstorage SQLite 3.x database
│   ├── http_mashable.disqus.com_0.localstorage SQLite 3.x database
│   ├── http_m.imdb.com_0.localstorage SQLite 3.x database
│   ├── https_api.twitter.com_0.localstorage SQLite 3.x database
│   ├── http_singularityhub.com_0.localstorage SQLite 3.x database
│   ├── http_singularityhub.disqus.com_0.localstorage SQLite 3.x database
│   ├── http_twitpic.com_0.localstorage SQLite 3.x database
│   ├── http_voices.washingtonpost.com_0.localstorage SQLite 3.x database
│   ├── http_www.accuweather.com_0 directory
│   │   └── 0000000000000001.db SQLite 3.x database
│   ├── http_www.accuweather.com_0.localstorage SQLite 3.x database
│   ├── http_www.cbc.ca_0.localstorage SQLite 3.x database
│   ├── http_www.forensicfocus.com_0.localstorage SQLite 3.x database
│   ├── http_www.forumlogr.com_0.localstorage SQLite 3.x database
│   ├── http_www.google.com_0.localstorage SQLite 3.x database
│   ├── http_www.iphoneworld.ca_0.localstorage SQLite 3.x database
│   ├── http_www.linkedin.com_0.localstorage SQLite 3.x database
│   └── http_www.youtube.com_0.localstorage SQLite 3.x database
├── app_geolocation directory
│   ├── CachedGeoposition.db SQLite 3.x database
│   └── GeolocationPermissions.db SQLite 3.x database
├── app_icons directory
│   └── WebpageIcons.db SQLite 3.x database
├── app_plugins directory
│   └── com.adobe.flashplayer directory
│       ├── .adobe directory
│       │   └── Flash_Player directory
│       │       └── AssetCache directory
│       │           └── YY3JJV4U directory
│       │               ├── 3C82B2A2455B252B8595FD0113249AA19D7E8BDD.heu data
│       │               ├── 3C82B2A2455B252B8595FD0113249AA19D7E8BDD.swz data
│       │               └── cacheSize.txt ASCII text, with no line terminators
│       └── .macromedia directory
│           └── Flash_Player directory
│               ├── adobe.com directory
│               │   └── flashplayer directory
│               │       ├── #cdn.widgetserver.com directory
│               │       │   └── settings.sol data
│               │       ├── #flashapps.ifg.net directory
│               │       │   └── settings.sol data
│               │       ├── #images10.newegg.com directory
│               │       │   └── settings.sol data
│               │       ├── settings.sol data
│               │       └── #s.ytimg.com directory
│               │           └── settings.sol data
│               └── #SharedObjects directory
│                   └── GPDJW6S3 directory
│                       ├── cdn.widgetserver.com directory
│
```

```
|                        |   ├── com.quantserve.sol data
|                        |   ├── syndication directory
|                        |   |   └── flash directory
|                        |   |       └── InsertWidget.swf directory
|                        |   |           └── wbx.sol data
|                        |   └── wbx_cookie.sol data
|                        ├── flashapps.ifg.net directory
|                        |   └── weather directory
|                        |       └── weather.swf directory
|                        |           └── TestMovie_Config_Info.sol data
|                        ├── images10.newegg.com directory
|                        |   ├── s7_newegg.sol data
|                        |   └── WebResource directory
|                        |       └── Themes directory
|                        |           └── 2005 directory
|                        |               └── Nest directory
|                        |                   └── genericzoomviewer.swf directory
|                        |                       └── #newegg directory
|                        |                           └── 16%2D102%2D144%2DZ02_init.sol data
|                        └── s.ytimg.com directory
|                            └── soundData.sol data
├── app_sharedimage directory
├── app_thumbnails directory
├── cache -> /app-cache/com.android.browser/cache broken symbolic link to '/app-cache/
|   com.android.browser/cache'
├── databases directory
|   ├── browser.db SQLite 3.x database, user version 24
|   ├── webviewCache.db SQLite 3.x database, user version 4
|   └── webview.db SQLite 3.x database, user version 10
├── lib directory
└── shared_prefs directory
    ├── com.android.browser_preferences.xml XML document text
    └── WebViewSettings.xml XML document text
```

In /app-cache/com.android.browser/cache:

```
app-cache/                    directory
└── com.android.browser       directory
    └── cache                 directory
        └── webviewCache      directory
            ├── 00684608      JPEG image data, JFIF standard 1.01, comment:
"CREATOR: gd-jpeg v1.0 (using IJ"
            ├── 00f02aa9      GIF image data, version 89a, 3 x 3
            ├── 0113650e      ASCII text, with very long lines
            ├── 01c6689f      ASCII C program text, with very long lines
            ├── 0249f797      PNG image, 46 x 20, 8-bit/color RGBA,
                              non-interlaced
            ├── 02d78554      GIF image data, version 89a, 468 x 60
            ├── 0305cad6      JPEG image data, JFIF standard 1.02
            ├── 0339028b      GIF image data, version 89a, 155 x 85
            ├── 036d8956      036d8956: GIF image data, version 89a, 15 x 15
            ├── 03bc67f9      ASCII text, with very long lines
            ├── 04e9f7f8      JPEG image data, JFIF standard 1.01
            ├── 056d50ab      HTML document text
            ├── 069360d7      JPEG image data, JFIF standard 1.02
            ├── 073f38ff      GIF image data, version 89a, 20 x 14
            ├── 074a5b68      ASCII text, with very long lines
            ├── 07f04406      PNG image, 200 x 52, 8-bit/color RGBA,
                              non-interlaced
            ├── 07ff1c11      PNG image, 132 x 29, 8-bit/color RGBA,
                              non-interlaced
            ├── 09fda0dd      GIF image data, version 89a, 32 x 11
            ├── 0aec9086      GIF image data, version 89a, 8 x 3
            ├── 0c24e90f      GIF image data, version 89a, 17 x 17
<snip>
```

Important Database Tables and Files

Local storage for supported web apps is shown in Table 7.5.

Cached geoposition data is shown in Table 7.6.

The geolocation permissions database is shown in Table 7.7.

Table 7.8 shows the browser database.

Table 7.9 shows the web view database.

And the web view cache database is shown in Table 7.10.

Table 7.5 Important Database Tables and Files from /data/data/com.android.browser/app_databases/http_www.google.com_0.localstorage

Database Tables/Files	Description
ItemTable	This table is a simple list of key/value pairs; however, potentially contains useful information for sites that were visited and takes advantage of the localstorage feature.

Table 7.6 Important Database Tables and Files from /data/data/com.android.browser/app_geolocation/CachedGeoposition.db

Database Tables/Files	Description
CachedPosition	• latitude—41.896888 • longitude=—87.799985 • altitude = • accuracy = 1368.0 • altitudeAccuracy = • heading = • speed = • timestamp = 1296479267929

Table 7.7 Important Database Tables and Files from /data/data/com.android.browser/app_geolocation/GeolocationPermissions.db

Database Tables/Files	Description
Permissions	This table is list of origins (web sites) and the permission for each (allow). For example, http://www.google.com and the value 1 means Google's web site has permission to access geolocation

Analyst Notes

Analyst notes for /data/data/com.android.browser:

- Check the WebpageIcons.db in app_icons if looking for a particular site and the site has a favicon.

Table 7.8 Important Database Tables and Files from /data/data/com.android.browser/databases/browser.db

Database Tables/Files	Description
Bookmarks	• _id = 662 • title = http://mobile.itworld.com/device/article.php?CALL_URL=http://www.itworld.com/security/135495/ddos-attacks-made-worse-firewalls-report-finds • url = http://mobile.itworld.com/device/article.php?CALL_URL=http://www.itworld.com/security/135495/ddos-attacks-made-worse-firewalls-report-finds • visits = 1 • date = 1296736862801
Searches	• _id = 4 • search = fogo de chao chicago • date = 1291401576968

Table 7.9 Important Database Tables and Files from /data/data/com.android.browser/databases/webview.db

Database Tables/Files	Description
cookies	• _id = 3912 • name = PHPSESSID • value = 25b5b5a8608795fa4ac45d2b872a20e5 • domain = mobile.itworld.com • path = / • expires = • secure = 0
formurl	• _id = 95 • url = http://en.m.wikipedia.org/wiki/Dime_(United_States_coin)?wasRedirected=true
formdata	• _id = 39 • urlid = 95 • name = search • value = Dime (United States coin)
httpauth	• _id = 1 • host = dev-computer-forensics.sans.org • realm = SANS - Restricted Access [Area - 39] • username = your-sans-blog-username • password = your-sans-blog-password
password	• _id = 2 • host = httpswww.netflix.com • username = your-netflix-username • password = your-netflix-password

Table 7.10 Important Database Tables and Files from /data/data/com.android.browser/databases/webviewCache.db

Database Tables/Files	Description
cache	• _id = 464 • url = http://profile.ak.fbcdn.net/hprofile-ak-snc4/hs267.snc3/23271_145853460360_2616_q.jpg • filepath = 00684608 • lastmodify = Thu, 01 Jan 2009 00:00:00 GMT • etag = • expires = 1299533415543 • expiresstring = Mon, 07 Mar 2011 21:30:00 GMT • mimetype = image/jpeg • encoding = • httpstatus = 200 • location = • contentlength = 2890 • contentdisposition = • crossdomain =

- The specific app databases can contain very useful information. For example, Google app database has previous search terms, many versions of cached "lon/lat/acc" with time stamps and more.
- The com.adobe.flashplayer directory contains not only "Flash cookies," which end in the .sol extension and can be parsed by log2timeline, but also some of the Flash .swf files.
- The browser database (databases/browser.db) contains a table called bookmarks, which is generally pre-populated with bookmarks from the wireless carriers. This same table also contains the web browser history. There is also a table called Searches, which contains Google searches made from the browser.
- The web view database (databases/webview.db) contains considerable information not only useful for a forensic examiner but also a security engineer. Cookies are visible and most are not secure, meaning they may be vulnerable to a cookie hijacking attack using a tool such as Firesheep. Form URL and data often contain sensitive information as do httpauth and password.
- The web view cache database (databases/webviewCache.db) provides the metadata about the cache files stored in cache directory.
- Most devices save the web view cache data as a subdirectory in /data/data/com.android.browser. However, the HTC Incredible moved this directory to a tmpfs (RAM disk) directory.

Contacts

App Info

This app is the main contacts app provided by Android. While there are many additional apps available, this app provides the core contact functionality.

- App Name: Contacts
- Package name: com.android.providers.contacts
- Version: 2.2
- Device: HTC Incredible
- App developer: Android

Directories, Files, and File Types

In /data/data/com.android.providers.contacts:

```
com.android.providers.contacts                          directory
├── databases                                           directory
│   └── contacts2.db                                    SQLite 3.x database, user version 309
├── files                                               directory
│   ├── thumbnail_photo_10014.jpg                       JPEG image data, JFIF standard 1.01
│   ├── thumbnail_photo_10194.jpg                       JPEG image data, JFIF standard 1.01
│   ├── thumbnail_photo_10199.jpg                       JPEG image data, JFIF standard 1.01
│   ├── thumbnail_photo_10202.jpg                       JPEG image data, JFIF standard 1.01
│   ├── thumbnail_photo_10203.jpg                       JPEG image data, JFIF standard 1.01
│   ├── thumbnail_photo_12450.jpg                       JPEG image data, JFIF standard 1.01
│   ├── thumbnail_photo_12827.jpg                       JPEG image data, JFIF standard 1.01
│   ├── thumbnail_photo_12832.jpg                       JPEG image data, JFIF standard 1.01
│   ├── thumbnail_photo_12833.jpg                       JPEG image data, JFIF standard 1.01
│   ├── thumbnail_photo_9508.jpg                        JPEG image data, JFIF standard 1.01
│   ├── thumbnail_photo_9509.jpg                        JPEG image data, JFIF standard 1.01
│   ├── thumbnail_photo_9566.jpg                        JPEG image data, JFIF standard 1.01
│   └── thumbnail_photo_9866.jpg                        JPEG image data, JFIF standard 1.01
├── lib                                                 directory
├── shared_prefs                                        directory
│   ├── com.android.providers.contacts_preferences.xml  XML  document text
│   └── ContactsUpgradeReceiver.xml                     XML  document text
└── SNtemp                                              directory
    └── 27386_604172803_5385_n.jpg                      empty
```

Important Database Tables and Files

There is only one database, contacts2.db, and it has over 30 tables. A few of the key tables are listed in Table 7.11.

Analyst Notes

Analyst notes for /data/data/com.android.providers.contacts:

- This app stores the Call Logs for the device in the calls table.
- There are over 30 tables in contacts2.db, so further inspection may be required. The data table contains additional values about contacts and the raw_contacts contains additional data about some contacts.
- The app is capable of storing contact information from many different accounts including Gmail, Exchange, Facebook, Twitter, and more. Some of the data stored include information from these other apps such as Facebook status messages.
- If pictures of the contacts are available, they are stored in the files directory and named thumbnail_photo_[NNNNN].jpg. In the reference HTC Incredible, there were over 200 images but duplicates were found.

Table 7.11 Important Database Tables and Files from /data/data/com.android.providers.contacts/databases/contacts2.db

Database Tables/Files	Description
accounts	• account_name = viaforensics • account_type = com.twitter.android.auth.login
calls	• _id = 1156 • number = 3128781100 • date = 1296780296202 • duration = 142 • type = 1 • new = 1 • name = viaForensics Corporate • numbertype = 3 • numberlabel = • raw_contact_id = 907 • city_id =
status_updates	• status_update_data_id = 14792 • status = installed Facebook for Windows Phone • status_ts = 1287597506000 • status_res_package = com.htc.socialnetwork.provider • status_label = 2130968576 • status_icon = 33685932
contacts	• _id = 907 • name_raw_contact_id = 907 • photo_id = • custom_ringtone = • send_to_voicemail = 0 • times_contacted = 19 • last_time_contacted = 1296780451343 • starred = 0 • in_visible_group = 1 • has_phone_number = 1 • lookup = 1598i2%3A40 • status_update_id = • single_is_restricted = 0 • ext_account_Type = com.htc.android.mail.eas • ext_photo_url = • display_name = viaForensics Corporate • default_action =

Media Scanner

App Info

This app scans and stores the metadata of media files available on internal and external storage.

- App Name: Media Store
- Package name: com.android.providers.media
- Version: 2.2
- Device: HTC Incredible
- App developer: Android

Directories, Files, and File Types

In /data/data/com.android.providers.media:

```
com.android.providers.media      directory
├── databases                    directory
│   ├── emmc-c7f80810.db         SQLite 3.x database, user version 90
│   ├── external-e0fd1813.db     SQLite 3.x database, user version 90
│   └── internal.db              SQLite 3.x database, user version 90
├── lib                          directory
└── shared_prefs                 directory
    └── ringtoneinit.xml         XML  document text
```

Important Database Tables and Files

The structure of each database is similar, as shown in Table 7.12.

Analyst Notes

Analyst notes for /data/data/com.android.providers.media:

- The database names contain the volume ID, if available. For example, on the reference HTC Incredible device, the eMMC FAT32 file system has a volume ID of 0xc7f80810.
- If a directory has a file named .nomedia, then the media store will not scan and record the metadata of files in that directory.
- If an image was deleted, the thumbnail likely still exists. Also, even if the metadata record is deleted, it is likely recoverable due to the YAFFS2 file system.
- Also scans for audio files, albums, etc.
- Other media scanners and apps exist, so check for those. One stores thumbnails on the SD card, which can provide an insight into deleted pictures and videos.

YouTube

App Info

YouTube is a video viewing web site now owned by Google, for which they have developed a native app for Android.

- App Name: YouTube
- Package name: com.google.android.youtube
- Version: 1.6.21
- Device: HTC Incredible
- App developer: Google

Table 7.12 Important Database Tables and Files from /data/data/com.android.providers.media/databases/

Database Tables/Files	Description
images	• _id = 88 • _data = /mnt/emmc/DCIM/100MEDIA/IMAG0074.jpg • _size = 873150 • _display_name = IMAG0074.jpg • mime_type = image/jpeg • title = IMAG0074 • date_added = 1295368758 • date_modified = 1295372358 • description = • picasa_id = • isprivate = • latitude = • longitude = • datetaken = 1295372358000 • orientation = 0 • mini_thumb_magic = 88 • bucket_id = -942500167 • bucket_display_name = 100MEDIA • favorite = • lock_screen =
videos	Fields similar to images table
thumbnails	• _id = 88 • data = /mnt/emmc/dcim/.thumbnails/(28)890943898-s=901931-fH=274-gH=160-mode=10-AG=0.raw • image_id = 28 • kind = 103 • width = 160 • height = 160

Directories, Files, and File Types

In /data/data/com.google.android.youtube:

```
com.google.android.youtube/             directory
├── cache                               directory
│   ├── GDataRequest.-1358025214        XML  document text
│   ├── GDataRequest.149614182          XML  document text
│   ├── GDataRequest.1718906282         XML  document text
│   ├── GDataRequest.307198247          XML  document text
│   ├── GDataRequest.-689089246         XML  document text
│   ├── GDataRequest.718990876          XML  document text
│   └── GDataRequest.-953243531         XML  document text
├── files                               directory
│   └── DATA_Preferences                data
├── lib                                 directory
└── shared_prefs                        directory
    └── youtube.xml                     XML  document text
```

Important Database Tables and Files

YouTube preferences, including device key(s) and watched videos in /data/data/com.google.android.youtube/shared_prefs/youtube.xml:

```
<?xml version='1.0' encoding='utf-8' standalone='yes' ?>
<map>
<int name="safe_search_mode" value="1" />
<string name="StrongAuth.deviceKey">AomSH9asdnA5DMqw/8mzHUDXdsaI15e0s=</string>
<string name="watchedVideos">osnUasdB9bUm-E,SunCPrwdsadO1NI,
qKrrHtY1231WcWA,E7ULR-asdayfNnk,aHmUZgssaoq123rIYA,JaecOddBxDFlas0</string>
<string name="StrongAuth.deviceId">AOuj_RqrF8oasdastTCOySdFNIaNV_M91X
-3MQMbBzzLassdTcAQQn8oYPMWZRK_PiTYMgB-T_rPECOyG4W2jd7zLT7TS2Q</string>
<string name="ratedVideos"></string>
<string name="MasfLogYouTubeApplicationVersion">1.6.21</string>
</map>
```

Information about specific movies watched saved in XML file in /data/data/com.google.android.youtube/cache:

```
<?xml version='1.0' encoding='UTF-8'?>
<id>tag:youtube.com,2008:video:E7ULR-yfNnk</id>
<published>2006-09-10T22:22:58.000Z</published>
<updated>2010-11-30T19:06:08.000Z</updated>
<category scheme='http://schemas.google.com/g/2005#kind'
term='http://gdata.youtube.com/schemas/2007#video'/>
<category scheme='http://gdata.youtube.com/schemas/2007/categories.cat'
term='Entertainment' label='Entertainment'/>
<category scheme='http://gdata.youtube.com/schemas/2007/keywords.cat'
term='Mime'/>
<category scheme='http://gdata.youtube.com/schemas/2007/keywords.cat'
term='Miming'/>
<category scheme='http://gdata.youtube.com/schemas/2007/keywords.cat'
term='Robot'/>
<category scheme='http://gdata.youtube.com/schemas/2007/keywords.cat'
term='Dance'/>
<title>Cool Mime! Tyson Eberly Mime Performance Part 2</title>
<content type='video/mp4' src='http://v12.lscache5.googlevideo.com/
videoplayback?id=13b50b47ec9f3679&amp;itag=18&amp;uaopt=
no-save&amp;ip=0.0.0.0&amp;ipbits=0&amp;expire=1293757989&amp;
sparams=id,itag,uaopt,ip,ipbits,expire
&amp;signature=C3885D4913EC51106910D8E99049F7D39F7C4AA6.D809F3290B0A6E0D8C83C28
F31261D64BDF0C680&amp;key=yta1
&amp;el=videos&amp;client=mvapp-android-
verizon&amp;devKey=ATEU_r3RX2afGwq_gCqiS2UO88HsQjpE1a8d1GxQnGDm&amp;
app=youtube_gdata'/>

<snip>
```

Analyst Notes

Analyst notes for /data/data/com.google.android.youtube:

- Examine the XML files in the cache directory and in the shared_prefs directory for information on videos viewed.
- A snapshot of the opening image to a video can often be found on the device using file carving or other techniques.

Cooliris Media Gallery

App Info

This app was developed for the Google Nexus One and provides a media gallery and scanner.

- App Name: Cooliris Media Gallery
- Package name: com.cooliris.media
- Version: 1.1.30682
- Device: Google Nexus One
- App developer: Cooliris

Directories, Files, and File Types

In /data/data/com.cooliris.media:

```
com.cooliris.media/      directory
└── databases             directory
   └── picasa.db         SQLite 3.x database, user version 83
```

More importantly, thumbnails are stored on the SD card:

```
/mnt/sdcard/Android/data/com.cooliris.media                 directory
└── cache                                                   directory
    ├── geocoder-cache                                      directory
    ├── geocoder-cachechunk_0                               data
    ├── geocoder-cacheindex                                 data
    ├── hires-image-cache                                   directory
    ├── hires-image-cache-1158935264581041381_1024.cache    JPEG image data, JFIF standard 1.01
    ├── hires-image-cache1585961800385347536_1024.cache     JPEG image data, JFIF standard 1.01
    ├── hires-image-cache1588208008548304680_1024.cache     JPEG image data, JFIF standard 1.01
    ├── hires-image-cache-1695915026582362443_1024.cache    JPEG image data, JFIF standard 1.01
    ├── hires-image-cache1826788044297674713_1024.cache     JPEG image data, JFIF standard 1.01
    ├── hires-image-cache1830742186312500388_1024.cache     JPEG image data, JFIF standard 1.01
    ├── hires-image-cache2087069753732167412_1024.cache     JPEG image data, JFIF standard 1.01
    ├── hires-image-cache2114895255670203853_1024.cache     JPEG image data, JFIF standard 1.01
<snip>
    ├── hires-image-cache9169278413697037975_1024.cache     JPEG image data, JFIF standard 1.01
    ├── local-album-cache                                      directory
    ├── local-album-cachechunk_0                               data
    ├── local-album-cacheindex                                 data
    ├── local-image-thumbs                                     directory
    ├── local-image-thumbschunk_0                              data
    ├── local-image-thumbsindex                                data
    ├── local-meta-cache                                       directory
    ├── local-meta-cachechunk_0                                data
    ├── local-meta-cacheindex                                  data
    ├── local-skip-cache                                       directory
    ├── local-skip-cachechunk_0                                MMDF mailbox
    ├── local-skip-cacheindex                                  data
    ├── local-video-thumbs                                     directory
    ├── local-video-thumbschunk_0                              data
    ├── local-video-thumbsindex                                data
    ├── picasa-thumbs                                          directory
    └── picasa-thumbsindex                                     data
```

Important Database Tables and Files

For this device, the picasa.db was empty, but presumably the databases will contain useful information.

Analyst Notes

Analyst notes for /data/data/com.cooliris.media:

- The real value in this app is that media discovered on the device is cached on the SD card in "/mnt/sdcard/Android/data/com.cooliris.media/cache" and should be examined closely.

Google Maps

App Info

This is the built-in Google Maps application used to view maps, search for endpoints, and even provide directions.

- App Name: Google Maps
- Package name: com.google.android.apps.maps
- Version: 4.4.0
- Device: HTC Incredible
- App developer: Google

Directories, Files, and File Types

In /data/data/com.google.android.apps.maps:

```
com.google.android.apps.maps/                  directory
├── app_                                       directory
│   ├── cache                                  directory
│   │   └── cache_r.m                          data
│   ├── debug                                  directory
│   └── testdata                               directory
├── cache                                      directory
│   └── webviewCache                           directory
├── databases                                  directory
│   ├── da_destination_history                 SQLite 3.x database, user version 1
│   ├── friends.db                             SQLite 3.x database, user version 19
│   ├── LayerInfo                              SQLite 3.x database, user version 2
│   ├── search_history.db                      SQLite 3.x database, user version 5
│   ├── webviewCache.db                        SQLite 3.x database, user version 4
│   └── webview.db                             SQLite 3.x database, user version 10
├── files                                      directory
│   ├── DA_DirOpt_en_US                        data
│   ├── DA_LayerInfo                           data
│   ├── DATA_LATITUDE_WIDGET_MODEL             data
│   ├── DATA_LAYER_10                          data
│   ├── DATA_LAYER_11                          data
│   ├── DATA_LAYER_13                          data
│   ├── DATA_LAYER_14                          data
│   ├── DATA_LAYER_15                          data
│   ├── DATA_LAYER_16                          data
│   ├── DATA_LAYER_18                          data
```

```
│   ├── DATA_LAYER_2                                        data
│   ├── DATA_LAYER_20                                       data
│   ├── DATA_LAYER_21                                       data
│   ├── DATA_LAYER_24                                       data
│   ├── DATA_LAYER_25                                       data
│   ├── DATA_LAYER_27                                       data
│   ├── DATA_LAYER_28                                       data
│   ├── DATA_LAYER_3                                        data
│   ├── DATA_LAYER_5                                        data
│   ├── DATA_LAYER_6                                        data
│   ├── DATA_LAYER_7                                        data
│   ├── DATA_LAYER_8                                        data
│   ├── DATA_LAYER_9                                        data
│   ├── DATA_location_history                               data
│   ├── DATA_OptionDefinitionBlock_en                       data
│   ├── DATA_Preferences                                    data
│   ├── DATA_PROTO_SAVED_CATEGORY_TREE_DB                   raw G3 data, byte-padded
│   ├── DATA_PROTO_SAVED_LAYER_STATE                        data
│   ├── DATA_PROTO_SAVED_RECENT_LAYERS                      data
│   ├── DATA_RemoteStringsBlock_en                          data
│   ├── DATA_Restrictions                                   raw G3 data, byte-padded
│   ├── DATA_Restrictions_lock                              empty
│   ├── DATA_SAVED_BGFS_3                                   data
│   ├── DATA_SAVED_BGFS_EXTRA_3                             data
│   ├── DATA_SAVED_BGSF_                                    data
│   ├── DATA_SAVED_REMOTE_ICONS_DATA_BLOCK                  data
│   ├── DATA_ServerControlledParametersManager.data         data
│   ├── DATA_STARRING                                       X11 SNF font data, MSB first
│   ├── DATA_SYNC_DATA                                      data
│   ├── DATA_SYNC_DATA_LOCAL                                data
│   ├── DATA_TILE_HISTORY                                   data
│   ├── DATA_Tiles                                          data
│   ├── DATA_Tiles_1                                        data
│   ├── DATA_Tiles_2                                        data
│   ├── DATA_Tiles_3                                        data
│   ├── DATA_Tiles_4                                        DBase 3 data file (45375 records)
│   ├── DATA_Tiles_5                                        data
│   ├── DATA_Tiles_6                                        data
│   ├── DATA_Tiles_7                                        data
│   ├── DATA_Tiles_8                                        DBase 3 data file (60175 records)
│   ├── event_store_driveabout                              data
│   ├── event_store_LocationFriendService                   data
│   ├── NavigationParameters.data                           data
│   ├── NavZoomTables.data                                  data
│   ├── nlp_GlsPlatformKey                                  data
│   ├── nlp_state                                           data
│   └── ZoomTables.data                                     data
├── lib                                                     directory
└── shared_prefs                                            directory
    ├── DriveAbout.xml                                      XML  document text
    ├── friend_service.xml                                  XML  document text
    ├── login_helper.xml                                    XML  document text
    └── network_initiated_prefs.xml                         XML  document text
```

This app also stores data on the SD card:

```
/mnt/sdcard/Android/data/com.google.android.apps.maps/      directory
├── cache                                                   directory
│   ├── cache_its.0                                         data
│   ├── cache_its.m                                         data
│   ├── cache_its_ter.m                                     data
│   ├── cache_r.0                                           data
```

```
|   ├── cache_r.1                                          data
|   ├── cache_rgts.0                                       Microsoft Document Imaging Forma
|   ├── cache_rgts.m                                       data
|   ├── cache_r.m                                          data
|   ├── cache_vts.0                                        data
|   ├── cache_vts.1                                        data
|   ├── cache_vts_GMM.0                                    data
|   ├── cache_vts_GMM.1                                    data
|   ├── cache_vts_GMM.10                                   data
|   ├── cache_vts_GMM.11                                   data
|   ├── cache_vts_GMM.12                                   data
|   ├── cache_vts_GMM.2                                    data
|   ├── cache_vts_GMM.3                                    data
|   ├── cache_vts_GMM.4                                    data
|   ├── cache_vts_GMM.5                                    data
|   ├── cache_vts_GMM.6                                    data
|   ├── cache_vts_GMM.7                                    data
|   ├── cache_vts_GMM.8                                    data
|   ├── cache_vts_GMM.9                                    data
|   ├── cache_vts_GMM.m                                    data
|   ├── cache_vts.m                                        data
|   ├── cache_vts_tran_GMM.m                               data
|   ├── ._speech_nav_0.wav                                 RIFF (little-endian)
data, WAVE audio, Microsoft PCM, 16 bit, mono 16000 Hz
|   ├── ._speech_nav_1.wav                                 RIFF (little-endian)
data, WAVE audio, Microsoft PCM, 16 bit, mono 16000 Hz
|   ├── ._speech_nav_2.wav                                 RIFF (little-endian)
data, WAVE audio, Microsoft PCM, 16 bit, mono 16000 Hz
|   ├── ._speech_nav_3.wav                                 RIFF (little-endian)
data, WAVE audio, Microsoft PCM, 16 bit, mono 16000 Hz
|   ├── ._speech_nav_4.wav                                 RIFF (little-endian)
data, WAVE audio, Microsoft PCM, 16 bit, mono 16000 Hz
|   ├── ._speech_nav_5.wav                                 RIFF (little-endian)
data, WAVE audio, Microsoft PCM, 16 bit, mono 16000 Hz
|   └── ._speech_nav_6.wav                                 RIFF (little-endian)
data, WAVE audio, Microsoft PCM, 16 bit, mono 16000 Hz
├── debug                                                  directory
└── testdata                                               directory
```

Table 7.13 Important Database Tables and Files from /data/data/com.google.android.apps.maps/databases/da_destination_history

Database Tables/Files	Description
destination_history	• time = 1295058395176 • dest_lat = 37786034 • dest_lng = -122405174 • dest_title = Coffee Bean and Tea Leaf • dest_address = 773 Market Street San Francisco, CA 94103 • dest_token = FbKRQAldyj60-CE--yMryKRCIQ • source_lat = 37791708 • source_lng = -122410077 • day_of_week = 6 • hour_of_day = 18

Important Database Tables and Files

While each database should be examined, on the HTC Incredible, two contained highly useful information. The first is the da_destination_history database as shown in Table 7.13 and the search_history database shown in Table 7.14.

Table 7.14 Important Database Tables and Files from /data/data/com.google.android.apps.maps/databases/search_history.db

	Description
suggestions	• _id = 140 • data1 = the stanford court, a renaissance hotel, 905 california street, san francisco, ca 94108 • singleResult = • displayQuery = The Stanford Court, A Renaissance Hotel, 905 California Street, San Francisco, CA 94108

The files directory also contains a significant amount of information. For example, the first part of the DATA_LAYER_24 file contains the following strings:

```
t,+0
XThe Stanford Court, A Renaissance Hotel, 905 California Street,
San Francisco, CA 94108
FQqpQAIdGS20-CHNignjYUhNwQ,CJ
$3.75;B
VWalking directions (beta): use caution.
Head southeast on Naglee Ave toward Cayuga Ave
3 %(
Balboa Park BART`
167 ft
37 secsRV
Turn left at Cayuga Ave
78aBo16F4yPZxvWb9KipKA
0.2 mi
3 minsRU
Turn left at Ottawa Ave
3 ((
KutrDTBAAz1iBqg0_dtz3w
167 ft
40 secsRW
Turn right at Delano Ave
paD-1LwjtwdrtiMP6pjAOw
0.3 mi
5 minsRV
Turn left at Geneva Ave
CHzTIqx_6bEUmrZ5e2dnBw
0.2 mi
4 minsR
#Millbrae-SFIA to Pittsburg/Baypoint
Balboa Park BART:
Powell St. BARTB
Pittsburg / Bay Point`
11 mins
Civic Center BART
us-ca-bart:CIVC
```

The data stored on the SD card is used for the turn-by-turn directions for the Google Maps Navigation and the turn-by-turn directions are time stamped:

```
ahoog@ubuntu:~/htc-inc/mnt/sdcard/Android/data/com.google.android.apps.maps/
cache$ ls -lah | grep speech
-rwxr-xr-x 1 root root 105K 2011-01-27 14:35 ._speech_nav_0.wav
-rwxr-xr-x 1 root root  81K 2011-01-27 14:34 ._speech_nav_1.wav
-rwxr-xr-x 1 root root 127K 2011-01-27 14:34 ._speech_nav_2.wav
-rwxr-xr-x 1 root root  61K 2011-01-27 14:33 ._speech_nav_3.wav
-rwxr-xr-x 1 root root  94K 2011-01-27 14:41 ._speech_nav_4.wav
-rwxr-xr-x 1 root root  67K 2011-01-27 14:41 ._speech_nav_5.wav
-rwxr-xr-x 1 root root 112K 2011-01-27 14:41 ._speech_nav_6.wav
```

Analyst Notes

Analyst notes for /data/data/com.google.android.apps.maps:

- The app stores a significant amount of information about maps, tiles, searches, and more in the files directory and should be closely examined.
- While each database may not contain information, both search_history.db and da_destination_history should be examined closely.
- While the shared_prefs direction contains some information, most is not useful to a forensic examination. However, the authentication token can be recovered, which may be of interest in a security review.
- The Navigation function caches map data on the SD card, as well as .wav files of the actual directions. If you look at the time stamps on the file, which are prefaced with a "._speech_nav," you can determine when the directions were provided and also hear the actual spoken directions.

Gmail

App Info

Google provides a native client for their Gmail service:

- App Name: Gmail (Google Mail)
- Package name: com.google.android.gm
- Version: 2.2
- Device: HTC Incredible
- App developer: Google

Directories, Files, and File Types

In /mnt/sdcard/Android/data/com.google.android.apps.maps/:

```
com.google.android.gm/                                 directory
├── app_sslcache                                       directory
│   └── android.clients.google.com.443                 data
├── cache                                              directory
│   ├── download                                       directory
│   │   └── .jpeg                                      JPEG image data, JFIF standard 1.01
│   └── webviewCache                                   directory
```

```
├── databases                                   directory
│   ├── downloads.db                            SQLite 3.x database, user version 100
│   ├── gmail.db                                SQLite 3.x database, user version 18
│   ├── gmail.db-journal                        empty
│   ├── mailstore.book@viaforensics.com.db      SQLite 3.x database, user version 56
│   ├── mailstore.personal@emailaddress.com.db  SQLite 3.x database, user version 56
│   ├── suggestions.db                          SQLite 3.x database, user version 513
│   ├── webviewCache.db                         SQLite 3.x database, user version 4
│   ├── webviewCache.db-journal                 data
│   └── webview.db                              SQLite 3.x database, user version 10
├── files                                       directory
├── lib                                         directory
└── shared_prefs                                directory
    ├── Gmail.xml                               XML  document text
    └── _has_set_default_values.xml             XML  document text
```

Important Database Tables and Files

The Gmail app stores a significant amount of information in SQLite databases and a sample of key tables is shown in Table 7.15.

Table 7.15 Important Database Tables and Files from /data/data/com.google.android.gm/databases/mailstore.book@viaforensics.com.db

Database Tables/Files	Description
conversations	• _id = 1343614283601791413 • queryId = 3 • subject = New Banking Trojan Discovered Targeting Businesses' Financial Accounts • maxMessageId = 1347608009807593988 • snippet = Forwarded message From: "Andrew Hoog" <book@viaforensics.com> Date ... • fromAddress = n 2 0 0
messages	• _id = 2 • messageId = 1338926826441746102 • conversation = 1338926826441746102 • fromAddress = "Hoog, Andrew" <book@viaforensics.com> • toAddresses = "" <us12268@somegraphxcompany.org> • ccAddresses = • bccAddresses = • replyToAddresses = • dateSentMs = 1276900125000 • dateReceivedMs = 1276900125971 • subject = viaForensics training packet

(continued on next page)

Table 7.15 Important Database Tables and Files from /data/data/com.google.android.gm/databases/mailstore.book@viaforensics.com.db *(Continued)*

Database Tables/Files	Description
	• snippet = Hello, Per our conversation with sandy, we need 11 packets by 10am monday. Th... • listInfo = • personalLevel = 0 • body = <p>Hello, Per our conversation with sandy, we need 11 packets by 10am monday. Thanks. Andrew </p> • bodyEmbedsExternalResources = 0 • joinedAttachmentInfos = • synced = 1 • error = • clientCreated = 0 • refMessageId = 0 • forward = 0 • includeQuotedText = 0 • quoteStartPos = 0 • bodyCompressed = • customFromAddress =

Analyst Notes

Analyst notes for /data/data/com.google.android.gm:

- Each configured Gmail account will have its own SQLite database, which will contain the entire e-mail content.
- Other databases such as downloads.db, suggestions.db, and gmail.db contain additional information.
- Some SQLite journal files may be recoverable.
- The cache/download directory stores downloads.
- The synced Gmail accounts are also referenced in the Gmail.xml in shared_prefs.

Facebook

App Info

This is the office Facebook app.

- App Name: Facebook
- Package name: com.facebook.katana
- Version: 1.2
- Device: HTC Incredible
- App developer: Facebook

Directories, Files, and File Types

In /data/data/com.facebook.katana:

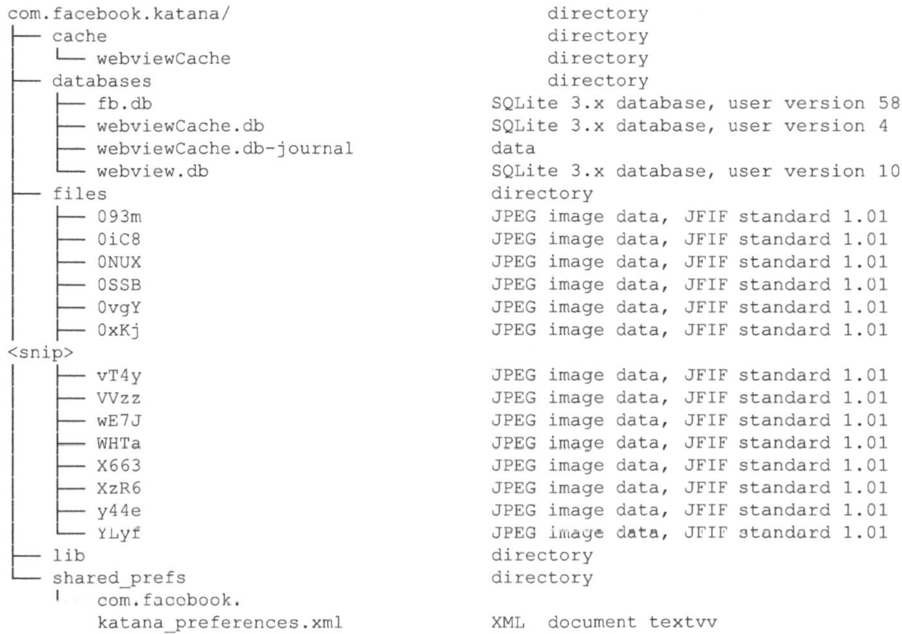

```
com.facebook.katana/                      directory
├── cache                                 directory
│   └── webviewCache                      directory
├── databases                             directory
│   ├── fb.db                             SQLite 3.x database, user version 58
│   ├── webviewCache.db                   SQLite 3.x database, user version 4
│   ├── webviewCache.db-journal           data
│   └── webview.db                        SQLite 3.x database, user version 10
├── files                                 directory
│   ├── 093m                              JPEG image data, JFIF standard 1.01
│   ├── 0iC8                              JPEG image data, JFIF standard 1.01
│   ├── 0NUX                              JPEG image data, JFIF standard 1.01
│   ├── 0SSB                              JPEG image data, JFIF standard 1.01
│   ├── 0vgY                              JPEG image data, JFIF standard 1.01
│   ├── 0xKj                              JPEG image data, JFIF standard 1.01
<snip>
│   ├── vT4y                              JPEG image data, JFIF standard 1.01
│   ├── VVzz                              JPEG image data, JFIF standard 1.01
│   ├── wE7J                              JPEG image data, JFIF standard 1.01
│   ├── WHTa                              JPEG image data, JFIF standard 1.01
│   ├── X663                              JPEG image data, JFIF standard 1.01
│   ├── XzR6                              JPEG image data, JFIF standard 1.01
│   ├── y44e                              JPEG image data, JFIF standard 1.01
│   └── YLyf                              JPEG image data, JFIF standard 1.01
├── lib                                   directory
└── shared_prefs                          directory
    └── com.facebook.
        katana_preferences.xml            XML  document textvv
```

Important Database Tables and Files

There is one primary database as shown in Table 7.16.

Analyst Notes

Analyst notes for /data/data/com.facebook.katana:

- The fb.db contains nearly all of the information and only three of the tables were profiled above. Full table list includes the following:
- albums
- info_contacts
- notifications
- android_metadata
- key_value
- perf_sessions
- chatconversations
- mailbox_messages
- photos
- chatmessages
- mailbox_messages_display
- search_results

Table 7.16 Important Database Tables and Files from /data/data/com.facebook.katana/databases/fb.db

Database Tables/Files	Description
friends	• _id = 125 • user_id = removed • first_name = FName • last_name = LName • display_name = FName LName • user_image_url = http://profile.ak.fbcdn.net/hprofile-ak-snc4/aa.jpg • user_image = ÿØÿà • intent = content://com.facebook.katana.provider.FriendsProvider/info_contacts/uid<snip> • birthday_month = 01 • birthday_day = 01 • birthday_year = 1929 • hash = -15123123123177976
user_statuses	• _id = 21 • user_id = removed • first_name = FName • last_name = LName • display_name = FName LName • user_pic = http://profile.ak.fbcdn.net/hprofile-ak-snc4/aa.jpg • timestamp = 1296367386 • message = geolocation, geolocation, geolocation…hmmm…
mailbox_messages	• _id = 13 • folder = 0 • tid = 1825710720339 • mid = 0 • author_id = removed • sent = 1290345224 • body = happy birthday! hope it was a fun day and that you have a wonderful year!

- default_user_images
- mailbox_profiles
- stream_photos
- events
- mailbox_threads
- user_statuses
- friends
- mailbox_users
- user_values
- The files directory contains a significant number of images from the Facebook app.

Adobe Reader

App Info

This is the official Abode Reader for PDF files

- App Name: Adobe Reader
- Package name: com.adobe.reader
- Version: 9.0.1
- Device: HTC Incredible
- App developer: Adobe

Directories, Files, and File Types

In /data/data/com.adobe.reader:

```
com.adobe.reader/                          directory
├── cache                                  directory
│   └── cache_file.pdf                     PDF document, version 1.1
├── lib                                    directory
└── shared_prefs                           directory
    ├── AdobeReader.xml                    XML  document  text
    └── com.adobe.reader.preferences.xml   XML  document  text
```

Important Database Tables and Files

The com.adobe.reader.preferences.xml preferences file:


```
<?xml version='1.0' encoding='utf-8' standalone='yes' ?>
<map>
<string name="recentFile0">/sdcard/dropbox/Android intro.pdf</string>
<string name="recentFile3">/mnt/sdcard/download/presentation-powerpoint.pdf
</string>
<string name="recentFile2">/mnt/sdcard/download/dinner-1.pdf</string>
<string name="recentFile1">/mnt/sdcard/download/file-1.pdf</string>
</map>
```


Analyst Notes

Analyst notes for /data/data/com.adobe.reader:

- Cached PDF files are stored in the cache directory.
- A list of recent files is stored in cache/com.adobe.reader.preferences.xml.

SUMMARY

While the acquisition of Android devices is the focus of much research, development, and discussion, it is really only half of the challenge of Android forensics. Analysis is needed with both logical and physical techniques. However, the amount of analysis needed after a physical acquisition is far greater. The goal of this chapter was to provide techniques that would allow a forensic analyst or security engineer to examine and extract data from acquisitions even if the file systems are not supported by forensic utilities. By leveraging existing forensic utilities, Linux commands and, at times, hex analysis, much of the data required for an investigation are available.

References

File times (Windows). (n.d.). Retrieved February 13, 2011, from http://msdn.microsoft.com/en-us/library/ms724290%28VS.85%29.aspx.

Carrier, B. (n.d.). Mactime output—SleuthKitWiki. Retrieved February 13, 2011, from http://wiki.sleuthkit.org/index.php?title=Mactime_output.

Casey, E. (n.d.). Misinterpretation of file system timestamps. Retrieved February 13, 2011, from http://blog.cmdlabs.com/2009/05/08/misinterpretation-of-file-system-timestamps/.

Debugging in Android with tombstones. (n.d.). Retrieved March 14, 2011, from http://crazydaks.com/debugging-in-android-with-tombstones.html.

Digital assembly: Adroit photo forensics—SmartCarving™. (n.d.). Retrieved February 13, 2011, from http://digital-assembly.com/products/adroit-photo-forensics/features/smartcarving.html.

Digital Detective—DCode. (n.d.). Retrieved February 14, 2011, from http://www.digital-detective.co.uk/freetools/decode.asp.

Epoch converter—epoch & unix timestamp conversion tools. (n.d.). Retrieved February 14, 2011, from http://www.epochconverter.com/.

Grundy, B. (n.d.). Linux LEO. Retrieved February 19, 2011, from http://www.linuxleo.com.

Kessler, G. (n.d.). File signatures table. Retrieved February 13, 2011, from http://www.garykessler.net/library/file_sigs.html.

Ross, A. (n.d.). digfor: Time and timestamps. Retrieved February 13, 2011, from http://digfor.blogspot.com/2008/10/time-and-timestamps.html.

Rovio—Angry Birds. (n.d.). Retrieved February 15, 2011, from http://www.rovio.com/index.php?page=angry-birds.

Scalpel: a frugal, high performance file carver. (n.d.). Retrieved February 13, 2011, from www.digitalforensicssolutions.com/Scalpel/.

What is my IP address. (n.d.). Retrieved February 19, 2011, from http://www.whatismyip.com/.

YAFFS debugging. (n.d.). Retrieved February 17, 2011, from http://www.yaffs.net/yaffs-debugging.

Index

Note: Page numbers followed by "f" and "t" denote figures and tables, respectively.

X

Y

Z

Lightning Source UK Ltd.
Milton Keynes UK
UKOW06f0152121214

242996UK00018B/449/P